RECONSTRUCTING THE CAMPUS

A NATION DIVIDED:
STUDIES IN THE CIVIL WAR ERA

Orville Vernon Burton, Editor

RECONSTRUCTING THE CAMPUS

Higher Education and the American Civil War

MICHAEL DAVID COHEN

UNIVERSITY OF VIRGINIA PRESS
Charlottesville and London

University of Virginia Press
© 2012 by Michael David Cohen
All rights reserved
Printed in the United States of America on acid- free paper

First published 2012
First paperback edition published 2026
ISBN 978-0-8139-5533-9 (paper)

1 3 5 7 9 8 6 4 2

The Library of Congress has cataloged the hardcover edition as follows:

Cohen, Michael David, 1980–
Reconstructing the campus : higher education and the American Civil War / Michael David Cohen.
  p. cm. — (A nation divided : studies in the Civil War era)
Includes bibliographical references and index.
ISBN 978-0-8139-3317-7 (cloth : alk. paper) — ISBN 978-0-8139-3318-4 (e-book)
1. United States—History—Civil War, 1861–1865—Education and the war. 2. Universities and colleges—United States—History—19th century. 3. Universities and colleges—United States—Admission—History—19th century. 4. Universities and colleges—Curricula—United States—History—19th century. 5. Education (Higher)—United States—History—19th century. 6. Educational change—United States—History—19th century. 7. United States—History—Civil War, 1861–1865—Influence. I. Title.
E541.C65 2012
973.7071'1—dc23
2012000870

For Mom and Dad
With love, gratitude, and admiration

Contents

	List of Illustrations	viii
	Acknowledgments	ix
	Introduction	1
ONE	Dwellers beside the Sea: Colleges at War	19
TWO	The Curriculum: Teaching the Arts of Peace and War	52
THREE	Admissions: Race, Class, Gender	92
FOUR	Admissions: Geography, Service, Morality	128
FIVE	College, Community, and Nation	153
	Conclusion	187
	Notes	197
	Bibliography	235
	Index	259

Illustrations

1. Seven colleges in 1861 — 15
2. Harvard University students guarding the Cambridge Arsenal — 30
3. Cornell College class of 1868 — 33
4. Institutions employing army officers as military professors — 64
5. University of Missouri students in military uniform with cannons — 66
6. University of Missouri in 1875 — 88
7. Students of the State Normal School in South Carolina — 122
8. Percentage of in-state college students — 131
9. Geographic origins of students at Wesleyan Female College — 136
10. Geographic origins of students at South Carolina College — 139
11. Lafayette College exhibit at the Centennial Exposition — 183

Acknowledgments

Writing a book involves many hours spent alone in an archive or at a computer. But it is hardly done in isolation. This book has benefited immensely from the advice, feedback, assistance, and support of many individuals and organizations. It began at Harvard University, where my readers guided me through the process of turning an idea into a dissertation. Nancy Cott, my adviser, continually impressed me with her intellectual rigor and wide-ranging knowledge. She helped me to clarify my arguments and to see the importance of my own findings. Julie Reuben contributed expert knowledge, careful readings, and kind encouragement. Susan O'Donovan offered original and insightful readings with unfailing enthusiasm. More recently, the Department of History and the Correspondence of James K. Polk Project at the University of Tennessee, Knoxville, have provided me a rich and welcoming intellectual home as I have refined my work into a finished book.

I thank those colleagues who read chapters and provided feedback: Drew Gilpin Faust, Roger Geiger, Katherine Reynolds Chaddock, Tom Chaffin, the late Martin Trow, and the members of the Boston-area History of Education Group, the Harvard history-of-education graduate student group, and the Harvard Nineteenth-Century Dissertation Group. Sarah Wadsworth read the entire manuscript. These colleagues' generosity with their time and expertise have made this a better book. Tom and Sarah, whom I consider both friends and mentors, and Martin, the mentor who first introduced me to the history of higher education at Carleton College, deserve special thanks for their unfailing support of my scholarship. Ellen Condliffe Lagemann, Peter Dobkin Hall, and Colin Burke provided helpful suggestions concerning this project. I thank Mary

ACKNOWLEDGMENTS

Ann Dzuback, Elizabeth Varon, and Robert Goler for their uncommonly thoughtful critiques as discussants at the conferences of the History of Education Society in 2006 and 2009 and the Organization of American Historians in 2010, where I presented research that led to this book.

An enthusiastic team helped turn my manuscript into a published book. I thank Richard Holway, Raennah Mitchell, Mark Mones, Ellen Satrom, and Emily Grandstaff for guiding me through the process; Joanne Allen for copyediting the book; William Nelson for creating its maps; and the anonymous readers of the University of Virginia Press for their helpful comments. I could not have asked for a more committed or more insightful reader than Aaron Sheehan-Dean, the then–series editor. His suggestions have made this book a significantly better work than the manuscript he first read.

Archivists and librarians provided invaluable help to me during my research. Without their thorough knowledge and unselfish labor, I would never have found some of my most important sources. I thank Sybil Mc-Neil, of the Wesleyan College Archives; Patricia Albright, of the Mount Holyoke College Archives; Mary Iber and her predecessor, Elizabeth Lawler Schau, of the Cornell College Archives; Gary Cox, of the University of Missouri Archives; Elizabeth West, of the University of South Carolina Archives; Kathryn Neal, of the University of California Archives; William Stolz, of the Western Historical Manuscript Collection; Kelli Hansen, of the University of Missouri Special Collections; Sara Przybylski, of the State Historical Society of Missouri; Edward Copenhagen, of the Monroe C. Gutman Library; Mary Jane Johnson, of the Phi Mu Fraternity Archives; and the entire staffs of the South Caroliniana Library, the Bancroft Library, and the Harvard University Archives. I thank the Department of History at the University of Minnesota, Twin Cities, for granting me access to that university's libraries. The staff of Wesleyan College deserves special notice for its uncommon hospitality during my visit. During my visit to Cornell College Richard Thomas helped me to understand its early history. Charles Sullivan kindly shared a Civil War image from his personal collection.

Several grants and fellowships have made my research and writing possible. I thank the Berenson family and Harvard University for the Richard A. Berenson Graduate Fellowship, the Charles Warren Center for Studies in American History at Harvard for two Summer Research Grants, and the Graduate School Fund at Harvard for the Graduate Society Dissertation Completion Fellowship. I thank the Department of His-

ACKNOWLEDGMENTS

tory at the University of Tennessee for a grant to cover publication-related expenses.

Last but far from least, I thank my family. Andrea Cohen, my best friend, has brought joy and balance to the years I have spent writing this book. The excitement of publishing it, though considerable, pales next to the dream come true of sharing my life with her. Marjorie and David Cohen, my parents, introduced my sister Caroline and me to America's past through visits to more historic sites, and more bookstores, than I can count. We have shared a love for history and for books ever since. Without their inexhaustible support, love, and confidence in my abilities, I could never have come so far in my scholarship. I cannot thank them enough for everything they have done to make this possible. To them, I dedicate this book.

RECONSTRUCTING THE CAMPUS

Introduction

> What do we care if we *were* expelled from college, Scarlett? The war's gonna start any day now, so we'd have left college anyhow.
> —Brent Tarleton in *Gone with the Wind*, 1939

When Americans think of the Civil War, few images come to mind more often than those from the epic film *Gone with the Wind*. We remember Scarlett O'Hara's early fright and growing fortitude as she loses and regains her estate. We remember Rhett Butler's dry cynicism about his compatriots' lust for war. And we remember, with incredulity, the African American servants who remain faithful to their masters through slavery and freedom. But we seldom remember the first lines of the film or the backstory they imply. As a turkey gobbles and horses laze in the sun, Scarlett's admirer Brent Tarleton defends his and his twin brother's academic failure.

This story of the war begins with college.

Brent's opening lines tell us a lot about higher education in the 1860s, probably more than the filmmakers intended. First, college was an important rite of passage for wealthy white men in the antebellum South. Nothing in the film suggests that the Tarleton twins aim for intellectual careers; clearly they intend to follow in their planter father's footsteps. Yet they have spent their formative years away from the fields, in the classroom. Scarlett's implied rebuke for their expulsion shows the value their society placed on formal education.

Second, Brent's dismissal of that rebuke points to the war's disruption of higher education. Patriotic young men, he believes, will leave their classrooms over the coming weeks and months to join the fight. The Tarletons may have misbehaved or failed their classes, but they would soon have left even if they had not been expelled. The departure of a large number of their classmates would have a devastating effect on colleges.

Finally, the exchange between Scarlett and her suitors implies that only men went to college. We hear nothing about the Southern belle's higher education.[1] Of these three implicit claims, only the last turns out to be false. Both white women and white men, albeit only a small minority of each, attended college in America before the Civil War. They did so for several reasons, but usually not for directly applicable professional training. The Southern planter class, in particular, enrolled primarily for social reasons. And the Civil War did indeed disrupt colleges. Throughout the nation, male students fled classrooms as they rallied to battlefields. In the South, physical and financial ruin posed additional challenges for colleges already starved for students.

Yet the Civil War did not destroy American higher education. Most colleges in the North stayed open through the war years. Most in the South reopened after the surrender. Some of the Tarletons' real-life counterparts—if, unlike the twins, neither expelled before the war nor killed during it—even resumed their studies after a four-year interregnum. But all was not the same. Like Scarlett's plantation, colleges after the war were very different places from before. This book tells the story of that change: how colleges responded to the war and what the war and its aftermath did to colleges. It argues that the Civil War affected higher education in two ways. First, colleges everywhere developed new relationships with the growing federal government that brought new funding, reshaped curricula, and gathered and spread information about American education. Second, wartime damage left Southern colleges with the need and the opportunity to rebuild themselves, often in new ways. With the support of state governments, colleges invented the new form of the comprehensive university and opened educational opportunities to previously excluded Americans. Though hardly gone with the wind, colleges in both the South and the North bore distinct marks of the Civil War.

By 1861 higher education in America already had a long history. Almost as soon as the Puritans arrived on the beaches of Massachusetts Bay, they resolved to establish a college. The legislature created Harvard College in 1636; classes began two years later. Other governments and denominations eventually followed suit. The Crown established the Anglican College of William and Mary in Virginia in 1693. Connecticut founded Congregational Yale College in 1701. Pennsylvania, New Jersey, New York, Rhode Island, and New Hampshire all founded colleges between then and the Revolution.

Most of the colonial colleges offered a narrow curriculum and served a narrow range of students. To be a college meant to award the bachelor of arts degree. An invention of thirteenth-century Europe, it denoted the completion of a fixed curriculum rooted in the classical languages and mathematics. Young men attended college to prepare for careers as ministers, doctors, lawyers, or civil leaders. Only ministers actually needed the degree (and only in some denominations), but college provided a level of respectability and classical knowledge that early Americans deemed valuable to other professionals and to politicians. College provided erudition rather than practical knowledge: professors taught law and medicine as liberal studies, if at all, leaving students to learn how to do their jobs elsewhere after graduation. Those who aimed neither for those three professions nor for political office had no reason to attend college. Of the 266 college alumni in New England before 1660, 85 percent were ministers and 11 percent were doctors or lawyers. Furthermore, the perceived need for college-educated men was so low that more than 40 percent of those men returned to England, often because they could not find work in the colonies.[2]

By the time of the American Revolution fewer than 1 percent of American men went to college.[3] Yet despite the miniscule demand, by building so many colleges colonial America had taken the first step toward widespread higher education. When the United States declared its independence in 1776, the new nation had nine institutions of higher learning. Geographic breadth and religious diversity among the colonies had facilitated that institutional growth. England, by contrast, had only two.[4]

As the Revolution shifted the center of government and reshaped Americans' ideas about the structure of society, it also interrupted and reshaped higher education. It especially impacted relationships between higher education and government. By the 1760s the governmental supervision that educators had imported from England had only increased. Colonial governments, which had founded the colleges and granted most of them monopolies, exercised control by granting charters, allotting funds, and holding seats on governing bodies.

Initially the Revolution intensified relationships between colleges and governments. In the years before the outbreak of war, conflict with the imperial government escalated. As a consequence, professors took their traditional goal of public service more seriously then ever. They chose sides. They taught their political perspectives to their students. Some published articles promoting or discouraging rebellion or became overtly politically active. Professors also used their knowledge of the classics and religion to develop the emerging nation's language of patriotism. Meanwhile, students debated political issues, participated in boycotts, and established cadet companies. Once war broke out, some enlisted in the Revolutionary armies. Even those who chose to stay at college met the war head-on when the armies commandeered college buildings, forcing the colleges to shut down or move.

Although the Revolution at first brought governments and colleges closer together, in the end it pushed them apart. The Americans' military success brought with it a new and weaker form of government. The state and especially national governments hesitated to interfere with institutions. Meanwhile, as states disestablished religion in the late eighteenth and early nineteenth centuries, now permitting multiple denominational groups, the main reason for granting educational monopolies disappeared. So governments stopped using their tools of control over colleges. Charters became automatic. State funding shriveled. In 1819 the U.S. Supreme Court placed an important symbolic limitation on state control of higher education: in *The Trustees of Dartmouth College v. Woodward* it denied New Hampshire's power to alter the college's charter without the latter's consent. The Court thereby established the legal notion of an independent college. Americans continued to see colleges as at least semipublic institutions because of their colonial history and their public-service functions, but governments no longer needed to have a direct hand in their founding or operation.[5]

With state monopolies abolished and governmental initiative obviated, higher education began to expand more rapidly. Towns, entrepreneurs, and philanthropists partnered with Christian denominations to set up small colleges across the country. The earliest ones opened their doors in the eastern states alongside the old colonial colleges. Williams College, for example, organized along Orthodox Congregational lines, began to compete with Unitarian Harvard for young Massachusetts men in 1793. Amherst College joined these two in 1821. During the colonial period, geography had determined where a man went to college. Now, with multiple colleges in a single state, student choice, institutional competition, and denominational diversity became important elements of higher education.

As Americans migrated west, they took their support for higher education with them. Many a frontier village consisting of little more than a church and a handful of houses rushed to build a denominational college. Pioneers considered colleges essential to spreading religion, learning, and civilization, as well as to raising land values and attracting business. Meadville, Pennsylvania, a village of only four hundred people, founded Presbyterian Allegheny College in 1815. Settlers had barely arrived in the new town of Oberlin, Ohio, when they began construction on its namesake Congregational college in 1833.[6] And citizens of Mount Vernon, Iowa, joined with the Methodist Church to found the Iowa Conference Seminary in 1853. Four years later, having secured a collegiate charter and a benefactor, they renamed the institution Cornell College.[7]

By then higher education had spread all the way to the west coast. Also in 1853, the Congregational and Presbyterian Churches jointly founded the College of California in Oakland. Mirroring the midwestern outlook, this college's vice president later claimed that only churches, common schools, and a religious newspaper had been higher priorities than a college for California's settlers.[8] Between 1800 and 1860, according to one historian's tally, Christian denominations founded 205 colleges; towns and entrepreneurs founded an additional sixteen without denominational support.[9] Many secondary or postsecondary institutions that did not seek permission from their state governments to award degrees—seminaries, academies, institutes, normal schools, and professional schools—spread opportunities for an advanced education still farther.[10]

Even as denominational colleges increasingly dotted the American landscape, state governments continued to play an active, if restrained, role in higher education. They retained seats on some colonial and new denominational colleges' governing boards. They also awarded the charters, albeit automatically, that authorized schools to grant bachelor's (and sometimes master's) degrees; this remained an important role because, as the census of 1860 noted, that authority continued to define a school as a *college*.[11] Some states also founded their own new colleges. The federal government generally stayed out of the education business, but federal land grants did help make the foundings of some state colleges possible. Institutions' names reflected their governmental origins: South Carolina founded South Carolina College in Columbia in 1801; Missouri founded the University of Missouri, also in a town called Columbia, in 1839. Thirteen state colleges or universities—the terms were essentially equivalent—existed by 1860.[12] But these actually differed little from denominational colleges. Legislatures provided little oversight and, except in South Carolina, Virginia, and Michigan, little money. After founding these colleges, the legislatures left them to operate independently.[13]

In total, the number of colleges in the United States rose from 9 at the nation's founding to as many as 467 in 1860. (Several dozen more opened but then closed for lack of money or students.)[14] But the proportion of Americans who attended college did not rise much. The nation's population multiplied along with its colleges, and most of the new institutions remained small. Of 123 colleges listed in an 1861 almanac, only 16 enrolled more than two hundred students and 47 enrolled fewer than one hundred.[15] The national college attendance rate was only about 1 percent on the eve of the Civil War, little more than it had been eight decades earlier, despite the proliferation of new institutions.[16]

The types of people who attended college, however, did change. The colonial colleges almost exclusively had educated middle-class white men who aimed to become ministers, doctors, or lawyers. (Colonial Yale College's president once gave a certificate to a bright girl indicating that had she been male, she would have gained admission.)[17] Although college remained unnecessary for and undesired by most Americans, between the Revolution and the Civil War a few new groups began to seek a higher education. As public primary and secondary education expanded in the Northeast and the Midwest, those interested in becoming teachers often attended either colleges or the new normal schools. Poor sons of farmers enrolled at New England colleges in hopes of avoiding agricultural wage labor by becoming ministers or teachers. In the South, the new state universities developed a reputation as cultural and social training grounds for the sons of planters. Fathers sent sons to those universities to meet their elite peers, to develop leadership skills, and to acquire the knowledge and social conservatism they deemed essential to upper-class status. Urban professionals' sons made up a significant minority on those campuses. Southern denominational colleges educated the sons of middling farmers and of businessmen, ministers, and other professionals.[18]

The restriction of higher education to white men also eroded over the antebellum years. In the 1830s Oberlin College, in Ohio, became the first college in America to admit students irrespective of either race or gender. A handful of other colleges, mostly in the Midwest, followed its lead in admitting African Americans, and Wilberforce University opened in Ohio in the late 1850s as the nation's first historically black college. Free Baptists opened the coeducational New York Central College, with both its student body and its faculty racially mixed, in 1849; ten years later Harvard hired Aaron Molyneaux Hewlett, a black man, to direct its gymnasium and teach physical education to its white students.

But these were exceptions. Higher education remained rare for African Americans. Most blacks were enslaved and lived in states where laws forbade so much as teaching a black person to read. When abolitionists tried to open a biracial college in Berea, Kentucky, in 1859, their proslavery neighbors forced them out of town under threat of violence. Southern colleges instead included blacks in roles that reproduced the hierarchy of the antebellum plantation: they either employed slaves themselves or permitted white students to bring their slaves along. Even as far north as New Haven, Connecticut, a movement in 1831 to establish a college for blacks met stiff and successful white opposition.[19]

White women's higher education, by contrast, expanded rapidly after 1830, taking several institutional forms. In the South, Protestant denominations and other groups founded women's colleges just as they had been founding men's colleges. Citizens of Macon, Georgia, and the Methodist Church founded the first, Georgia Female College (later renamed Wesleyan Female College), in 1836. The bachelor's course, Southern educators believed, prepared elite women to be good wives, just as it prepared elite men to be good planters and public leaders. Knowledge of classical literature signified both men's and women's membership in a social class. Midwesterners founded some women's colleges but primarily educated women in coeducational institutions such as Oberlin. Iowa's Cornell College admitted both genders from its founding. For some midwestern women, as for some men, college was an entryway into teaching in the new public schools.[20]

Very few actual colleges in the Northeast admitted women before the Civil War. But women there did attend postsecondary seminaries that did not seek collegiate charters from their states and thus did not grant degrees. These included Mount Holyoke Female Seminary, founded in South Hadley, Massachusetts, in 1836. Women's seminaries also coexisted alongside coeducational and women's colleges in the Midwest and eventually even in California. By 1855–56 Oakland's Seminary for Young Ladies and the male College of California were making efficient use of limited resources by sharing a commencement, a catalogue, two faculty members, and probably several trustees.[21]

Another change in college student populations resulted from the slow emergence of public secondary education. At the same time that colleges were spreading across the country, public school systems were forming in the Northeast and the Midwest. By the 1830s state governments had begun to craft laws to mandate, and bureaucracies to coordinate, common (i.e., free primary) schools. Most Southern states, by contrast, did not establish public schools until after the Civil War. Southern youths preparing for college studied under private tutors, at denominational or independent schools, or on their own.

The expansion of public schooling facilitated the growth of higher education. It also shaped the form that growth took. On the one hand, free primary schools ensured widespread literacy and a large pool of adolescents who could, in theory, attend college down the road. On the other hand, high schools remained relatively scarce. Many northeastern communities established them: by 1865, 70 percent of Massachusetts residents had access to a high school, even if few actually attended one. But they were much less common in the Midwest. Antebellum public schools thus took boys and girls through the primary grades but usually not through the secondary course, which they needed before beginning college.[22]

In the absence of public high schools, college founders outside the Northeast built secondary schools right into their colleges. They called these schools *preparatory departments.* Some colleges, including Cornell College and the University of Missouri, also established primary departments for younger children.[23] Because preparatory departments enrolled both future collegians and young people who desired a secondary education but had no plans to enter the college course, they usually comprised most of a college's student body. The term *college,* then, now denoted, not necessarily an institution that taught exclusively bachelor's students, but rather one that offered a bachelor's program, often along with secondary and sometimes primary curricula. The younger students were just as much a part of a college as the older ones. Letters, faculty minutes, and other records often referred to students without specifying their preparatory or collegiate status. In this book, unless I specify otherwise, I include both when discussing colleges' student populations.

Despite the proliferation of institutions and the modest diversification of their student populations, college curricula in the early nineteenth century remained remarkably similar to Harvard's in the early seventeenth. Students learned Greek, Latin, mathematics, rhetoric, and moral philosophy, sometimes supplemented with smaller amounts of history, the modern languages, and the sciences. There was little difference between men's and women's curricula. Both secondary schools and colleges for women strove to match the standards of men's institutions, including solid training in the classics, and increasingly they succeeded. Though women's courses sometimes varied in length from the men's four-year bachelor's curriculum—some seminaries required fewer years for a diploma, and Wesleyan required five for a degree—these differences meant little, because few college students stayed through the senior year.[24] As in the colonial period, few colleges offered direct occupational training. Lawyers and doctors learned their professions either in separate professional schools or on the job. Those who went to college did so to gain respectability and honor.[25]

INTRODUCTION

Beginning early in the nineteenth century reformers at a few colleges experimented with new types of curricula. Their efforts sparked debates over the purposes of higher education. But in the end they produced no widespread curricular change. Thomas Jefferson, founder of the University of Virginia, believed in the value of science both for strengthening the mind and for practical pursuits. He believed that college, while primarily an intellectual experience, should prepare students in a practical way for the medical and legal professions. It also should educate politically informed citizens. To further these ends, Jefferson designed a university comprising eight schools. Each taught a different subject area, such as the classics, the sciences, medicine, or law. Students enrolled in the school or schools of their choice. In essence, Jefferson created a modern university in 1825. But the concept did not catch on. Few other Southern educators attempted to build multicollegiate universities before the Civil War; none succeeded. The University of Virginia remained unique in its structure and curriculum.[26]

Others experimented more modestly with the curriculum. Starting in the 1820s a number of colleges added scientific classes to the prescribed course. Union College in New York offered students the choice between an arts and a scientific course; one offered more classical language classes, the other more science classes. In 1827 Amherst began designing an alternative course that omitted the classics altogether in order to teach "Chemistry and other kindred branches of Physical Science by showing their application to the more useful arts and trades," but it abandoned the project two years later.[27] By then the president and faculty of Yale College had issued an influential report critiquing curricular reform.

The Yale Report of 1828 answered a proposal that Yale stop teaching the classical languages. But in that response the professors addressed more broadly the choices of various colleges to reduce requirements in Latin and Greek, introduce new subjects, and permit students to choose their courses. They did not object to all curricular reform. While they did not believe that a college should teach professions or trades, they acknowledged that new liberal subjects could enhance students' learning. Over the past century, in fact, Yale itself had added new courses in science and other areas. But the new subjects, they stressed, must not come at the expense of the classical curriculum. Students still needed to study Latin, Greek, and mathematics.

The authors of the Yale Report made both psychological and social arguments for the classical curriculum. First, the traditional subjects built mental "discipline" and "furniture." A young man emerged from four years of classical study with powers of reasoning and general knowledge that would serve him well in any of the learned professions. Those abilities, not particular scientific or professional knowledge, were the aim of a college education. Second, a college needed to attract students in order to survive, and it needed to teach a socially valued curriculum in order to attract students. Americans of the professional classes believed knowledge of the classics and mathematics essential to identification as an educated individual. If Yale no longer required those subjects, men might not enroll their sons; if a Yale degree no longer connoted that knowledge, that degree might lose its prestige. To remain useful to its students and to remain solvent and respected, a college needed to retain the classical curriculum.

The Yale Report, which appeared in pamphlet form in 1828 and in the *American Journal of Science and Arts* in 1829, had a nationwide impact. The large number of Yale graduates involved in founding the new midwestern colleges helped to spread the report's conservative philosophy of higher education. Curricula, to be sure, did not remain static. Educators continued to experiment with new courses, especially in the sciences. Union College's notion of parallel courses spread, as other institutions tried to attract young men who were uninterested in Greek and Latin or young women whom some deemed unfit for them. These courses led to the bachelor of science, bachelor of literature, and bachelor of philosophy degrees. But the prescribed bachelor of arts curriculum rooted in the classical languages and mathematics remained the defining feature of a college education for the next third of a century. Even the alternative degree programs followed prescribed curricula and usually required the classics, only fewer classes in them.[28] A few colleges hired professors of law, medicine, or divinity, and a few colleges of agriculture opened their doors. But those were the exceptions. Most young men obtained their occupational training either in noncollegiate institutions or on the job through practice or apprenticeship.[29] Like their colonial predecessors, men and women who attended college did so for the classical education that many considered valuable to certain categories of people.

In 1860, then, hundreds of small colleges taught a classical curriculum to mostly white men, women, and children. These students came, for the most part, from elite families in the South and from more diverse backgrounds in the North. They attended college to affirm their social standing, to discipline their minds, or to gain entry into a narrow range of professions, but not for practical job training. State governments had

INTRODUCTION

founded several colleges, but religious denominations, boards of trustees, and professors made most of the decisions regarding higher education. Educators had built new colleges and admitted some new types of students, but they usually preserved the curriculum and institutional form of two hundred years earlier. Reform had come slowly.

The Civil War changed all that.

The historian Merle Curti, during World War II, looked back on the impact of earlier wars on American intellectuals. He believed that impact to have been significant. Wars, he observed, had helped to break down barriers between intellectuals and the general public. During the Civil War, for example, many professors had set aside their usual research to promote national goals and contribute their expertise to the military effort. More generally, "wars provided sharply posed problems for the leaders of American intellectual life." Those problems, he asserted, had played a key role in shaping the future of intellectual institutions.[30] Curti provided little evidence for this assertion. But it offers a useful starting point. The present book looks at colleges' responses to the problems created by the Civil War.

Higher education underwent substantial reform during the Civil War and Reconstruction. The number of colleges continued to grow, reaching 514 (plus 110 seminaries and similar institutions for women) by 1877.[31] Both institutions and their students diversified. Some of the small, classical colleges grew into universities offering a variety of academic, professional, and practical curricula. New subjects ranged from medicine to engineering and from teaching to agriculture. The universities enrolled students from outside their traditional demographic bases, especially women and lower-class Americans. For the first time, a significant though small number of African Americans went to college. Both the state and federal governments played more active roles in higher education, helping to fund colleges and universities and influencing their curricula. Contemporary observers realized that they were living in a period of educational transformation. The philosopher Ralph Waldo Emerson wrote of universities in 1867, "A cleavage is occurring in the hitherto firm granite of the past, and a new era is nearly arrived."[32]

Historians since Curti have uncovered several of the origins of higher education's transformation in the second half of the nineteenth century. They have noted the antebellum precedents for the much more extensive postbellum reforms, the effect of Congress's passing a college funding bill in 1862, and the European roots of the American research university.[33] A few, following Curti's lead, have recognized the impact of the Civil War on colleges. Willis Rudy collects in one book chapter the wartime stories from numerous institutional histories. Robert F. Pace, in a chapter, and Joseph M. Stetar, in an article, focus on Southern colleges. Pace traces the war's impact on male student culture; Stetar, on institutional development. John R. Thelin, in his survey of American higher education, briefly notes that the war enabled Congress to pass the funding bill in 1862 and had a broader impact on Southern colleges. And Martin Trow goes so far as to declare the Civil War "the watershed" for higher education's transition from elite to mass access because of the funding bill, though he does not explore the relationship between the bill and its wartime context.[34]

More often, the Civil War remains curiously absent from the history of higher education. Some authors give the topic no more than a couple of sentences.[35] Laurence R. Veysey, writing on the origins of the university, begins his narrative in 1865 and cursorily dismisses the war as a cause for change. Frederick Rudolph, in his survey of American higher education, uses the war chiefly as a chronological marker: he highlights the differences between antebellum and postbellum higher education but suggests no concrete way in which the war promoted change. Both he and Christopher J. Lucas, author of another survey, note the physical and financial damage the war did to Southern colleges but conclude that the afflicted institutions remained stagnant or backward-looking as a result. "Reconstruction in the South," Lucas argues, "would hardly touch academic institutions at all."[36] I argue otherwise. Throughout the nation, and especially in the South, the Civil War and its consequences promoted major educational reform.

Historians not focusing on education, of course, often have described the Civil War as a major—*the* major—watershed of American history. In 1869, two years after Emerson noted the "cleavage" in higher education, the former Harvard professor George Ticknor wrote, "The civil war of '61 has made a great gulf between what happened before it . . . and what has happened since."[37] The massive modern literature on the war and its aftermath emphasizes several key changes in American life that the war enabled or accelerated. African Americans escaped the bonds of slavery to become legally free laborers and citizens. The Northern victory firmly established the Constitution as unbreakable and the federal government as the supreme power of the land. That government expanded significantly in both size and strength. Abraham Lincoln and the Republican Party described the nation in new terms that emphasized equal opportunity,

INTRODUCTION

free labor, and democracy. Men and women began to identify themselves primarily as Americans rather than as citizens of their individual states.

Yet historians continue to debate the degree to which the Civil War brought real, lasting change. While most agree that the government expanded, they do not agree on the extent or longevity of its expansion. Some question whether growing nationalism actually overcame localist traditions. And historians vigorously debate whether and for how long legal freedom and citizenship brought real changes to the lives of former slaves. The end of federal enforcement of Southern blacks' rights in 1877 powerfully calls into question the ultimate effect of the war.[38]

Furthermore, historians are only beginning to discover the impact of the Civil War on Americans' daily lives and civilian institutions. A war involving millions of soldiers and resulting in hundreds of thousands of deaths,[39] the end of slavery, and the physical devastation and attempted reconstruction of the South was sure to affect Americans in diverse and unexpected ways. We understand some of these effects fairly well. Historians of gender have debated the changes in women's lives that arose from the war. Enabled or forced to take on new roles during the conflict, and occasionally to challenge men's authority, some women channeled their energies afterward into new activities even as they returned to their traditional responsibilities.[40] Historians also have studied the wartime home front. Intellectuals' discussions of national issues, civilians' contributions to the war effort, and the proximity of battles to Southerners' doorsteps made the war a part of each American's life.[41]

We know much less about the war's impact on institutions and facets of life that lacked an obvious link to the military effort. Until recently, some historians assumed that life in the North went on much as before.[42] But both before and after Appomattox, both in the North and in the South, Americans lived in a country largely defined by a military conflict and its resolution. Anything they did was very likely affected by that context. Several recent historians have uncovered evidence of these effects. Sven Beckert, for example, has shown the key role of the Civil War in reallocating power among New York City capitalist elites. Cheryl A. Wells has shown that battlefield experiences temporarily reshaped many Americans' understanding of time. Other writers have traced the war's effects on reading, the family, children, black schooling, religion, and machine politics. By drawing connections between the military and political events of the Civil War era and the cultural and institutional histories of the larger society, these historians are helping us to understand better the broad impact of the war. Most of them argue that the Civil War brought major and lasting change to Americans' lives and institutions. (Wells, who argues that Americans returned to their antebellum notions of time after the war, is an exception.)[43]

In the following chapters, I tell the history of higher-education reform in the context of the military, political, social, and economic history of the Civil War and Reconstruction. By bringing together these two stories of change in the 1860s and 1870s—in other words, by bridging educational history and general American history—I shed new light on both the origins of the transformation of higher education and the effects of the war on civilian life and institutions. The contemporaneity of Emerson's "cleavage" in higher education and Ticknor's "gulf" of the Civil War was no coincidence. In the early 1860s colleges, like all other American institutions, made decisions within a world consumed by war. After 1865 they continued to operate amid sweeping political and social change. Both the war itself and the hardships that followed it imperiled many colleges' very survival. The threat of closure had played an important role in colleges' policies during peacetime,[44] and that threat was far greater during and right after the war. Professors and trustees had no choice but to take into account the events going on outside their colleges' gates. Politicians, meanwhile, included colleges in their plans for shaping the postbellum nation. I argue that colleges' and governments' practical responses to difficult and fluid conditions during the Civil War era drove some of the most important educational reforms of the late nineteenth century. Merle Curti's hypothesis was right: the Civil War did break down barriers between colleges and the public, and the challenges it posed did shape colleges' futures. Its impact was both profound and lasting.

Although educational reform never ended, crucial changes in college curricula, institutional structures, admissions policies, and relationships with governments began or accelerated within a clearly defined period. I therefore focus on this long Civil War era, which lasted from Abraham Lincoln's election in 1860 until the end of Reconstruction in 1877. Where necessary, I extend the narrative into the early 1880s. In order to explore in depth colleges' experiences and policy decisions, I selected seven representative institutions as case studies. I include national-level data where possible, and some parts of this story take place in exposition exhibit halls or the halls of Congress rather than college lecture halls. But most of my evidence comes from the seven colleges.

I selected colleges to represent both the different regions of the country and the different types of colleges at the beginning of the Civil War (fig. 1).[45] The war affected life in all parts of the country, albeit to varying

INTRODUCTION

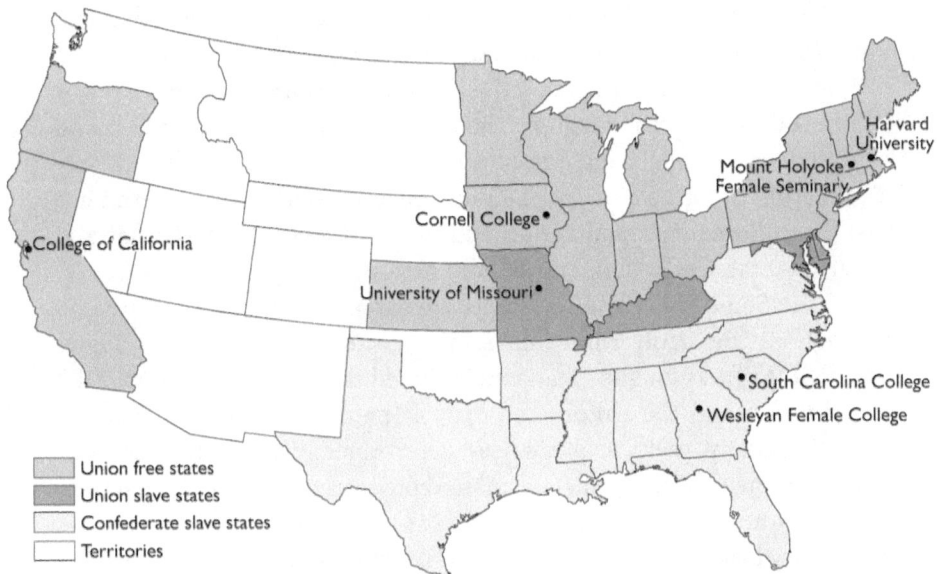

Fig. 1. The United States and the Confederate States in 1861, with seven representative colleges

degrees, so this book looks at colleges in both North and South, East and West. Harvard University in Massachusetts, the centuries-old Unitarian college for men, was one of the handful in the United States that already had begun to add professional schools to the classical core. The College of California, Wesleyan Female College in Georgia, and Cornell College in Iowa were among the hundreds of denominational colleges that appeared in the early and middle nineteenth century. California educated men; Wesleyan, women; and Cornell, both. South Carolina College and the University of Missouri typified the male state universities that characterized the South. Because women in the Northeast attended seminaries rather than degree-granting colleges, I include Mount Holyoke Female Seminary in Massachusetts.

The Civil War and Reconstruction had two types of effects on colleges. First, they induced the federal government to play a larger role in higher education. During the war and in its wake Congress passed a series of laws funding certain types of colleges and providing supplies and personnel for certain types of curricula. Congress also established a bureau to collect and disseminate information on education. These actions were part of a general expansion of the federal government that began as it mobilized for war and continued, albeit somewhat abated, after the conflict's end. Legislators aimed to address perceived educational needs that had grown out of the war. In particular, they encouraged military education in civilian colleges after witnessing the Union's unreadiness to fight a major war in 1861. Colleges throughout the nation modified their curricula and provided institutional data in response to these new federal policies. They also recruited war veterans to their campuses. Together the government and the colleges reshaped higher education to meet the curricular and governmental needs of the postbellum nation.

In the South the war affected colleges in additional ways. Here and throughout this book, I use the term *South* to refer to the area where the Civil War was fought. That area included the slave states of both the Confederacy and the Union (see fig. 1); the proximity of the war, far more than states' political allegiances, determined the challenges colleges faced.[46] Some Southern colleges suffered physical damage or destruction. Others endured takeover by the Union or the Confederate army for use as military bases or hospitals. Rampant inflation of the Confederate currency posed financial challenges to both institutions and students. The presence of armies made it difficult for young people to travel to college. After the war, the emancipation of 4 million African American slaves and the politics of Reconstruction and Redemption forced many colleges to redefine their constituencies. Therefore, much more changed at Southern colleges because of the war than at Northern ones. As they rebuilt themselves after the surrender, Southern colleges developed a new institutional form, the comprehensive university. Some elements of this form, such as medical schools and agricultural courses, had appeared at a few colleges earlier, but it took the war to bring full-fledged universities to the South. At the same time, as they responded to economic and political changes, colleges diversified their student populations, admitting students from lower wealth levels and, sometimes, African Americans. As a consequence of the war, then, Southern colleges initiated reforms that Northern colleges already had begun. Southern colleges came more closely to resemble Northern ones in their curricula, structures, and student populations. The Civil War affected higher education everywhere, but in the South it provided the opportunity for a new beginning.

The structure of this book is both chronological and topical. Chapter 1 examines the immediate impact of the Civil War on colleges. As students enlisted in the armies, monetary inflation accelerated, and armies commandeered some college campuses, the increasing federal role in education and the war's greater impact on the South began to materialize. The remaining chapters take the story beyond 1865. Chapter 2 looks

INTRODUCTION

at college curricula, which diversified as colleges, sometimes aided by a state or federal government, added graduate, professional, practical, and military education to their classical courses. Southern colleges in the 1860s invented the new institutional form of the comprehensive university. Chapters 3 and 4 look at different aspects of college admissions. The political, economic, social, and military conditions of the 1860s and 1870s led colleges, especially in the South, to admit several new types of students and help them afford their education. Finally, chapter 5 traces colleges' burgeoning relationships with their local communities and the national government. By the end of Reconstruction colleges had begun to offer outreach programs and to work with the government to publicize higher education on a national level.

Between 1860 and 1877 several of the key features of twentieth-century higher education emerged: multicollegiate universities, practical curricula, military training, more diverse student populations, expanded financial aid, closer relationships with governments, and outreach to the local and national communities. As historians have shown, these reforms grew in part out of a dialogue among educators about the value of classical traditions, practical training, and the European university model. But they also came in part—often primarily—as practical responses to national events. The Civil War, by reshaping the federal government and by forcing colleges to reform, helped to build our modern system of higher education.

ONE

Dwellers beside the Sea
Colleges at War

When Sallie Love received her college diploma, she may well have heaved a sigh of relief. Few knew the difficulties of attending college in wartime better than she. When the Civil War broke out, the Love, Mississippi, native was attending the State Female College in Memphis, Tennessee. Upon the surrender of Tennessee's Fort Donelson to Northern troops in February 1862, however, the college closed, fearing a Union invasion. Love briefly returned home, then enrolled at Berryman College in Hernando, Mississippi. But one afternoon that summer she and her classmates watched the Confederate army retreat through the streets of Hernando; that night Union troops entered the town and began looting. The college immediately disbanded, and Love left for home the next morning.

Sallie Love's father, however, was determined that she should obtain a college education. So he, Sallie, and his enslaved driver set out for the train station in the middle of the night, fearing encounters with Union troops during daylight. The Loves boarded the last train south before the Northern army shut down the line and made their way to Marion, Alabama, intending to enroll Sallie in the Judson Institute. But the very night they arrived, they learned that Union troops were headed in their direction. The institute would likely close. So they fled by boat, then carefully made their way to Macon, Georgia, home of Wesleyan Female College. They arrived there on Christmas Eve, 1862.

Love remained at Wesleyan for a year and a half. But at the end of the summer vacation in 1864, the Union general William T. Sherman's march through Georgia made it too dangerous for her to return there. So she enrolled instead at Aberdeen Female College in Aberdeen, Mississippi.

There, at the fourth college she had attended and the fifth to which she had traveled, Love finally graduated in June 1865. Her and her father's time, money, and risk to their lives paid off in the form of a liberal arts degree.[1]

Sallie Love's circuitous wartime journey underscores the challenges of attending college, especially in the South, during the Civil War. Someone less determined than she or her father would have given up much earlier. Her journey also underscores the challenges colleges faced in staying open amid battles and troop movements. Love witnessed the closure or impending closure of three institutions. At the same time, though, her story reveals that some students and families valued higher education enough to defy invading armies and that some colleges managed to keep classes in session. The Civil War did not destroy American higher education, though some individual institutions closed, temporarily or permanently. But the war did engulf and impair it for the duration. The experience changed it forever.

Between 1861 and 1865 colleges across America refashioned themselves as vehicles of war. Even as the war did severe harm to some institutions, they harnessed the strengths of a college campus and adapted these to serve wartime needs. The combination of colleges' willing contributions to the war, combatants' attempts to make use of the colleges, and the unforeseeable and uncontrollable effects of the war both hindered and changed higher education. After the war ended, colleges would continue to adapt to recover from wartime damage and to serve a nation changed by civil war.

When the Civil War began in 1861, America's college communities reacted in varied ways. Many students, along with a few professors, rushed off to join the fight. Others left to participate by peaceful means, such as nursing wounded soldiers or taking up farmwork vacated by enlisted relatives. Many stayed on campus but sought other ways to contribute to the military effort. Virtually all remained keenly aware of the war, often discussing or writing about the sectional crisis both before and after Fort Sumter. But many students and professors resisted the pull of the war. They continued attending classes, teaching them, and going about the daily activities of a college as in peacetime. Women's colleges, to some extent, became microcosms of the antebellum world, refuges from the disrupted world surrounding them. Colleges in the Far West, separated from the front by high mountains and an unfinished railroad, hardly noticed the war.

Most colleges, however, could not escape the nation's greatest conflict. Whether they embraced the war or not, students and professors east of the Rocky Mountains found their lives dramatically changed. For even as they decided whether to support or resist the Union or the Confederate cause, other actors and accidents were making the decision for them. At least as much as students', professors', and trustees' intentional contributions to the Civil War, the actions of state and national governments and the incidental effects of war helped to shape the direction of higher education.

During the Civil War government officials began directly to influence America's colleges. Colleges had always considered themselves public institutions and had educated many of the men who governed the United States, but not since the Revolution had national or state legislation affected them so dramatically. Now state governments and both national ones conscripted young men. Governments enlisted professors for intellectual or other wartime service. In the South, armies even took control of college campuses when they needed the buildings for their own use. Governments' actions during the war had little to do with higher education as such. They drafted young men regardless of their student status and commandeered college buildings for their convenience rather than their teaching facilities. Thus, governments and colleges began to craft partnerships. They shared each other's resources to achieve military goals. These partnerships would last. Beginning during the war and increasingly after it, governments and colleges would work together to achieve not only military but also educational and political goals.

Of course, neither governments nor colleges could fully control the fortunes of war. Even as colleges looked for ways to contribute and as governments took advantage of colleges' human and material resources, the war affected colleges in ways that neither colleges nor governments intended. Battles destroyed campuses. Male enlistments resulted in women's increased representation in student populations. Inflation made college more expensive. The movement of armies, as Love discovered, made simply getting to college a risky prospect. These accidental effects of the Civil War on America's colleges influenced them, in both the short and the long term, as much as the developing government partnerships and more than professors' or students' intentional involvement in the war. And unlike the government partnerships, which affected colleges throughout the Union and the Confederacy, these accidental effects occurred primarily in the South, the region where the war was fought. As a result, though the war affected higher education everywhere, it played a particularly strong role in shaping the colleges of the South—from the first shot at Fort Sumter to well beyond the surrender at Appomattox.

Even before the Southern states began to secede, the impending crisis was felt on college campuses. Students watched the sectional conflict over slavery develop in the 1850s. Conversation often revolved around political developments. At Mount Holyoke in 1853, "constant" talk of the Fugitive Slave Law and the Kansas-Nebraska Bill enlivened the campus. Students feared for the nation, going so far in 1854 as to hold a day of mourning for the difficult times. They closed the blinds in their dormitories and draped black badges and aprons over their doorknobs. The associate principal, in a lecture on national politics, implored students to pray for the country.[2] Six years later the students and faculty held their own mock presidential election. The results revealed some diversity of opinion on campus. Although Mount Holyoke enrolled only three women from slave states, the Southern candidates John C. Breckinridge and John Bell together polled 21 votes. That said, Abraham Lincoln won handily with 246 votes out of 299 (an 82% victory at Mount Holyoke that exceeded his 49% in the Union states and his 63% in Massachusetts). When Republican students learned that Lincoln had won the real election, they held a victory procession; disappointed Democrats tried unsuccessfully to blow out their lamps.[3]

Political conversations often took on a more academic character. Colleges were places of organized, methodical discussion both in and out of the classroom. Professors and students applied this academic ethic to the political and social questions of the day. As war seemed increasingly likely, students at Mount Holyoke wrote about the evils of war in their essays. For one composition assignment, a Southern and a Northern roommate wrote essays in favor of and against the Fugitive Slave Law. Another time, perhaps to teach skills of argumentation or perhaps to proselytize, a teacher at the seminary required a proslavery Southern student to recite to her class the antislavery arguments presented in a moral science textbook. To the Southerner's credit, a Northern classmate thought she made her case as well "as if she were convinced of its truth."[4]

A handful of Southerners and Northern Breckinridge or Bell supporters furnished some diversity of opinion at Mount Holyoke's Massachusetts campus, but in the future Confederacy students' discussions were more one-sided. Southerners had founded colleges there in part to ensure their sons' proslavery upbringing, which they considered essential for the

South's ruling class but which they could not expect from Northern colleges. These schools enrolled few or, as in the case of South Carolina College, no Northerners. Discussions on the eve of the Civil War thus entailed not so much a debate as unanimous enthusiasm for white Southern views. Shortly after the presidential election of 1860, South Carolina students attended a "political demonstration" that surely did not congratulate Lincoln on his victory. The following February, they attended another demonstration, celebrating the birth of the Confederacy.[5]

South Carolina College president Augustus B. Longstreet, uncle and political mentor of the future Confederate general James Longstreet, did not hesitate to teach South Carolina's students his own proslavery, states' rights opinions. His biographer argues that Longstreet's influence made them particularly enthusiastic Confederates after secession. Other faculty members freely expressed their extreme states' rights views in class lectures. Meanwhile, Georgia's Mercer University made proslavery views even more explicitly a part of the curriculum. In 1860 Mercer initiated a formal course in slavery, through which the faculty hoped to fit young men "to defend the institutions of their country."[6]

More often, organized debates over politics and slavery took place outside the classroom and away from professors. Literary societies, which first had appeared during the colonial period, dominated the social life of antebellum colleges. Next to the colleges' narrow classical curriculum, these societies provided an important social and educational forum for students. There they practiced debating, oratory, and parliamentary procedure, skills that served many alumni later in life. Debate topics ranged from history to education to local and national politics. Students thus both reflected on what they had learned in class and incorporated the study of current events into their academic experience.[7]

As the Civil War neared, students increasingly debated the political issues surrounding the sectional conflict. Students' choice of debate topics reflected their sectional and ideological makeup. Many Southern colleges had debated slavery during the 1850s (the proslavery side usually won) and some continued to debate related issues, including secession, during the 1860–61 academic year. But at South Carolina College, where the student body seems to have agreed that slavery was right, federal authority was wrong, and secession was the solution, these issues evidently were not open for debate. The closest students came was such questions as whether a government should prioritize "justice" or "Policy" and whether the United States should "maintain a standing army."[8]

At colleges in the Union states, both free and slave, the questions of the day were less tidily resolved. Revealing the diversity of opinion among white Northerners at the beginning of the war, both pro- and antisecession students made their voices heard at Cornell College in Iowa and the University of Missouri well into 1861. In addition to the mock congresses and orations that stirred Cornell's campus, the men of the Amphictyon Society regularly debated questions of slavery, politics, and secession. In April 1860 they considered the "political expedien[cy]" of the decade-old Fugitive Slave Law, and in January 1861 they asked whether secession would "be detrimental to the domestic & political institutions of the Northern states." Despite Cornell's not enrolling any students from slave states, the society president declared the negative debaters victorious. In April 1861 he could not decide who won when students debated whether the U.S. government should "recognize the Southern Confederacy."[9] Unlike South Carolina College students, who followed their college president in cheering for states' rights and the Confederacy, Cornell students debated the sectional issues and sometimes disagreed with the Lincoln administration.

Debates at Cornell, though two-sided, were tame. Not so at the University of Missouri. That border state harbored large numbers of both Unionist and secessionist Americans. With more than one hundred thousand slaves and a long border on the Mississippi River, Missouri easily could have joined the Confederacy. By the end of 1861, in fact, Union military forces and a renegade secessionist governor had created two state governments, one Union, one Confederate.[10] In a state with divided loyalties and an uncertain future, students at the university contentiously debated sectional questions in the months before the war.

The Athenaean Literary Society quickly became a microcosm of border-state politics. In some cases its members moved ahead of national debates on questions of sectionalism. As early as April 1860 they debated whether the Southern states should secede from the Union. They debated the same question again that fall, as well as, ominously, whether "the Southern youth who would kill Abraham Lincoln would be by future generations regarded the Brutus of America." In January 1861 they debated the secession question yet again—this time after it had begun—and "after a lengthy discussion," the society voted in favor of the seceded states' decision.[11]

Lest it appear that University of Missouri students agreed on secession, Unionists made their voices heard. The strength of their opposition became clear after the beginning of hostilities. On April 19, one week after the firing on Fort Sumter, a student introduced into the Athenaean

Society a resolution that it opposed Lincoln's war policy and supported Missouri's secession. But an opposing student successfully got that pro-Confederate measure tabled. Debate seems to have grown increasingly contentious thereafter. By the end of the year "the question of the dissolution of the Union" had grown so divisive that the society amended its constitution to forbid debate on the issue.[12] Through a gag rule, these students sought to maintain order in a sharply divided university and state.

Another organ of student opinion, the student newspaper or magazine, provided an outlet for a small group of editors to broadcast their views. Not all editors chose to do so. Harvard's complained shortly before Fort Sumter that college monthlies from Virginia, North Carolina, South Carolina, and Kentucky said nothing about military preparations or the founding of the Confederacy. The frustrated Bay Staters could explain that absence only by citing the popular opinion that politics had no place in a student paper. But the *Virginia University Magazine* did promote war, as did the *Harvard Magazine* itself. The Harvard editors expressed fascination at the "excitement and whirl of mad passion" in both North and South following Lincoln's election. They predicted and welcomed a war. Both Southern blacks and "Northern backs" had endured the "slave-driving lash" for too long. The time had come for "the reconstruction of the republic by force." Such a war would bring freedom to Northerners and rightful "subjugation" to white Southerners. Far ahead of the Northern curve, these students believed that the war "promised deliverance" to the slaves, for "the bondsman who takes refuge with us will find his safety."[13] A college brought youths together and encouraged them to analyze and debate important questions; the hothouse atmosphere of a college during a national crisis thus made youths passionate and sometimes radical in their sectional views. They discussed secession, assassination, and emancipation months or years before most Americans. And some, with high hopes, eagerly anticipated the Civil War.

Students were not the only members of college communities who had the sectional conflict on their minds in the 1850s and early 1860s. While students discussed and sometimes debated issues of national politics, faculty members also participated in the discussion. Sometimes, as noted above, they incorporated political questions into their courses. They thus adapted the curriculum to help their students understand the sectional crisis. At Mount Holyoke, although teachers rarely mentioned slavery, they permitted students to write about the Fugitive Slave Law and their fear of war for class compositions, and one teacher asked a Southern student to recite antislavery arguments. In 1854, when students held a day of mourning for the precarious condition of the country, they received a teacher's encouragement. Afterward, the associate principal addressed the students on the political issues of the day and encouraged them to pray for the nation. Her remarks likely reflected a distinctly Northern perspective, for she excused Southern students from attendance.[14] Harvard's African American physical-education instructor, Aaron Molyneaux Hewlett, may also have influenced students' views. The experience of training under a black man—one whose daughter later married the abolitionist Frederick Douglass's son, perhaps an indication of his own politics[15]—may well have fostered a sensitivity toward the rights of blacks and may have helped to develop the then radical interpretation of the war expressed by the *Harvard Magazine* editors.

But professors did not confine their comments to the college campus. Setting a pattern that would continue after the beginning of hostilities, they stepped onto the public, political stage. After the American Revolution, when some professors had tried to shape public opinion, a gulf had developed between colleges and the polity. But during the 1840s and 1850s some Southern professors and other intellectuals came to believe that their mental superiority entitled them to a role of moral leadership. Attempting to guide the formation of a better society, they published articles and made speeches promoting economic, political, and educational causes. The defense of slavery figured prominently on their agenda.[16] After Lincoln's election and the Deep South's secession, more academics decided to give up their relative isolation from public affairs. Moving from the classroom to the pulpit and from the study to the town square, they tried to use their intellectual authority to control the crisis. Their advice to the public ranged from reasoned caution to warlike exuberance, and their success in guiding their communities varied greatly. Still, in both North and South, the Civil War led these professors to refigure themselves as community leaders.

President Longstreet of South Carolina College was among the first scholars to seek a public role in the crisis. South Carolina did, after all, take the lead in both secession and armed conflict. Eyeing the state around him, Longstreet addressed its citizens in January 1861 with a pamphlet, *Shall South Carolina Begin the War?* In it he considered how his state should respond if President James Buchanan were to send a naval ship into Charleston to collect the taxes. Most South Carolinians supported firing upon that ship. Longstreet decried this as "the most dangerous, useless, ill-advised measure" imaginable. Currently, South Carolina was fighting a "defensive," "constructive" war. The national government was the aggressor, and South Carolina stood a good chance of attracting allies among other Southern states. Everything, he observed, was going according to plan.[17]

Were South Carolinians to fire upon a ship of the U.S. Navy, however, they would ruin everything. South Carolina would become the aggressor. The Northern states would unite against South Carolina, the Southern states would shy away from its aid, and the national government would have an excuse to launch "a war of extermination." This, Longstreet argued, was precisely what the "enemy" wanted. Sending a tax collector was merely a ruse to tempt South Carolina to start a war it could not win alone.

Longstreet urged his fellow citizens instead to proceed with caution. The tax collector was coming to collect federal taxes. So let him. He advised sending South Carolina's tax collector to meet him: they would converse as "the Collectors of two sovereignties . . . in the spirit of courtesy and kindness." The Palmetto State would pay its taxes, and that money would buy it time to secure allies in the South and in Europe. Then it would be ready for a war. Now, even if the navy did come to reinforce its forts, South Carolina might as well let it. The state was powerless to prevent it. Some might consider forbearance a sign of cowardice; those people, Longstreet charged, were "fools." "Let the first shot come from the enemy," he warned his audience. *"Burn that precept into your hearts, if you despise all else that I have written."*[18]

Longstreet acknowledged that most South Carolinians disagreed with him. But, he pointed out, "the correctness of opinions is not to be estimated by number . . . but by the standard of reason."[19] As a college president, he saw himself as the voice of reason and believed that the people and politicians of South Carolina should carefully consider his analysis of their situation.

Longstreet thus attempted to influence war policy. Although few professors would take such explicit (or condescending) political actions, during the war others did follow him in assuming roles of community leadership. But the question of South Carolina's starting the war in January became moot. President Buchanan did not send a ship to collect the taxes. By February six states had joined South Carolina to form the Confederate States of America. In April the new president of the United States dispatched a ship to supply Fort Sumter in Charleston Harbor. At that point, with the support of the Deep South, South Carolina fired, and the Civil War began.

College students and professors immediately involved themselves in the war. Most of them, especially the students, responded with enthusiasm for their sections. The women of Wesleyan Female College ended the school year in July with a concert featuring such pieces as "When Tyranny Condescending" and a hymn, "To Our Gallant Southern Soldiers," set to the tune of the "Marseillaise." The student newspaper chided the states of the Upper South for taking so long to join the Confederate cause. Students at the University of Missouri had banned debate on secession in their literary society, but they felt free to express their opinions elsewhere. Declaring their willingness to take up arms against Republican rule, one group of students attempted to erect a Confederate flag on campus—to the consternation of several faculty members. They ultimately reached a compromise, placing the flag in the street just outside the university entrance.[20] Meanwhile, colleges from Ohio to New England held flag-raising ceremonies for the Stars and Stripes. Professors not only permitted these pro-Union displays but often participated. At Brown University in Rhode Island, for example, faculty, clergy, and a former governor delivered speeches "deprecating civil war" but pledging readiness "to meet its necessity, and to uphold any measure which should have for its object the preservation of the national government." Columbia College in New York City showed its support for the Lincoln administration at commencement in June by awarding an honorary doctor of laws degree, in absentia, to the president.[21]

Right after Fort Sumter, the *Harvard Magazine* published a rousing call to patriotism. "As in the earlier Revolution," an editor observed, Americans were turning all their efforts to the national crisis. "The plough is left in the furrow, the hammer on the anvil, and strong-handed and stout-hearted men, fired with the true spirit of freedom, are rallying to the support of the government." College men did no less: "The voice of Harvard is for War!" Even those who until the first shot had advocated "conciliation and compromise" now fully supported the military effort. If anyone at Harvard did question the rightness of the war, that "traitor" kept his mouth shut—and rightly so, argued the editor. "It is not a time to prate of an honest difference of opinion. . . . Who respects or regards the scruples of a pirate, or his apologist?" He proudly published the names of the six Harvard men who already had joined the Union army.[22]

Of course, if Harvard spoke with one voice, it did so because Southern students had left when the war began. The editor who named the six Harvardians who had joined the Union army declined to name the fifteen who had joined the Confederates. Some of his coeditors remained gracious enough toward their Southern erstwhile schoolmates to apologize for the offence and print their names in the next issue. The war had begun to challenge bonds of school and friendship. Classmate prepared to fight against classmate, and those remaining on campus quarreled over how firmly to put national before college loyalties.[23]

At Cornell, students and professors turned community leaders expressed their enthusiasm for the Union cause together. Students had debated the Confederacy's legitimacy early in 1861, but after Fort Sumter supporters of the Union and of war made the most noise. When news of Lincoln's call for troops arrived in Mount Vernon, Iowa, students and professors joined townspeople around a huge bonfire. Professors delivered patriotic speeches. The next day, Linn County formed its first company. Enthusiasm permeated the area, with more volunteering than the company had room for. The chosen ones organized into Company K of the First Iowa Volunteer Infantry. One-fourth of them were Cornell students.[24]

The Civil War affected colleges most directly and most visibly through student enlistments. Both the Union and the Confederacy needed (and eventually required) young men to fight for them. Colleges were full of young men. So men's and coeducational colleges contributed their most valuable resource—their students—to the Cause. Both early enthusiasm and the opprobrium of the draft led large numbers of these young men to volunteer. Peer pressure surely contributed to these numbers. College populations consequently decreased. Some colleges shut down in the absence of pupils. Coeducational schools' populations became increasingly female, and a few all-male colleges began admitting women to avoid closure. Some professors encouraged enlistments, as at Cornell, while others resisted them, knowing the potentially disastrous effect on their institutions. But professors' wishes had little influence on students' decisions. Those who wanted to leave the classroom for the battlefield did so regardless of what their instructors said. The college environment, which in peacetime had fostered strident discussion of sectional issues, now mobilized young men for war.

Some colleges had no cause to worry about student enlistments. The military did not admit women, so enlistments did not directly affect women's colleges. Few soldiers came from beyond the Rocky Mountains, so colleges there suffered few, if any, student losses.[25] In 1862 a professor reported that some students had left the College of California. He did not explain why; they may have volunteered. Even if they did, however, they were few in number, and their departure did not produce a drop in the student population.[26]

Enlistments did affect colleges east of the Rockies. Men's and coeducational colleges there saw numerous students depart for the front.[27] Twenty-one Harvard men enlisted within a month after Fort Sumter, some of them without even notifying the school. (One of these, the future jurist Oliver Wendell Holmes Jr., remained sufficiently committed to his collegiate duties that he wrote his class poem at Fort Independence in Boston. He returned to Cambridge to deliver it on Class Day before enlisting.)[28] Even those who remained in town served the Cause. In late April 1861 the governor, who chaired Harvard's board of overseers, called on Harvard men to guard the Cambridge Arsenal (fig. 2). Professors recruited students for the job and excused them from some classes. A few seniors obtained the faculty's permission to join the troops in Boston Harbor for some practical training. And many of their classmates determined

Fig. 2. Harvard University students guarding the Cambridge Arsenal in an 1861 drawing by Frederick B. Allen. (Courtesy Charles M. Sullivan)

to start preparing to fight even before they left campus. Eager to become "effective soldiers," students petitioned to institute a drill. The faculty and the Harvard Corporation, which shared governing power with the overseers, obliged: they replaced gymnastic exercises with the faculty-led College Drill Club as of May 1. No fewer than 352 students—including the freshman Robert Todd Lincoln, son of the president—signed up. The law school, meanwhile, established a similar club. For a time, even as the first enlistees headed south, most Harvard students could get a taste of war without actually leaving.[29]

Of course, soon they did leave. Harvard sent a good share of its students to the front. Five hundred eighty-three members of the classes of 1861 through 1868 enlisted in the Union forces. Seventy students of the early 1860s joined the Confederate military. Including alumni, 1,311 Harvard men fought for the Union, and 353 for the Confederacy. Two hundred nine of those gave their lives. Yet Harvard was large enough that enlistments did not threaten its existence. Enrollment fell from 912 in 1860–61 to a low of 770 in 1862–63. Then it began to recover, and growth accelerated after 1867.[30]

Enlistments affected smaller colleges more dramatically. After Company K left Mount Vernon, Cornell College students continued to sign up for other units. By October 1, 1861, at least one hundred of them had enlisted. A student later recalled that nine Iowa regiments eventually included "considerable numbers" of Cornell men. Sixty-two members of the Amphictyon Society served, as did fifty-nine members of the Adelphian Society. Some of these scholar-soldiers achieved military distinction. None became generals or colonels, but Cornell furnished at least ten captains, six adjutants, ten lieutenants, and a quartermaster.[31]

The faculty and trustees appear to have supported or even encouraged their students to leave. When professors led the town in celebration of the war and Lincoln's call for troops, the message to their students was clear. When the trustees reported to the Methodist Episcopal Conference at the end of the 1861–62 academic year, they too celebrated rather than lamented the loss of those "true patriots." The fortuitous fact that new matriculates had offset the enlistments made it easier for them to take such a positive perspective. But the trustees did express concern that enrollment might decrease in the coming years.[32]

Indeed, enlistments had a sharp, if delayed, impact on the student population of Cornell College. That impact included an incidental but important result: not only the size but also the gender makeup of the college changed. In 1861, excluding children in the primary department, the student body actually grew slightly, from 320 to 322. But a year later it dropped to 213, a 34 percent decline. The number of male students, in particular, fell, from 173 to 80, a 54 percent decline. With 133 girls and women, this made females during the 1862–63 academic year the majority for the first time. Thereafter the population recovered, with large increases in both male and female enrollments. But men remained a minority until after the war.[33] As late as 1868 half the college's graduates were women (fig. 3). Other colleges experienced similar changes. Oberlin College became mostly female during the war. Virginia's Roanoke College and Iowa's Grinnell College admitted women for the first time (the latter against opposition from its dwindling male student population).[34]

When they enlisted, Cornell's scholar-soldiers risked both their education and their lives. Some returned after the war to complete their studies. Others were not so lucky. If the college kept a list of its Civil War casualties, that list has not survived. But one alumnus recalled that some of his schoolmates never made it back to Iowa. Others "came home crippled for life."[35]

Cornell College, unlike some of its students, survived the war. Like nearly all Northern colleges, it had the good fortune to be located far from the battles. Its coeducational student body also helped it to survive. Although the number of women declined slightly in the middle of the war, plenty remained to carry on the work of the college. Their presence and tuition money saved Cornell from any concerns about closing. The continued enrollment of some males, including young boys in the primary and preparatory departments, also helped. The primary department remained at least half male every year except one.[36] But other colleges lacked some or all of these fortunate circumstances.

South Carolina College suffered much more acutely from students' leaving for the war front. To start with, more students volunteered. The college reflected the Confederacy as a whole. With a much smaller white population than the Union, the new nation needed many more of its white men to enlist: four-fifths of those of eligible age by the end of the war versus half in the North. Ultimately virtually the entire military-aged male student population of South Carolina College joined the Confederate forces. And unlike at Cornell and many other Northern colleges, here males of military age made up the entire student population. There were almost no coeducational colleges in the South, and South Carolina College had no primary or preparatory department.[37] So the men's departure had greater consequences there than at Cornell.

Fig. 3. The Cornell College graduating class of 1868. (Photograph courtesy Cornell College Archives, Mount Vernon, Iowa)

RECONSTRUCTING THE CAMPUS

With enthusiastic and universal support for the Confederacy before the war even began, South Carolina College's students were only too eager to join the fight. By March 1861, with the faculty's approval, they had formed a drill company called the College Cadets. Governor Francis W. Pickens, who served as president of the board of trustees, supplied them with muskets from the state arsenal. At first they just marched around town and enjoyed the attention of the public.[38] When they learned in April of the federal intention to resupply Fort Sumter, however, they decided to do something. The students asked President Longstreet for permission to march to Charleston to defend the harbor from the Union invasion. Longstreet, the man who earlier had advised South Carolinians against just such behavior, denied their request. But nearly all of them went anyway. Pickens accepted their temporary enlistment.

The attack on Fort Sumter was a rare bloodless encounter in the Civil War; the students soon returned to campus. But they had set a pattern that would continue, namely, dedication to homeland before homework. During the summer vacation, many of them served with the Confederate army in Virginia. They remained somewhat dedicated to their studies, though, for they returned for fall classes. The faculty, evidently miffed by students' repeated departures from Columbia, readmitted them but denied senior ex-soldiers the right to compete for honors.[39]

Discouragement from the faculty did not prevent the students from returning to the war front. When they heard about another planned Union invasion of Charleston Harbor in November 1861, the students met and resolved to head to Charleston again to defend their state. This time they did not ask permission. The entire student body left. Revealing a strong sense of solidarity, even the seniors went, though most of them had opposed the decision. Governor Pickens, again contradicting the faculty, approved the students' action.

The faculty worried that their college, bereft of students, had reached its end. The only reason they did not officially close the school was that they lacked the authority; only the trustees could make that decision. But their worries proved exaggerated, at least for the time being. The Union navy never arrived in Charleston Harbor, but invaded Port Royal, farther south, instead. Pickens ordered the students' company there; he and the other trustees awarded seniors their degrees in absentia. The faculty, meanwhile, kept the college going by adjusting the calendar. They persuaded the trustees to extend the registration period for the second semester. By late January seventy-two students had been discharged and had returned to campus, down from 143 a year before. They were enough, and classes resumed.

But not for long. On March 8, 1862, the governor issued a conscription order.[40] Unlike much later in American history, when college attendance and good grades earned young men deferrals from the Vietnam War draft, even the brightest students were eligible for conscription during the Civil War. South Carolina's draft covered men aged eighteen to forty-five; the Confederate national draft that followed it a month later, men aged eighteen to thirty-five. The latter exempted professors, but neither exempted students. Nor did the Union draft of twenty- to forty-five-year-olds that came in March 1863.

Some Southern college leaders lobbied against the drafts. They asked state or Confederate officials to exempt all students, those under twenty-one, or those studying medicine. Usually their pleas met with flat refusals. Roanoke College did persuade the Confederate secretary of war to let students complete the academic term during which they turned eighteen, though he required students to drill and protect the area in exchange for that concession. In 1864 President Jefferson Davis exempted current juniors and seniors at the University of North Carolina from the draft. The university president's account of the school's precarious status and the student and faculty losses it already had suffered evidently impressed him (though not enough to exempt all students for the current session and upperclassmen for the duration, as the college president had asked). But these were exceptions. Governments expected young men to serve. Some students could avoid the draft by buying a substitute, as some did at Yale College, or by paying a fee, and others were disabled, underage, or exempted as the sole support of a mother; some, once drafted in the towns where their colleges were located, temporarily escaped service by proving residency elsewhere. But many who remained on campus in 1862 or 1863 faced the real possibility of forced military service. The only way to escape that fate, ironically, was to do just what they had been avoiding until then: enlist as volunteers.[41]

The state draft applied to all but twelve students at South Carolina College. The student body again met to plan its actions. Deciding that the only way to avoid the opprobrium of the draft was to volunteer, all but three or four students did just that. Not even those three or four showed up for class the next day. After spending the day waiting in empty classrooms, the faculty gave up. Because the trustees rejected a motion officially to close the college, the faculty advertised for students. They found only nine. They nonetheless finished the term with that miniscule class. Student enlistments had all but shut down South Carolina College. Other war-related events would soon finish the job.[42]

Enlistments stripped colleges of their adult male students. At some colleges, as at South Carolina, they reduced the student population almost to zero. Yet students could contribute to the war effort without actually taking up arms. Many of those students who did not enlist, including many women, found other ways to participate in the Civil War. Colleges helped to mobilize them by promoting types of war work that could occur on campus. Other types of noncombatant service, however, contributed to the colleges' depopulation.

Not all students who abandoned their campuses in the 1860s were men. Women could not join the military, but many had good reason to leave. Sallie Love, whose story begins this chapter, left four colleges to evade enemy troops before she graduated from Aberdeen Female College. She kept trying, moving from one college to another until she graduated. Those who lacked her determination went home without a degree.

Not only mortal fear led women to leave school. Although they could not fight, many women gave up their studies, at least temporarily, to perform other types of war work. Men who joined the army left civilian jobs undone. Many Cornell women had brothers who enlisted, forcing them to return home to work on family farms. Hence the college's enrollments for both genders fell in 1863, though much less precipitously for women.[43]

Women left Mount Holyoke for a variety of reasons. One returned home to war-torn Missouri after losing contact with her family there. At least one student was forced to leave upon her enlisted father's death, probably for financial reasons. Another left to care for her brother, who had returned home from the war ill. Other women left to take a more active role in the Union war effort by heading to the front as nurses. A teacher later remembered "our army of hospital nurses." It is unclear exactly how many served as nurses and how many of those who did were current students rather than alumnae. The best-remembered among students, Caroline Cutter, was an 1861 graduate who immediately joined her surgeon father in North Carolina, where she died of a fever.[44] Although Mount Holyoke did not endure the shrinking student population common at men's colleges, a number of women did leave school owing to a combination of reasons, including financial woes, to fill in for male relatives at home, and to care for the ill at home or in military hospitals.

Students did not need to leave campus to contribute to the war. Although many chose or were forced to depart for war-related reasons, those who remained also served. Students on campus joined the war effort most visibly, if perhaps not most usefully, by drilling. The College Cadets at South Carolina College and the College Drill Club at Harvard marched around campus when they were not away fighting a real war. Missouri's students petitioned for a military company, leading to the formation by June 1861 of a company led by Professor Edward F. Fristoe that probably also included townsmen. Even the far-off College of California had formed a cadet company for its preparatory students by 1864. Numerous other colleges established drill companies for their male students, often by student initiative.[45]

Some colleges developed more elaborate student military organizations. The president of the University of Alabama, aiming both to train future officers and to justify continued college attendance, just before the war enlisted all students in a cadet corps that he hoped could help resist a Union invasion or suppress a slave rebellion. The University of Virginia also became primarily a military school. Colleges in Ohio formed units of the Home Guard that trained on campus in case they were needed to defend the state. The governor called on them for duty several times in 1862 and 1863, though the closest they came to combat was escorting captured Confederates to prison.[46]

Drilling was not confined to men. In 1863 or 1864 the faculty of Wesleyan organized its female student body into two companies, the Bonnell Blues and the Freeman Guards, after the college president and custodian. They wore uniforms consisting of their regular homespun dresses, paper hats, and sashes identifying their companies, blue for the Blues and green for the Guards. Those young women selected as officers wore paper epaulets. Armed with artificial guns, they marched around Macon in military fashion, commanded by the president's son and led by a local child hired as their drummer. On one occasion the college invited local citizens to watch the women drill, hear a prowar speech, and eat strawberries. After this patriotic "Strawberry Festival," the women marched in formation back to their dormitory. The Blues and the Guards may not have contributed to any Confederate victories, but possibly they helped maintain patriotic sentiment in Macon. At the very least, they considered their own role serious and important.[47]

By organizing young women into military units, Wesleyan's faculty and students pushed the boundaries of mid-nineteenth-century gender conventions. They were not alone in doing so. Beginning early in the war, adult women in some Southern cities formed armed groups to defend their homes. With so many men away fighting or dead, they had little choice. A group of Virginia women in 1864 even asked the Confederate secretary of war (unsuccessfully) to authorize an entire regiment of women. In addition, hundreds or thousands of Confederate and Union women joined the armies disguised as men. Their reasons ranged from patriotism to desire for adventure to love for a soldier to financial need.[48] These women issued no calls for gender equality or the permanent inclusion of women in the military. Rather, they did what they felt was necessary and permissible in an extraordinary situation.

At Wesleyan, the armed women negotiated a delicate boundary between those changes that they believed necessary in wartime and those that remained beyond the pale. Sallie Love, like her classmates, found drilling invigorating. Hearing the male speaker at the Strawberry Festival extol the student-soldiers' "stern faces" and "formidable weapons," she proudly "clutched my helpless wooden gun as I listened!" But on hearing that her roommate once had masqueraded as a male to join the army as a drummer boy, Love was deeply distressed: "To think I was rooming with that style girl." Though the story turned out to be a hoax, her reaction illuminates the strange new waters students navigated in wartime.[49] Amid the possibility of an even greater subversion of gender roles—women in the actual army—young women's taking up fake arms on a college campus became an acceptable, even celebrated, change.

College women also did more conventional, and practical, war work. These other ways in which women contributed to the war effort from the beginning, in fact, likely made their military activities seem more palatable by the second half of the conflict.[50] They included raising money. In July 1861 Wesleyan music students performed the operetta *The Flower Queen* for the benefit of the Soldiers' Aid Society of Macon.[51] Mount Holyoke's class of 1864, instead of buying the traditional class badges, pooled their funds to donate $175 to the U.S. Christian Commission for its work with wounded and ill soldiers. In thanks for their generosity, the organization awarded each donor a Christian Commission badge, which she found attached to her diploma.[52]

More often, college women contributed in kind. Students at Mount Holyoke spent many hours knitting and sewing items to send to the soldiers, to military hospitals, and to Christian Commission fairs for sale. Three hundred young women gathered in a room to work, turning the seminary into a veritable textile factory. Teachers and more experienced students instructed the rest in the task at hand. Sometimes, as the students worked, teachers would take the opportunity to lecture them on etiquette. Even outside the supervised work sessions, students carried their knitting bags with them at all times, using every free moment to continue the work. In this fashion they made socks, mittens, drawers, slippers, and bandages. Along with these they sent pins, buttons, needles, thread, and occasionally "jellies and other delicacies" to break the monotony of army rations.[53] To help boost the soldiers' morale, a group of Mount Holyoke students and South Hadley townspeople organized "a society . . . to write cheering letters to the soldiers." (Oberlin women took this one step further, hiding a note in the toe of each sock they knitted.)[54] No doubt, many a soldier appreciated a kind missive as much as warm clothing.

Mount Holyoke students also supported the soldiers in less tangible ways. At commencement in 1862, for example, the principal instructed graduates to encourage men they knew to fight for the Cause.[55] But by far the most common war activity at the seminary, with the possible exceptions of sewing and knitting, was prayer. Mount Holyoke, founded with a Christian mission, incorporated prayer into its curriculum throughout the day and week. Thereby it sought to induce conversions among the student population.[56] Now, in a time of war, the faculty put the religious custom into national service. During the 1850s students had prayed for a nation in crisis. Now they prayed for the soldiers.

They prayed constantly. News of relatives' deaths made prayer necessary for students to make it through a trying time. In 1862 a teacher suggested that students reserve one evening each week to pray for the soldiers. By 1864 the faculty had formalized her suggestion. Students attended an optional fifteen-minute prayer meeting, led by a teacher, every evening. Each day they focused on a different object of prayer; on Tuesdays they prayed for the nation and the soldiers. Students could offer up notes for prayers for relatives in the military. All this supplemented individual prayers throughout the days, weeks, and years of the war.[57] With their hands and with their hearts, students—male and female, Southern and Northern—did what they could to support their nations' causes.

Just as faculty members joined students in debating sectional issues before the war, some played an active role in the conflict once it began. That role was not the same everywhere. At Cornell College, professors led Mount Vernon's celebration of Lincoln's call for troops, at least implicitly (and successfully) encouraging their pupils to enlist. At South Carolina, they explicitly (and unsuccessfully) attempted to prevent students from joining the fight, fearful of their institution's fate. Faculty members elsewhere tried (also unsuccessfully) to get students exempted from the draft. At Mount Holyoke, free from the question of enlistments, they led female students in prayer for the men defending their country.

Wesleyan's faculty used the college facilities to help those in need. By 1863, with declining enrollment owing to wartime inflation and the difficulty of travel, they opened the college dormitory to war refugees. Some were girls or young women who shared rooms with students. As many as five slept in a single room. Adult men and women also found refuge in dormitory rooms. Families who could afford to paid the college rent, helping the college to survive financially with fewer students.[58]

Some professors played more active roles in the war. The Columbia College political scientist Francis Lieber, who earlier had taught at South Carolina College, wrote a new code of war for the Union government and pro-Union propaganda for the Loyalist Publication Society. The recently founded National Academy of Sciences facilitated scientists' contributions to the war effort; it and other learned societies published articles on topics ranging from ballistics to medicine. Some professors joined the armies. The rhetorician Joshua L. Chamberlain, lying to Maine's Bowdoin College about a research trip to Europe, accepted a commission in the Union army and rose to the rank of major general. The College of California trustee John C. Frémont also served as a Union major general; as a trustee, he presumably needed to make no excuse. William L. Broun, formerly a mathematics professor at the University of Georgia and now a Confederate major, oversaw the administration of a mathematics and science examination for officers in the Ordnance Department. In 1861 and 1862, Harvard granted leaves of absence to two professors so that they could join the Union army. Edward F. Fristoe, the University of Missouri mathematics and astronomy professor who had led students in military drill in 1861, left campus early in 1862 to join the Confederates.[59]

South Carolina College professors, despite their resistance to student enlistments, served the Confederacy in both combative and noncombative capacities. Charles S. Venable, the professor of mathematics and astronomy, actually joined the army. He became a colonel on General Robert E. Lee's staff and served at Gettysburg. He resumed his academic career after the war, accepting a new position at the University of Virginia.[60]

Venable's colleagues, though also supportive of the Confederacy, were unwilling to abandon the college. Much like fathers who struggled with competing responsibilities to nation and family as they decided whether to join or remain in the armies,[61] these men tried to balance their responsibilities to nation and school. Early on, both Robert W. Barnwell Jr. and Maximilian LaBorde decided to volunteer in the military hospitals. Realizing, however, that the college could not afford to lose two professors—one-fourth of the faculty—Barnwell agreed to stay through the term. He joined his colleague that summer. By the fall of 1861, though, neither wanted to return. Barnwell informed the trustees that "the welfare of the noblest blood" outweighed his commitment to the college. The patriotic board, agreeing that removing him from the hospital "would seem to be indefensible," allowed him to stay. He returned later that fall. But when the students left to defend Charleston in November, he took the opportunity to leave for the hospital again. Citing his "conflict of duties" between the college and the army, he even offered his resignation to the trustees so that he could stay with the troops. They refused his resignation, however, and he returned again the following March.[62] Meanwhile, LaBorde became chairman of the faculty but still escaped campus enough to establish four hospitals in Virginia. He also founded the Central Association for the Relief of South Carolina Soldiers. These men did not fight, but they saved lives—and Barnwell lost his to illness.[63]

Two other professors contributed their expertise to the war effort while remaining mostly on or near campus. Between 1862 and 1864 the chemistry and geology professor Joseph LeConte wrote a pamphlet for the military on the production of niter, a key ingredient in gunpowder; arbitrated between the Confederate government and the owners of niter mines; and oversaw the production of medicine for the army at a factory near Columbia. He then received appointments as chemist and professional assistant to test sources of niter, a position that involved both research in his college laboratory and travel throughout the Confederacy, and as consulting chemist at Columbia for the Niter and Mining Bureau. He later claimed to have worked for the government at first because he needed extra money due to inflation, but afterwards to "support . . . the cause." Meanwhile, probably owing to the Union blockade of Confederate ports, the South Carolina government asked the science professor John LeConte, Joseph's brother, to prepare a pamphlet on the extraction of salt from seawater. John then served as superintendent of the niter works at Columbia.[64] Whether armed with a pen, a beaker, a scalpel, or a sword, more than half the South Carolina faculty served the Confederate cause.

All parts of college communities contributed to the war effort. Male students took up arms. Female students supplied the soldiers with medical care, socks, letters, and prayers. Although some professors tried to prevent their pupils from joining the fight, others encouraged them. Some even joined the younger men on the battlefield or in hospitals.

Trustees, at a minimum, permitted all this to happen; some, such as Frémont when he took an officer's commission and Pickens when he armed and then enlisted South Carolina's students, played a more active role. Students, professors, and trustees happily participated in the Civil War. Governments, by mustering in young men and by welcoming professors' contributions, facilitated colleges' participation.

Not all the war's effects on colleges were voluntary. Students and professors joined the war effort, but they could not control it. With a war going on around them—literally, in the South—colleges inevitably underwent unexpected and undesired changes. These ranged from the challenging to the destructive. Although all the colleges I focus on still existed after the war, some took a long time to recover from its damage. In the South, as we will see in later chapters, the accidental effects of the war, along with the actions of governments, would shape higher education for many years to come.

Even before colleges started losing their students to the war, they lost something else dear to them: public attention. All colleges, and especially young ones, relied heavily upon private donations.[65] They also relied, therefore, on a public perception of colleges' importance. Months before the war started, that began to wane. Americans did not come to think colleges unnecessary. They simply thought about them less. The College of California suffered from this sudden shift. In the fall of 1861 Professor Martin Kellogg traveled through New England soliciting donations to the struggling Pacific college. He had a great deal of success—until South Carolina seceded. With the national crisis on people's minds, plus the financial panic that followed, few considered a college three thousand miles away a priority. "Northern men," Kellogg reported to the trustees, "feel that they must bend all their energies now to the great task of saving the country." "Colleges," consequently, "are pushed quite out of sight." In his report he referred to college fundraising as "the cause."[66] But most Americans had another cause on their minds. Combined with the loss of tuition from students who left to enlist, the drop in donations hurt colleges.

So did inflation. By the end of the war prices in the Union were 75 percent higher than in 1860. The Confederacy fared much worse. Whereas the United States financed the war primarily with loans, the Confederate States financed 62 percent of the war by printing more currency. This policy resulted in devaluation and thus rampant inflation. By the end of the war, prices in the South had risen by 9,000 percent.[67] Virtually everyone suffered from want, including college communities.

Northern colleges faced relatively minor hardships from inflation. Students at both Cornell College and Mount Holyoke wore simpler clothing owing to the high cost of fabric. At Mount Holyoke, students suffered great disappointment when served pumpkin pie for dessert instead of the more expensive apple or mincemeat pie.[68] But inflation also produced more serious effects. Harvard's president noted the "poverty and want" his students faced as prices rose. In 1864, owing to the rising cost of living, Mount Holyoke's trustees increased faculty salaries; to pay for the raise, they increased tuition as well. They acknowledged that the change would prevent some students from returning but saw no alternative.[69] Inflation forced them to sacrifice poorer students' education to ensure their employees a living wage.

Severe Confederate inflation and the Union blockade magnified these problems. Most male students avoided dealing with inflation because they joined the army. Not so for women. At Wesleyan, students started wearing homespun clothing owing to the high cost and low availability of professionally produced goods. The scarcity of gas for lamps forced them to burn lard; the scarcity of paper forced them to share sheet music and memorize the songs. More important, in the spring of 1862 the trustees responded to inflation by raising tuition and fees. They continued to do so over the next three years. At the beginning of the war tuition and fees totaled $210; by the end they were more than $1,100.[70] Chapter 3 examines in depth the consequences of inflation for Southern colleges. For now, suffice it to say that the rise in tuition made it difficult for many to attend.

The war unleashed much more destructive forces than high tuition or pumpkin pie. Some colleges, almost all of them in the South, endured physical destruction or military takeover.[71] The extensive damage to the College of William & Mary included the burning of its Main Building by Union troops. The nation's second oldest college did not permanently reopen until 1888. Troops armed with torches completely destroyed Cumberland University in Tennessee and the Virginia Military Institute, forcing them to construct new facilities when they reopened after the war. Even those Southern colleges fortunate enough to avoid battle sometimes suffered inconvenience or damage from a military presence. Columbian College (now George Washington University), in the nation's capital, was commandeered by the Union army and converted to barracks and hospitals as soon as the war began; professors moved classes into their homes. And in 1864 the Confederacy's chief surgeon at Macon repeatedly requested that Wesleyan turn over its buildings for use as a military hospital. Given that the government had converted many public buildings into hospitals, including hotels, factories, courthouses, and other colleges, his requests probably came as little surprise. When the faculty refused, he threatened to take the buildings by force. The college hired a lawyer to fight the attempt. Later the same year, after Sallie Love went elsewhere owing to Sherman's march through Georgia, Wesleyan briefly closed for the same reason. In the end, Sherman decided against entering Macon, and the college reopened.[72] The Confederacy did not take over Wesleyan. But it was one of the lucky ones.

In March 1862 South Carolina College saw virtually its entire student population go to war. It took only a few months for the Confederate government to deal the final blow to the enfeebled college. That summer the government asked the chairman of the faculty to turn over the campus for use as a military hospital. When he refused, the authorities repeated the request to the executive committee of the trustees. When the committee also said no, the national government applied to the governor. He granted the request. South Carolina College became a hospital. No classes met that fall.[73]

The Confederacy had turned the college, against its will, to wartime purposes. It remained a military hospital for the rest of the war. The professors, though, did not stand idly by. The trustees told those who had not left for service on the battlefield or in other hospitals that they could remain on campus. Chairman LaBorde contributed his own labor to the hospital that had closed his college. But he, his colleagues, and the trustees also complained. In May 1863 they asked the Confederacy to return control of the college to them. Not surprisingly, the military denied the request. Thereafter, the faculty and trustees began describing the agreement as one of the trustees' renting out the college buildings to the government. That interpretation allowed them to makes lists showing which buildings they had rented out and which ones they had not. But the occupiers cared little about those lists, continuing to occupy buildings regardless of whether their hosts thought they had rented them. The trustees also attempted to collect rent payments, without success.[74]

Ironically, the Confederate occupation ended up saving the college from destruction. On February 17, 1865, people far more dangerous than doctors arrived in Columbia: Union soldiers. General Sherman, having completed his march through Georgia and turned north, had reached South Carolina's capital. His troops began pillaging the city. Worse, both they and fleeing Confederate troops set it ablaze. Hundreds of buildings burned, but not those on the campus of South Carolina College. LaBorde's biographer claims that he saved the college. Another professor claimed that his own wife played a key role. But most likely the presence of a hospital protected the campus from Sherman's forces. Some Union soldiers were recuperating there, a fortunate circumstance for the college. Even so, several times college buildings did catch fire, probably due to flying sparks, forcing doctors to move their patients outside. Doctors, professors, and soldiers all helped to put out the flames. As for plunder, a local paper speculated that the professors living at the college remained safe simply because they owned little worth taking. The army arrested John LeConte, the professor overseeing the Confederate niter works, but released him after a few days.[75]

With the Confederate occupiers gone, the college's fate rested with Union military policy. President Lincoln preferred to respect private property and conduct a war against the governments of the Confederacy and its states. But he acknowledged that the military sometimes needed to target private property. The new Union code of war written in 1863—by a former South Carolina College professor—authorized seizure or destruction in such cases. This policy, as interpreted by Sherman and other commanders, legalized the destruction of property at least to supply their troops and possibly to demoralize Confederate citizens.[76] It also legalized the seizure of South Carolina College when Columbia's occupiers needed a headquarters. In addition, the Confederacy already had militarized the college by turning it into a hospital. So had the professors who had conducted scientific and medical work for the Confederacy on campus. They had sacrificed any protection due to private property. Furthermore, all colleges stood at the boundary between public and private. Whether founded by the state, as South Carolina College had been, or by a religious denomination, as Cumberland University (which was occupied by Union troops before being burned by Confederate ones)[77] had been, colleges always had served a public role. Union commanders, like the Confederate authorities who turned both courthouses and colleges into hospitals, evidently deemed colleges sufficiently public facilities to justify their seizure.

The Union army therefore took over the campus, making it the headquarters for the commandant of Columbia, and remained in control of part of the campus until at least 1874. (Unlike the Confederacy, the Union did pay rent.) Meanwhile, people left homeless by the burning of Columbia stole into the college dormitories, where they remained for a decade.[78] Even as efforts began to reopen the college, it continued to deal with occupying forces. The campus had survived the war, but it had lost its students, part of its faculty, and dominion over its property.

The University of Missouri also became a military camp. Like South Carolina College, it found itself in a war zone. At first, though, it seemed to have escaped the armies' paths. A local newspaper reported in July 1861 that the spring term had been "the most prosperous and successful" ever, despite "the political troubles and financial embarrassments of the Country." Some predicted that the university would remain a refuge from the war. Their optimism proved premature. Missouri may have been a Union state, but that did not make its institutions immune to Union occupation. In addition to forming dual Union and Confederate governments, the state endured invasions by both sides and became a field for guerrilla tactics.[79] The university at Columbia was only too convenient a base in a contested and violent area. During the fall of 1861 several units of troops arrived, set up camp, and left. On January 2, 1862, the military presence became permanent. University facilities served numerous purposes. The grammar school became a hospital; the president's house, military headquarters. Other buildings served as courtroom, barracks, prison, quartermaster's department, and stables. Before the army's departure in August 1865, it occupied every room on campus except those housing the chemistry equipment.

Classes ceased temporarily a couple of times, but remarkably, the professors kept the university open for at least part of every academic year. The army accommodated their needs, vacating the main building so that they could hold classes. This is not to say that college life went unhindered. With so many students enlisted in the military, enrollment dropped from 168 at the beginning of the war to only 23 in 1862–63, with only 1 graduate in 1863. With tuition income so small and no financial support from the state government, the university stayed open only because dedicated professors worked without pay.[80]

With the university under military authority, its faculty and its governing board of curators had to assure the occupiers of their allegiance. South Carolina College's loyalty to the Confederacy went without saying; a border-state school's loyalty to the Union did not. On February 3, 1862, therefore, General Henry W. Halleck, commander of the Department of the Missouri, ordered that all officers of the university either take a loyalty oath or lose their positions. He cited the federal land grant with which the state had founded the university as a reason to "expel from its walls all persons who by word or deed favor, assist, or abet rebellion." And he did just that. While most took the oath, a Confederate-leaning curator and the treasurer resigned. Professor Fristoe took the opportunity to join the Confederate army.[81]

The Union troops, though not a hostile force as in South Carolina, caused a great deal of physical damage to the campus. Prisoners held in the main building cut holes in the floor while trying to escape. Soldiers chopped down most of the trees, removed classroom fixtures, packed up and shipped away the geological collection, and burned or sold—to local blacks and poor whites in exchange for whiskey—hundreds of books from the library. Soldiers even broke into and stole from the rooms where chemical apparatus were stored, the only rooms the military did not officially occupy. A committee appointed by the board of curators to assess the damages placed their total value at more than three thousand dollars by February 1863.[82] The University of Missouri stayed open during most of the war, and it got along better than South Carolina College with the occupying force. But it still suffered heavily from the experience.

As the war dragged on and hardships mounted, some students and professors grew disillusioned with the war and their political and military leaders. That colleges served the nation does not mean that college communities were of a single mind. They shared the mixed opinion about the Cause—either nation's cause—that permeated the country around them. Colleges during the Civil War never garnered the attention as repositories of dissent that they did during the Vietnam War a century later.[83] But some members of college communities, amid the general atmosphere of prowar patriotism, did question the rightness of the war or of their leaders. After 1862, as the deaths mounted and, in the Confederacy, the future looked increasingly grim, they began more vocally to criticize their nations.

Not all students and professors cheered their national leaders at the beginning. Augustus B. Longstreet, the president of South Carolina College who had taken South Carolinians to task for their haste in starting the war, turned a critical eye to the Confederate leadership after it began. Although a steadfast Confederate, he remained uncertain about President Jefferson Davis's motives. A republic, he told Methodist worshippers in June 1861, always risks turning corrupt. Only religion can prevent that. Davis's absence of religious motives pointed to danger. Although he did not list specifics, Longstreet observed that the Confederacy already had made mistakes in "our conduct and our code" that could turn it as corrupt as the U.S. government it had just rejected. He called on the citizens of the new nation to ensure that that did not happen by allowing their religion to guide their votes.[84] As he had before the war, Longstreet used his authority as a college president to recommend political behavior and point out pitfalls as the new nation established itself.

Over time, some people in Northern and Southern colleges grew overtly critical of their leaders. In effect, they resisted the war's use of higher education for its own ends. Cornell College had always harbored mixed opinion. The men's literary society had debated federal policy in the first months of 1861; it continued to do so after the declaration of hostilities. In May 1862 the society considered whether "war [is] ever justifiable"; that October it debated the wisdom of the president's recent Preliminary Emancipation Proclamation. In each case the negative position won. More ominously, in January 1863 the society debated whether "our government in her present struggle [will] be sustained." Again the negative won.[85]

At commencement that July the debate turned violent. Two students, one male and one female, wore Copperhead (antiwar) pins to the occasion. Supporters of the war responded by de-pinning the offenders. The altercation ended in a lawsuit, in which the Copperheads charged their opponents with assault and inciting a riot. But the loyalists won, the court ruling that they had acted properly against disloyal Americans.[86]

At Harvard, students expressed their opposition through private talk and public silence. In late 1862 the initial loud support for the Union cause began to subside. In April 1863 nothing remained but "a low murmur of timid, trembling patriotism." While none vocally opposed the war, some now read and discussed approvingly "Copperhead speeches" about "the *despotism* of our National Administration." A Lincoln supporter declared this talk "seeds of treason," excoriating his schoolmates for not taking a strong public stance in favor of Lincoln and against all who criticized the administration. He feared Harvard's rejection of real patriotism in favor of *"heartless indifference."*[87]

Down South at Wesleyan, one student was both vocal and specific in her criticism of the war effort. She did not criticize the Cause, but rather the men fighting for it. In her commencement speech, presented in 1864 before her classmates and invited citizens of Macon, Stella Marshall celebrated the "honorable" nature of war and the righteousness of the Confederate cause. She even predicted "victory over our ruthless and brutal invaders." But she followed that prediction with a sharp criticism: "No Southern *woman* has ever had the shadow of a doubt on this issue, nor has she ever shrunk from any sacrifice in her power to contribute *her* share towards the advancement of our cause. Would to God the same could be said of every *man* in the South."[88] Three years of war and little reason for optimism, along with refugees in the dormitories and lard in the candles, evidently had worn Marshall's patience thin. Without actually opposing the Confederacy, she now used her public position on a college stage, as commencement speaker, to criticize rather than contribute to the war effort.

Some students felt that college life isolated them from the war. At men's and coeducational colleges this was impossible. A man at "secluded" Hamilton College in New York, "so much removed from marching regiments, and mass meetings, and flying banners," did claim in October 1861 that "if it were not for the daily papers, we would almost forget there was a war."[89] But the feeling could not have lasted long. Even if men wanted to avoid the war, which most did not, peer pressure and eventually the draft made them constantly think about the possibility of fighting. Southern schools under military occupation, such as South Carolina and Missouri, could hardly isolate their inhabitants from the war. But women's colleges were different.

Women sometimes described college as a refuge from the war. Kathleen M. Carruth felt disconnected from the war at Mount Holyoke even though her father served in the officer corps. A Wesleyan alumna later recalled that her parents had sent her and her sister to the Georgia college "for safe-keeping until the close of the war." Once there, students were forbidden to read newspapers. In some ways that campus became a walled-in microcosm of the antebellum Southern world that the war was destroying. As white students studied (and drilled) in dresses, preparing for their presumed future lives as plantation mistresses, they enjoyed the service of (probably enslaved) African American servants. Unlike some Southern colleges, Wesleyan generally prohibited students' bringing their own slaves to campus. During the war, though, the sisters nonetheless brought their slave mammy along. With her tying their shoes and combing their hair, they lived a life remarkably similar to that on an antebellum plantation.[90]

Students such as Carruth, however, were in the minority. Her classmate Ellen C. Parsons expressed a more measured opinion. She agreed that students at Mount Holyoke could temporarily forget about the war while picking flowers or being serenaded by male students from nearby Amherst College. But the blissful forgetfulness never lasted long. For "always, we were like dwellers beside the sea, and the undertone we heard was war." Most surely agreed with her that colleges stood at least beside the sea, if not engulfed by the tide.[91]

For better or worse, nearly all colleges had come to serve war-related purposes. The Civil War context largely defined college life in the early 1860s. And some students, in the end, reflected on the war as a positive experience. Parsons felt that Mount Holyoke students, by virtue of attending college in wartime, had graduated with more "maturity" than they would have otherwise. The experience, she believed, had taught the women "unquenchable courage . . . , quiet endurance, fervent devotion, [and] strong, winning service for education and for Christ." If women learned all that on campus during the war, men who fought learned even more. When South Carolina College students returned from military service in early 1862, even the faculty that had opposed their enlistment acknowledged the improvement in their work ethic. War had produced a class more "distinguished for industry" than almost any the college had known.[92]

Patriotic participation, government cooptation, and mere accident refashioned colleges to serve the needs of war. As the war neared its end, both college leaders and government officials began to consider longer-term changes in higher education. Colleges needed to serve not only the immediate needs of war but also the peacetime needs of a postbellum world. These needs continued to reshape higher education after 1865.

Plans for postbellum change began even before hostilities ended. As early as 1864 Cornell College started looking for a way to give back to those who had fought to preserve the Union. The trustees set up a fund to provide free tuition to disabled soldiers and orphans of soldiers.[93] Meanwhile, men in Washington began to set long-term educational policy. Most partnerships between governments and colleges during the war— enlisting students, employing professors, and taking over college property—had little to do with education and served the governments more than the colleges. But in 1862 Congress passed a law explicitly about higher education. The Morrill Land-Grant College Act, which provided federal funding for certain types of colleges, sought to create a system of higher education that would serve America well beyond the war years.

When General Robert E. Lee surrendered at Appomattox Court House, Virginia, on April 9, 1865, American higher education lay in an uneven state. A few colleges, such as the College of California, continued almost as if nothing had happened. Others carried on knowing they had contributed to the war and probably glad they no longer risked further intrusion. Mount Holyoke had sent its share of nurses to the front and Harvard its share of soldiers; both mourned the deaths of friends or family. Wesleyan, closed briefly during Sherman's march, had reopened and could look forward to lowering tuition and replacing the refugees in its dormitory with students. Cornell had become primarily a college for women but now rightly expected war veterans to begin filling its classrooms. Still other colleges had suffered from the war and looked forward to a challenging recovery. Missouri had struggled to stay open amid soldiers and army livestock. South Carolina had not held a class in nearly three years. The college turned hospital at least had escaped destruction by Sherman's troops, and soon a new governor would look into reopening and re-creating the defunct state college.

American higher education had survived the Civil War by serving it. Through military service, hospital work, and clothing production, colleges had contributed to the needs of a nation at war. By enlisting male students, soliciting professors' expertise, and commandeering college buildings, state and national governments had coopted college communities for their causes. Physical damage and monetary inflation had challenged the survival of colleges and their students. These experiences immediately and visibly changed colleges, especially in the South.

After the surrender, longer-term consequences of the war began to surface. The Civil War, it turned out, did not only steal men and raise the cost of fabric. It helped to change colleges' policies in such seemingly unrelated areas as curricula and admissions. It did so while building new relationships between colleges and governments, as the federal government grew much larger and more watchful than ever before. The war ended after four years, but its most important effects on higher education took longer.

◁❧· TWO ·❧▷

The Curriculum
Teaching the Arts of Peace and War

On September 30, 1859, the lawyer and failed senatorial candidate Abraham Lincoln spoke to the Wisconsin State Agricultural Society at its annual fair in Milwaukee. Although conceding that he was "in no sort a farmer" himself, Lincoln pointed to what he saw as some of the most important issues of the day relating to agriculture. He speculated on the value of new technologies and internal improvements for growing and transporting produce. He compared the meanings of free and slave labor. And, toward the end of his speech, he broached the question of education for farmers. "Cultivated thought," he argued, could make possible more "*thorough* work" in agriculture. He looked forward to a time when people would value agricultural learning above all other types: "This . . . conforms to what must occur in a world less inclined to wars, and more devoted to the arts of peace than heretofore. Population must increase rapidly—more rapidly than in former times—and ere long the most valuable of all arts, will be the art of deriving a comfortable subsistence from the smallest area of soil."[1]

In terms of educational expansion, Lincoln was prescient yet mistaken. In the coming years and decades, agricultural training would grow far more important in America's colleges. So, too, would other forms of vocational training, for engineers, teachers, doctors, lawyers, and scholars. The emergence of universities that taught these occupations alongside the undergraduate classical curriculum was among the most important developments in higher education in the late nineteenth century. Yet, contrary to Lincoln's expectation, training in these arts of peace did not come at the expense of the art of war. War, of course, dominated his presidential administration. And even as colleges added programs in civil vocational training, they also added military curricula. Lincoln, in fact, signed a law that promoted the expansion of both agricultural and military education in colleges. The experience of war fostered the growth of curricula for both peace and war.

Most colleges survived the Civil War. In the North, they generally managed to stay open through the conflict, albeit with fewer students and perhaps an unbalanced gender ratio. In the South, most colleges that closed during the war reopened after it. While they might struggle with a continued military presence and physical damage to the campus, they nevertheless resumed the work of teaching and learning. That work, however, had changed. Students after the war did not learn exactly the same material as their antebellum predecessors. College curricula, and with them institutional structures, changed rapidly beginning in the 1860s. The war encouraged both educational and political leaders to explore new goals and forms for higher education. In an effort to ensure colleges' survival and their value, they redesigned curricula to better serve a postbellum nation.

The Civil War drove two major changes in college curricula. One involved teaching the art of war; the other, the arts of peace. Both stemmed, in part, from the Morrill Land-Grant College Act of 1862. First, colleges began to conduct military drill and teach military tactics. These jarring additions to the classical curriculum grew out of the new partnership between colleges and the federal government that began during the Civil War. During the war, the government forced colleges to give up their students and buildings to serve military needs. Beginning with the Morrill Act and increasingly after the war, the partnership became less one-sided. As the federal government grew increasingly powerful and attentive to many aspects of American life, it partnered with colleges in ways that related more to education and that benefited both the colleges and the government. In terms of curricula, colleges and the government cooperated to expand military training. They combined their resources to turn civilian colleges into training grounds for soldiers. Students learned new skills as the nation prepared for the next military crisis.

More happened in the South. Military education, in part a federal project, spread throughout the country. But just as the war's immediate impacts had disproportionately affected colleges in the states where the war was fought, the war also affected Southern curricula more in the long term. Southern colleges had endured many more government intrusions and accidental effects of the war. More students had enlisted in the military. The Confederate and Union armies had taken over some campuses. Some colleges had faced physical destruction. Because of all this damage, Southern colleges had to rebuild after the surrender. State governments recognized that need and, albeit sometimes reluctantly, provided state colleges with the necessary resources. Given the chance to start almost from scratch, these colleges expanded and diversified their curricula to appeal to postbellum students. In addition to adding the military lessons that appeared everywhere, Southern colleges now became universities.

The Morrill Act and Nurseries for Soldiers

Both changes began with the Morrill Land-Grant College Act. The law that Lincoln signed in 1862 helped spark both the expansion of military education everywhere and the emergence of universities in the South. Ironically, the man whose name the law bears, like Lincoln, never attended college. Justin S. Morrill's regret about this fact helped the self-educated son of a Vermont blacksmith rise to the fore of a movement to develop educational opportunities for the next generation of America's farmers and laborers. But he did not begin that movement.

In the early nineteenth century, a new type of college had begun to appear. Americans concerned with the education of the working and farming classes and eager to make use of recent innovations in agricultural science had founded several schools to teach scientific methods. The first agricultural school, the Gardiner Lyceum, opened in Maine in 1823. Others followed, some with the word *college* in their names. New York's surveyor general proposed the establishment of a state agricultural college as early as 1819. Although the legislature repeatedly rejected such proposals, the citizens of Ovid finally obtained a charter for the New York State Agricultural College in 1853. Funded initially by private subscriptions, it obtained a state loan three years later and opened in 1860. Michigan established its government-sponsored State Agricultural College in 1855. By the late 1850s, however, these institutions formed a very small sector of American higher education.[2] Some, wanting to change that, decided that the federal government should get involved. As early as 1848, Congress had received—and ignored—a petition to fund state agricultural and mechanical colleges.[3] It continued its longstanding policy of educational laissez faire. Now Morrill, having won a seat in the House of Representatives, began pushing for a new policy.

In December 1857 Morrill introduced a bill to fund a nationwide system of land-grant colleges. He proposed that the federal government donate a large area of land to each state. The state would sell the land and use the income to endow one or more colleges teaching agriculture and mechanics (i.e., engineering). Systematic in nature and national in scope, this program would go far beyond the few grants the government previously had made to support the foundings of state colleges.

Convinced that farming remained central to the American economy, Morrill heavily emphasized the agricultural part of the bill. He cited the need to reverse the recent decline in production and the promise of experimental science to furnish a solution. If Americans already built schools for soldiers, he argued, they certainly should build schools for farmers, who contributed much more to the nation. His arguments worked. Despite opposition from Southern and western politicians, the bill passed both houses. This paved the way for the most extensive federal foray into education to date—until President James Buchanan vetoed the bill, describing it as an unconstitutional usurpation of power by the federal government that would spell "the end of the Republic." Lacking a two-thirds majority in Congress, Morrill had to wait for a new president.[4]

Three years later, with Lincoln in the White House and the Southern opposition gone from Congress, Morrill tried again. In December 1861 the House took a brief break from war matters as he proposed a new version of his land-grant bill. For the most part, this was the same one that had passed Congress before. Each state would receive thirty thousand acres of federal land or land scrip for each representative or senator it elected to Congress. The state must manage and sell this land. Once it did so, it must use the income to support one or more colleges offering instruction in "such branches of learning as are related to agriculture and the mechanic arts," in addition to the traditional "scientific and classical studies." The state could, if it chose, use some of the income from land sales to buy land for experimental farms. It could not use the income to buy or construct college buildings; the state, the town, donors, or the college itself had to contribute these. Each year, the state or college(s) must submit to the federal government a report on the college's "progress," "improvements or experiments," and "State agricultural and economic statistics." States had until 1864 to accept the grant. (Congress later extended the deadline to 1869 or three years after a new state entered the Union.)[5]

Addressing his colleagues the next June, Morrill used many of his old arguments for the importance of agricultural (and, to a lesser extent, mechanical) education. The nation must commit itself to educating the laboring classes, who undergirded its prosperity yet who had little need for a classical education and could not afford college tuition. Government-sponsored, free or inexpensive agricultural colleges were the answer. A federal commitment to agricultural education would "elevat[e]" the reputation of agriculture itself. It also would improve agricultural output as farmers learned the newest scientific methods, benefiting the nation that consumed farm produce, the farmers who grew it, and the governments to which the farmers paid higher taxes. The bill also would reverse the worrisome pattern of migration from rural to urban areas and encourage settlement of the West by educated young farmers, the most desirable settlers.[6] Agricultural higher education run by the states and indirectly funded by the federal government, in short, would make smarter farmers and better farms and would ensure a prosperous, agriculture-based nation.

But Morrill framed these old arguments with a new one. The 1862 bill was not quite the same as the one he had promoted in 1857–58. This land-grant bill came in wartime, and although Morrill conceded that it lacked "the pepper and spice of party or sectional politics," it served the needs of war. In addition to agriculture, mechanics, science, and the classics, the Morrill Act of 1862 required colleges funded by federal land grants to teach military tactics.[7] In the 1850s Morrill, like Lincoln, had resented Americans' undue attention to military rather than agricultural learning. Now he wanted to bring them together.

Early in his speech, Morrill reminded his colleagues how ill prepared the North's volunteer army had been at the start of the war. The U.S. Military Academy served the nation well enough in peacetime, but it simply was not enough when the nation "suddenly" needed to raise "a large army." Had a bill like this one been in place in 1861, he speculated, "the young men might have had more of fitness for their sphere of duties, whether on the farm, in the workshop, or in the battle-field." Americans had learned the importance of military education in peacetime the hard way. More and more young men were anxious to study military tactics. The state and federal governments needed to do their part, building "nurseries" to make those young men into capable state militias. Land-grant colleges could fill that need. Then the nation would be ready the next time disaster struck.[8]

Morrill returned to the subject of military training throughout his lengthy speech. He also ended with this topic, in an apparent effort to shame his colleagues into supporting the bill. Americans had fervently defended their country in 1861, but, accused Morrill, their government had not properly prepared them. It had "long assumed that military discipline was . . . [as] spontaneous" as patriotism, an assumption that had cost many lives. Congress must not make the same mistake again. Before the next war, it must support colleges teaching military tactics. Both agricultural improvement and military preparation served the national interest. Government-supported higher education could accomplish both.[9]

By the time the bill came up for a vote in June 1862, its chances of passage likely were helped by other late actions of Congress. Both houses recently had passed the Homestead Act, awarding free land to western settlers. The House of Representatives also had passed the Pacific Railroad Act, allocating federal land and loans to complete a line of transportation across the country (the Senate later approved it).[10] Congress, in the midst of war, had gotten into the business of funding national development focused on the West. Morrill's bill, which facilitated the training of farmers and workers as well as soldiers while promoting the sale of western lands, contributed to the same project.

The bill passed the House with only a little difficulty. The Committee on Public Lands reported it with a negative recommendation. On the House floor, however, although one representative tried to prevent the vote, it passed easily, 90 to 25. The Senate, which took up the bill first, seemed to pose more difficulty. Senators debated at length about the impact on western states and territories of awarding land scrip within their borders to eastern states that had little federal land. But none expressed opposition to the educational goals of the bill. During three weeks of debate, no one even mentioned the military provision, though curiously, one senator objected to the bill on the grounds that it had nothing to do with the war. After much heated exchange between eastern and western senators, the bill finally came to a vote, passing by a solid majority of 32 to 7. On July 2, 1862, Lincoln, still committed to agricultural education but as aware as anyone of the need for a well-trained military, signed the Land-Grant College Act into law.[11]

Military training, of course, was not new. Morrill acknowledged this in his speech. But before the 1860s it seldom had appeared in the curricula of civilian colleges. Soldiers-to-be had either attended military academies or forgone formal training. In colonial America, young men who joined the British or the colonial army had learned how to fight by fighting. Even officers had learned on the job by observing their superiors, as George Washington did during the French and Indian War. Several military schools did open during the Revolution. Then, in 1783, Congress began considering how to build a more thorough and permanent system of military education. A series of rejected proposals ended with the opening of the U.S. Military Academy at West Point, New York, in 1802.

Primarily an engineering school, it did not offer much practical officer training before the Civil War.

Meanwhile, many other military academies opened, mostly in the South. State governments organized some, including the Virginia Military Institute and the Citadel in South Carolina. Others were private ventures, such as the American Literary, Scientific, and Military Academy, a school in Vermont that combined military training with a classical curriculum. A handful of existing civilian colleges also added military studies. South Carolina College organized a cadet corps in 1824, but it did not last. The Harvard Washington Corps, which students initiated and the faculty endorsed, marched around Cambridge from 1811 to the 1830s. But none of these antebellum efforts forged a real connection between college and the military. Even the Southern military academies had no formal connection with the army. Not a single general officer before 1860 had attended West Point. Most military men continued to view higher education as unnecessary for, if not harmful to, future officers.[12] Those who did obtain formal military training did so in separate institutions created for that purpose.

College students, however, sometimes developed their martial skills even without their professors' sanction. During the Revolutionary era, college men organized companies of cadets. At the beginning of the nineteenth century, the sons of the founders rebelled against their professors in a sort of generational war. And the military values of Southern culture permeated antebellum campuses. Students at South Carolina College learned their social class's honor code through regular duels on campus. At the University of Virginia, a student might challenge a classmate, a Charlottesville resident, or even a professor to a duel if he felt slighted. Students there also banded together to rebel against the faculty; Thomas Jefferson, the university's founder, displayed rare anger when he learned that his own nephew had participated in one such rebellion.[13]

The onset of the Civil War brought military education to many college campuses. Americans began to realize that military skill would determine the future of the nation. As we saw in chapter 1, college students and professors were no exception. Both before and after the fighting began, many colleges established drill companies by either student or faculty initiative. Eager young proto-Confederates at South Carolina College formed the College Cadets on campus, then marched to Charleston to defend Fort Sumter. Harvard established the College Drill Club in response to a student petition. University of Missouri students probably drilled alongside Columbia residents. The College of California drilled its preparatory students. Wesleyan Female College even organized its women into military companies with artificial guns and paper hats.

The real push for military education came after the surrender. The wartime experiments at South Carolina, Harvard, Missouri, California, Wesleyan, and elsewhere reflected a growing national sense of the military's importance. Of course a war, especially one that consumed the nation for four long years, persuaded many that military preparation was important and perhaps might have shortened the conflict. The Morrill Act codified that belief and offered colleges a financial incentive to act on it. Beginning with this law, the Civil War forged the link between formal education and military service that neither antebellum academies nor student initiative had managed to establish. It moved much formal training from military academies into civilian colleges. Using the provisions of this law and others that followed it, professors made military instruction a formal component of the college curriculum. Colleges and Congress partnered to develop an intelligent and physically capable male citizenry who would plant the nation's crops, build its machines, and, when necessary, defend its interests on the battlefield.

The new law had an immediate effect. Even before the war ended, some states organized agricultural and mechanical colleges. Because the law did not specify that the money must go to state-owned institutions, many denominational colleges greedily eyed the Morrill funds.[14] They reminded state legislatures about their agricultural and mechanical programs, or else created them, in the hopes of winning the money. The College of California, for example, responded to the Morrill Act by establishing a Mining and Agricultural College, also known as the Department of Science and the Arts, in 1864.

In compliance with the new law, would-be land-grant colleges prepared students for the battlefield, as well as for the farm and the mine. In California's new college not all students had to study military tactics; the Morrill Act did not require them to. But engineering students could choose to concentrate on military engineering. This course of study taught "Military Tactics, Fortification, Ordnance, and Gunnery." Curiously, students who chose this course did not receive a degree as their schoolmates studying civil or topographical engineering did.[15] Perhaps the trustees were reluctant to give military-related training the same prestige as civil vocational education; in any event, those trustees complied with the letter of the federal law and hoped their efforts would pay off.

The trustees failed to get their college recognized as the state's land-grant institution, but not for want of effort. They reprinted and sent to legislators the section of the catalogue describing the Mining and Agricultural College. They cited as precedent Connecticut's awarding its land-grant money to Yale College's Sheffield School of Science. They even offered to seat the governor and other state officials on the board of trustees and to give free tuition to qualified students selected by the legislature. Meanwhile, the new department's director visited Sacramento twice to lobby the lawmakers. But these efforts failed. The lawmakers postponed action until the following session; after the trustees memorialized them again later in 1864, they denied the request.[16] The College of California did not become a land-grant college during the Civil War.

Although the trustees failed to win land-grant status for their college, they did not close the school or end military education there. The Mining and Agricultural College remained open. It offered few classes through the 1860s, owing to the small number of students, a depression in the mining industry, and probably the lack of government support.[17] But military training, instigated by the wartime atmosphere and the federal law that grew out of it, remained a part of the curriculum.

In fact, military higher education continued to expand after the war. One conflict may have ended, but Justin Morrill had warned his countrymen that they must ready themselves for another. Four years of war had convinced them that he was right. To defend the country, to enforce Reconstruction, and to earn the Morrill Act money, more civilian colleges added military tactics to their curricula through the late 1860s and 1870s. Training citizen-soldiers became a key function of colleges.

With the war over, states could devote more time and resources to such civil tasks as expanding higher education. By the end of 1865, twenty-one states had accepted the federal land grants. Five years later, all thirty-seven had done so. Colleges rushed to compete for the money. By 1879 states had designated forty-three land-grant institutions.[18] If a college failed to win the federal funding, often it added military training to its curriculum anyway. By 1873 every college in this study except Mount Holyoke had introduced, and most had kept, military training.

The College of California now intensified its military offerings. By 1867 the preparatory College School, which enrolled the large majority of California's students, required weekly drill and lessons in tactics.[19] Then in 1869 the state took over the college and renamed it the University of California. Since the legislature already had awarded the land-grant money to the (then nonexistent) state university, the college turned university finally got that money. In accordance with the Morrill Act, the legislature and the governing board of regents made military training an even more important part of the curriculum. The regents demonstrated this commitment symbolically by electing the former U.S. general in chief George B. McClellan as the university's president. McClellan did not take the job, but his election nonetheless highlighted the expanded role of military education at the school.[20]

On a more practical level, the legislature in 1870 required that the faculty organize all male students into the University Cadets, who would receive military instruction and participate in drill. The state provided arms for the cadets' use. The legislature also required the faculty to recommend capable young men to the governor for military commissions. The president began to give the students "Military Lectures." A military professor and a commandant, the latter a major in the army, made up the new Military Department. All four college classes now spent three hours each week in military lessons, clad in military uniforms.[21]

Students' opinions about all this are unclear, but the general public applauded this feature of the state university. The agriculture professor, after speaking to audiences around the state, reported that "the development of the Military Department meets with universal approval." He, and apparently his audiences, interpreted military education as an effort to bring the university "into direct contact with the people."[22] Preparing to defend those people in a crisis, California's young men attended college in a distinctly postbellum atmosphere.

Postbellum efforts to expand military education extended beyond Oakland and Sacramento. Politicians in Washington continued to promote military curricula. In 1862 Congress had included a military provision in a bill concerned primarily with agricultural education. In the late 1860s and early 1870s it included educational provisions in laws concerned with the military. These new laws provided support for civilian colleges interested in offering military training to their students. The overwhelming response revealed colleges' interest in preparing the country's citizen-soldiers.

During the Civil War, the United States built a volunteer and conscript army of unprecedented size. After that army defeated the rebels, the nation's military needs changed. It still needed a substantial army to preserve peace and, after 1866, to govern the South under congressional Reconstruction, but it did not need the same massive mobilization as in wartime. Therefore, early in 1866 Congress set to work on a bill to determine the size and specifications of the peacetime army.

During the debate in the Senate, discussion eventually turned to higher education. Senator John Sherman of Ohio (whose brother, William T. Sherman, had run a Louisiana military academy before becoming a Union general)[23] introduced the following amendment: "That for the purpose of promoting knowledge of military science among the young men of the United States, the President may, upon the application of an established college or university . . . with sufficient capacity to educate at one time not less than one hundred and fifty male students, detail an officer of the Army to act as president or superintendent of such college or university." The amendment capped the number of appointments at twenty and mandated their distribution across the country according to population. Through this amendment, which he claimed had the support of many officers and the Senate's military committee, Sherman hoped to establish a network of "*quasi* military" colleges. By training "thousands of young men throughout the United States" in military skills, these officer-headed colleges would do more for America's defenses than any militia.[24]

Sherman's colleagues supported the amendment's goal, but some questioned its precise method. America would benefit from teaching young men to defend their country. But did that goal require officers to run the colleges? Would Harvard or Yale, asked one senator, consent to install an army officer as its president? Sherman responded that at least one or two Ohio colleges would, but this reassurance failed to convince his audience. So the Senate amended Sherman's amendment, adding the words "or professor": a college could request an officer either as its head or merely as a military teacher.[25]

This revision transformed the amendment. The original version would have created a network of military colleges under the leadership and financial support of the army, in effect using federal money to reinforce the antebellum system of formal military training. The revised version created something new: it provided federal support for the expansion of military instruction at civilian colleges. Along with the military provision of the Morrill Act, it enabled the relocation of military education from military academies to civilian colleges. In addition to supporting land-grant colleges teaching military tactics, the government would pay the salaries of military professors at colleges that did not receive their primary support from the government and did not meet the other requirements of the 1862 law. The amended bill passed both the Senate and, after some interhouse wrangling over other parts of the bill, the House of Representatives. President Andrew Johnson signed it into law on July 28, 1866.[26]

THE CURRICULUM

The president and the War Department worked out the details of the new policy. To satisfy the law and to distribute its benefits as broadly as possible, the government would apportion the officers regionally according to congressional representation and send at most one officer to each state. After a few years, they decided to appoint as professors only first lieutenants of artillery. They further stipulated that each appointment must last only three years, though a single college could have different officers for consecutive three-year terms.[27]

Congress, meanwhile, followed this law with others. In an army-funding bill of 1870 it permitted any retired officer who so desired to serve as a professor in any college. It thus expanded the pool of potential officer-professors.[28] Also in 1870, Congress passed a joint resolution authorizing the secretary of war to issue small arms or field artillery to colleges, on bond, for use in classes taught by officers dispatched under the law of 1866. The War Department allowed each college two cannons plus as many muskets as it had students.[29] This law further defrayed colleges' expenses in building military curricula: the government now paid for both teacher and supplies. Together, the three laws helped make military training a common feature of civilian higher education.

As it created these programs to teach college students to fight, Congress may have been watching developments in Europe. Military training in Europe did not occur in civilian universities, but several national governments were promoting its expansion elsewhere. Elite secondary schools in the United Kingdom had begun adding courses that prepared students for the military colleges' entrance examination in the late 1850s. The Royal Commission on Military Education, which the government appointed in 1868, lauded these courses and recommended in its report of 1869–70 that other schools copy the most effective ones. Prussia, whose army much of the world viewed as a model, in 1868 began an expansion of the cadet schools in which it trained most officers. And Russia extensively reformed its military education system in the 1860s, driven by the poor state of its officer corps in the Crimean War, of 1853–56.[30] While legislators in Washington responded primarily to the lessons of the Civil War, they may also have wished to ensure that American military education kept up with that in the rest of the world.

American colleges, some already having begun to teach military tactics during and after the war, happily accepted the government's help. The War Department had begun to receive requests for officers by 1868.[31] During the 1872–73 academic year, fifteen officers were teaching military tactics to college students. A year later, the number rose to nineteen.

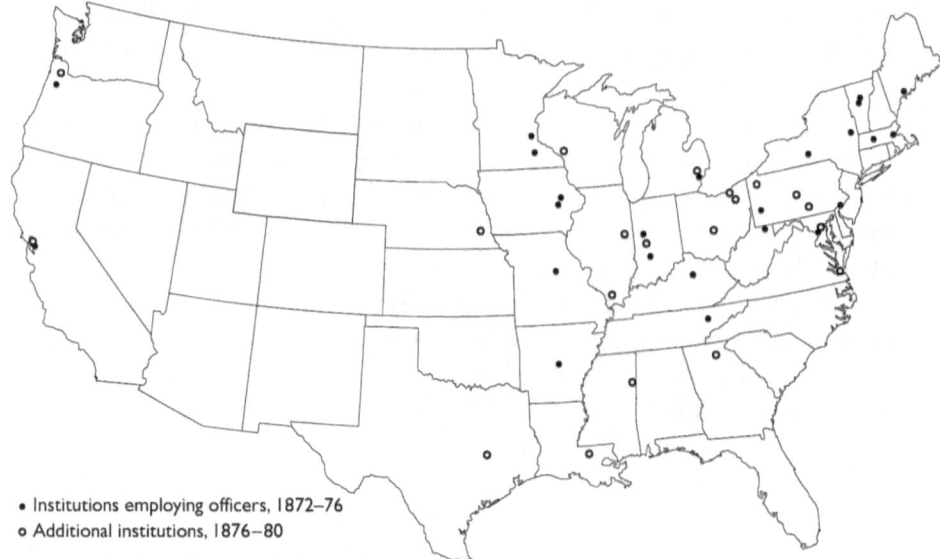

• Institutions employing officers, 1872–76
o Additional institutions, 1876–80

Fig. 4. Institutions employing army officers as military professors under the laws of 1866 and 1870 and the amendment of 1876, 1872–80

The colleges employing these officers spanned the country, from Maine to California and from Minnesota to Arkansas (fig. 4). Only one officer taught in the former Confederacy any year before 1876, first at East Tennessee University and then at Arkansas Industrial University. The War Department may have hesitated to support the military training of former rebels, but the region's stronger tradition of military academies likely deterred civilian colleges from requesting officers. Two or three officers each year taught at military institutions, in line with Senator Sherman's original intention, and another one or two taught at civilian secondary schools. The large majority, however, joined the faculties of civilian colleges.[32] Evidently, those colleges needed only a little encouragement and a free salary to add military tactics to their curricula.

So many colleges responded, in fact, that the government could not accommodate them all. As early as 1874 the War Department denied a request for an officer from the University of South Carolina, probably either because active appointments had reached the maximum of twenty or because no officer was available.[33] In July 1876 Congress responded to the high demand by raising the maximum number of officer-professors to thirty. The War Department immediately began appointing more. Now even former Confederate states received officers, three of them in

1876–77 and four in 1877–78. The latter year, the total number reached the new limit.[34] Yet still more colleges applied for military professors. A conference of college presidents in 1877 recommended the addition of military courses to state colleges' curricula, possibly prompting further applications.[35] In the early 1880s the secretary of war again had to deny requests. And by a curious coincidence, the secretary now making those decisions was Robert Todd Lincoln, the president's son who as a freshman two decades earlier had enrolled in the new military instruction at Harvard.[36] During the war, students such as he had eagerly prepared to join the fight; faculties had obliged by introducing military courses. In the war's aftermath, college leaders and national politicians saw a need to train America's young men in case of a future military conflict. Through curricular reform supported by a series of federal laws, they increasingly partnered to provide that training.

The University of Missouri was among the first colleges to take advantage of the new legislation. It had good reason. The border state of Missouri, positioned between and claimed by both the Union and the Confederacy, had endured invasions by both armies. Guerrilla warfare had wreaked havoc across the state. Even the university itself had lived through three and a half years of military occupation. No wonder the faculty wished to teach Missouri's young men to fight. As early as 1867, President Daniel Read recommended the teaching of military tactics in a new school of agriculture and mechanical arts.[37]

By that time Congress had passed the first law offering to dispatch army officers as college professors. Missouri took up the offer, making military training a much larger part of the curriculum than Read had first proposed. General Richard W. Johnson arrived in the fall of 1868. As professor of civil and military engineering and tactics, he taught the new engineering course for seniors and led all students in a compulsory military drill. Johnson left after a year, but another officer replaced him. His department, even before the federal government offered to send guns and artillery, owned a collection of arms for students to use in practicing their fighting skills.[38] The university probably took advantage of the congressional joint resolution thereafter. In 1875 Company G alone of the University Cadet Battalion, which comprised the students at the School of Mining and Metallurgy, counted in its armory ninety-nine muskets, forty rifles, four swords, two drums, two fifes, and a flag.[39]

Military drill became a key part of Missouri students' lives (fig. 5). In the early 1870s they were spending forty-five minutes each morning and

Fig. 5. University of Missouri students in military uniforms with cannons, guns, and swords, ca. 1876. (Courtesy State Historical Society of Missouri, accession number 024346)

one hour each evening drilling. They also had to purchase a blue military uniform to wear during drill, unless they could prove financial hardship. The faculty soon found a solution even for poor students: they could wear their uniforms all the time, thereby saving money on civilian clothes.[40] The look of the American college campus was changing. No longer did it consist solely of classrooms, dormitories, and young people lost in intellectual study or youthful disorder. Students increasingly spent their time in military uniform, drilling and learning how to fire rifles. Even with the occupying troops of the war years gone, campuses in Missouri and elsewhere now resembled military camps as much as classical colleges.

This is not to say that students welcomed drill. Their enthusiasm for it did not quite equal their professors'. As soon as Missouri established the drill, the faculty began to receive constant requests for exemptions, which they often granted. But the military professors showed less sympathy for students who did not show up for drill or misbehaved once there.

THE CURRICULUM

They assigned demerits to these young men: four for one absence, ten for two. One student earned forty demerits for a single military infraction of particular gravity. That was a serious penalty, for one hundred demerits meant expulsion.[41] Whether the students liked it or not, military training had become an essential component of higher education.

The University of California, which had instituted military training without the benefit of the new laws, eventually took advantage of them. Until 1876 it had no need for Congress's offer to provide an officer, for it had its own military professor. But when he announced his resignation, the regents wasted no time in applying to the War Department for a free replacement. They also asked the government to send arms. The War Department complied with both requests. A brief conflict accompanied the officer's appointment—the regents wanted him also to teach mathematics, which he refused—but in the fall of 1877 Lieutenant George G. Greenough took his place on the university faculty.[42] The state and federal governments now partnered in training young scholars to defend their country should the need arise.

Cornell College also took advantage of the new laws. Doing so took some persistence in its case. President William F. King first requested an officer-teacher in 1871, but the War Department apparently denied that request. Possibly it already had dispatched the maximum of twenty. After a second request the next spring, the secretary of war promised to send an officer but did not. A third request, that fall, had the same result.[43] Finally, in early 1873, after a fourth request, the War Department agreed to dispatch Lieutenant Isaac T. Webster as professor of military science and tactics. He arrived at Cornell in March and began organizing the new military department. Uniformed drill began that spring.[44]

King also obtained arms from the government. For those, he received multiple offers. Besides the federal War Department, the Iowa militia offered to send rifles, artillery, ammunition, and swords. It was already supplying Grinnell College and the Iowa State Agricultural College. The catch was that if Cornell accepted these arms, its students would become a company of the militia. That meant, in theory, that the federal government could muster them into service in a crisis. King worried about that possibility and apparently turned down the state's offer. (Three years later, the faculty again considered and again rejected forming the students into a militia company.) He accepted arms from the federal government instead. Except for a monetary bond, those came with no strings attached.[45]

The military curriculum grew increasingly complex over time. Within a year of Webster's arrival, he added an artillery drill and lectures for the juniors and seniors. In the spring of 1874 his students took a formal examination. And in 1877, under Webster's successor, commissioned student officers began doing reading on tactics and giving weekly or semiweekly recitations.[46] Military training had entered the academic heart of the curriculum.

Cornell went one step further than many colleges. Unlike California and Missouri, it did not confine drill to young men. To be sure, only male students enrolled in the military department, a restriction implied (though not required) by the federal law. But soon after Webster organized that department, the faculty began planning a parallel "*Gym.* drill" for the women. It began in the fall of 1873 with a female professor in charge. The two drills met simultaneously. As with the men, the faculty appointed student officers from among the women.[47] Cornell was not preparing women to defend their country in war, but it followed wartime Wesleyan in giving young women much the same military-influenced education as men. And Cornell was not alone. Five years later, at female students' request, Iowa State Agricultural College created its Ladies' Military Company. By the early 1890s the University of Nebraska, St. Olaf College in Minnesota, and Utah Agricultural College had followed suit. Utah, like Cornell, made women's drill mandatory. Even the University of Missouri, which only recently had admitted women as students (see chapter 3), established an armed drill company for women in the 1880s after they petitioned for one.[48] Colleges and the government had added military training to the civilian curriculum to prepare men to fight in another national crisis. At some schools, though, it had become an essential part of the college experience for all students.

As at Missouri, students at Cornell almost immediately tried to get out of drill. Men presented a variety of excuses for exemption, from physical disability to paid employment to "Conscientious Scruples." Women too petitioned for exemption. In both cases, the faculty at first often granted the requests. But in 1876 they resolved to grant exemptions only for disability, if the student had a surgeon's note, or for "the best of reasons."[49] Military training was now part of college; like other subjects, it was mandatory. Students may have come to college to study Latin and algebra, but once there, they had to learn arms use and military discipline too. Colleges, states, and the federal government saw to that.

Some colleges, of course, did not receive federal support for military education. These colleges, not surprisingly, tended to have less extensive military curricula. But even without public funds or army personnel, some colleges did institute military lessons. California taught military engineering and drilled the preparatory students before the state takeover brought Morrill funds. Harvard, which received neither Morrill funds nor a federal officer, established a Rifle Corps in 1875 at the suggestion and under the command of the gymnasium superintendent, Frederick W. Lister. Lister, a retired Civil War officer, drilled students "according to the latest United States tactics" and taught them to use "the national weapon." The student newspaper endorsed his effort to train students for "the position of the soldier." Over time, however, the corps became as much a recreational as a military organization. Members began to refer to it as the "Rifle Club" or "team" and took more interest in winning competitions against other teams than in becoming good soldiers. Even so, Lister continued to drill them.[50] Military lessons had become part of the curriculum.

South Carolina College, now renamed the University of South Carolina, also tried to add military classes. There the absence of federal support was more debilitating. And military training there acquired unique political significance. When the Civil War ended, African Americans in the South gained their rights at the point of a gun as much as at the point of a pen. Whatever the law said, ongoing violence between Republican blacks and Democratic whites determined the racial and partisan balance of power. Colleges offering military instruction contributed, at least symbolically, to young men's ability to carry on that violent struggle. Nowhere was that contribution more important than at the University of South Carolina. Between 1866 and 1880 that state university changed from a white to a black to a white institution. Depending on who held power in the statehouse, it served the needs of Democrats or Republicans. Preparing students to fight gave it a controversial political role.

When the University of South Carolina reopened after the war, prospects looked good for its designation as a land-grant institution. The Morrill Act excluded states in rebellion, but President Johnson readmitted South Carolina to the Union in 1865. The lenient policies of presidential Reconstruction required only that 10 percent of voters pledge their loyalty and that the state ratify the Thirteenth Amendment, abolishing slavery. So the state became eligible for the Morrill Act funds. But for the actions of Congress, South Carolina likely would have accepted the land grant and given the income to its state university.[51] But Congress, when it reconvened the next winter, rejected the president's Reconstruction plan. The Radical Republicans, in control, refused to seat Southern delegations, then voted to require much more stringent criteria for readmission to the Union under the Reconstruction Act of 1867, which they passed over Johnson's veto. In the meantime, military governors would rule the ex-Confederate states. Congress also passed a joint resolution reiterating that those states (except Tennessee) could not receive land scrip until they were readmitted and revoking the scrip already issued or about to be issued to several of them. South Carolina, as a result, lost its eligibility for a land grant until it reentered the Union again in 1868. At that point, the Republican legislature gave the money, not to the state university, but to a new agricultural and mechanical institute for blacks affiliated with Claflin University in Orangeburg.[52]

Federal law, then, neither mandated nor funded military education at the University of South Carolina. But the trustees chose to begin it nonetheless. Evidently the military needs of the past half decade and the precedent of students' drilling on campus early in the war had made military work appear relevant to the civil training of young white Southern men. Rule by a resented military force could not have hurt martial sentiment either. As at California, a military curriculum first appeared in the engineering department, titled the School of Mathematics, and Civil and Military Engineering and Construction. High enrollment in that school indicated student interest, though we cannot know which part of this broadly defined school students found most appealing. Owing to students' poor preparation in mathematics, it is unclear whether its sole professor even had time to cover engineering, civil or military.[53]

If the mathematics professor did find time to teach military engineering in the late 1860s and early 1870s, symbolically he contributed to an undeclared war that was going on in the Reconstruction South. The Thirteenth Amendment may have declared the slaves free, but whites quickly turned to violence to withhold from blacks any meaningful freedom. Riots began in South Carolina immediately after the war. As blacks gained power in the state government, whites' attacks grew more intense. Beginning in 1868, they turned to the Ku Klux Klan, a terrorist force born in Tennessee two years earlier, to intimidate African Americans seeking rights and political power. Blacks defended themselves through Union Leagues, political turned paramilitary organizations dedicated to the Republican Party. The Republican state government reorganized the militia into an armed body of nearly one hundred thousand blacks in 1869 and 1870, prompting the Klan to escalate its campaign of terror. South Carolina saw a lull in white violence in 1871 and 1872, owing partly to the deployment of federal troops and prosecutions of Klan members under the Enforcement Acts of 1870 and 1871 and partly to the simple fact that the Klan had succeeded in intimidating many blacks. But violence flared up again after a year.[54] Paramilitary politics ruled the postbellum South. While engineering lessons probably did not help students conduct vigilante warfare, they did symbolically involve the university in a political war of racial violence. The same white men who a few years earlier had defended the Confederacy and slavery now were taking military lessons at their state university, while former slaves continued to fight for their freedom.

Then things changed. In 1873 the trustees opened the University of South Carolina to black students. After most whites left in protest, African Americans became the majority of the student body (see chapter 3). If the university were to offer military training now, it would be helping these young people to affirm their citizenship, a status blacks tied closely to military service.[55] It also would be teaching them to defend themselves and their rights against white violence. University training would ready potential recruits for the militia and Union Leagues. And in 1874 the Republican, mostly black legislature decided to do just that.

By then the government already was supporting military training for black South Carolinians. The land-grant institute at Claflin University had hired a military professor in 1872. When the legislature considered a bill to create a military professorship at the state university, however, it nonetheless set off a flurry of debate in Columbia's newspaper. The bill called for the establishment of a school of military tactics within the university. The trustees would request an army officer, under the law of 1866, to head the new school. Readers of the *Columbia Daily Union-Herald*, for a variety of reasons, questioned the wisdom of the bill. One, tired of fourteen years of military "pomp and circumstance," hoped the university would concentrate instead on "training for civil . . . life." The same correspondent cited the student rebellion against military training at Bowdoin College in Maine as evidence of its general failure in civilian institutions. A group of teachers from Aiken, South Carolina, in a letter titled "Teaching Versus Fighting," argued that the state should devote its resources to the common schools, not the state university. The former represented "the *real* interests of our people." One reader did express support for the bill. Perhaps revealing pessimism about its chances, however, this correspondent wrote under the impotent pseudonym "Blank Cartridge."[56]

None of these readers mentioned the violent political context in which the legislature considered the bill. Nor did they mention the race of most students at the university. But surely they knew. Training students meant training black students, and training black students meant helping young black men to claim their status as citizens and to sustain Reconstruction through force. Efforts to deny them such training, whatever the justifications, served white conservative interests. Writers obscured the question of race and violence with questions of primary education and civil training.

In the end, neither side unambiguously won the debate. The legislature passed the bill; the trustees, with the faculty's support, requested a federal officer. But no officer arrived.[57] The War Department's letter of denial has not survived. Probably it denied the request because appointments had reached the maximum of twenty, because the region already had received its quota, or because no officer was available. The secretary of war may well have considered the political realities of the South when deciding not to assign an officer to the black university. He earlier had assigned one to Howard University in Washington, DC, and he later assigned one to the Hampton Normal and Agricultural Institute in Virginia, but a much more explosive political climate surrounded the University of South Carolina than surrounded either of those black schools.[58] In any event, South Carolina's state university did not train African Americans to fight. But like academic leaders elsewhere, those at this civilian college wanted to establish a military curriculum. More than at most colleges, as this one's mission and constituency changed through the 1860s and 1870s, that curricular debate took on political meaning.

By the end of Reconstruction, military training had become an important part of the college experience. Not only had formal training grown much more common but much of that training had moved from military academies to civilian colleges. Nearly every college in this study had added military studies to its curriculum. The expansion of military education—and the federal government's expanded involvement in it—signaled the beginning of a gradual militarization of American culture. Although the Union army quickly contracted after the war and the Reconstruction army left the South in the 1870s, the Civil War had convinced many Americans of the importance of the military. That lesson led politicians and college leaders to expand military education as insurance against another crisis. Later in the century, the military began to play a more visible role outside college campuses, as troops suppressed labor strikes, the country fought a jingoist war against Spain, and colleges trained football players who exhibited the rugged traits of warriors.[59] The intertwined military and cultural legacies of the Civil War thus unfolded over several decades. As the places where Americans educated their men of arms-bearing age and their future leaders, colleges became an early and lasting target of new policies that reflected the militarized culture and aimed to build a safer nation.

From College to University

The Civil War did more than encourage colleges to provide military training. That project, driven by the federal government, affected colleges in all parts of the country. But in the South, the war affected curricula more fundamentally. Schools such as the University of Missouri and South Carolina College emerged from the war having lost students, endured military occupation, suffered physical damage, and temporarily shut down. They needed to rebuild, and that need gave them the obligation and the opportunity to rethink what they taught. These Southern colleges, with the support of their state governments, took that opportunity to make big changes. The Civil War facilitated the emergence of the Southern university.

Of all changes in American higher education during the second half of the nineteenth century, few were more visible, and none more fundamental, than the emergence of the university. At its base a structural innovation, the university also brought new purposes and new constituencies to the American college.

Before the Civil War, with few exceptions, colleges were small, monocentric teaching institutions. Every student enrolled in a single unit and followed the single prescribed curriculum that led to the bachelor of arts degree. This was true even of most institutions called universities. Though a college might offer one or two slightly modified courses leading to the less prestigious bachelor of science, literature, or philosophy degree, students in those courses still followed an intellectually oriented curriculum that included the classics. Professors' work, meanwhile, consisted entirely in undergraduate teaching. Graduate students did not exist, though some colleges conferred master's degrees on alumni automatically. (At the University of Georgia, for example, to receive his master's an alumnus needed only show up at commencement three years after graduation, pay a small fee, and prove that he had not served prison time; Harvard offered a similarly automatic master's.)[60] Faculty members who conducted research did so by personal choice or to improve their teaching, not because colleges valued research itself. Professors did not strongly identify with their disciplines, often alternating between academic and other jobs and, especially before the antebellum period, switching among subjects depending on colleges' teaching needs.[61]

After the Civil War, this started to change. To be sure, classical colleges did not disappear. Most institutions of higher learning remained small. As late as 1881 only twenty-six of the country's more than six hundred colleges enrolled more than two hundred students. Colleges continued to focus on undergraduate education, including the bachelor of arts course built around the classical languages.[62] But many colleges began to do more, diversifying their curricula and developing more complex institutional structures. Meanwhile, faculty began more stringently to define and distinguish their disciplines. Now they identified with specific disciplines and departments, even conducting research as part of their job. While Americans of the nineteenth century did not always draw a clear linguistic distinction between a *college* and a *university*—founding bodies sometimes scratched their heads over which title to use—both contemporary advocates and later historians have identified these more complex institutions as the true universities.[63]

Two basic types of universities emerged in the late nineteenth century, from somewhat different origins: research universities and comprehensive universities. The famous research universities began to appear in the 1870s. Historians of early universities, beginning with Laurence R. Veysey in his landmark study of 1965, have devoted most of their attention to these institutions. Between 1865 and 1910 academics and journalists argued for the establishment of a new form of higher education. They wanted to replace the classical college, with its emphasis on mental discipline and moral piety, with a different educational core. Some preferred a utilitarian model. They believed that training in such learned professions as law and medicine and in such working-class occupations as agriculture and engineering, along with teaching and research in the sciences, would serve the public better than the classical curriculum. Supporters of utilitarian universities tended to promote the introduction of election: students who chose their own studies could focus on the subjects most useful to them later in life.

Other promoters of the research university emphasized the type of abstract research common in German universities of the mid- and late nineteenth century. A number of these scholars and writers had studied in Germany. While they tended to overlook the educational philosophy behind those institutions, they admired and brought back to America the Germans' careful study of scientific and historical evidence. In science especially, they wanted to replace rote memorization and recitation with laboratory-based courses that emphasized experimental inquiry and the evolving nature of scientific knowledge. Still other university supporters, mostly humanists, focused on the teaching of "liberal culture." The American university, they argued, must provide more than utilitarian training or cold research. A graduate should emerge with aesthetic discernment, moral sense, emotional receptiveness, and social cultivation. As time passed, and especially after the turn of the century, these several schools within the research university movement merged into a single, more complex notion of the university.[64]

The research-university movement grew out of several cultural, economic, and intellectual impulses. Veysey emphasized three: the desire to equal European cultural accomplishments, the need to attract more students, and the availability of funds from industrial benefactors and other sources. A turnover among colleges' leadership after the Civil War also helped to bring reform-minded men to power. Supporters of the research university, even as they sought to increase enrollments, wanted to raise the standards of admission and student accomplishment. And academics, concerned with the moral training and mental development of America's youth, saw the university as a way to reconcile those goals with advanced study and academic research.

The expansion of knowledge itself also drove the growth of research universities. Such discoveries as Darwinian evolution motivated further scientific inquiry by professors and graduate students. Even more important, these discoveries transformed some scholars' notions about the nature of science and science pedagogy. The publication of Charles Darwin's *On the Origin of Species* in 1859 led some scientists to question the prevailing notion of science as a series of immutable laws that researchers must identify and students must memorize. They began to reconceive of science as a process of hypothesis, experimentation, and the reshaping of theories. The notion of science as an ongoing research process promoted the teaching of science in a laboratory by the people involved in research, that is, by professors in a research university.

Beginning in the 1870s, reformers founded a few of these universities with research at their center and graduate and vocational training as major educational goals. By far the greatest early success was the Johns Hopkins University in Maryland. Founded in 1876 through the munificence of its namesake, Johns Hopkins devoted itself so completely to research and occupational education that its trustees almost chose not to admit undergraduates. It immediately became the symbol of the German-style university in America. But it was as exceptional as it was prototypical. For one thing, it was the only research university south of the Mason-Dixon Line. For another, unlike most research universities, it did not evolve out of an old classical college. Of the fourteen founding members of the Association of American Universities in 1900, nine had existed as colleges before the Civil War. Owing to European influence, the need for students, new sources of funding, and other factors peculiar to each school and locality, Northern colleges such as Harvard and California transformed from centralized teaching colleges into expansive, internally diverse research universities.[65]

Harvard started to become a university even before the war. *University* first became part of its name in 1780. More important, it established the Harvard Medical School, its first professional school, in 1782. This was followed by the Divinity School in 1815; the Law School in 1817; the Astronomical Observatory, a research unit that enrolled a small number of students, in 1839; and the Lawrence Scientific School in 1847.[66]

In the 1860s Harvard's presidents began to push for its expansion into a German-style university with the classical college at its center, research as its focus, and occupational training as a key goal. In 1863 President Thomas Hill told the governing boards that the time had come to "make Harvard College a University in reality as in name." He argued that the United States could sustain only "one University of the highest grade" and that Harvard stood in the best position to assume that role. A year later, he denounced Americans' "dependence" on European universities for graduate education as "disgraceful and injurious." America needed its own university committed to the production of knowledge. Hill made some progress. Under his leadership, Harvard established the Dental School and the School of Mining and Practical Geology. A donor provided land and money for an agricultural school.[67] But the most important changes were still to come.

Charles W. Eliot, who became president in 1869, guided the centuries-old college into its new life as a research university. In his view, Harvard's faculty and governing boards had not paid enough attention to professional studies. With the exception of divinity, Harvard and other institutions had "been notoriously scanty, hasty, and unsystematic" in their professional training. He set out to change this. Under his leadership, Harvard expanded its legal curriculum from eighteen months to two years and added practicing lawyers to the faculty. It extended the medical curriculum from one year to three and supplemented the lectures with laboratory and clinical work. Eliot also wanted to make the bachelor's degree a pre-

THE CURRICULUM

requisite for the Divinity and Medical Schools—a change that would have disqualified four-fifths of current students—but the governing boards did not enact that measure.[68]

Eliot also led Harvard forward in practical and scientific learning. Formerly the chair of Harvard's engineering department, Eliot as president oversaw the establishment of a four-year course leading to a degree in civil engineering. The agricultural and horticultural school, named the Bussey Institution for its founding donor, opened in 1871. It awarded degrees for three years of study in farming, horticulture, agricultural chemistry, applied zoology, quantitative analysis, and entomology. The mining school continued to award the degree in mining engineering for four years of study.[69] Students could prepare at Harvard for an increasing number of professions and trades.

Just as important, Harvard made research a key part of its identity. In 1872 the university began admitting students for the doctor of philosophy and doctor of science degrees. It stopped awarding the master's degree automatically to college graduates, now instead requiring one additional year of study. Even the bachelor's course changed to fit the research-university model. The introduction of elective courses had begun under Hill and continued under Eliot. By 1872 students were filling fourteen elective slots in their schedules from more than seventy choices.[70] By expanding occupational training, introducing research degrees, and instituting student choice, Harvard had become a research university.

The College of California also grew into a university in the 1860s. The trustees began diversifying its curriculum and expanding its structure in 1864, when they opened the Mining and Agricultural College. Besides mining and agriculture, that college taught mechanics, architecture, shipbuilding, surveying, navigation, and civil and military engineering.[71] But it enrolled few students; the College of California remained primarily a classical institution.

It made the real transition after the war. Even before the college formed its new department, the state government had appointed a committee to explore the possibility of forming a state university. Lobbying by the head of that committee, in fact, had helped convince the legislature to deny the college land-grant status: he wanted that distinction for the new school.[72] Now lawmakers decided to move forward and build a state university, which would receive the federal money. But that plan required starting from scratch—obtaining land, buying or constructing buildings, attracting students, and hiring professors—and remained only a plan.[73]

Meanwhile, the college had purchased a large area of land outside Oakland known as Berkeley. But it could not afford to move the college to the new site. Heavily in debt, it could not even pay its professors.[74]

In 1867 the trustees came up with a solution: they donated the college to the state. The institution then could take advantage of both the college's students and land and the state's money. In offering the college to the government, the trustees stipulated that it must establish at Berkeley "a University of California, which shall include a College of Mines, a College of Civil Engineering, a College of Mechanics, and a College of Agriculture, and an Academical College."[75] They aimed not only to save the College of California but also to use state and federal money to build a multicollegiate university with the old classical college as its "germ."[76]

The legislature was only too happy to accept an offer of free land. In March 1868 it passed the Organic Act, creating the University of California. Despite some stumbling blocks—the college's faculty questioned the state's commitment to the liberal arts, and quarrels over the legality of the transfer reached the state supreme court—the deal went through. University of California classes began in the college's old buildings in Oakland in the fall of 1869. They moved to the new Berkeley campus four years later.[77]

The University of California lived up to its name. Besides the academic curriculum in the College of Letters, it offered a range of professional and practical courses in affiliated schools. The governing board of regents established the Agricultural College in 1869. One year later, it opened the Mechanic Arts College in the Mechanics' Institute of San Francisco. With free classes scheduled in the evenings and on weekends to allow laboring men and women to attend, this division immediately attracted huge crowds, exceeding the lecture hall's capacity of five hundred.[78] Meanwhile, the state university absorbed or affiliated with several previously independent professional schools: Toland Medical College in 1870, the California College of Pharmacy in 1873, and the California College of Dentistry in 1873. Although this university did not meet the highest standards of the German model—the faculty bemoaned its meager postgraduate offerings—it did have the extensive structure and diverse curriculum of a university.[79] In California as in Massachusetts and elsewhere in the North, educational (and, in this case, political) leaders had converted a classical college into a research university.

For a variety of cultural, intellectual, and pragmatic reasons, these Northern colleges became universities after the Civil War. But they did not become universities *because* of the war. Although the war contributed to the economic boom that created the wealth Northern schools drew on in the form of private donations, for the most part Northern research universities developed independently of the war.[80] They probably would have become universities even if the Civil War had not happened.

Not so for Southern universities. Indeed, the famous Northern research institutions were not the only universities. As much attention as they have received from historians, few research universities on the German model appeared before 1900. The Association of American Universities included only fourteen members that year; all except Johns Hopkins were in the Northeast or the West. At the same time, though, other universities were appearing throughout the United States. These did not always have as strong an ideological basis as the research universities, nor were they as complete a departure from classical colleges as Johns Hopkins or Harvard. Perhaps for these reasons, they have received less historiographic attention. But these *comprehensive universities,* as the historian John R. Thelin has labeled them, differed enough from classical colleges and shared enough with research universities to constitute a second, much larger group of postbellum universities.[81]

As some Northern institutions began to emulate the German universities, other colleges adopted some of their curricular innovations without their complete structural or research basis. Instead of building graduate programs and directing resources toward faculty research, these new universities simply added undergraduate vocational schools onto the old classical college. Along with the diversification of the curriculum came student choice. Students could elect to study the classics; traditional learned professions such as law, medicine, and divinity; or emerging occupational fields such as agriculture, engineering, and mining. Few colleges before the Civil War had offered such an array of studies; occupational training had taken place outside colleges, either in independent professional schools or in the workplace. Now, without elevating these studies to the postgraduate level, comprehensive universities combined them institutionally with the classical college. The effort resulted in what Thelin calls "a smorgasbord for student choice." These were horizontally oriented universities with multiple undergraduate colleges alongside each other, not vertically oriented ones with doctoral training at the top.[82]

Unlike research universities, comprehensive universities spread throughout the country. Some, such as the University of Pennsylvania and Temple University in Philadelphia, grew alongside research universities in the Northeast. But others sprang up in the South. Kentucky University, the University of Louisville in Kentucky, Tulane University in Louisiana, Vanderbilt University in Tennessee, and Washington College in Virginia all had undergraduate vocational schools alongside their colleges of liberal arts.[83] So did the postbellum state universities of South Carolina and Missouri. These vocational schools expanded rapidly. By 1890, 36 percent of all undergraduate degrees earned at men's or coeducational colleges and universities, and 39 percent of those earned in the South, were in professional or practical subjects.[84]

Several factors contributed to the national emergence of comprehensive universities starting in the 1860s. First, colleges needed students. Even more than the research universities, undergraduate-focused institutions changed in order to survive. With sluggish enrollments threatening insolvency, these colleges added what they believed to be popular subjects in order to attract young men and (especially to normal schools) women. Second, some comprehensive university founders worked from a genuine egalitarian impulse to spread learning to previously excluded social groups. Third, Congress passed the Morrill Act. The income from the land grants helped to build some comprehensive universities.[85]

In addition to these national factors, regionally specific conditions drove the growth of comprehensive universities. Closely tied to local demographics and occupational needs, these institutions developed in response to changes in their states' underlying economic structures and, in the South, the physical environment. Open-access Temple University could succeed because many Pennsylvanians lacked preparatory education but needed skills to earn an income. Turn-of-the-century Northeastern College in Boston, which included polytechnic, engineering, and automotive schools, designed its educational program around technological innovation.[86] These Northern comprehensive universities, much more directly than the research institutions, filled the practical needs of a changing society. In the South, which during the 1860s and 1870s endured unparalleled physical trauma accompanied by sudden changes to its economy, society, and polity, physical and economic conditions played an even greater role in the establishment of universities.

The Civil War made Southern comprehensive universities possible. The war generated the physical and economic conditions that persuaded college leaders and state governments to expand those colleges' curricula and reshape their structure. Whereas European and American intellectual philosophies combined with the need to attract students and the expansion of philanthropy to create the Northern research universities,

THE CURRICULUM

the practical problem of rebuilding colleges after a war motivated the building of Southern comprehensive universities. Both South Carolina's and Missouri's stories illustrate the war's key role in their transition from classical colleges to comprehensive universities.

When the Confederate armies surrendered, South Carolina College had not held classes in nearly three years. All the students had left in the spring of 1862, the Confederate army had turned the college into a military hospital that summer, and the Union army had made it the commandant's headquarters in the winter of 1865. The latter army remained in control.[87] It did not take long, however, for postwar politicians to start thinking about reopening their state college—with some big changes.

At first, prospects for the college's reopening looked bleak. Besides the absence of students and the military occupation, the president had resigned in 1861, and two other professors had left or died since. The school's and the state government's coffers were low. Any chance of obtaining rent from the Confederate occupiers evaporated when the Confederacy ceased to exist (the faculty estimated that the Confederacy owed the college nearly $100,000).[88] Yet the situation improved quickly after the surrender. The army vacated some buildings within a year, though it maintained a limited presence on campus until at least 1874. A professor had performed the president's duties since his departure, and the trustees appointed a permanent chairman of the faculty soon after the war. The board had little trouble replacing the lost faculty members.[89] But the dearth of money and students posed a greater challenge. Even with classrooms and teachers restored, the resumption of college exercises would require committed and creative action.

The state government took that action. President Johnson appointed Benjamin F. Perry, a South Carolina College trustee, as the state's new governor. Perry determined to reopen the college, but on a new model that he believed would better serve his postbellum state. The war, he argued, had left South Carolina's young white men both poor and poorly educated. It had destroyed their fathers' fortunes and kept them away from secondary school. These potential students could not pass an entrance examination that presumed a complete secondary education. They could not easily afford the old tuition. And they had little reason to struggle to pay it if their only reward would be a classical degree that would not help them find work. Moreover, the war had left the state treasury bare. South Carolina simply could not afford to reopen the college on the same model as before. The war had not ended politicians' commitment to higher education, but its social and economic consequences now forced them to reevaluate the form state-sponsored higher education took.

So Perry and the legislature looked for a new model of higher education, one the state could afford and its young men would pay for. With these purely practical considerations in mind, they decided that a university structure—decentralized, vocational, and choice-driven—best satisfied the requirements of economy and appeal.[90] The war finally had made Jefferson's University of Virginia, theretofore a unique university among the South's many classical colleges, an attractive model. (Hopes for funding under the Morrill Act, though for the time being unfulfilled, probably also influenced the politicians' decision to change the curriculum.) On December 19, 1865, legislators passed a law transforming South Carolina College into the University of South Carolina. By then a new governor had succeeded Perry, but he endorsed his predecessor's proposal and happily signed the bill. The renamed institution opened three weeks later.[91] And not only the name changed. The university's structure, curricula, and funding differed in important ways from those of the college.

To make the University of South Carolina attractive to the state's youth, the new law expanded and diversified the curriculum. South Carolina College, like most antebellum colleges, had comprised a single unit. All students had enrolled in the one college and taken the same classes. They had studied under professors of logic, rhetoric, and philosophy of the mind; Roman literature; Greek literature; moral philosophy; sacred literature and evidences of Christianity; natural and mechanical philosophy; chemistry, mineralogy, and geology; and mathematics and astronomy. After completing the prescribed four-year curriculum in these academic subjects, they had received the bachelor of arts degree.[92]

The 1865 law establishing the university split apart the college. Emulating Virginia, it divided the University of South Carolina into eight schools teaching different subject areas. Each school employed only a single professor, and most bore titles similar to those of the old departments. But one was quite new: the School of Mathematics, and Civil and Military Engineering and Construction. This school, at least in theory, included practical job training informed by scientific knowledge. While coursework at first focused on elementary mathematics owing to the poor preparation of the school's students, the expectation of practical training likely appealed to young men in the depressed Southern economy of 1866. In any event, the politicians hoped it would. They also added pharmaceutical and agricultural studies to the chemistry and geology school and authorized the trustees to hire an instructor in law, medicine, or "any mechanical or practical pursuit."[93] When the trustees failed to act, the legislature in December 1866 mandated the establishment of medical and law schools. By the next year, the university's faculty included six professors of medicine and one of law. The University of South Carolina continued to teach the classics, but now it also trained the state's young white men to earn a living. By doing so, the editor of a local newspaper observed, the university might help to revive South Carolina's shattered economy.[94]

When the legislature responded to postbellum conditions by establishing a university, it did more than reorganize the college and add new subjects. It also gave students the opportunity to choose their studies. The elective principle previously had been as uncommon in the South as in the North. It drastically changed the undergraduate experience. Instead of following a single, prescribed course of study, each student chose six schools within the university that interested him. Once he completed the two-year curricula of four schools and the first year of two more, he received his bachelor's degree. If he completed the full curricula of all eight schools, he received a master's. But he also could choose to study fewer subjects, in which case he would graduate from those schools but not receive a degree from the university.[95] Whether a young man wanted the prestige of a college degree or practical knowledge in a subject related to his future vocation, the new university could serve his needs. "The conversion of the South Carolina College into a University," legislators asserted, "will meet its great demand" in a way the old classical college could not.[96] Curricular freedom, they hoped, would attract a large number of students whose interests lay outside the classical curriculum of the antebellum college.

While legislators tried to make the university more attractive to men impoverished by the war, the faculty tried to make admission easier for them. Nineteenth-century colleges did not practice selective admissions as we know them today, under which colleges admit only the most academically gifted applicants from a large pool. So few people applied to college that such a policy was impossible. But colleges did want to ensure that their students had the basic academic preparation necessary to begin a college course. So would-be students, on arriving at a college, took an examination. This covered what they should have learned in a high school, with a private tutor, or through self-guided study. If they passed, they could begin college; if not, they could study further and try again the next year. South Carolina used such an examination before and during the Civil War.[97]

After the war, the faculty set aside the entrance examination. Given the need for students and the poor preparation of most young men, they had little choice but to waive it for all entrants in January 1866. They reinstated the test the next fall, but only for minors. Any man eighteen or older gained admission by virtue of his age, regardless of his academic background. This decision hampered educational goals, requiring professors to spend more time on basic material. It was this policy that prevented the mathematics and engineering professor from getting to engineering the first year. But the faculty subordinated these concerns to the need to attract students. Evidently they were unhappy with the results, for after one year the faculty and the trustees agreed to reinstate an examination for all applicants.[98]

Politicians also saw the university structure as a way to save money. The Civil War had nearly exhausted public funds, forcing legislators to choose a frugal system of education. Before the war, they had awarded South Carolina College an annual appropriation of about twenty-six thousand dollars—a difficult prospect after the war. A university with elective courses, Governor Perry argued, would eliminate the need for such a large sum. Tuition income would replace it. At the old college, with every student paying the same tuition for the same courses, tuition income had not covered all the institution's expenses; hence the need for the large state appropriation. But at the new university each student studied as many or as few courses as he liked. The cost to the student depended on the number of schools in which he enrolled. The elective principle thus masked a tuition increase. Those who enrolled in three schools, the normal full course load, paid more than the antebellum tuition. On the other hand, those who could not afford or did not desire the full course could enroll in only one or two schools, at a lower cost, thus contributing to the university's income. "Relief to the treasury" after a costly war, one professor observed, was one of the main reasons for establishing a "self-sustaining" university.[99]

The plan did not quite work. The legislature did reduce its appropriation for the university to eighty-six hundred dollars. But income from modular tuition did not meet expectations. Enrollment remained small. In the fall of 1866, with fewer than seventy students, the university's treasury contained less than fifty dollars. Meanwhile, professors received a low salary of one thousand dollars. By 1870 the legislature had responded by increasing funding even beyond its antebellum levels.[100] Thereafter, as political control in South Carolina left conservative white hands and then returned to them, the university's structure and constituency underwent additional changes. The white university became a black university, then a white agricultural college, then a white university again (see chapter 3). In no sense did the immediate postbellum reform settle the institution's fate. But the financial condition of the state college and government and the economic and educational needs of white constituents following the Civil War had motivated the governor and the legislature to create South Carolina's first true state university.

The Civil War furnished a similar opportunity for the University of Missouri. There, no one imagined that the establishment of an expansive university would save the state money. On the contrary, both the legislature and the new president recognized that the project would require a large investment. But the very damage the university had suffered during the war convinced the legislature of the need to make that investment.

The University of Missouri exited the war in nearly as bad a condition as did South Carolina College. Although the faculty had managed to hold classes during part of every year, enrollment had plummeted, and the Union army had occupied most of the campus since the winter of 1861–62. The campus was in a dismal state. The occupiers had left the buildings dirty and damaged. Trees, classroom fixtures, library books, the geological collection, and chemistry equipment had disappeared. To cap it all off, shortly after the war the president's house accidentally burned down.[101]

Financial problems compounded the low enrollment and physical damage. The state had appropriated no tax money for the university since 1839. The small endowment returned poor dividends. The university was twenty thousand dollars in debt and could pay its faculty only in low-value warrants. The mere sixty-nine students, less than half the prewar enrollment, provided little in the way of tuition income. Still, the university had two causes for hope. The first was the Morrill Act. Missouri's legislature had yet to accept a land grant, but the president and curators hoped that once it did, it would award the new money to the old university.[102]

The other cause for hope was a new state constitution. Early in 1865 a constitutional convention of farmers, merchants, and professionals met in St. Louis. It appointed a committee on education, which recommended the establishment of a statewide educational system. The committee argued that training in "the benefits of free government" was essential to ensuring "the liberty of the people" in Missouri's future. Furthermore, "the desolations and dangers of a terrible civil war" and the end of a slave-based economy that had stifled learning had created a unique opportunity to build an educational system. To this end, the committee proposed an article creating both public schools and a state university supported by the public-school fund. The state university, divided into multiple "departments or colleges," would offer courses in agriculture, science, and teaching. The convention adopted the proposed article, and Missouri's white voters ratified the constitution in June. The document thus provided a legal basis for the revitalization of the state university, but nothing more concrete. It did not specify a timeline for the project, only that it would occur "as soon as the public school fund will permit."[103] As with the land grant, the state legislature needed to act. Until it did, the future looked bleak for the war-ravaged school.

That bleak outlook, however, provided just the motivation and leverage the university's leader needed to make the legislature act. In 1866, following the president's death, the board of curators offered the position to Daniel Read of the University of Wisconsin. Read hesitated to take the job. Looking around at the decrepit campus and uncertain finances, he had doubts about the institution's prospects. But he was optimistic about the possibility of state support. Like the framers of the new constitution, he saw the wartime damage as an opportunity for revitalization with government backing. So he used the constitutional promise and the poor shape of the university to force the state government into action.

Read appeared before Missouri's legislators in January 1867. He reminded them of the university's "dilapidated" condition, the state's longtime policy of "doing nothing whatever for it," the constitution's promise of funding, and the recent establishment of the public-school fund. He was ready to lead the university, he told them, but only if he could "make it a seat of learning, worthy its high designation." That required money. So he issued an ultimatum: if the legislators appropriated tax money to support and expand the university, he would accept the presidency. If they did not, he would turn down the job. He returned to Wisconsin to await their decision. Evidently the ultimatum worked, for the legislature appropriated ten thousand dollars to rebuild the president's house plus an annual grant (from the public-school fund) of 1.3125 percent of the state's revenue. Over the next nine years this amounted to $136,000 in state support.[104]

The new funding altered the University of Missouri in several ways. Not least important, it could now pay its faculty. Guaranteed income and the state's blessing also allowed the institution to expand and diversify its curriculum over the next decade. Although a university in name, until then it had been essentially a classical college. The only professional programs at the start of the war had been a normal course and a scientific-agriculture diploma program for students taking the regular college course. The latter had ceased when the chemistry professor teaching it left in 1861. Neither had constituted a separate unit of the university.[105] The income born out of wartime hardship, however, made the school a true comprehensive university in its curriculum and structure. Quoting Ezra Cornell, founder of New York's land-grant university, Read declared, "I would found an institution where any person can find instruction in any study."[106]

In his first report as president, Read recommended the establishment of new schools and departments, including a law college, a normal school, and a college of agriculture and mechanics incorporating schools of engineering, analytical chemistry, and mining and metallurgy. Most of these became a reality within the next decade: the College of Normal Instruction in 1867, the Agricultural and Mechanical College in 1870, the School of Mining and Metallurgy (in Rolla, Missouri) in 1871, the Law College in 1872, and the Department of Analytical and Applied Chemistry in 1873. The university also established the Medical Department in 1872. The agricultural college and the mining college took advantage of the Morrill Act income, which the legislature awarded the university in 1870. The agricultural college, located on the Columbia campus in Boone County, received an additional founding donation of ninety thousand dollars from that county.[107]

Literally reconstructing the campus, the university erected new buildings to house the vocational schools (fig. 6). The Normal Building went up in the corner of campus; the Scientific Building, primarily for the Agricultural and Mechanical College, near the center. The university also built new bridges and walkways to improve the appearance of the campus, a cosmetic but significant action given the damage done during the war.[108] The college at Columbia had dramatically and visibly changed: the county, the state, and the nation had joined hands after the war to build it into a university.

The Universities of South Carolina and Missouri were not alone. Other Southern colleges underwent similar transformations. Three small colleges in Kentucky, for example, found themselves defunct or stillborn at the end of the Civil War. Transylvania University and Kentucky University, denominational colleges, had both seen their buildings converted

Fig. 6. University of Missouri in 1875, including the Scientific Building, used by the Agricultural and Mechanical College, and the Normal Building. (*Boone County Atlas*, 1875; courtesy State Historical Society of Missouri, accession number 029537)

into military hospitals, then one of them destroyed by fire. The Agricultural and Mechanical College, which the state government recently had established using the Morrill Act funds, remained little more than a piece of legislation. Surveying the situation, an alumnus of Kentucky University proposed a merger as a solution to all three schools' problems. By combining their resources, including public money, not only could they survive but they could do something previously impossible, namely, build a comprehensive university. The two denominational colleges and the state legislature all approved the plan. In 1865 the new, state-sponsored Kentucky University opened with colleges of arts and sciences, divinity, law, and agriculture and mechanics.

A few years later, a Methodist minister in Tennessee surveyed the many Methodist colleges in the Upper South that had closed during the war. Those that had managed to reopen in the late 1860s continued to struggle in 1870. He proposed a solution similar to Kentucky University's: by combining their resources, several Methodist conferences could together establish one large university on a more solid foundation than any small college sponsored by a single conference would have. That university could offer courses in both classical and professional subjects. The conferences agreed. Cornelius Vanderbilt offered a donation to support the university, and Vanderbilt University was born. The founders wanted to establish a graduate-only university, more similar to Johns Hopkins than to South Carolina or Missouri. But with few graduates of other colleges prepared to pursue further studies, that proved impossible. The institution that opened in 1875 was an undergraduate comprehensive university, like virtually every other university in the South. It included departments of law, medicine, divinity, and the arts.[109]

The Confederacy's top military leader led another school from classical college to comprehensive university. Robert E. Lee accepted the presidency of Washington College in Lexington, Virginia, only months after the war's end. That school had faced its own wartime trials: the Confederate army had used it as quarters and a hospital in 1862, then Union troops had damaged and robbed it during an attack on Lexington in 1864. Lee quickly set to work, not merely restoring the college to its antebellum health but expanding its scientific and practical offerings. He wanted to teach Southerners to apply scientific research to farming and industry. Though his attempt to create an agricultural school failed, under his leadership the college did establish schools of civil and mining engineering, business, applied mathematics, and applied chemistry, as well as a program in printing and journalism. Attracted by the new practical curricula and by Lee's name, the student body increased rapidly. In 1870, upon Lee's death, the trustees recognized both his contribution and the school's new direction by renaming it Washington and Lee University. The famous general's support for practical higher education encouraged educators elsewhere in the South to introduce similar reforms at their institutions.[110] The comprehensive-university model was becoming a common feature of Southern higher education.

The Civil War brought universities to the American South. As college and state leaders looked for ways to reopen or rejuvenate colleges that had suffered physically and financially during the war, they turned to the new model of the university as a solution. That trend had begun in the North for different reasons. Research universities along the German model were appearing in the northeastern, midwestern, and far western states. Without a crisis in Southern higher education to spark major change, universities might well have bypassed that region. The Civil War gave Southern leaders the opportunity and motivation to establish their own universities, albeit of a different kind. The war thus led the South to imitate to some extent an emerging Northern model.

Colleges in the late 1870s looked very different from colleges twenty years earlier. Before the Civil War, colleges had provided young men and women with an undergraduate classical education. Each college had consisted of a single unit that offered a single course of study (or several very similar ones). Starting during the war and accelerating after it, many colleges diversified their curricula and expanded their structures. After the shock experienced by a nation that went to war unprepared, colleges began to train their students in military skills as well as civil subjects. In between Greek recitations and geometry examinations, students marched in uniform and fired cannons. At the same time, colleges built themselves into universities with multiple academic and vocational curricula. In the South, they did so in response to the damage caused by the war. With multiple units, vocational education, daily drill, and federal officers joining faculties, the war's impact on colleges was very apparent.

The curricular reforms of the Civil War era, in effect, helped to expand the role of higher education in American life. The militarization of American culture and the increasing attention to collegiate occupational training made colleges seem more relevant. They now served an array of purposes that many Americans considered important to the military and economic life of the nation. Congress had passed the Morrill Act and the legislation supplying army officers and arms to encourage colleges to pre-

THE CURRICULUM

pare the expert farmers, engineers, and soldiers that the country needed. As colleges added courses in these disciplines and in teaching, mining, law, medicine, and pharmacy, they accepted their new role as venues for training in the subjects the nation deemed useful, not merely those professors and trustees deemed timeless. In other words, they became more democratic institutions, guided by the priorities not of a few elites but of the nation as a whole.

Colleges also became more reflective of the nation in another regard: their students. Some curricular reforms rested, in part, on a belief among college and state leaders that they could attract new types of students. To an extent they were right. New social groups did begin to attend college in the 1860s and 1870s. But the reasons were complex. Vocational training played a part. Courses were useful to more people and even promoted the Republican Party's ideal of equal economic opportunity. Professors and trustees also modified admissions and financial-aid policies to make new groups' attendance possible. And the simple exigencies of war—where, for example, a student could travel without encountering a hostile army—influenced students' decisions about whether and where to attend college.

THREE

Admissions
Race, Class, Gender

In October 1876 South Carolina's governor received a letter from Grandison Harris, a justice of the peace in Augusta, Georgia. Harris wished to send his son to study law at the University of South Carolina. He wrote to the governor, who chaired the board of trustees, to inquire about admissions procedures and tuition fees. There was nothing especially unusual about his letter. The legislature recently had established the law school as part of its building a comprehensive university. Given Harris's own profession, it is not surprising that he wanted his son to study there. What was remarkable here was not the letter but the writer: Grandison Harris was black.[1]

A lot had changed in the American South. Now a former slave could become a justice of the peace.[2] A lot had changed at the University of South Carolina too. After enduring military takeover and near destruction during the war, then structural and curricular reinvention right after it, the university underwent still more change in the following years. The state's Reconstruction and Redemption governments reshaped the state university, most starkly with regard to who attended it. By 1876 Judge Harris could consider enrolling his son. Missing pages from that year's extant catalogue conceal whether the younger Harris actually attended, but in any event other blacks did. And although South Carolina was unique, it was not alone. No other college changed so completely as it did, but others did begin to enroll new types of students. Some of the changes to admissions were permanent, others temporary. Even as colleges remade curricula, the Civil War and the events that followed it also changed who went to college.

The term *admissions* can be somewhat misleading. Colleges in the nineteenth century did not practice selective admissions as we know them today. They lacked both the need and the ability. So few Americans pursued a college education that colleges usually could admit all qualified applicants. And for the most part they had to: they needed the tuition money. The notion of selecting from among a large number of academically qualified applicants did not take root until the twentieth century and remained uncommon until after World War II, when economic prosperity and rising high-school graduation rates helped to drive a massive increase in applications. Even on the rare occasion that a nineteenth-century institution tried to admit only the best scorers on an entrance test—as the State Normal School in South Carolina did when it opened in 1874—it found the policy impracticable. The small number of applicants and the poor condition of South Carolina's public schools forced the Normal School to admit ill-prepared students.[3]

Yet, nineteenth-century colleges did not welcome everyone. They practiced forms of selective admissions, just very different forms from today's. These fell into three general categories. First were academic criteria for admission. While colleges could not choose only the best applicants, they did want to ensure that matriculates had the necessary preparation to begin college studies. So they administered a test to all prospective freshmen on the material that freshmen already should have mastered. Passing the test—not scoring the best—gained one admission. Despite South Carolina College's temporarily waiving this test to accommodate students' time away from school during the war, the entrance test (and a new equivalent credential, the high-school diploma) remained an important part of college admissions in the late nineteenth century.[4]

Second, and most important, colleges established social criteria for admission. With few exceptions, colleges admitted only those belonging to certain social groups. Most restricted admission to one gender, usually men. Especially before the Civil War, very few admitted African Americans. The cost of tuition, room and board, transportation, and lost work often produced a class and geographic admissions screen: neither the poor nor the distant could afford to attend. These admissions policies and financial requirements restricted both who received a college education and which college a particular student attended.

Finally, colleges established moral admissions criteria. Nineteenth-century colleges, even to some extent the state universities, were Christian institutions with a moral and religious agenda. They aimed to train not only good scholars but also good people and good Christians. To that end, they tried to ensure that only well-behaved youths with good prospects for moral success joined their communities. Thus they usually required applicants to submit testimonials to their moral character and sometimes recorded students' religious status on matriculation. This chapter examines changes in three social criteria for college admission—race, class, and gender—during and after the Civil War. Chapter 4 examines two more social criteria—geography and veteran status—as well as moral criteria.

The war strongly influenced admissions practices, especially social admissions. But it did so unevenly. As with curricula, the war affected college admissions much more in the South than in the North. And as with curricula, the war pushed colleges in the Confederate and border Union states in the direction Northern ones already were heading. By the middle of the nineteenth century, Northern colleges had begun to admit increasing numbers of nontraditional students. They educated much more economically and sexually diverse student populations than a half century before. The state universities and women's colleges of the South, by contrast, remained homogeneous and elite. The challenges of war and the politics of Reconstruction changed that. They accelerated reform in the North and brought it to the South. Southern universities not only diversified curricula but also sought out and successfully attracted new types of students. They became economically diverse, coeducational, and occasionally biracial. By the end of Reconstruction, Southern student populations more closely resembled Northern ones. In both regions, they more closely resembled the population of the nation as a whole.

Diversity in Northern Colleges

By the time of the Civil War, Northern student populations already were growing more diverse. Only about 1 percent of Americans attended college, little more than in the colonial and Revolutionary eras. But those who did attend no longer were only white men from the professional classes. Since the 1830s several Northern colleges had followed Oberlin College in admitting African Americans, either alongside whites or, at Wilberforce University, in an institution founded specifically for them. Most Northern colleges, however, remained closed to blacks, and most blacks did not live in the North. Only a symbolic change had begun.

White women's higher education was expanding much more rapidly, as women's seminaries opened in the Northeast and as more midwestern colleges copied Oberlin's coeducation than copied its biracialism. The feminization of schoolteaching and a belief in gender equality contributed to some of these decisions, but economic expediency often directed reform. College students were a precious commodity in the rural Midwest. Entrepreneurs knew that if they depended entirely on men, they would cut in half their pool of students and therefore their chances of avoiding bankruptcy. Setting up separate schools for men and women, on the other hand, would have cost too much. So to maximize revenue and minimize costs, they made their colleges coeducational. The founding of Lawrence University showed how economics could triumph over ideals. The founding donor Amos A. Lawrence insisted that the school admit men only. But he lived far away in Massachusetts. The ministers and professors actually setting up the school in Wisconsin knew that they could not raise enough money without admitting women. So they founded a coeducational college without telling Lawrence. They simply omitted female graduates from the commencement photograph.[5]

Antebellum Northern colleges also enrolled students from a broad range of social classes. Poor men became a major constituency of New England colleges between 1800 and 1860. Younger sons of farmers, unlikely to inherit land, began to see college as an alternative to agricultural wage labor. With a college education, they hoped to earn more secure livings as ministers or teachers. They obtained financial aid from churches, local charitable associations, or, after 1815, the American Education Society (AES). The AES pooled resources from across New England to support hundreds of poor male students every year. Colleges in the recently settled Midwest attracted large numbers of men from small towns and rural areas, including poor men hoping to enter the ministry. And the women at colleges and seminaries in the North came chiefly from the middle and lower classes.[6] In gender and class, Northern colleges achieved a high level of diversity before the Civil War.

These trends toward increased diversity continued during the 1860s and 1870s. The war accelerated them, first by facilitating the entrance of new types of students and then by providing a political language that justified the change. As we saw in chapter 1, the loss of male students to the military led coeducational colleges to develop increasingly female student populations. So many men left Cornell and Oberlin Colleges to enlist that women and girls there became the majority for the first time. Grinnell College introduced coeducation during the war. The Civil War expanded opportunities for women at midwestern colleges because those colleges needed women in order to survive.

The war's dramatic effects on the gender of enrollments proved temporary when men returned to campuses. Men regained the majority at Cornell College in 1865. But the experience with a primarily female student population, along with the gradual increase in women's enrollments since the 1830s, bolstered colleges' support of coeducation. College leaders from Iowa to California applauded that cause after 1865. Even in New England, some men's colleges began to admit women. The political atmosphere of the Civil War era now influenced college leaders' thinking about gender. The Union had defeated the Confederacy in the name of freedom and equality. Equal access for all Americans to education logically followed. The rhetoric of equal opportunity that was key to Republicans' arguments about economic and political rights also crept into educators' arguments about college admissions.

At postbellum Cornell, both students and college leaders celebrated gender equality. At its quarter-centennial celebration in 1882 a former professor and trustee touted the "equal privileges" the college always had offered to women and men. In the 1860s both the men's and the women's literary societies debated whether the genders should study together. In both societies the affirmative side won. The women also decided that education should prepare women for professions; the men, that women should be able to serve in public office. To be sure, gendered life in practice was neither free nor equal. The faculty strictly regulated social interactions between male and female students, with restrictions on women's activities (such as their need to secure parents' permission to attend the state fair) sometimes more stringent than those on men's.[7] Students addressed male classmates by their last names and females by their first. But women played active and celebrated academic roles. Cornell had a female salutatorian in 1869, and women gave master's orations in 1869 and 1872. Cornell hired female faculty members with equal pay to men's, even naming a woman as full professor in 1871.[8] What had begun before the war continued after it.

Coeducation continued to spread to new institutions. In 1870, one year after the University of California became a state institution, the board of regents opened it to women. Dean Martin Kellogg attributed the decision to the unfairness of excluding women and the fiscal impossibility of founding a separate university for them. The need to prepare teachers for the state's public schools probably also contributed to the regents' decision; most teachers outside the South were now female, and most women who made teaching a profession attended colleges or other institutions of advanced education. But Kellogg emphasized principle, not practicality. Defending coeducation in an address in 1876, he invoked the language of democracy that Abraham Lincoln had used at Gettysburg in 1863: the state university "was of and for the people of the whole

State.... Why should THE DAUGHTERS OF THE STATE Be [sic] denied its privileges?"[9] Lincoln had described a "government of the people, by the people, for the people" to rally Americans behind a war for the restoration of the Union and the emancipation of blacks.[10] Kellogg mimicked his wording to convince Californians of the educational rights of another disadvantaged group.

Even some degree-granting colleges in the Northeast began to educate women, though seminaries such as Mount Holyoke remained. New York Central College and Bates College in Maine, both coeducational, were among the very few that had admitted women before the war. Now New York's Vassar College in 1865 and Massachusetts's Smith and Wellesley Colleges in 1875 opened as women's institutions. Cornell University opened in New York in 1868 with a stated commitment to teach "any person" who qualified for admission. It soon fulfilled that promise by admitting its first female student in 1870 and admitting women on a regular basis beginning in 1872.[11]

Even Harvard took steps toward coeducation. Its development into a university permitted it to begin teaching women in some units without admitting them to the core undergraduate college. It admitted women to the zoologist Louis Agassiz's lectures in 1861 and to a variety of nonresidential lecture courses beginning in 1863. Harvard intended these courses for schoolteachers, among others, so women's admission made sense. For the time being, the Harvard Corporation was unwilling to go further. It rejected two women's applications to the Medical School in 1866, one to the Divinity School in 1869, and one to the Lawrence Scientific School in 1870. But when the agricultural and horticultural college opened in 1871, the corporation admitted women to its courses in horticulture, agricultural chemistry, and entomology. In June 1874 Harvard began administering examinations to women in classical and literary studies. Finally, Harvard in 1879 established the coordinate women's institution that in 1893 became Radcliffe College. Through a series of tentative steps, America's oldest college opened its doors to women.[12]

Some Northern colleges also admitted token numbers of black students after the war. A decline in racism linked to the Civil War's ultimate abolitionist goal may have facilitated their admission. Harvard's first black student, Richard T. Greener, entered the university in 1865 after his former employer convinced the administration of the young man's intellectual promise. He got along well with his white classmates, won the Boylston Prize for Oratory, and graduated with honors in 1870.[13] Cornell's trustees, who had briefly admitted but then dismissed a black man in 1858–59—they had justified his dismissal by citing the existence of Wilberforce and their concern about harming it by competing for black students—declared in 1870 that race would no longer bar a person from admission. Two or three African Americans enrolled in the 1870s, at least one of them a former slave. The faculty expelled a white student who left campus because he had been seated near a black man.[14] Neither college, though, became racially integrated in a meaningful way. Most blacks at Harvard were staff, not students: in addition to the black gymnasium director hired just before the war, many African Americans served food in the dining hall.[15] Northern colleges continued to resist admitting African Americans as students. Racial reform proceeded at its sluggish antebellum pace.

Class was a different matter. As before the war, Northern colleges admitted many men and women who came from humble origins and struggled to afford tuition. Mount Holyoke's principal reminded the trustees in 1873 that Mary Lyon had founded the seminary not for "the poor [who] are crushed, [or] the rich [who are] enervated" but "for the middle classes." Another teacher argued that they should enable women of "any class" to enroll. Elsewhere, college leaders welcomed the poor with the Republican language of free labor and equal opportunity: they celebrated young people who determined to improve their lot through hard work. California's Dean Kellogg found that the "best students very often come from common ranks," because those who "work their way are apt to make a good use of their time and opportunities." Harvard's president wanted to attract "young men of ability and of sterling character, who help give a high and manly tone to all their fellow-students" but who lacked the money to purchase a college education.[16] Colleges continued to seek students from a variety of economic strata.

Poor men and women accepted the invitation. In 1872 Mount Holyoke's principal noted the large number of students who struggled to pay tuition. The University of California received inquiries throughout the 1870s from prospective students, their parents, and their teachers expressing the young men's interest in attending despite their poverty.[17] Colleges wanted to enroll them, and they wanted to come. But college attendance required both tuition payments and time away from paid work. With the AES circumscribing its activities, the responsibility for funding paupers' education fell increasingly to the colleges and the students.[18]

Colleges made paupers' education possible by expanding financial aid. During the early 1860s donors endowed twenty-two scholarships for needy students at Harvard, bringing the total to thirty-nine. A "general beneficiary fund" supported additional poor men. But these were sufficient in neither number nor size. Some students received only twenty dollars, when tuition was seventy-five excluding room, board, and textbooks. Other needy men got nothing.

The president continually called on the trustees and on philanthropists to improve aid. And they responded. The Northern economic boom cultivated by the war, which had made possible the donations that paid for the expansion of colleges into universities, also brought in donations for financial aid. Soon after the war, five individuals and an alumni class donated money for new scholarships. The number of scholarships continued to increase thereafter, reaching seventy in the classical college alone by the fall of 1870. By the late 1870s Harvard was spending nearly thirty thousand dollars annually on undergraduate grants and loans. The founding donor of the agricultural and horticultural college stipulated that it not charge tuition for "poor and meritorious students." Perhaps most important of all, other philanthropists donated money to build a new dormitory and dining hall where students could live and board cheaply. The president claimed that that project saved poor students as much money "as the total income of the scholarship and beneficiary funds."[19] In its tuition, living costs, and financial aid, Harvard was becoming increasingly receptive to an economically diverse student body.

Other colleges also helped out their students. By the fall of 1871 Mount Holyoke's trustees had both set up a dedicated "education fund" and authorized additional spending from the general funds to enable the attendance of "deserving pupils who need pecuniary assistance." The funds covered up to half their tuition and board. The principal awarded aid to about twenty to thirty women each year, often giving out more than the trustees had allotted for the purpose. Justifications for the unauthorized spending, which included recipients' status as the daughters of ministers or missionaries and the inherent rightness of admitting young women of talent, became a regular part of her annual report. The University of California, now a state-run, tax-supported institution, used public funds to go even further than Harvard or Mount Holyoke. Anxious to serve the public and to avoid the exclusionary practices the regents associated with other universities, legislators eliminated tuition for undergraduates one year after the university opened.[20] The construction of a German-style research university, they believed, required expanding access along with the curriculum.

Yet financial aid was insufficient. Students were poor enough and numerous enough that many still struggled to survive without a regular income. Financial pressures forced some at Cornell College and many at Mount Holyoke to end their education prematurely. Others stayed in college by combining study and paid work. Cornell students taught, farmed, or even preached during vacations or weekends. Cornell's student newspaper claimed in 1870 that most students at western colleges had to work for pay. Many colleges, especially those teaching agriculture, gave them jobs right on campus. Harvard hired students to do agricultural labor, as did Cornell University and the state universities of Illinois, Iowa, Maine, Massachusetts, and Wisconsin.[21] These universities had established agricultural curricula, often with the support of Morrill Act funds, to educate those with limited means. Their leaders reaffirmed that commitment by instituting work-study options that both provided occupational practice and enabled young people to attend. Since early in the nineteenth century, colleges throughout the North had educated an economically diverse population of students. They continued that tradition after the war, putting both rhetorical and financial resources into attracting poor men and women.

Altogether, social admissions criteria in the North changed only moderately after the war. The war accelerated antebellum trends toward greater inclusion with respect to gender, class, and, to a much lesser extent, race. It contributed to the admission of women by temporarily robbing colleges of men and perhaps contributed to the admission of blacks by tempering racist attitudes. Its effect on class-based admissions policies went in both directions: the financial strains of war led schools such as Mount Holyoke to raise tuition, but the war ultimately helped the Northern economy and therefore facilitated philanthropy that supported financial aid. The Morrill Act, passed in wartime, created a new type of institution that made special efforts to enable poor people to attend. Republicans' celebration of equal opportunity, free labor, and democracy gave educators a language with which to defend their newly diversified admissions policies. The war's effects were complex and important but not transformative. Northern colleges mainly experienced continuity.

New Diversity in Southern Universities

The Civil War affected admissions policies much more dramatically in the states where it was fought. As they responded to the challenges of war and Reconstruction, Southern college leaders built institutions that not only taught different things from before but taught them to different people. At the comprehensive universities, these two changes were tightly interwoven. The new schools of agriculture, mining, engineering, and teaching appealed to new types of students. These included poor men, women, and sometimes blacks, people who before the war might have attended Northern denominational colleges but rarely Southern state colleges.

The South had not experienced the same diversification of student populations as the North between 1800 and 1860. Colleges there consistently educated an elite and relatively homogenous group of people. State universities prepared planters' sons to fulfill their inherited roles of economic prosperity and political leadership. Women's colleges prepared their future wives to be intelligent companions and plantation mistresses. Some men's and women's colleges even reproduced the plantation hierarchy by employing slaves directly or permitting students to bring theirs with them. Denominational colleges for men contributed some class diversity to the Southern student population by educating middle-class whites with aspirations of professional success. The peculiar circumstances of the South, then, were that upper-class men, middle-class men, and upper-class women attended different types of colleges and that middle-class women and the poor attended none.

The elite institutions, the most distinctive colleges of the antebellum South, underwent dramatic changes during and after the Civil War. By the late 1870s they were no longer so elite. These colleges relaxed their admissions policies, most notably with respect to economic class. In some cases the change was permanent. Admitting an increasingly diverse array of students, many Southern colleges lost their unique status as the last preserve of socially exclusive higher education. They began to look much more like Northern colleges. As they made this transition in the context of Reconstruction, their students sometimes used the same Republican rhetoric of equal opportunity and free labor that Northern reformers used to defend diversification.

Wesleyan Female College, the University of Missouri, and the University of South Carolina all moved toward greater diversity during the Civil War era. But each followed a unique path. Wesleyan responded to the war and Reconstruction as conservatively as conditions allowed. Missouri enacted more substantial change, admitting more poor Southerners after the war than before it and admitting women for the first time. South Carolina took the steepest route of all. There the poor, women, and even formerly enslaved African Americans won the opportunity for a higher education. These different paths justify a separate look at each school. Despite their differences, one thing was clear: as Judge Harris recognized, after the war Southern colleges on the whole served very different constituencies from those they had served before.

Wesleyan's Conservative Reform

Some colleges survived the Civil War with minimal change to their student populations. This was true of women's colleges in particular. Because women did not fight in the war, these institutions lost far fewer students, and were more likely to stay open, than men's colleges. In fact, the desire to preserve Southern antebellum life made women's colleges resilient. As we saw in chapter 1, some saw them as sanctuaries from the war and microcosms of the halcyon world of days past. Also, women supported the war effort through work on campus. Students at Wesleyan raised money by putting on an operetta and helped sustain local support for the Confederate cause by marching in uniform. With fewer reasons to leave and more reasons to stay than at men's colleges, traditional students remained at women's colleges.

Women's colleges in the antebellum South shared three characteristics: all students were white, all were female, and nearly all were wealthy. The Civil War changed none of this. Opening women's colleges to either African Americans or men probably never entered trustees' minds. Wartime turbulence and the South's economic woes did challenge these colleges' class elitism, but Wesleyan's leaders nonetheless made only minimal changes. They preserved Wesleyan as primarily a community of elite young women preparing for an elite lifestyle.

First of all, women's colleges remained racially exclusive. Wesleyan, like every other antebellum college in the South, educated only whites. Like most other Southern colleges, it continued to do so after the war. The white trustees and the Methodist synod had no desire to spark a racial revolution. Only blacks and the most radical white politicians—who sometimes controlled state universities but could not control denominational colleges—did. If anything, given widespread fears that racial intermarriage and violence would follow emancipation, Wesleyan's governing bodies had yet another reason to exclude blacks.[22] Besides, emerging from an era when laws had forbidden whites from teaching blacks even to read, offering them a college education required both a mental revolution of which few whites were capable and preparation that few blacks had.[23] Wesleyan remained a white campus.

Second, women's colleges remained women's colleges. The South almost always had educated its women separately from its men. There were exceptions. Blount College in Tennessee, perhaps the first coeducational college in the country, enrolled five young women in the first decade of the nineteenth century. Mississippi College opened in 1830 as a coeducational institution and the following year awarded the first college degree ever to a woman. But few schools emulated these. Instead, Georgia (later Wesleyan) Female College opened in 1836 as the nation's first college for women only. It, not Blount or Mississippi, set the pattern for Southern women's higher education. By 1860 every Southern state except Florida had at least one women's college. Tennessee had five; Georgia, at least ten; and North Carolina, thirteen. Meanwhile, few new coeducational colleges appeared. Even Blount (renamed East Tennessee College) had stopped admitting women by 1809; Mississippi followed suit in 1850. Higher education for Southern women had taken root, but almost always in segregated environments. Men studied the classical curriculum in some colleges to prepare for their careers as planters or professionals; women studied it in others to become intelligent, appealing, and pious upper-class wives. Americans increasingly believed that men and women shared equal intellectual gifts, but for educational purposes in the South, equal did not mean together.[24]

The Civil War did not challenge women's colleges' gendered identity. Wesleyan's campus did become temporarily mixed during the war. Male and female refugees joined the students living in the college hall; they included prominent local families to whom the college rented rooms to offset rising costs and declining tuition receipts.[25] But these wartime measures did not last, and Wesleyan never admitted men as students.

Finally, antebellum women's colleges of the South educated a socially and economically elite clientele. To start with, many poor Southern women were illiterate. The 24 percent of adult white women in the South (23% in Georgia) who could not read obviously could not attend college.[26] But even those who could read had little opportunity or motivation to pursue a higher education. Poor women in the North, like their male counterparts, might work their way through college by teaching in the common schools. They might also view college as a path to high-school teaching. In the South, teaching remained primarily a masculine profession. That meant that (1) lower-class women could not as easily teach their way through college and (2) a college degree did not carry the promise of a teaching job. The gendered purpose of the colleges also helped make women's higher education a socially elite program. These colleges prepared wives, not workers. They trained planters' and professionals' daughters in the culture of their class. A poor woman who needed to work and would never live on a plantation had no use for training in the culture of the Southern belle.

Wesleyan did admit a very few women of moderate means. The Everett Scholarships supported four or five students each year who could not afford tuition. Beginning in 1860, the college offered free tuition to the daughters or wards of clergymen in the Georgia Methodist Conference. Twelve took advantage of the offer that year. The faculty allowed five others to attend at no charge for unclear reasons. So during the 1860–61 academic year twenty-two attended Wesleyan for free. Yet ministers' daughters were not exactly working class, and one recipient of an Everett Scholarship belonged to the Everett family itself. That left at most 9 truly poor students out of a population of 219.[27] They hardly made a dent in Wesleyan's aristocratic milieu.

Then the war came. It tried the college, its students, and their families both emotionally and financially. The inflation that spread across the South and the difficulty of travel in wartime had reduced the student population to half its prewar level by the end of the conflict. The social makeup of the student body, however, did not change. Wealthy young women continued to populate Wesleyan's campus. Many of the most prominent families of Macon sent their daughters there during the war.[28] Students from outside the city often represented the Confederacy's slaveholding elite. The father of Sallie Love, the traveling student whose story begins chapter 1, owned more than one hundred slaves.[29]

Not only did Wesleyan continue to educate the South's elite class, but in some ways the wartime campus re-created the plantation world in which its students had grown up. The college tried to teach frugality and simplicity, discouraging elaborate dress and forbidding shopping in town or bringing personal slaves to campus. But at least two African Americans, probably enslaved, served the students in the dining hall and the living area. The father of the preparatory students Ella and Clara Burton, a slaveholder and a captain in the Confederate army, even persuaded the president to make an exception to the rule about personal slaves. Aged thirteen and twelve, the sisters were so accustomed to enslaved help that they could neither tie their own shoes nor comb their own hair. After seeing their "neglected appearance," the captain sent Frances, their slave mammy, to care for them.[30] They re-created the plantation hierarchy on the campus. In the midst of civil war, the women's college remained an institution of and for the antebellum slaveholding elite.

As the war continued, even the wealthy found their wallets getting thin. Inflation of the Confederate currency began almost immediately, as the Southern government financed the war through the extensive printing of scrip. By the fall of 1862 prices had reached six times their prewar levels.[31] Colleges were not immune. As the dollar fell and prices rose, the trustees needed to act to keep Wesleyan solvent. Thus the cost of a college education, like everything else, drastically increased. Even more than in peacetime, only the wealthiest families could afford to send their daughters to college.

Costs began rising in 1862. Noting "the great advance in the price of provisions," the trustees raised the cost of board three times that year, then stopped printing the price schedule because they knew they would need to raise it again. Their meeting minutes reflected no discussion of providing an affordable education. The trustees aimed instead to keep Wesleyan financially sound.[32] Still, for the time being they were acting conservatively. At the start of the war tuition cost $60; room, board, and washing, $150 more.[33] Had fees kept pace with general inflation, by 1863 they would have climbed to four digits. Instead, they reached only $70 for tuition and $230 for room, board, and washing, a mere 43 percent increase overall and less than one-thirteenth the Confederate dollar's inflation rate. The lowering of the real cost of attending Wesleyan probably did not attract middle- or lower-class Confederates, for they had no more reason to attend now than before the war. But it did allow elite but hurting families to keep their daughters enrolled. During the 1862–63 academic year the student population was about the same as two years earlier.[34]

In 1863 fees rose more sharply. The trustees had little choice. Inflation accelerated that year, especially after the summer military defeats at Gettysburg and Vicksburg. The shrinking physical size of the Confederacy, by concentrating its currency in a smaller space, helped drive up prices. The high costs of provisions forced Wesleyan to close early for the summer. When classes resumed that October, prices were nearly twenty times what they had been before the war; a year later, following the capture of Atlanta, they reached twice that.[35]

The trustees now began listening to the faculty, who had been advocating matching fees to inflation since the summer of 1862. Professors' income, after all, depended on tuition receipts. Furthermore, President John M. Bonnell argued on behalf of the faculty, "a sudden turn of the fortunes of war, or a failure in some wanted source of supply," could force Wesleyan to shut its doors at any time. The college needed to increase its funds.[36] In June 1863 the trustees raised tuition to $100 and board to $330. In August they raised board again, to $50 *per month,* and linked it thereafter to the cost of provisions. As a result, board rose to $75 in

January, $80 in February, and $100 in March 1864.[37] The next catalogue listed tuition for 1864–65 as $150 and board as $950 per year, but even before classes began, the trustees raised tuition again, to $300, and redefined board *in kind*. Room and board now cost "136 pounds of *bacon,* and 340 pounds of *flour,* and 16 bushels of *corn;* or the equivalent of these, if paid in other provisions or in currency." This policy kept college fees in a direct relationship with inflation. The trustees also, in November 1864, granted the faculty's request to make French an optional course, with an additional charge. The lucrative elective principle, adopted by universities after the war, helped professors to survive in a bad economy. Finally, in March 1865 the trustees transferred the power of setting tuition and board to the faculty, expecting professors to increase costs.[38] Faculty records have not survived, but presumably they did just that.

In sum, tuition and board rose from $210 at the beginning of the war to more than $1,100 at its end. The big jumps came in 1863 and 1864. The goal of the trustees and the faculty was institutional survival, not economic diversity. And the effect of their actions was dramatic. Wesleyan's enrollment fell by one-fourth during the first year of the war, then rose over the next two years, but in 1864 it dropped by more than half, from 245 to 112.[39] Few could still afford the price. Ella and Clara Burton, the sisters whose slave mammy had joined them on campus, had to leave about this time, their family's fortune depleted.[40] William T. Sherman's Atlanta campaign and his subsequent march through Georgia compounded the effect, as invading and pillaging troops kept students from returning.

Those students who remained at Wesleyan still came from the Southern elite. If anything, higher costs had made the college more exclusive. And it remained exclusive after the war. The student population recovered as fees fell to near their prewar levels.[41] But in 1868 those students included the daughters of Georgia's chief justice and other prominent citizens.[42] Upon graduation, these young women looked forward to "wear[ing] long trains, go[ing] to parties and do[ing] everything exactly as we like," noted a student commencement speaker in 1877.[43] The need to work for a living, let alone the possibility of not being able to afford those long trains, applied to few of her classmates. Two years earlier, another commencement speaker had divided her graduating class into those who would marry and those who would seek "fames"[44]—the latter category implying professional employment, but with emphasis on status, not earning power. Neither student speakers nor college catalogues ever mentioned occupational preparation or economic advancement as an educational goal.

ADMISSIONS: RACE, CLASS, GENDER

These students began at the top and came to Wesleyan as part of their elite upbringing. Those below the top generally stayed away.

As before the war, a few relatively humble women did study at Wesleyan during Reconstruction. The faculty granted at least one woman in 1866 an extension on her tuition "until she could pay us from her own earnings."[45] Since 1860 the college had offered free tuition to the daughters of Methodist ministers; immediately after the war, it expanded this policy to include all "daughters of Clergymen, living by the ministry, or . . . indigent daughters of deceased Confederate soldiers."[46] This policy continued until a decade later, when it was limited to the daughters of clergymen only. Wesleyan was, after all, a Christian college. The trustees, most of them ministers themselves, understood both the school's religious mission and the low income of a minister relative to a planter.[47] But now the trustees also supported the Lost Cause of the South. Free tuition for dead soldiers' poor daughters no doubt helped the college's reputation and probably gave hope for the future to some young women and their mothers. Also, the Southern teaching profession had remained mostly male before the 1870s, but with public schools now opening in the South, teaching opportunities for women were growing. During the 1870–71 academic year one-third of Southern teachers were female.[48] Wesleyan could now prepare young women for those jobs.

Any nonelite students who attended Wesleyan, however, remained a small and largely invisible minority. A student commencement speech of 1875 exposed their invisibility. The same year that one speaker divided her classmates into the to-be-famous and the to-be-married, Eugenia Jones titled her speech "Hard Times." In it she described the hard times that Southerners had experienced since the Civil War "devastat[ed] and la[id] waste every thing the people had by assiduous [effort] collected." She acknowledged the difficulties of "the merchant, the banker, the railroad contractor, . . . the school girl," and "the working man." But Jones clearly addressed workers as a foreign group—not her family and not her classmates. For students at Wesleyan, hard times meant forgoing the purchase of new dresses and, she quipped, taking final examinations. For workers, hard times meant reduced wages and debt. She implored them to avoid debt by avoiding the use of credit, without offering advice on how to do that.[49] If any of her fellow graduates were from the working class, Jones seemed unaware. The antebellum ideal of the Southern belle survived the Civil War.[50] Women's colleges such as Wesleyan continued to enable and institutionalize it.

In the end, the Civil War brought no permanent change to admissions at Wesleyan. The trustees had responded to the Confederate defeat by opening the college to a few poor women deemed especially worthy, the daughters of those who had died for the Cause. But that step toward economic diversity was both small—Wesleyan remained primarily an elite college training those already well off to become intelligent, cultured wives—and temporary. In 1875, with most dead soldiers' orphaned daughters now grown up, the trustees ended the offer of free tuition.[51] Despite nearby battles and heavy inflation, Wesleyan had survived a decline in enrollment and made it through the war with no lasting change in its student population. It remained the preserve of the Southern elite that its antebellum founders had made it.

Class and Gender at the University of Missouri

The Civil War sparked much greater change at the University of Missouri. Enrollment rose abruptly after 1865 as the school began to admit more diverse cohorts of students. Just as the war provided the opportunity and the motivation to convert the institution into a comprehensive university, it simultaneously encouraged the faculty and curators to loosen admissions criteria. Whereas Wesleyan only slightly reduced economic barriers, Missouri grew substantially more open with regard to both class and gender.

Until the Civil War, admissions policies at Southern state universities resembled those at denominational women's colleges. Without exception, they admitted only whites. With few exceptions, they admitted only one gender—in this case men. The University of Alabama became one of the exceptions in the 1830s, when it permitted students of the Alabama Female Institute to attend its lectures in mathematics and science. The University of Missouri became another in 1841, when the female Columbia College was rechristened a branch of the university. But these exceptions were as brief as they were rare. The Columbia-Missouri connection lasted only two years. The colleges returned to being strictly single-gender institutions.[52]

Men's colleges were somewhat more diverse economically. Men derived professional opportunities from higher education that women did not, so some youths from the middle classes did attend college. But these sons of modest farmers and urban professionals tended to enroll at denominational colleges, making the state universities bastions of the plantation elite. If a nonelite Southerner did enroll at a state university, he likely struggled to meet expenses and felt like an outsider. The future author Edgar Allan Poe, for example, son of actors and foster son of a merchant, acquired the reputation of "a beggar" at the University of Virginia in 1826. Partly owing to the upper-class expectation of a student's paying not only for tuition, books, room, and board but also for a servant (if he did not own a slave), Poe quickly fell into debt and left the university after less than a year.[53]

Still, a few middle-class men did study at state universities. Missouri made it relatively affordable for them to do so. Antebellum tuition, at thirty-one dollars, was half that of either Wesleyan or Virginia. The university provided no dormitories, but the catalogue estimated room and board with private families at just over one hundred dollars per year. These charges compared favorably with those at some other state universities.[54] But they were still substantial. On top of these, students and their families lost the income the students would have made working for pay or on family farms. College, while more affordable at Missouri than at Wesleyan, meant a financial sacrifice that many could not afford.

The University of Missouri provided for the education of some poor youths. A privately endowed fund supported about a dozen Boone County students who demonstrated academic talent, moral character, and financial need.[55] The board of curators also could select some "indigent students" to attend free of charge but for a "contingent fee of one dollar." Surviving sources do not indicate how many took advantage of the offer.[56] Some probably relished the opportunity to achieve an education beyond their means, but free tuition could only do so much. The university did not pay for students' room and board, let alone reimburse them for lost income while they studied. Furthermore, Missouri may have done the same as the University of Virginia, which awarded many of its scholarships not to the truly poor but to elite men whose fathers had fallen on hard times.[57] It is unclear whether Missouri's aid programs significantly expanded diversity.

The faculty and curators deserved little blame for limiting financial aid. They lacked the resources to support many poor students. The name University of Missouri is somewhat misleading, and not only because of the absence of a university structure. Although many states established state universities in the first half of the nineteenth century, only Virginia, South Carolina, and Michigan provided significant state funding.[58] Missouri gave its university next to nothing: after a large initial grant to build the institution in 1839, the legislature had not awarded it another dollar by 1861.[59] Essentially a private college created by the state, the University of Missouri suffered the same financial challenges as denominational colleges such as Wesleyan. Neither could afford to educate many paupers. Students meant tuition, and tuition meant survival.

The war ruined that equation. If paying students meant survival, enlisting students threatened death for the university. It managed to stay open at least part of every year during the war, but just barely. In the first year enrollment plummeted from 168 to 40. In March 1862 the curators noted the dearth of students, the lack of state funding, and their inability to pay the faculty. The Union troops occupying the campus did nothing to temper their gloom. So they shut down the university. When they reopened it the next fall, only 23 students enrolled.[60]

The curators seemed uncertain about how to revive the school's income in wartime. They did not need to deal with extreme inflation as in the Confederacy, but they did adjust tuition. At first they lowered it: from $30 in 1861 to $25 in 1862 and $20 in 1863. They probably hoped that more young men would come if they charged less. That strategy having only limited success, however, in 1864 they raised tuition to $42 ($32 for freshmen).[61] They probably hoped to compensate for inflation and get what money they could from the few students they had.

The military surrender found the school in an abysmal state, both physically and financially. As we saw in chapter 2, the newly appointed president, Daniel Read, used the university's hardships to persuade the legislature to fund repairs and the creation of an expansive comprehensive university. But a university could not operate without students, and these had been in short supply for several years. The postbellum economy did not bode well for their return. The Civil War had ruined the South economically. Former slaves emerged from the war free but penniless. Landless whites outside the border states had only worthless Confederate currency. And even landowning whites suffered. Three billion dollars' worth of human property had either run away or been legislated out of existence. The land remained, but its value plummeted in the absence of forced labor. In 1867 it was worth only about one-fifth as much as before the war.[62]

Nor could planters bring in much monetary income. Crop failures in 1865 and 1866 devastated both white landowners and black laborers. New laws prevented planters from collecting old debts, while they fell into debt themselves. Finally, federal law now required former masters to pay their black workers with cash they did not have. Those former masters eventually solved this dilemma with the exploitative sharecropping system. But production in some areas did not return to antebellum levels for decades. Facing such difficulties, many planters considered getting out of agriculture altogether. Low on funds, the old elite could not easily afford to send its sons to college.[63]

The University of Missouri's leaders understood this. They had to design an institution that people could actually attend. So when they built a comprehensive university in the 1860s and 1870s, they made it affordable—and not just for the suffering elite. The legislature, the curators, and the faculty created a university that was accessible and attractive to a broader economic range of Missourians. They helped their old constituency to attend in hard times but also reached out to new types of students.

The very creation of a comprehensive, land-grant university altered the student body. The Agricultural and Mechanical College and the School of Mining and Metallurgy opened the door for a new class of young people to study in Columbia. The classical college before the Civil War had not actively excluded men of the laboring classes, but few, even if offered free tuition by a friendly curator, had been able to afford the cost of housing and lost income. Besides, young men who had neither inherited land nor aimed for the learned professions had had little reason to study a classical curriculum designed to turn the sons of the elite into gentlemen. The new agricultural, mechanical, mining, and metallurgy curricula, by contrast, prepared young men for paying occupations.

The university included two entire colleges devoted to manual forms of labor, in addition to the law, normal, and arts colleges. These aimed higher education specifically at the laboring classes. One student described the agricultural college's mission in terms that reflected the Republican Party's ideals of free labor and equal opportunity: "to educate, develop and direct the intellectual and physical powers of the industrial classes." With all lectures in the university open to students in that college, it could become a back door for poor farmers into a practical *and* classical education.[64]

Of course, designing a curriculum for nonelites did not in itself make that curriculum affordable to them. The legislature, the curators, and the faculty understood this. With a flurry of cost-cutting measures for students, they used the university's new tax support to make higher education possible for whoever desired it. First, with the opening of the normal school in 1867, the legislature adjusted the free-tuition policy. Instead of an uncertain number of poor men studying the classics for free, now each county could send one needy and talented student to the normal school every two years, free of charge. The beneficiary had to teach for at least two years in the Missouri public schools following graduation. According to one observer, though, this law was "devoid of results."⁶⁵ Evidently young people did not take advantage of the opportunity.

More importantly and successfully, the legislature in 1872 drastically reduced tuition. It increased state funding to compensate. Senator James S. Rollins, who proposed the law—and who also happened to be president of the board of curators—claimed to have made the university "substantially free" to any Missourian between fourteen and twenty-five. In fact, for state residents the law replaced the forty-dollar tuition with a ten-dollar entrance fee plus a maximum ten-dollar library fee. That is, it cut tuition in half. The law's passage revealed Missouri politicians' commitment to education for the masses across party lines. While the rhetoric of raising "the industrial classes" drew on the ideology of the Republican Party, which had held power in Missouri after the war, the election of 1870 had given Democrats control of the legislature. Rollins himself was a Democrat.⁶⁶ Men of both political stripes wanted to make a university education available to the common people of their state.

The response on campus was jubilant. When they learned that the law had passed, students celebrated late into the night—and not only because their own tuition bills would go down. "Virtually free" tuition, some students believed, would make the state university "the grand culminating point of the public school system of this State." The student newspaper predicted a record enrollment the next year, as youths from all over Missouri who previously had been kept out only by the high tuition rushed to Columbia to study.⁶⁷

The newspaper was right. Enrollment had recovered since the war; during the 1871–72 academic year, the inaugural year of the School of Mining and Metallurgy in Rolla, the combined enrollment at the Columbia and Rolla campuses had reached 321. But with the drop in tuition it instantly doubled, to about 660. Many of the new students matriculated in the Agricultural and Mechanical College, whose population jumped from 51 to 138, and the School of Mining and Metallurgy, which grew from 28 to 75.⁶⁸ In achieving these enrollment figures, Missouri outperformed many land-grant colleges.⁶⁹ It had found the right formula: twenty dollars made all the difference for many middling or poor Missourians as well as the old elite.

The curators also looked for ways to make housing more affordable. Missouri had no dormitories. In 1868 the curators acknowledged that the high cost of room and board in town prevented many young men from attending, so they built three cottages for students looking to economize.

Residents shared expenses for food. The cost of room and board in the cottages was less than half what it was in town, $1.50 to $2.00 per week compared with $4.00 to $5.50. Students responded decisively: as enrollment rose, the cottages filled to capacity. By 1871, the curators had purchased a mansion and two adjacent cottages to serve as more cheap student housing. Students kept coming, one of them claiming that interest in the cottages was so high that the curators could have filled three times as many.[70] Continuing the literal reconstruction of the campus that had begun with academic buildings for the vocational schools, the university kept adding new buildings to expand access as well as curricula.

Several other measures combined with reduced tuition and inexpensive housing to make it possible for poorer youths to attend the university. Opportunities for campus work helped some agriculture students. Starting in 1870, when the Agricultural and Mechanical College opened, it permitted students to earn money toward tuition and expenses by working on the university's farm or garden. At the mining and metallurgy school a few students could avoid tuition altogether: any county that currently had no students enrolled in the university could send one to this school free of charge. Many young people still could not afford to attend, and some who did enroll had to leave owing to financial difficulties.[71] But in the decade after the Civil War, spurred by the need to mend the war-torn campus, the legislature had made higher education in Missouri increasingly accessible to students from humble backgrounds. And many poor youths did come.

The same structural changes opened the university in another respect. Starting in the 1860s, women attended Missouri's state university. When President Read demanded that the legislature fund the institution, he sought to build a variety of professional and practical units, including a normal school to prepare teachers for Missouri's public schools. After all, some had begun to envision the university, in the words of the student newspaper, as "the grand culminating point of the public school system of this State."[72] And if it were to educate Missouri's schoolteachers, it had to educate women. As female teachers became more common in the South after the Civil War, some prepared for their jobs at colleges such as Wesleyan, but others turned to the normal schools that were springing up around the country. Because of the large number of these female prospective teachers, normal schools usually admitted both women and men. At many of these schools, the majority of students were women. Missouri followed the national pattern, admitting women to the College of Normal

Instruction one year after it opened, in 1868. The curators seemed quite anxious to attract female students: by 1870 they were offering women reduced tuition. Men paid $40; women, only $7.50.[73]

Admission to the normal school paved the way to the rest of the university. After a year, the curators discovered that having women on campus "did no manner of harm," so they let female normal students attend lectures in the College of Letters and Sciences. The women marched in as a group, flanked by two professors "as guards." When even this radical policy triggered no disaster, in 1870 the curators took the final momentous step and admitted women to all branches of the university. Over the next few years women enrolled in a variety of courses. In 1872 the first woman received her bachelor's degree; four years later one graduated as valedictorian. The faculty and the curators now celebrated their own wisdom in admitting women. The state university, they argued, should educate both "the teachers of our race" and good wives skilled in farming, landscaping, and gardening. They also justified coeducation through women's influence on men. By educating "wives and daughters" in agriculture, they hoped through those women to spread an appreciation for agriculture among men.[74]

The Civil War provided the opportunity for these changes in admissions policies. The need to rebuild the University of Missouri after physical damage from occupying troops and to attract students in an era of financial hardship allowed President Read to demand a multipurpose university with increased state funding. That structure and that funding facilitated the broadening of the curriculum and the diversification of the student body. Reduced tuition allowed planters' sons to attend despite the loss of family fortunes. Vocational curricula, along with reduced tuition, made the university attractive and affordable to young men and women of the middle and lower classes. The war changed both the subjects the university taught and to whom it taught them.

South Carolina: Reconstruction and Redemption

The University of South Carolina changed the most of all. Its experience revealed both the enormous change that could come out of the Civil War and the fragility of some types of change. Wesleyan survived the Civil War with minimal reforms in admissions. It opened very slightly with respect to class and not at all with respect to gender or race. Missouri went much further, opening with respect to both class and gender. But South Carolina proved that the Civil War had enabled even greater change, at least temporarily. At South Carolina the war did not initiate change directly, as at Missouri. Here, political Reconstruction, which reached its apogee in the state of South Carolina, transformed admissions. A Republican legislature with an African American majority opened that university to the poor, to women, and to formerly enslaved blacks.

Before the war, South Carolina College fit the same Southern model as Wesleyan and Missouri. It educated one race, one gender, and for the most part one class: whites, men, and elites, especially planters' sons. The first two admissions criteria were easy enough to enforce. Slavery occupied most blacks. State law in South Carolina, as elsewhere, prohibited even teaching them to read. The census of 1860 reported that only 365 free blacks had attended school in the state during the past year, compared with 46,226 whites. Higher education was out of the question. White women, meanwhile, attended separate women's colleges, such as Methodist Female College in Columbia.[75]

South Carolina's fees ensured an almost exclusively wealthy student population. Besides tuition, rent, and board, the catalogue listed additional fees for fuel, washing, lighting, use of the library, and a servant. This last expectation underscored the institution's presumption that its students came from a privileged social stratum. So did the comprehensive annual price tag of $240.50. It surpassed Missouri's by more than one hundred dollars, though it was only moderately high by Southern standards. That figure actually underestimated the cost of attendance, since students also had to pay for books, clothing, furniture, and travel between home and school. Beyond that, as at Missouri, families sacrificed income by allowing their sons to attend school instead of working. Few young men had either the financial ability or the financial incentive to attend college. Not surprisingly, then, most students at South Carolina came from heavily slaveholding areas.[76]

At South Carolina as elsewhere, a few young men of moderate means did enroll. Five scholarships supported "young men of more than ordinary merit and attainments, whose circumstances require that they should be aided in their College course." The catalogue explained, "They are . . . not simply aids to indigence, but compliments to excellence." A man who wanted a college education but could not pay for it had to demonstrate superior talent or diligence to his wealthier peers. But if he met this higher standard, the college (or the wealthy alumni who had endowed the scholarships) would give him a hoist as he pulled himself up by his bootstraps.[77]

More important, the state government offered some young men a free education. In accordance with a law of 1857 the commissioner of education in each county could nominate one promising but needy man to study at the college free of charge. The state and local governments thereby cooperated to make higher education in South Carolina an option for a small but slightly more diverse group of young white men. Students seem to have shared that vision and done their part to further it. The two student literary societies each annually chose a "beneficiary"; one also waived membership dues for students receiving financial aid. The members of a year's class sometimes pooled funds to pay the college expenses of one of their own.[78] South Carolina College, like other antebellum Southern men's colleges, served primarily the economic elite. But the alumni, faculty, legislature, and students helped a small number of more modest South Carolinians to attend their elite institution.

The Civil War and Reconstruction opened South Carolina College in all three respects: class, gender, and race. As early as April 1861 the faculty discovered that they would be hard pressed to maintain the college with the old student population. That month, defying the college president's instructions to remain, the students deserted the campus to defend Charleston Harbor. They went to war again that summer and again that fall. When they took longer to return the third time, the faculty worried that their "departure . . . will peril the existence of the Institution." Although many of the students eventually did return, they all left when the governor called for a military draft the next March. The faculty then decided that the admissions requirements needed revising. Because of the enlistment of many young men and the financial hardship of many others, they resolved to make it easier for those of "limited means" to attend. But their decision became a moot point when the Confederate military took over the college that summer for use as a hospital.[79]

The school that reopened in January 1866 was in many ways a different institution. South Carolina College had become the University of South Carolina. Instead of the old four-year prescribed curriculum, students now chose from among eight two-year schools modeled on the University of Virginia. The curriculum included such practical studies as pharmacy, engineering, and mechanics. And the school was smaller than before, with only forty-nine students at the end of the first term.[80]

Most of the first postbellum students had served in the Confederate military. That experience in "the severe school of the soldier," as one student put it, could be neither forgotten nor ignored. Many had lost a limb and got around on crutches. And in some ways their recent past served them well in college. The faculty unanimously applauded students' hard work and desire to learn, as well as their good discipline. The discipline probably owed much to students' military service. At the same time, having spent the past couple of years on the battlefield instead of at a preparatory school, these men arrived at Columbia ill prepared for college work. In order to attract students, the faculty forwent the entrance examination in the first semester. Once classes began, they discovered that they had to begin instruction at a very low level to accommodate the new student population.[81]

But few of these students were poor. The faculty temporarily eliminated academic admissions requirements, but the trustees did not eliminate or reduce tuition. In fact, they raised it. In 1862 tuition and fees had totaled $240.50; in 1866 they surpassed $320.[82] This increase was less than the 75 percent inflation in the Union currency by the end of the war but still large enough to render higher education even less attainable than before for those of modest means.[83] And while some colleges offered financial incentives for veterans to attend (see chapter 4), South Carolina did not. The war had exhausted four of the school's five scholarships. Although each county could still send one young man for free, many did not do so, probably because of the high cost of travel, room, and board. The veterans who enrolled, a professor observed, were the same young men who would have attended South Carolina College had the war not intervened.[84] They were those who could afford it.

Students' curricular choices reflected their elite social origins. For the first time, students at the University of South Carolina could choose their classes. Options included such vocational studies as engineering, pharmacy, and mechanics. Presumably, upwardly mobile youths of the working or middle classes would have enrolled in such courses. Yet only nine took chemistry, which included pharmacy, and eight enrolled in the natural and mechanical philosophy and astronomy school. (The mathematics and engineering professor did not record his school's enrollment.) Meanwhile, sixteen signed up for Latin, thirty for Greek, and twenty-eight for rhetoric and literature.[85] Most of these students sought a classical education, the traditional collegiate program that prepared them for careers as doctors, lawyers, ministers, or planters.

Yet young men of limited resources soon began to infiltrate the university's halls. They struggled to pay tuition but chose to struggle nonetheless. In 1868, for instance, a graduate student complained that despite working for pay, he could not afford to purchase bedclothes, let alone pay the fifteen-dollar library fee. Four years later, law students' financial problems had become such a concern that a professor, without prior approval from the president or the trustees, reduced the law curriculum from two years to one. Asking students to postpone employment another year, he worried, "would have driven all such Students from the University."[86] These students may not have come from the lower classes, but they had less wealth than traditional matriculates. These middle-class men had begun to sway curricular policy. The state government had created a comprehensive university in part to attract new types of students. Now the faculty had no choice but to shape a curriculum that appealed to the increasingly diverse student population.

The big changes were still to come. In 1873 the university remained racially and sexually exclusive. It had taken only small steps toward economic diversity. Nonetheless, a revolution had been going on on campus. Radical Reconstruction had arrived in South Carolina. Enfranchised blacks, now the majority of the state's voters, had elected an overwhelmingly Republican and mostly black legislature in 1868. In 1873 more than 60 percent of its members were black. Federal troops and especially black militamen guaranteed their ability to govern. Owing to the damage Sherman's troops had done to the statehouse, that legislature was meeting in the university chapel. White students, derisive and fearful of the new government, sat in the gallery watching their state get transformed. Having reversed South Carolina's political hierarchy, the legislators strove to topple other institutions of racial discrimination. It was difficult work. They created the Land Commission to help poor blacks and whites purchase land, but corrupt administration hampered its influence. They tried to ban racial discrimination in public accommodations, but white legislators, who retained a slight majority in the Senate, blocked that measure.[87] Now they turned their eyes, inevitably, to the white university surrounding them. There, at least for a while, they effected concrete and drastic change.

South Carolina's legislators may have known about recent experiments elsewhere in the South. Before the Civil War, blacks' role at Southern colleges had been limited to service as slaves. After the war, blacks remained on some campuses (including Wesleyan) as paid servants,[88] but for the first time others enrolled as students. Many supporters of blacks' education promoted the founding of separate colleges for them, such as Howard University in Washington, DC, and Claflin University in Orangeburg, South Carolina. Others tried teaching the races together. Near the end of the war some white Kentuckians who had tried to open a biracial college in 1859 decided to try again. Their first attempt had foundered against powerful local white opposition, but a new regime offered new possibilities. Berea College opened in early 1866. It admitted students regardless of race or gender. During the 1866–67 academic year Berea enrolled ninety-six blacks and ninety-one whites in the primary and preparatory departments. College classes began three years later; the second graduating class, of 1874, comprised two blacks and two whites. Meanwhile, Straight University in New Orleans, though organized in 1869 primarily to educate African Americans, enrolled both black and white students in a law school directed by a black man.[89] Enabled by the Civil War, these institutions' founders had built a Christian college and a comprehensive university on Reconstruction principles.

Soon state governments in the South began exploring the possibility of educating blacks and whites together. Some proposals went nowhere. In Mississippi, black legislators in 1870 suggested to the governor that he integrate the state university. After the chancellor threatened the entire faculty's resignation, however, the governor instead promoted the development of separate colleges for blacks. In Louisiana, the legislature in 1873 ordered Louisiana State University to integrate, but to no effect: the university's president chose to lose state funding rather than admit blacks.[90]

Arkansas's state university was the first in the South actually to implement biracial education. That state's Reconstruction government opened Arkansas Industrial University in 1872 without admissions restrictions based on either gender or race. The state superintendent of education, an African American, signed its charter and chaired its board of trustees. At least two black men enrolled. They did not, however, participate equally with whites in university life. Rather than allowing them to attend classes with white students, the president taught them privately. Nor did these men stay long. After only one year the legislature decided to open a separate normal school for blacks and make the state university an all-white institution.[91] The first experiment in state-sponsored biracial Southern higher education had failed. But South Carolina's black politicians were ready to try again.

In 1873, only months after Arkansas abandoned biracial higher education, South Carolina moved to establish it. The legislature appointed a black majority to the board of trustees, which in turn declared the University of South Carolina "the common property of all our citizens without distinction of race." The trustees published this resolution in a local newspaper.[92] It made the university a very different institution. Before the Civil War, South Carolina College had acculturated the plantation elite, helping to perpetuate the racial hierarchy of a slave society. It had excluded those who were excluded from the ruling class: women, poor men, and blacks. African Americans instead had endured, in the words of George W. Murray, a former slave who attended the university under the new policy and later served in Congress, "cruel and relentless training for the benefit of others."[93]

Now the university served a political and social purpose diametrically opposed to the antebellum college's. In theory, it brought black and white Americans together in their formative years on the basis of equality. In practice, few whites chose to attend. It offered former slaves, less than a decade earlier legally barred from learning to read, all the educational opportunities previously available only to white students. It offered them training for their *own* benefit. Despite blacks' inevitable lack of preparation, the trustees resolved not "to abridge, reduce or suspend any of the schools of the University." Matriculates could study law, medicine, engineering, or the arts. While together in Columbia, blacks (and a few whites) could now form their own social and professional networks. To accommodate students' backgrounds, and probably anticipating private secondary schools' reluctance to admit African Americans, the trustees created a preparatory school within the university. The trustees believed this to be the only way to "meet . . . the educational wants of the people of this State." For if tax money was to support the university, it had better meet the needs of the people—all the people.[94]

They really did mean *all* the people. Easily overlooked amid the racial revolution in Columbia was another, gendered revolution. Women began to study at the university. Historians most often view Reconstruction as an effort to reshape the racial lines of Southern politics, economics, and society. But efforts to re-create the South after the Civil War introduced the possibility of other types of change. Many Americans began to rethink traditional gender roles.[95] Nowhere, perhaps, were the results so visible as on college campuses being rebuilt after the Civil War. White women in Columbia, Missouri, took their places in normal classrooms, then in all classrooms, at that city's university. And in Columbia, South Carolina, at a university transformed in its purpose and constituency by Radical Reconstruction, both African American men and women now arrived on the campus.

Educational change at the primary and secondary levels made black women's higher education possible. During Reconstruction, African Americans throughout the South were busily building a network of schools for their children. Schools needed qualified teachers. While Northern missionaries filled part of the need, Southern normal schools and colleges had to supply the remainder. So both Northern philanthropists and Southern state governments sponsored black normal schools after 1870. African American communities often initiated the foundings, but legislatures continually voted to fund the black institutions during and, in most cases, after Reconstruction. By the turn of the century, Southern states were funding about twenty black normal schools. Owing to the increasingly feminine gendering of the teaching profession, black normal schools, like white ones, usually admitted both women and men.[96]

Responding to the needs of South Carolina's primary and secondary schools, the legislature in 1873 voted to establish a normal school on the university's campus. It opened the following year. A "strictly professional" institution, in the words of its catalogue, the State Normal School enhanced the professional and practical offerings the university had developed since the Civil War. Students went there to learn to teach; they even took a pledge that they would teach in South Carolina's public schools after leaving. Like the university proper, and in keeping with its goal of furnishing teachers for black schools, the State Normal School admitted students without regard to "race, color or previous condition of servitude." Unlike the university, but like other normal schools, it admitted both men and women (fig. 7). Women, in fact, comprised twenty-five out of thirty-one students in 1874 and the entire graduating class in 1877.[97] In stark contrast to the white male student population of the antebellum years, both men and women and both blacks and (a few) whites now studied on the same campus.

In addition to the more visible changes in race and gender, efforts at class expansion also were afoot. Of course, the establishment of a university for blacks was itself a class project. Former slaves were both a class and a race. But policymakers also redesigned financial policies. And in the end, however momentous the admission of blacks and women, those changes proved temporary. Expanded opportunities for youths without inherited wealth, on the other hand, lasted.

When in 1873 the trustees declared that blacks could attend the University of South Carolina, they understood that an administrative fiat was not enough. Few former slaves could afford to pay annually more than one hundred dollars in tuition and fees. (One student, James J. Durham, obtained some money for tuition from his father—the white man who previously had owned him and his mother. Few former slaveholders, however, were so generous.)[98] So the trustees took another radical step: they eliminated tuition and nearly all fees. Even rooms became free. Students

Fig. 7. Students of the State Normal School at the University of South Carolina, with, possibly, Principal Mortimer A. Warren at right, ca. 1875. (Courtesy University of South Carolina Archives)

had to pay only for board. The trustees refashioned the university as "the crown of the free schools of the State. . . . The way is now provided in which children may, from every rank and position in life, obtain a full education, to the highest extent possible."[99] This was a far cry from the antebellum training ground for elite white men. South Carolina only recently had developed a public school system thanks to black citizens' initiative; the state constitution of 1868 guaranteed black and white access to the same schools.[100] The state university now took its place at the top of that system. South Carolina College's old purpose had been to preserve elites' social status. The University of South Carolina's new purpose was to help any South Carolinian, but especially the most disadvantaged, to achieve theretofore unheard-of economic stability and social standing.

There was no mistaking the partisan nature of these reforms. As part of Radical Reconstruction, the use of lower and higher education to expand economic opportunities for poor blacks and whites was very much a Republican project. Students writing to a Columbia newspaper pointed this out. They contrasted Republican support for state-sponsored "universal education" with Democratic hopes to exclude blacks from the university and to "abolish the free schools" altogether. Equal opportunity, these students understood, benefited not only former slaves but the poor of both races. If the Democrats got their way, "the colored man will know his place, and the poor white man be counted even lower."[101] Under Republican rule and guided by the ideals of equal opportunity and free labor, the university now opened its doors to all.

And they came. Large numbers of poor and black students enrolled. Not all were among the most disadvantaged of Southern blacks. The first African American to enroll, medical student Henry Hayne, was South Carolina's secretary of state. Of the seven black students in the classical collegiate program the first year, six had transferred from Howard University and one from Amherst College. These young men had already begun college but had been forced to leave their home state of South Carolina to do so. Now they could return. Richard T. Greener, Harvard's first black graduate, also came to Columbia. He joined the university as both a law student and, as professor of moral philosophy and literature, the school's first black faculty member.

But blacks with little or no prior education also came. They entered the preparatory school, which accounted for nearly half of the university's students during integration. Owing to the preparatory students' quick and eager work, in the second year a relatively enormous freshman class of twenty-nine entered the college proper. Across campus, the normal school also enrolled students with little or no educational background. In a state where 98 percent of blacks had been enslaved in 1860, these students surely included many former slaves.[102] They used their new access to higher education to achieve ambitious goals. George Murray became a schoolteacher and then a congressman. James Durham, a minister with some prior schooling, became both a medical doctor and secretary of the South Carolina Baptist Convention after studying at South Carolina and two other black universities.[103] The legislators' and trustees' actions made a real difference in the lives of some black Americans.

As African Americans came to the university, most whites left. These included professors. Four faculty members resigned as soon as Hayne enrolled; a fifth followed a few months later. At least one of these was furious about the new students and "evil leadership." The trustees fired three more professors, presumably owing to their attitude toward (or perhaps treatment of) black students. One of those fired, Robert W. Barnwell Sr., had served on the Confederate Senate—hardly an indication of his support for Radical Reconstruction. Five other professors stayed. The trustees hired Greener to fill one vacancy but filled all the others with white men.

Most white students at the university showed as little predilection for studying alongside blacks as some professors showed for teaching them. They began withdrawing as soon as Hayne enrolled. During the 1873–74 academic year, along with the seven black students in the classical collegiate program, only three whites from before integration remained and two new whites entered. The total university enrollment numbers by race are unknown, but students' observations suggested that within a year blacks had become a majority.[104] Those whites who did remain, presumably supporters of Reconstruction, got along well with their black schoolmates. Although blacks and whites did not sleep or eat together, one black student reported that they did "study together, visit each other's rooms, play ball together, [and] walk into the city together, without the blacks feeling honored or the whites disgraced." Despite fears to the contrary, some students wrote to a local newspaper, "there is no war of races nor other chimeras."[105] Socially, things went better than many had expected.

Economically, integration was more of a challenge. The legislature soon discovered that not even free tuition and housing were enough to make higher education affordable for the new students. These young freedpeople were destitute; college was their way to start life from scratch. Most had no money for such basic necessities as food and clothing. Those unable to live in free college housing (probably because it was full) had to pay rent. Some were supporting families.

So in addition to making tuition and housing free, the legislature in 1874 established a new scholarship program. It allotted each county one or more scholarships, the total starting at 32 and increasing to 124 over four years. County residents competed for these scholarships by taking a written examination. Each winner received a stipend of twenty dollars per month, on condition of satisfactory academic progress, on which to support himself. Some had to stretch it further: recalled one recipient, "With that I supported my family and myself."[106] During the 1874–75 academic year the state spent more than eleven thousand dollars to fund 57 scholarships.[107] Clearly, the board of trustees and the Republican legislature were committed to providing a higher education to those who wanted one, going so far as to pay young people to study.

Yet even that was not enough. Students with neither scholarships nor personal funds came to Columbia to take advantage of a free higher education. And they needed money. In the fall of 1875 twenty students signed a petition to the faculty asking them to "perhaps suggest some plan whereby we may obtain assistance" in order to "obtain board and other needful things." The following spring, forty-four signed a petition to postpone the final examination until December. They were "totally unable to meet our [financial] obligations" and thus needed to set their books aside and spend the next six months earning an income.[108] The Reconstruction financial-aid policies at the university reveal legislators' commitment to make higher education inclusive with respect to race and class, as well as the value many poor and black South Carolinians attached to higher education. But they also reveal the structural barriers to rapid change. However committed the government and some of its constituents were, transforming the university into a vehicle for African Americans' economic improvement was not an easy task.

And it failed. The final blow to racially integrated higher education came not from financial challenges but from the changing politics of the postbellum South. In 1876–77, owing to white discontent, Republican disunity, violent intimidation, and massive fraud—in two counties Democrats received more votes than the total number of voters—white Democrats won control of the legislature and the governorship. Meanwhile, on the national stage an apparent electoral compromise led to Republican Rutherford B. Hayes's winning the disputed presidential election but his party's forswearing further efforts to protect blacks' rights in the South. On taking office, Hayes ordered the removal of federal troops from the South Carolina statehouse. In control of the state government and free from federal pressure, Democrats now set to work "redeeming" South Carolina from the Radical Republican policies they abhorred.[109] Redemption included undoing Reconstruction politicians' racial project in higher education. The new regime promptly shut down the integrated University of South Carolina, and the school entered its second period of dormancy in two decades.

It took four years for the school to reopen. In 1879 a former professor asked the governor's permission to open a biracial, coeducational day school on the university campus. He hoped thereby "to show [blacks] that there is no intention to deprive them of their educational privileges." But that was precisely the Redeemers' intention. This day school seems not to have opened. Instead, the campus reopened in 1880 as the South Carolina College of Agriculture and Mechanics, an all-white institution. Because the coeducational normal school did not reopen, the college also became all male.[110] It would become a university again a few years later, but a white, male one. No more women would attend until 1893; no more blacks, until 1963.[111]

South Carolina now relegated blacks' education to a separate institution. In 1872 the legislature had awarded the state's income from the Morrill Act to a state agricultural and mechanical institute for African Americans affiliated with Claflin University. Owing to poor management, little of the money actually reached the institute, but officially in 1877 Claflin became the only state-supported college for blacks. Some Columbia students transferred there. Two years later, legislators reduced their support for black education still further, transferring half the Morrill funds to the yet-unopened college for whites in Columbia and giving that college's treasurer control over the funds designated for the black institute. This higher-education policy paralleled the Redeemers' permitting black public schools to remain open—despite the state constitution's mandate, few had integrated—but providing little funding.[112] The government sponsored institutions for both whites and blacks but made no pretense of equality.

Racial and sexual integration in Columbia had failed, but one change in the student population survived: the South Carolina College of Agriculture and Mechanics remained open to the poor. As its new name suggested, the college now taught subjects that middle- and working-class men, as well as men born into elite families that had been ruined by the war, might find useful. (The institution was renamed South Carolina College in 1882 but continued to teach agriculture and engineering.) The first year, for example, students included both the son of a former governor and a farm boy who had never used a chalkboard and had to find a job to pay for room and board. Lax admissions standards ensured that any white man could matriculate and that academic work stayed at an elementary level.[113] The trustees chose to concentrate on the parts of the curriculum that they believed most appealed to white men without substantial wealth or prior education.

Most important, tuition remained free. A mostly African American legislature and board of trustees had abolished tuition to promote the education of former slaves as well as poor whites. They had drawn on the Republican ideology of equal opportunity and free labor. The white Democratic Redeemers now in South Carolina's capitol rejected that purpose and part of that philosophy, but they retained the policy. Students paid only a ten-dollar matriculation fee and, if they wished to live on campus, the cost of room and board. (At first, the college may have required students to work at its farm and workshop in exchange for their education.)[114] Prospective farmers and mechanics thus could afford to study in Columbia. Ironically, the educational legacy of Reconstruction in South Carolina was that a college education became attainable for a wider range of white men.

The postbellum state universities of Missouri and South Carolina made higher education more feasible for Southerners with limited financial resources. And they were not alone. As they built themselves into affordable comprehensive universities, colleges throughout the South were striking down financial barriers to attendance. In 1870 the new federal Bureau of Education began collecting data from colleges, including tuition figures. That year, eighty-five Southern colleges charged a mean annual tuition of more than $120. In 1880, 112 colleges charged an average of only $43. Eight charged nothing at all, up from none in 1870. And not a single Southern college in 1880 charged $200 or more, down from at least seventeen a decade earlier.[115] With both colleges and families struggling in a defeated and war-ravaged region, schools that continued to limit admission to the wealthy had little chance of survival. To fill their classrooms and their coffers, Southern colleges taught new curricula and sought out new types of learners.

By 1880 many colleges in the South had lost their distinctive elite student populations. As in the antebellum and postbellum North, a young person without a lot of money but with aspirations for either a lucrative profession or a working-class job could gain practical training or a classical education before seeking employment. Sometimes, at least temporarily, Reconstruction state universities even admitted women or African Americans. They were joined by universities such as Howard, Claflin, and Straight that opened during Reconstruction to educate primarily or exclusively black students. Northerners and, to a lesser extent, Southerners applied to education the language of equal opportunity that had emerged through the Republican Party's defense of free labor. As a result of their efforts, student populations in the South and the North now more closely resembled each other and the nation as a whole. Both were changing in other ways too.

FOUR

Admissions
Geography, Service, Morality

William H. Lynch, a lieutenant in the Thirty-second Missouri Volunteer Infantry (USA), returned to his home state in August 1865. But instead of going to his hometown of Houston, he headed one hundred miles north to Columbia. There he enrolled at the University of Missouri. He spent the next year studying Greek, Latin, mathematics, and surveying. He won election as an officer in one of the student literary societies. He attended local churches and a Sunday school. He paid university tuition with his army wages.

In several ways, Lieutenant Lynch was a typical student of post–Civil War America. He appears not to have had much money; in his diary he listed army wages as his only financial resource.[1] He also joined many veterans who went to college after the war. His church attendance fit with the religious atmosphere and requirements of many colleges. Finally, he made an increasingly common choice when he enrolled at a university in his home state.

The Civil War influenced more than the racial, gendered, and class makeup of college students. It affected two other social facets of admissions. By making travel difficult, raising the cost of housing, and promoting the establishment of modern state universities, the war led students more often to select institutions in their own states. The growth of institutions in the West also enabled more young people to attend college near home. Complicating the usual image of the war's nationalizing American culture, colleges became more locally based, their students less geographically diverse. Meanwhile, by creating a large population of veterans, the war raised the question of how they would readjust to civilian life and rejoin the civilian economy. Both college leaders and state legislators saw higher education as one solution, especially for veterans who had suffered injury or illness on the battlefield. So, much as they partnered to create universities for farmers and engineers, colleges and governments also partnered to provide and pay for higher education for veterans. By rewarding military service with educational opportunity, they attracted men who shared the maturing experience of war and who often were older than traditional students.

The war brought localized enrollments and veteran students to all parts of the country. Until 1860 colleges in some areas had been drawing increasing numbers of students from a distance, but the Civil War ended those regional trends. Thereafter colleges everywhere attracted more of their students from within their own states. The influx of veterans, of course, was a national phenomenon. Men from all states had fought in the war—on one side or the other—so colleges everywhere welcomed veterans as students after 1865. Both Northern and Southern state governments helped the veterans to attend.

As colleges admitted new types of students, they faced the question of whether to hold these students to the same moral and religious expectations as their relatively homogeneous antebellum populations. On these moral criteria for admission, in contrast to social criteria, college leaders decided against change. They continued to require applicants to prove their moral character. Denominational colleges also continued to stress their Christian mission. Nonreligious youths could attend, but they knew to expect attempts at conversion. Even as students arrived with nontraditional class, gendered, and racial backgrounds, more local origins, greater maturity, and the experience of fighting in a war, professors and trustees expected them to behave and believe as college students always had.

Geography: The Emergence of the Local College

Historians often emphasize the Civil War's nationalizing impact on American life. Secession forced the Union to build a stronger federal government that could win a difficult war and that afterward would play a much more visible role in states' and individuals' activities. The experience of fighting the war, the Union's military and ideological victory, Lincoln's idea of a free nation premised on the Declaration of Independence, and the project of reincorporating and reconstructing the former Confederacy promoted a new national identity. Americans began to see themselves primarily as Americans, rather than as Missourians or New Yorkers, and to use *United States* as a grammatically singular term: this was one nation, not a union of independent states. The Fourteenth Amendment to the Constitution made that vision official, declaring Americans to be citizens of the nation, not just of their states. Meanwhile, the citizens who had rallied around the federal government during the war looked on it afterward with more favor and less suspicion than before.[2]

The nationalization of American life had important consequences for higher education. The curricular and admissions reforms discussed in chapters 2 and 3 reflected colleges' increasing attention to the needs of the nation as a whole. Chapter 5 discusses additional consequences of nationalization, and especially the expansion of the federal government, for colleges. But a look at where Americans chose to go to college reveals a simultaneous and paradoxical trend: the localization of higher education.

Localization went hand in hand with nationalization. The national government expanded after the war, but so did state governments. Educational and entrepreneurial institutions spread across the country, but by doing so they made each community more self-sufficient. Federal and Confederate troops crisscrossed two nations, but the consequent difficulty (and the expense) of civilian travel encouraged many men and women to stay where they were. All these factors led colleges after the war to draw their students increasingly from their own communities and states. Robert H. Wiebe, in an alternative narrative to postbellum nationalization, has described America through most of the nineteenth century as a collection of "island communities." He argues that even in the 1870s, despite economic and political threats to those communities' autonomy, their residents nostalgically celebrated that autonomy.[3] College enrollments show further that during the 1860s and 1870s higher education became more of a local activity than it had been before.

Before the Civil War, American colleges drew their students from a broad geographic base. Although nearly all colleges had been founded by local communities and congregations or by state governments, they did not remain local or state institutions. Over the first half of the nineteenth century, colleges in the South and in New England attracted increasing numbers of students from outside their states. The historian Colin B. Burke, though he does not continue his analysis past the Civil War, documents the earlier shift in his thorough statistical study of antebellum higher education.[4]

Antebellum Southern colleges were growing more geographically diverse. In the first decade of the nineteenth century, only 14 percent of students in Southern colleges came from beyond state borders (fig. 8). By the 1850s the figure had risen to about 33 percent.[5] Few of these traveling

ADMISSIONS: GEOGRAPHY, SERVICE, MORALITY

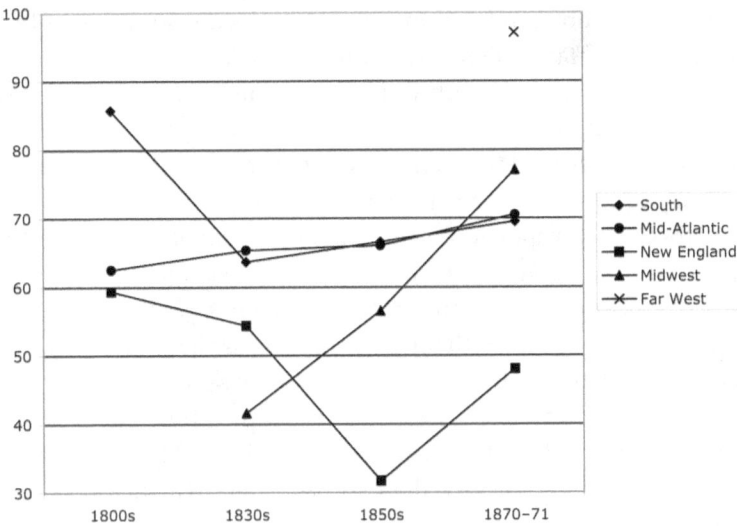

Fig. 8. Percentage of in-state college students in the South, the Mid-Atlantic, New England, the Midwest, and the Far West, 1800–1871. (Data derived from Burke, *Collegiate Populations*, 109, 117, 121, 123, 128; and U.S. Bureau of Education, *Inquiry*, 45–58)

scholars came from the North, but many came from distant parts of the South. South Carolina College and Wesleyan Female College, for example, enrolled students from Mississippi, Louisiana, and other distant Southern states but none from any Northern state.[6] Southern colleges were not national institutions, but they were regional.

New England followed a similar pattern. Colleges there began the century with far more students from out of state than those in the South, about 41 percent. The small geographic size and hence closer proximity of states in the region help to explain the higher figure. But by the 1850s that figure had risen substantially, to about 68 percent. Right before the war, Mount Holyoke Female Seminary drew 70 percent of its students from outside Massachusetts. Harvard drew 42 percent from outside the state, a major shift at a school that in the first decade of the century had drawn 82 percent of its students from within it. Some students at both schools even came from states about to secede from the Union. One hundred eighty future members of the Confederate military attended Harvard in the 1850s, and another seventy in the early 1860s; the large majority of these came from the future Confederacy.[7] As in the South, in New England colleges increasingly attracted young people from distant locations over the antebellum period.

The shift did not extend elsewhere. Out-of-state students in Burke's sample for mid-Atlantic colleges fell from about 37 percent in the first decade of the nineteenth century to 34 percent in the 1850s, a statistically insignificant change. In the Midwest, student populations actually become more local. Too few colleges existed there in the first decade of the century to form a statistically useful sample, but between the 1830s and the 1850s the proportion of students from *within* the states of their colleges rose from about 42 percent to about 57 percent. Cornell College was an extreme case. During the 1858–59 academic year 90 percent of its collegiate and preparatory students listed Iowa as their home (excluding preparatory students, as Burke does, reduces the figure to 89%).[8] The explanation for the midwestern exception is simple: more colleges existed there by the 1850s. With hundreds of college foundings in the antebellum period, many students for the first time had the *option* to attend an in-state school.

During and after the Civil War, colleges everywhere became more local. In 1872 the newly established federal Bureau of Education published data it had collected on the geographic origins of college students during the 1870–71 academic year. The contrasts with the numbers for the 1850s are striking. The Midwest had continued its trend toward localization: now 77 percent of students came from within the states of their colleges. The figure for mid-Atlantic colleges, barely rising before the war, now crept up to 71 percent.

More surprisingly, the South and New England also grew more local, reversing their antebellum trends. Southern colleges in 1870–71 attracted 70 percent of their students from within their own states, an increase of about 3 percent over the 1850s; New England colleges, 48 percent, an increase of about 16 percent. Put another way, 76 percent of students from the Midwest now attended college in their home states, 67 percent from the Mid-Atlantic, 65 percent from the South, and 67 percent from New England. (With both miles and mountains separating them from the rest of the nation, the new colleges of the Far West drew 97% of their students from their own states, and 88% of students from the region attended colleges in their home states.) Nationally, 69 percent of students attended colleges in their home states in 1870–71, compared with 56 percent in the 1850s.[9] After the Civil War, students across the country increasingly chose colleges near home.

The shift toward in-state college attendance, especially at Southern and New England colleges that before the war had been growing more cosmopolitan, had several causes. For one, new colleges in the West affected old ones in the East. The frenetic pace of college founding between the Revolution and the Civil War continued after 1861. Some states and territories, such as Nebraska and Idaho Territory, built their first colleges in the 1860s and 1870s, making it possible for men and women on the frontier to enroll at nearby institutions.[10] As a result, formerly diverse eastern colleges had to fill their classrooms with eastern students.

The Civil War also promoted localization, in part by fostering the development of universities. As universities added scientific and occupational schools to their classical colleges, practical job training became one of their major activities. As chapter 3 shows, these new schools attracted nontraditional students. Less affluent men and women who aspired to (or already had begun) occupations in such fields as small-scale agriculture, engineering, mining, and teaching began to enroll. These students, more than their antebellum predecessors, tended to come from the local area. First-generation college students unaccustomed to the tradition of traveling far for their education had little reason to do so—or to spend money on room and board—when they had an adequate school nearby and could live with their families. The same was true for working adults who wished to improve their vocational knowledge or qualifications, especially if they needed to continue working while attending classes.

Local residents, consequently, made up a particularly large portion of the new schools' student populations. During the 1870–71 academic year 97 percent of normal, agricultural, and mining students at the University of Missouri hailed from Missouri, compared with 91 percent of academic students. In 1876–77 all six students at Harvard's agricultural college lived in the Boston area.[11] And when the University of California opened its Mechanic Arts College in the Mechanics' Institute of San Francisco and scheduled classes on evenings and weekends, the board of regents was deliberately making that college accessible to the working men and women of the city. Though the university did not record the hometowns of the five hundred–plus students who flooded the lecture hall, undoubtedly they lived and worked nearby. The first graduating class pointed to its local roots when it wrote to the regents thanking them for having "displayed a knowledge of the needs of the community."[12]

Besides offering practical curricula and flexible schedules that appealed to local residents, many of the new universities were *state universities*. Antebellum state universities, though founded by state governments, had operated independently of legislatures and survived primarily on income from tuition and philanthropy. They had charged the same tuition to all students, sometimes at rates higher than many denominational colleges'.[13] But after the war the state designation began to mean something. We saw in chapters 2 and 3 that wartime damage, financial ruin, and the politics of Reconstruction and Redemption led Southern state governments to take a much more active role in funding, shaping, and regulating their state universities. The passage of the Morrill Act and the emergence of research universities led some Northern states to do the same. In developing these institutions after the war, state governments saw their own constituents as the logical beneficiaries. No state actually barred nonresidents from its university, but universities and governments did adopt the rhetoric of educating their own citizens and sometimes adopted tuition policies that favored those preferred students.

The University of California illustrated the change in geographic rhetoric that accompanied the transition to modern public higher education. The old College of California, founded and controlled by the Presbyterian and Congregational Churches, not only attracted students from many locations but even celebrated the diversity of culture and experience they brought to the campus. An advertisement for the college's preparatory school in 1868 quoted California newspapers that lauded the presence of young people from multiple states and nations. The *San Francisco Mining and Scientific Press,* for example, in an endorsement quoted in the *Placer Herald,* argued that "the advantage gained by sending a son where the thoughts and experiences of students from Washington Territory and Idaho, from Nevada, Mexico and the Sandwich Islands, are intermingled with the fertile minds of those from every county of California, is incalculably great."[14] The college took advantage of students' varied backgrounds through the Sociedad Literaria Castellana de California. This faculty-led student organization brought together students from Latin America and the United States to study Spanish literature.[15] It also suggested an openness to the substantial Spanish-speaking population of California, a state that until 1848 had been part of Mexico. College leaders used students' geographic and cultural diversity to enrich the education of all students.

When the College of California became the University of California in 1869, the rhetoric changed. Although the first catalogue of the preparatory school after the transfer of authority from church to state did promote the school's multistate and multinational student body, support for geographic and cultural diversity ended there. Dean Martin Kellogg explained in a speech in 1876 that the state university "was of and for the people of the whole State [of California]."[16] The new rhetoric translated into new policy. When, in 1870, the legislature created five scholarships for needy and talented students, it stipulated that recipients must "be *bona fide* residents of California" who had attended school in the state. In addition, the Sociedad Literaria Castellana disappeared when the state took over.[17] Its elimination signaled a discounting of the cultural contributions of both Latin Americans and Spanish-speaking Californians. The university now existed to educate the people of one state and one native language, not to facilitate or draw on a geographically and culturally diverse learning community.

The effects on enrollment were stark. In 1867 the College of California had drawn 15 percent of its students from outside of California. Nearly half of those had come from foreign nations, including nineteen students from Mexico and one from Panama. By the 1872–73 academic year, with the new state-university rhetoric, the in-state scholarships, and the closing of the preparatory school (a move that favored applicants who had attended California's English-language high schools), out-of-state enrollment had fallen to 4 percent and international enrollment had ceased altogether.[18] The state university truly had become an institution "of and for" Californians.

The University of Missouri introduced similar, pro-Missourian policies. Though it always had been technically a state institution, only after the war had damaged its campus and decimated its student body did President Daniel Read convince the legislature to fund it. Read also argued, in a speech in Indiana in 1869, for a state's special commitment to educate its own citizens in its state university. For young people to seek an education in another state, he believed, was shameful to their own. The board of curators evidently agreed that a university funded by Missouri tax dollars should serve primarily Missouri citizens. In 1872 the board introduced an unfamiliar concept: different tuition levels depending on one's home state. Students from outside Missouri paid forty dollars, as before. Missourians, however, paid only twenty. This new policy at first glance appears to have had a major effect on the student population: out-of-state enrollment instantly dropped from 7 percent to 3 percent. The drop, however, included some unscrupulous students from outside the state who simply began listing Missouri as their home. Unable to distinguish true Missourians from imposters, the curators abolished the new policy after five years.[19]

The Civil War and Reconstruction also promoted the localization of college attendance in more direct ways than through supporting the growth of universities. For one thing, secession and the war hardly fostered friendship between the North and the South. Students from the Confederate states left Northern colleges as soon as the war began. They

RECONSTRUCTING THE CAMPUS

were not likely to return after their defeat, nor were Northerners likely to march into once-enemy territory to attend college. But beyond sectional animosity, the war and Reconstruction impacted students' college choices in ways that primarily affected the South. There, the military battles and economic hardships that accompanied the war prevented students from traveling long distances for their education, even within the Confederacy. Sallie Love's experience, chronicled in chapter 1, illustrates the war's impact: with travel increasingly dangerous and colleges continually closing because of troop movements, she journeyed to five colleges in four states before graduating from one in her home state of Mississippi. The resulting hesitancy to travel far to attend college lasted beyond the end of hostilities. Reconstruction politics also sometimes contributed to localization. The war's direct impact on the geography of college attendance is best seen through the stories of individual institutions. Wesleyan and South Carolina are excellent examples.

Like other Southern colleges, antebellum Wesleyan educated a mostly in-state but broadly Southern student population. On the eve of war, during the 1860–61 academic year, 21 percent of students came from Macon; 62 percent, from elsewhere in Georgia; and 18 percent, from the rest of the South (fig. 9). Not surprisingly, given both cultural differences

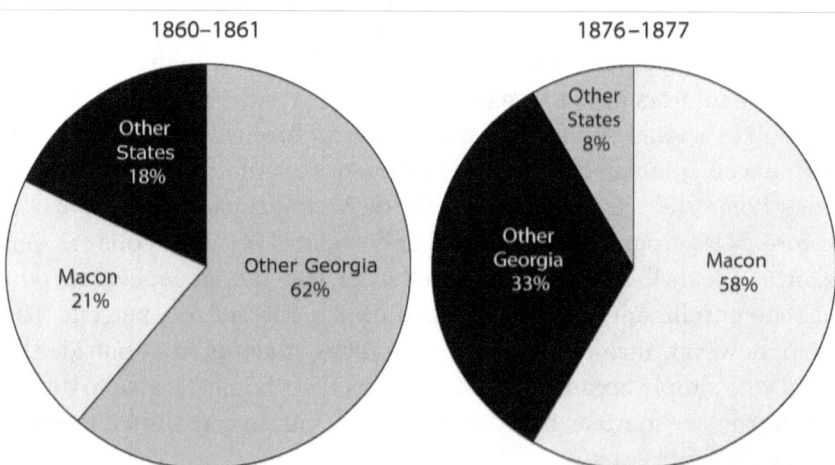

Fig. 9. Geographic origins of students at Wesleyan Female College at the beginning and end of the long Civil War era, 1860–61 and 1876–77. (Data derived from catalogue of Wesleyan Female College, 1860–61, 13–21, and 1876–77, 13–17; data for 1860–61 exclude students who studied only music, drawing and painting, or ornamental work, whose place of origin the catalogue did not identify)

and the existence of female seminaries and coeducational colleges in the Northeast and the Midwest, none came to Wesleyan from states that were to remain in the Union. Three years later little had changed: 30 percent came from Macon; 52 percent, from elsewhere in Georgia; and 18 percent, from everywhere else. Aside from one Missourian, they all called the Confederacy home.[20]

Then the war arrived. The Union army began to threaten Macon, home to a Confederate armory and arsenal, in the summer of 1864. On July 30 and 31, while students were away on vacation, defenders repulsed a Union raid on the city led by General George M. Stoneman Jr. Meanwhile, General William T. Sherman laid siege to Atlanta, which fell on September 1. By Wesleyan's opening day, October 3, Confederates were destroying Union depots near Atlanta and Sherman was contemplating a march of destruction toward the coast that would bring his forces perilously close to Macon. Though Sherman did not attempt to capture the city when he reached it in mid-November, he did order a diversionary attack while troops destroyed nearby railroad tracks. Wesleyan closed for two or three weeks amid the turmoil. Parents had reason to hesitate before sending their daughters to college in Georgia that fall.[21]

If the military danger did not dissuade parents from sending their daughters to Wesleyan, the financial danger did. Responding to rampant inflation, the trustees raised costs in 1864. Tuition rose, but room and board rose far more. Because Macon residents could live at home with their families, the increase disproportionately affected those from out of town or out of state. The military and financial barriers thus combined to keep away long-distance students. The percentage of students from Macon now increased from 30 to 51; the percentage from outside Georgia fell from 18 to 6. Put another way, although the total student population fell by slightly more than half in 1864, the attrition was not even: the number of students from Macon dropped from seventy-four to fifty-seven, while the number from out of state plummeted from forty-three to seven.[22]

After the war ended, the difficulties of getting to and paying for Wesleyan eased. Battle had ceased by the summer of 1865. Families no longer needed to worry so much about the hazards of travel. Meanwhile, the trustees lowered costs to only slightly above their prewar levels. By the fall of 1865 tuition was $60, the same as five years earlier; room and board, at $165, exceeded prewar rates by only $15. Prices gradually increased as time passed, but even in 1876–77 costs were only $80 for tuition and $200 for room and board. Cost did not seem to prohibit those from far away from enrolling. In addition, while the provision for free tuition for clergymen's and (until 1875) fallen soldiers' daughters did not include free housing, neither did it restrict tuition waivers to local residents.

Yet those from afar still did not come (see fig. 9). The proportion of Wesleyan students from Macon, 21 percent right before the war, fell below 50 only twice in the twelve years of Reconstruction. Those from outside Georgia, 18 percent before the war, only twice surpassed 10.[23] It became the norm for students to call Macon home and reside in town with their parents; students now referred to the "walk home from school" as a daily trek.[24] Wesleyan had to some extent become, to use a modern term, a commuter college. The women of the South, who had grown accustomed to attending college near home, maintained this new preference. The Civil War, having cut Wesleyan off from its Georgian and Southern clientele, left as its legacy a more local orientation of the nation's oldest college for women.

The difficulty of traveling in wartime and Confederate inflation had a similar impact on the University of South Carolina. But there postbellum politics also helped shape the student body. Attempts to expand access with regard to race and wealth level had an unintended consequence. They combined with wartime challenges to make the university *less* diverse geographically. By the 1880s South Carolina College had acquired a state, even local constituency.

The old South Carolina College followed the antebellum pattern with a primarily South Carolinian but still broadly Southern constituency. During the 1859–60 academic year 16 percent of the student body came from outside the state—below average, but still significant (fig. 10). The following year, the number fell slightly, to 12 percent. These students came to Columbia from as far away as Florida and Louisiana, but none came from any Northern or border state. On the other hand, only 2 percent of the student body—that is, three students—resided in Columbia itself. The great bulk of students came from elsewhere in South Carolina; nearly all of them lived in the dormitories.[25] Higher education merited a short journey and the cost of a room, but most young men did not need to stray far from their families. Representatives of the rest of the Deep South and the emerging Confederacy provided diversity within class and ideological bounds.

When the war began, the student body changed less in its makeup than in its size. Enrollment fell by half in 1861, from 143 to 72, as young men volunteered for the Confederate military. In terms of geography, students' origins became somewhat more local. Now 10 percent came from

ADMISSIONS: GEOGRAPHY, SERVICE, MORALITY

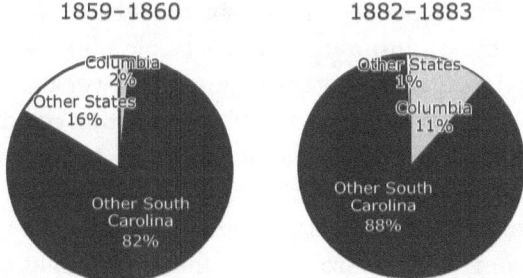

Fig. 10. Geographic origins of students at South Carolina College before and after the long Civil War era, 1859–60 and 1882–83. (Data derived from catalogue of South Carolina College, 1860, 12–17, and 1882–83, 18–23)

Columbia, 83 percent from the rest of South Carolina, and 7 percent from elsewhere in the Deep South.[26] The hazards of traveling through a war zone no doubt kept some long-distance students away. In addition, many young men who had not yet enlisted likely preferred to return home to protect their families or fill in for relatives or overseers who had joined the military. In any event, the war soon became such a priority that few young men from anywhere in the South could justify academic study. South Carolina's military draft in the spring of 1862 and the college's conversion into a hospital that summer shut down the school.

When it reopened in 1866 as the University of South Carolina, despite the grander name it was a more local institution, with 18 percent of students hailing from Columbia and only 3 percent from outside the state. The trend continued through the early years of Reconstruction. By 1869–70 Columbians made up 48 percent of the student population, and non–South Carolinians only 2 percent—a single student. As at Wesleyan, the rising cost of room and board likely discouraged out-of-towners from attending. Young men from Columbia, living with their families, could more easily afford to come. In fact, room and board apparently were such a financial strain that, despite the law permitting each county to send one student to the university free of tuition, many counties in the late 1860s and early 1870s did not.[27] Merely the cost of living in Columbia, never mind studying there, prevented distant young men from attending. Financial barriers had made the university a local institution.

In the early 1870s students from a distance began to make a comeback. In 1870–71 out-of-state students made up just over one-quarter of the student population and included young men from as far away as Texas and Pennsylvania. Columbians, meanwhile, dropped below one-third of the total. Why this happened is unclear, but whatever the reason, the new trend did not last. Just as the school at Columbia was again starting to become a regional, and potentially national, university, changes to the admissions policies abruptly halted and reversed that trend.

In 1873 the trustees opened the university to African Americans. In doing so they effectively closed it to non–South Carolinians. We might expect otherwise. Although racial prejudice ensured the withdrawal of most white students, blacks from across the South might have enrolled. Probably many non–South Carolinian freedpeople with some education and an intellectual inclination would very much have liked to enroll. Indeed, Grandison Harris, the justice of the peace who wanted to send his son to the law school, hailed from Georgia. But the attractions for South Carolinians and the barriers for most others were too great. First, like Missouri and California, South Carolina made it clear in promotional literature that it intended this free university for the citizens of South Carolina.[28] Second, travel expenses kept others away. Finally, African Americans were making great efforts to reconstitute families that slavery had dispersed.[29] Unless they could bring entire kinship groups to Columbia, those from far away were unlikely to go themselves.

When the trustees instituted free tuition and housing in 1873, they did more than open educational opportunities to lower-class and black Americans. They created a new relationship between the state and individuals' education. Just as California and Missouri were doing in different contexts, South Carolina was developing a modern state university. No longer an independent college with state funding, it now became a mechanism through which South Carolinians funded one another's education. This new conception of higher education accompanied the construction of a public school system in South Carolina; legislators described the university as the "crown" on that system. One scholar has noted that the Reconstruction university embodied "the nation's first attempt to educate Negroes from the level of the 'A-B-C's' all the way to the classics." In fact few states, and none in the South, had ever set out to educate *any* of their citizens that fully.[30] Now it was being done in California with the Morrill Act funds and in South Carolina with state revenue alone. Reconstruction politics in South Carolina gave birth to a new state role in education.

With the university refashioned as part of South Carolina's public school system, the incipient trend toward a regional student body reversed. By the mid-1870s the university had again become a state and largely local institution. In 1875–76, with nearly two hundred students, it had its largest student population in more than twenty years. Of those, 37 percent came from Columbia; 59 percent, from elsewhere in South Carolina; and only 4 percent, from the rest of the country.[31] The university had once again become a local and state institution, as well as, in a sense, one of the first modern public universities.

Though the Redeemers expelled African Americans from the university in 1877, they retained the principle of a free state college. They also continued to educate South Carolina citizens almost exclusively. In 1881–82, a year after the school reopened as the South Carolina College of Agriculture and Mechanics, not one student came from out of state. Only one did the next year, a Marylander who "came to Columbia with a Circus that disbanded," leaving him stranded and in need of a new career (see fig. 10).[32]

South Carolina College too had embarked upon a new career. It had entered the Civil War as a cultural training ground for an economically narrow but geographically broad Southern class, and it had emerged from the war, Reconstruction, and Redemption as quite the opposite: a source of educational and occupational opportunity for a relatively broad economic stratum of South Carolina's white male citizens. Throughout the country, colleges during and after the Civil War increasingly educated local student populations. Men and women interested in a college education increasingly selected colleges near their homes.

The GI Bills of the 1860s

The localization of college enrollments after the Civil War had exceptions. Cornell College was one. There, after a dip during the war, enrollment from outside Iowa during the late 1860s and 1870s exceeded prewar levels. More than twice as many non-Iowans attended Cornell in the late 1860s as had a decade earlier. The increase was even higher for male students.[33] Cornell's anomalous pattern points to another nationwide change in college student populations. The Civil War created a sizeable population of veterans ready to return to civilian life. It also left many children fatherless and without the support of their fathers' income.

Some veterans now looked to colleges to prepare them for new careers. These included former students who returned after fighting in the war. Cornell College and New York's Union College were among those that welcomed back men who had interrupted their studies for military service.[34] Other veterans saw their return to civilian life as a reason to attend college for the first time. Confederate veterans, most of them with little prior education, made up the majority of the University of South Carolina's students after the war. William Lynch headed directly from the battlefield to the University of Missouri. Cornell University's earliest classes included veterans wearing military coats dyed to resemble civilian garb. And postbellum Harvard enrolled veterans of both the Union and Confederate armies.[35] These men found attending college attractive solely because of the potential intellectual and professional rewards. But some colleges and state governments created additional financial incentives. They made it easier for veterans, and sometimes orphans of veterans, to get a college education.

The GI Bill of Rights famously offered free college tuition to veterans of World War II. When Congress passed that law in 1944, it demonstrated national respect for those who had served their country. But eighty years earlier, governments and colleges had established similar policies that revealed a heightened respect for veterans after the Civil War. Veterans of even earlier wars had received some government benefits, but those had been inconsistent and almost entirely confined to money or land. Between 1776 and 1832 Congress passed a series of laws granting pensions to Revolutionary War veterans or their widows. Most states gave land bounties to Revolutionary soldiers, usually in an attempt to spur enlistments. Congress awarded federal land to those who had fought in the War of 1812 and the Mexican War but did not offer them pensions until many decades later. It did establish a home in Washington, DC, in the 1850s to care for disabled veterans, but that served only a small number of men.[36]

The Civil War led to a vast expansion of veterans' benefits. Far more Americans had participated in that war than in any before it. The country developed a stronger sense of the military's importance—a sense that prompted the growth of military courses in colleges—and began to value war veterans' service more highly. The federal government built a much larger pension system than it had before, first for disabled veterans and survivors and eventually for all who had defended the Union. Between 1861 and 1890 the Pension Bureau dispersed more than seven hundred thousand pensions, more than five times the total dispersed before then; in 1893 pensions accounted for more than 40 percent of the federal budget. With its newfound generosity Congress finally established pension systems for veterans of the War of 1812 and the Mexican War in 1871 and 1887, respectively. And this time veterans' benefits included services in addition to money. Congress created a much larger system of homes for disabled, elderly, or otherwise unhealthy Union veterans. Across the country these homes ultimately served more than one hundred thousand Civil War veterans. Former Confederate states, meanwhile, built homes for their own veterans; Virginia also provided artificial limbs to amputees. In the late 1880s and 1890s these states began awarding pensions to the Confederate veterans excluded from the federal bounty.[37]

In addition to pensions and healthcare, veterans for the first time received educational benefits. Three states passed laws offering at least some veterans a free college education. In 1864 Virginia awarded free tuition, housing, and laboratory use at the state university to any disabled Confederate veteran of good character from the state who could not afford those expenses. The same year, Ohio's legislature passed a law providing free tuition at state-supported colleges for Union veterans from Ohio who had enlisted as minors. They could study without cost for the length of time they had served in the military before turning twenty-one. Two years later Ohio extended this program by offering public funding to any college that gave free tuition to veterans. Georgia passed a law in 1866 providing free clothing, books, board, and tuition at the University of Georgia or any of four other colleges to indigent disabled Confederate veterans from Georgia under the age of thirty. In exchange, recipients promised to teach in the state's public schools for the length of time they had studied at taxpayers' expense. Veterans accepted the offer, leading a student to remark that the state university's campus resembled a military camp. A fourth state took similar but abortive action on behalf of another constituency affected by the war. In 1868 Arkansas's Reconstruction legislature voted to give scholarships to the *children* of Union veterans at the yet-to-be-formed state university. Because the university did not open until after a new legislature had redesigned its charter, this provision never took effect.[38] But in Virginia, Ohio, and Georgia, taxpayers rewarded men for their service with an advanced education.

The increased respect for veterans and the desire to help them were not confined to politicians. Individual colleges established similar policies without state compensation. Indiana-Asbury College offered free tuition to all veterans "who come well recommended." Valparaiso University in Indiana admitted wounded veterans free of charge. The University of Virginia, Ohio University, and Mercer University in Macon, Georgia, did the same even before the new state laws required or publicly funded the programs. And while Mercer educated disabled veterans for free, Macon's other college educated their departed comrades' daughters: Wesleyan offered free tuition to the indigent daughters of men who had died fighting for the Confederate cause.³⁹ No public funds supported that effort. The Methodists who ran the college evidently thought it the right, or at least the popular, thing to do.

Cornell College took a more active approach to attracting and supporting veterans. In 1864 the trustees voted to establish a Soldiers Fund to pay for disabled veterans and soldiers' orphans to study at Cornell. But they did not simply ask local citizens to donate. At the suggestion of some Iowa soldiers, the trustees sent the college's president south collecting subscriptions for the fund from the soldiers themselves. With the permission of the War Department and possibly even the blessing of President Lincoln, President William F. King met with eighteen Iowa regiments in General Sherman's army. The troops pledged about thirty thousand dollars to support their comrades' education. Amid soldiers' rush to return home when the war ended, the college managed to collect only about fourteen thousand. But that sum lasted more than a quarter-century, paying veterans' and orphans' tuition and, when necessary, the cost of board and books. The college did not record the number of veterans who attended, but the amount spent from the fund by 1878 would have covered more than 360 years of tuition or more than fifty years of tuition and board. King recalled that "numerous" veterans took advantage of the fund. Cornell's postbellum classes thus included both former students who returned after the war and men who had not attended college before and without this aid probably never would have.⁴⁰

Besides the financial incentive for the wounded, another factor brought veterans to Cornell after 1865. According to the president and a student turned soldier, Cornell students and alumni who served in the army spread their college's reputation among the troops. These soldiers' and officers' "splendid record, their education and social quality, united to make the college favorably known to their comrades, and they thus drew to its halls many gallant fellows who wanted a higher education, when their army life was over."⁴¹ Evidently the war gave Cornell a national reputation. This helps to explain the increase in male enrollment from outside Iowa. Having learned about Cornell from its students around the campfire, discharged veterans headed to Iowa for college; the Soldiers Fund, which was not restricted to Iowans, made their attendance possible. This also suggests that many of those veterans who enrolled in college after the Civil War, at Cornell and elsewhere, may not have considered doing so before the war. Military service brought together the well educated and the uneducated, those who talked about their college experiences and those who listened with interest. Army campfires, where some American men heard about college life for the first time, likely served as recruitment sites both for specific institutions and for college in general. In yet another way, the Civil War facilitated new diversity among college entrants.

The enrollment of veterans affected the age distribution on college campuses. Antebellum colleges had enrolled students from a wide range of ages. Twenty-three percent of midwestern students in the 1850s began college after their twenty-first birthday; another 23 percent, before turning 17. The figures for New England were about 17 percent and 15 percent, respectively. Now, at some colleges veterans temporarily tilted the age scale upward. By 1869 the average age for Cornell men at graduation was twenty-four, with the oldest male graduate twenty-eight years old and the youngest twenty-two. (Unfortunately, Cornell did not record age figures for earlier years.) Three years later, with veterans' enrollment apparently winding down, the average age at graduation (for all students, including women) fell to just under twenty-one years, the lowest in Cornell's history.[42]

At the same time that veterans were arriving on campuses, some colleges began to seek out older students for academic and political reasons. Mount Holyoke's faculty, convinced that older students did better in school and were more likely to graduate, encouraged young women to wait before applying to the seminary. The principal happily reported in 1876 that the average age at graduation had increased to twenty-two years and four months, though like Cornell College, she did not provide any earlier figures for comparison.[43]

The University of South Carolina faced particular pressure to maintain a mature student population. When that university became a tuition-free, primarily black institution in the 1870s, it easily could have become a school for young teenagers. Drawing its students from a recently enslaved people, it could not rely on an established network of secondary schools or private tutors to provide cohorts of well-prepared, traditionally aged applicants. Thanks to antebellum prohibitions against slave literacy, most adult freedpeople had no more education than children. Indeed, the legislature accused the university of awarding scholarships to a "crowd of youngsters." But the faculty disputed the criticism. They pointed out that not only did the university have a minimum graduation age of nineteen but its students surpassed that by several years. The average age of seniors on scholarships was twenty-two; that of freshmen on scholarships, eighteen and a half. Even the preparatory school enrolled students as old as twenty-three.[44] Under pressure to make the school a real university with real university students, the faculty awarded scholarships to mature men. For several reasons, including the recruitment of veterans, mature students became a larger part of college populations right after the war.

As students got older, they presented colleges with a new and probably unexpected question: might college students wed? Some did, or else they arrived already married. As early as 1863 a Mount Holyoke senior wed during spring vacation, just before her husband joined the army as a chaplain. She stayed through graduation, then joined him on the front. The next year, a twenty-five-year-old woman enrolled while her husband served in the navy. Her letters mentioned no difficulty gaining admission. A married woman enrolled in Harvard's coeducational lecture course in philosophy in the fall of 1869. And for the 1871–72 academic year a married woman, possibly along with her husband, enrolled as a preparatory student at the University of Missouri.[45]

At Cornell College, however, the question of married students raised qualms among the faculty. With students well into their twenties by the late 1860s, some chose to marry before graduating. But at a school that still strictly limited social interactions between male and female students, student marriages were bound to cause problems. When the faculty learned in March 1868 that a male junior intended to marry, they resolved—after reaffirming the rule prohibiting men from escorting women to public events—that if he did so, he would face expulsion. The junior married anyway; the faculty rejected a petition by students that they reconsider his dismissal. By late 1871 the prohibition of married students had become "the usual law." The faculty did grant an exception that year, but they granted no exception a year later when younger students followed their older schoolmates' example. On learning that two students "of tender years and immature judgment" had "by a matrimonial alliance contrary to the common law of College life, brought disrepute upon the College and virtually placed themselves outside of the relation of students," the professors immediately dropped them from the rolls.[46] The faculty expected students to postpone marriage until after college. They welcomed older students and veterans, but when it came to students' behavior, they were far less flexible. Antebellum expectations of students' behavior survived.

Science, Virtue, and Christ: Morality at Postbellum Colleges

Besides an academic examination, colleges in the nineteenth century relied on two types of criteria for selective admissions, which I call social and moral criteria. Social criteria for admission related to who a potential student *was*. These restricted or encouraged entrance according to class, race, gender, geography, veterancy, and age. Moral criteria, on the other hand, related to how an applicant *behaved* and what he or she *believed*. These criteria fell into two intertwined categories: moral character and religion. Antebellum colleges usually required each applicant to present evidence of good character in the form of a testimonial from a teacher, tutor, clergyman, or other authority. Because colleges were in the business of training the whole student—of preparing a mature, intelligent, and moral adult—they wanted to begin with youths who showed promise in all respects.

Most antebellum colleges also had a strong religious tone. Christian denominations had founded the large majority of colleges during the eighteenth and nineteenth centuries. These institutions hoped to train good Christians. College life involved mandatory church attendance, classes in religion, and the expectation that students imbibe the laws of Christianity. They might not require a declaration of faith from matriculates, but young people who were not prepared to devote a large portion of their days to worship and Bible study would not find most colleges to their liking. The extent to which denominational colleges taught those denominations' specific principles varied; over time, colleges found that they needed to remain *broadly* Christian in order to attract enough students to stay solvent.[47]

State universities gave religion a smaller role in their curricula and general tone. All colleges were Christian institutions, but the universities that Southern states founded in the first half of the nineteenth century did not require the same religious commitment of their students, or even of their faculty, as the denominational colleges. The University of Virginia had no religious observances at all. An early president of South Carolina College publicly criticized church authority. South Carolina did require evidence of "good moral character" from its applicants, but unlike with denominational colleges, prospective students did not need to consider their level of Christian devotion when selecting a state university.[48] The division here lay not along regional boundaries, as with social criteria for admission, but instead along lines of governance.

Unlike social criteria for admission, moral requirements did not change in the 1860s and 1870s. They might well have. Colleges in the South that had educated socially uniform student populations now attracted economically, sexually, and sometimes racially diverse clienteles. Older students, including veterans, began to enroll all over the country. Some institutions drastically expanded their curricula, adding a variety of professional and practical schools to their old classical colleges. Their introduction of the elective principle suggested an acknowledgment of postbellum students' relative maturity. Colleges, then, might have reformed their moral and religious character to fit the educational goals of their new students and new curricula. But they did not. Just as Cornell's faculty admitted adult students but did not let them marry, colleges everywhere admitted new social types of students but retained the traditional moral and religious expectations. The old division remained: denominational colleges were broadly Christian in their curricula and tone, while state universities were committed to moral character but only minimally religious. This was one facet of higher education that the Civil War did not change.

Colleges continued to require evidence of good moral character from their applicants. Cornell and the College/University of California required written testimonials. The University of South Carolina did too in the 1860s, then possibly let the requirement lapse until reinstating it for preparatory students in 1875. Harvard required testimonials at its new mining and agricultural colleges. Mount Holyoke practiced an even more thorough method of moral selection: the seminary admitted all students on a "probationary" basis. During the first three weeks of the school year they had to demonstrate "maturity of character." If they did not, they faced removal.[49]

At state universities the moral part of admissions remained relatively small. At some it included little more than the character testimonials. Students at South Carolina took the standard "evidences of Christianity" course, but catalogues and other promotional literature said nothing else about religious life. The by-laws approved by the trustees in 1866 and 1869 required students to follow "the obligations of morality and religion" and affirmed the university's goal of producing "refined and elevated Christian gentlemen," but the trustees did not consider that goal important enough to put it in the catalogue.[50] Students' rushing off to war against the faculty's wishes and returning as matured veterans may have tempered the adults' attempts to police their morals. The new normal school required testimonials of good character as well as aptitude for study, but its circular and catalogue renounced any "religious test" for admission. The state's future teachers did not need to declare their faith.[51] Moral and religious expectations were somewhat higher at the University of Missouri. It required daily chapel worship, at least for men, until 1876, when the faculty began to exempt some students "for various reasons."[52] But as before the war, these policies were mild compared with those at denominational colleges.

ADMISSIONS: GEOGRAPHY, SERVICE, MORALITY

Colleges founded under religious auspices remained committed to their students' moral and religious condition. Although Harvard reformed its religious requirements in 1869, it merely reduced the Sunday church requirement from two services to one and allowed parents to monitor their own sons' church attendance if they spent Sunday together. Harvard's monitors continued to check all other students' attendance at church. Mandatory daily prayers also continued. In 1870 the faculty decided to exempt students living two-fifths of a mile or more from campus from daily morning prayers, a significant change.[53] But religion remained important enough for prayers to be required of the rest.

Cornell's founders had built the college to do God's work, and Christian lessons continued to permeate its campus. Students had to attend daily chapel and Sunday morning church. Professors also led Bible classes on Sundays. In some years professors led an additional weekly prayer meeting and students led another daily prayer. On top of all that, revivals enlivened campus nearly every year from the 1850s to the 1880s—more often and more successfully "than in any non-college community in Iowa," according to a former professor and trustee. Each February, Cornell observed the national prayer day for colleges.[54]

Because religion was central to life at Cornell, it attracted students who were either religious already or open to conversion at the revivals. Of the fourteen men in the class of 1869, four were sons of ministers, and all professed religion by the time they graduated. Students showed their religious commitment by incorporating it into extracurricular activities. The meetings of the student literary societies, especially the women's, regularly included prayers, devotional exercises, scriptural recitations, and addresses by invited clergymen. Students did question the large number of mandatory religious services, but they revealed in their own activities a shared commitment to Christian observance.[55] Cornell remained, in its rules and its students, a devotedly Christian community.

The women's colleges remained at least as focused on religion as Cornell. Wesleyan's catalogues of the 1870s announced the college's "most constant attention to the moral and religious training of our pupils." Professors could not watch them all quite as constantly as before, because more students now lived with their parents and commuted, but when they were on campus, students submitted to strict religious requirements. They had to take six years (including the preparatory year and the five-year collegiate program) of courses in the Bible or the evidences of Christianity. They also began and ended each day with a prayer service. As at Cornell, revivals were a part of college life, and students endeavored to convert their classmates. Sallie Love became one such convert, baptized a Methodist while at Wesleyan. The religious curriculum inspired many Wesleyan alumnae to embark on missionary careers. As one woman wrote gratefully in the student newspaper, the professors "assist us in the prosecution of virtue and science."[56]

Religion formed an even larger part of life at Mount Holyoke. As we saw in chapter 1, students at the seminary constantly prayed, both in private and in formal gatherings with teachers. In 1862 a student complained in her diary about having attended nine religious meetings and a church service in one day—"too many meetings for profit"—and having endured no fewer than twenty-three prayers. Worries about the nation and its soldiers motivated many of those prayers, but the religious curriculum hardly abated after the war. In the 1870s and 1880s every day still began with mandatory devotionals and ended with an optional prayer meeting. On Sundays students had to attend church services (the seminary reserved one-third of the seats in South Hadley's church) and Bible lessons. The faculty made Sunday Bible study optional in 1870 but also instituted six weeks of mandatory daily Bible study. The seminary hired its teachers based primarily on their religiosity.[57] In the words of one alumna, a central lesson of a Mount Holyoke education was "to believe in a wise and loving Creator" and not "to question God's beneficence." Or as the president of the board of trustees succinctly told the students, "This is a school for Christ."[58]

Mount Holyoke did not exclude non-Christians. On the contrary, the faculty welcomed them—as potential converts. Students announced their religious views at registration; the teachers used this information to proselytize. They held some prayer meetings exclusively for the nonreligious and others integrating them with Christians. Religious students, encouraged by their teachers, tried to convert their classmates. As elsewhere, formal revivals swept through the town and the campus. Altogether, Mount Holyoke achieved an excellent rate of conversion, which the principal reported each year to the trustees. It began the fall term of 1869, for instance, with fifty non-Christians. After a year of constant effort that ended with a "deep and general" revival, three-fourths of those had converted. The next year, even without a revival, the community converted thirty-five of fifty-one non-Christians.[59]

Each of these colleges, despite changes at most of them in curricula and admissions, retained its secular or religious character. One college in this study did not. The University of California, the only one of the seven colleges to undergo a major change in governance, was also the only one to recast the role of religion. This was no coincidence. Its experience shows the determinative relationship between a college's governance and its religious atmosphere. Before 1869 religion was central to the denominational College of California. Professors, the catalogue noted, aimed "to form characters sincere, manly, and unaffectedly Christian." College rules guaranteed evangelical control of the board of trustees and evangelical church membership of the president and a majority of the faculty. The college celebrated the national prayer day for colleges and held meetings at which local citizens joined students in prayer.[60] Students had to attend Sunday church, daily prayers, and biblical instruction from professors or local clergymen. As at Mount Holyoke, the faculty surveyed students' religious views. The vice president, in language similar to that used to describe Wesleyan and Mount Holyoke, asserted that the college sought through its religious and academic curriculum to produce "disciples of science, who are at the same time disciples of Christ."[61]

When the College of California became the University of California, that changed. The college's trustees began to worry when they learned the makeup of the state university's governing board: "Roman Catholics, Jews, and indifferents or Skeptics—but no minister of the Gospel." Their fears proved well founded. The university still required character testimonials, but the religious mission and curriculum evaporated once the state took over. The first catalogue made no mention of religion besides the traditional course for seniors in natural theology. Even that disappeared within a few years.[62] And with the establishment of the Mechanic Arts College in 1870 the university took on hundreds of adult night and weekend students, over whose lives outside the classroom it had no control. Unlike the denominational trustees, the state government did not require students to be disciples of Christ. Science and perhaps virtue were enough.

Religion eventually disappeared from many private colleges and universities too. But that came later. As academic leaders shaped their institutions into expansive universities dedicated to scientific, professional, and graduate instruction, they tried to incorporate the traditional religious mission of higher education into those new activities. Southern leaders, especially, tried to keep religion in their schools in order to preserve something of the lamented antebellum culture. Only at the turn of the century, when disciplinary specialization and progressive science made the unity of divine truth an untenable ideal in universities, did those attempts end in failure.[63] Despite the influx of new types of students, colleges retained their moral and religious character well after the Civil War.

By the end of Reconstruction more diverse types of individuals were attending college. Very few did overall: only 4–5 percent of Americans as late as 1900.[64] Not until the twentieth century did higher education carry enough prestige and economic value to attract a large portion of America's youth.[65] But the change began in the 1860s and 1870s. College students now came from different social origins from those before the war. In 1860 Southern state universities and women's colleges still had attracted social elites from a broad geographic swath of the South. Now the state universities educated a broad economic stratum of local and state residents. Some had become coeducational or even biracial. Northern colleges, too, had become even more socially diverse than before the war, as well as geographically narrower. Colleges everywhere offered admission and, sometimes with state support, financial aid to Civil War veterans or their orphaned children. Denominational colleges, however, continued to apply traditional moral and religious expectations to the new types of students.

Colleges, in cooperation with state and federal governments, had begun to serve a more diverse group of Americans. They did so through varied curricula, university structures, financial aid, and new social criteria for admission, each of these sometimes supported by public funds. But the colleges and governments did more than this to bring higher education to the people and to public attention. During the 1860s and 1870s colleges reached beyond their gates, not only bringing in different types of students but also providing services for Americans besides their students. Meanwhile, the federal government participated in education in new ways.

FIVE

College, Community, and Nation

In a Pennsylvania hall in 1876, adults leafed through examination papers by Lincoln University students. But they were not professors at the African American university. They were not even on the Chester County campus. Nearby, others watched children engaged in a kindergarten lesson. But they were neither teachers nor parents. They were not even in a school building. These viewers were tourists. They were attending the Centennial Exposition in Philadelphia, at which American institutions of many kinds, including colleges and schools, displayed their accomplishments. Lincoln's exhibit taught attendees about the work of black college students. A mock kindergarten attended by local orphans showcased the latest methods of early childhood education.[1] Educational institutions, in cooperation with the federal government, used the exposition to spread knowledge about recent developments in American education. That joint project reflected the expansion of colleges' connections with local and national communities and the intensification of their relationship with the federal government after the Civil War. As Reconstruction came to a close, the exposition served as both a demonstration and a culmination of the changes the Civil War had brought to higher education.

American colleges always had maintained concrete relationships with communities beyond their student populations. Towns and their churches had founded most antebellum colleges. State governments had founded most of the rest and often retained seats on the governing boards of both denominational and state-founded institutions.[2] But few formal programs had involved colleges with their broader communities. Colleges had served the general public only indirectly, by educating public leaders and certain types of professionals.

During and after the war, colleges began to develop strong connections with the federal government. Paradoxically, at the very time when colleges were educating increasingly *local* student populations, they did so through a curriculum designed in cooperation with *national* authorities. Through the Morrill Act of 1862, the government agreed to use public funding to support colleges that met certain criteria. Through the legislation of 1866 and 1870 to supply army officers and arms, the government supplied its own personnel and equipment to colleges that offered courses it believed contributed to the national interest. Meanwhile, some state governments gave new money and attention to their state universities. By providing this support, national and state legislators gained the power to define the nature of colleges' indirect public service. Colleges began to train not only doctors, lawyers, ministers, and teachers but also farmers, engineers, and citizen-soldiers. They introduced curricular and admissions policies that expanded the role of higher education in American life.

After the Civil War, colleges also began to operate more explicitly in the public arena. I use the term *public* in two of its senses: "of or relating to the people as a whole" and "carried out or made on behalf of the community by the government or state."[3] Colleges increased their involvement with both their local communities and the federal government. First, they reached out to the populations of their cities and states, providing services for people besides their enrolled students. In other words, they began to provide direct, as well as indirect, public service. Some Southern colleges began these programs in response to the same wartime and Reconstruction conditions that spurred them to reinvent curricular and admissions policies. Second, the federal government began to collect data on education to a much greater extent than ever before. This new activity came as part of a general expansion of federal authority during and after the war. For the first time, the national government included a large bureaucracy and became involved in many areas of American life. Colleges joined with the new bureaucracy, including at the Centennial Exposition, to disseminate information about themselves and about American education as a whole.

In the introduction I mentioned Merle Curti's 1942 assertion that wars had broken down barriers between intellectuals and the public. That assertion turns out to be true for the Civil War, but in a more fundamental and lasting way than Curti realized. Through local service and federally supported publicity, colleges after the war built permanent links to communities beyond their students. In doing so, they became important cultural and economic resources for their communities and important partners of the federal state.

From the Closet to the Field: University Outreach

The Civil War stimulated direct public service at America's colleges. College leaders and individual faculty members looked for ways they could help the nonstudent public. Wesleyan Female College turned part of its dormitory into a refugee shelter. South Carolina College professors wrote a pamphlet on the production of saltpeter for gunpowder and mended soldiers' wounds. Mount Holyoke Female Seminary teachers led students in knitting socks for soldiers. These colleges used their resources—sturdy buildings, scientific expertise, and captive students—to reach beyond their gates to serve the wartime needs of the larger public.

Having begun to serve their communities during a crisis, colleges continued to do so after it. Colleges of the postbellum South and North began to establish outreach programs that brought both cultural and practical services to nonstudent populations. Americans who had neither signed an enrollment form nor paid tuition began to have contact with colleges' employees and resources. In a sense, colleges were taking the opening of admissions to its logical, democratic conclusion. Removing social admissions requirements and reducing or eliminating tuition meant, in theory, that *anyone* could become a student. Public lectures and farm visits by professors meant, in theory, that *everyone* could. The university, no longer limited by brick walls or enrollment numbers, could become truly universal.

But the road from wartime service to postbellum outreach was neither straight nor single. Trustees and professors did not simply preserve wartime programs. Outreach programs of the 1860s and 1870s arose from several considerations. As with curricular, structural, and admissions changes, these differed by region. In the former Confederate and border states where the war had been fought, institutions developed outreach programs as part of the war-inspired reforms we saw in chapters 2 and 3: the formation of university structures, the expansion of public funding, and the admission of new types of students. The programs they designed reflected these origins. In the North, colleges developed different outreach programs for different reasons.

University outreach had its roots in public lecture series unconnected with colleges or universities. In both England and America, individuals and mechanics' institutes had offered lectures on scientific topics to whoever cared to listen since the late eighteenth century. Starting in the 1820s the lyceum circuit institutionalized public lectures. New organizations such as the Lowell Institute in Boston and the Peabody Institute in Baltimore became centers of adult education in the antebellum years. In the 1870s, the Chautauqua Literary and Scientific Circle spread learning to diverse classes of Americans and Canadians through lecture and reading courses on a variety of liberal and practical subjects. Anna Ticknor's Boston-based correspondence school also extended learning. Historians of university outreach have argued that these noncollegiate institutions, along with the influence of English universities that began introducing extension lectures in the 1860s, led directly to the American university extension schools of the last quarter of the nineteenth century.[4] But the Civil War, by encouraging community service and promoting curricular reform, initiated the first stage of university outreach in the United States.

Outreach began at the University of South Carolina in 1867. That year the faculty started giving weekly public lectures. They lectured on the same disciplines they taught, with topics ranging from astronomy to medicine to poetry. The citizens of Columbia responded with enthusiasm. The lectures consistently attracted a large and attentive audience, though a newspaper account intimated that attendees were more intellectually inclined than the average townsperson. In any event, the lectures ended after a single winter.[5] But public lectures would return to Columbia several years later in a very different political and educational context.

By 1875 the University of South Carolina had changed drastically. Under the control of a Republican and mostly African American legislature, it now educated Americans who had been born slaves. It helped them to attain higher intellectual and professional status than their parents might have dreamed of. And as they built this comprehensive university and opened it to previously excluded students, professors took these projects one step further. As at the white university eight years earlier, they inaugurated a course of public lectures. This time, those lectures took place in the African Methodist Episcopal Church, a center of black cultural life. Having brought some black Southerners to the university, they now brought the university to the rest. Indeed, the first lecture was titled "Education for all the people, the great want of South Carolina." No one in attendance could mistake the professors' goal. Subsequent lectures covered such academic topics as "Animal Life" and the "Life and Character of Milton." In addition to the faculty, politicians and the university's first black graduate delivered lectures. A newspaper described one of the lectures as "scholarly" and the audience as "large and intelligent."[6] In effect, the faculty had created another school of the university in the spiritual heart of the black community.

The University of Missouri, too, established outreach programs as part of its state-sponsored expansion. It became a true university during the late 1860s and early 1870s as President Daniel Read steered the creation of vocational schools. It also introduced public lectures. To reflect "the threefold relation existing between themselves, the students under their care and the state," the faculty in 1877 began delivering lectures "of sufficiently popular character" to interest the local community. Topics ranged from Latin to art to evolution. The lectures attracted large enough audiences that the faculty continued them beyond the first year and published the second year's lectures so that even more people could profit from them.[7]

Missouri also introduced another type of outreach program, one resulting from the university's new public funding. When Read had convinced the state legislature to fund the university's expansion by stressing its dire need after wartime damage, Boone County also had contributed. It had donated ninety thousand dollars for the university to purchase farmland and erect a building for the Agricultural and Mechanical College, which opened in 1870.[8] Though always formally a state institution, the university until then had relied on income from tuition and philanthropy rather than taxes. As this changed, the curators may well have expected their new government patrons to ask for something in return.

In 1874 the local government called in its favor—in effect, if not in intention. The county wrote to the board of curators asking to lease thirty-seven acres of the university's land. On that land it wished to "erect . . . Good & suitable buildings for the accommodations of the County Poor, Together with a ward for the Treatment of the Sick of Said County Poor & a ward Suitable for the treatment of pay patients." The county's new patronage of the university had enabled its representatives to turn to the university for help in serving local needs. The curators, either understanding their civic responsibility or feeling financially obligated to the county, responded the same day with a unanimous decision: they would lease the land for a token fee of one dollar per year for ninety-nine years. They did stipulate that the poorhouse and the hospital be made of brick and stone, that the curators approve the building plans, that the land be well landscaped, and that no one be buried there.

Most important, the curators offered the county something it had not asked for. Besides land, they offered labor. They insisted "that the care, medical treatment and management of the sick and invalids in the poor House and hospital shall be vested absolutely and exclusively in the Professors of the Medical Department of the University, who shall furnish all needed medical attention, advice and service without charge."[9] Records do not indicate whether the curators asked the medical faculty before offering its services or whether the plan was actually put into practice. Assuming that it was, professors at that two-year-old school of the new university left their classrooms to contribute their expertise directly to the nonstudent public. This was a new type of outreach, not intellectual lectures but practical services. (It may also have met an educational need by giving medical students practical training.) It recalled the South Carolina professors who had cared for wounded soldiers at the hospital on campus and elsewhere during the war. The Missouri professors remained on university property, but in effect the school reached beyond its walls to spread its benefits to more people.

Teaching their enrolled students remained the primary responsibility of professors at these Southern comprehensive universities. But just as it shaped curricular, structural, and admissions reform, the Civil War led them to develop outreach programs and shaped the forms those programs took. As with curricular and structural change, outreach happened in the North too, but for different reasons. Harvard, California, and other Northern universities established programs that brought their resources to an outside audience. They did so as part of their growth into research universities, and California also did so to serve the practical needs of state citizens in keeping with its new status as a state university.

The emergence of research universities promoted outreach programs at Maryland's Johns Hopkins University and throughout the North. Johns Hopkins, whose president wanted instruction to be "entertaining, if not serviceable," to a broader audience than enrolled students, began offering public lectures as soon as it opened in 1876. These included lectures directed specifically at members of certain professions and trades, including bankers, lawyers, teachers, and charity workers. In 1861 the Harvard Corporation instructed a professor in the scientific school to deliver lectures on "technology" to both enrolled students and the public. The expanding university also created several museums. Some served only research purposes and did not display their collections to the public.[10] But the Museum of Comparative Zoology, which the Swiss faculty member Louis Agassiz founded in 1859, served a greater variety of functions.

Agassiz designed the Museum of Comparative Zoology primarily to serve the needs of a growing research university. With most of its extensive holdings hidden from public view and accessible only to those working in Harvard's laboratories, it helped the university to produce knowledge. But the museum did more. Agassiz was aware that similar museums in Europe invited the public to view their collections. As he helped to build a German-style research university in America, he imported the public natural history museum as well, with improvements. Instead of simply opening the entire collection to public view, he selected a small portion of it, then arranged and labeled these items so as most effectively to teach visitors about the patterns of nature. He believed that those patterns, "direct proof of the existence of a thinking God," would inspire in visitors admiration for the divine. In addition, the museum loaned specimens to public schools for use in natural history instruction.[11]

The University of California established particularly extensive outreach programs. These grew out of its development as both a research university and a state university. Like Harvard, it established a museum with botanical, mineral, and fossil collections; whether it opened this museum to the public is unclear. Professor Joseph LeConte, formerly of the University of South Carolina, delivered a series of lectures titled "Religion and Science" (which he first had given to a Bible class at his old institution) to a public California audience, then published them in book form.[12]

Meanwhile, one member of the faculty was extending the university's outreach beyond intellectual lessons and beyond the Bay Area. In June 1870 the regents resolved "to transfer the Agricultural College of the university from the closet to the field, and make its instruction of practical value to the people of the State." To this end, they sent Ezra S. Carr, professor of agriculture and medicine, across the state to lecture for free on agriculture, horticulture, zoology, meteorology, and every other subject taught in the Agricultural College. Between lectures, Carr was to observe local farmers at work and suggest improvements to their techniques. This was quite a change from only eight years earlier, when a majority of the faculty had rebuked their colleagues for leaving campus to lecture. Now Carr's job included spreading the knowledge he had gained from study, research, and experience to those Californians engaged in the business of agriculture. Through him, the regents sought to make the university a key economic resource for the state. Both the farmers and the state, through increased productivity, would gain.[13]

Carr dutifully headed off on his statewide lecture tour. The next fall, he reported on his activities during the summer vacation: "I have . . . given nine addresses, at seven state and district Agricultural Fairs, six lectures and addresses before the State and two county teachers Institutes; and four addresses on different public occasions. To accomplish this I have travelled about two thousand miles, [and] have spoken in San Francisco, Oakland[,] Pacheco, Marysville, Valley's, Sacramento, San Jose's, Stockton, Jackson, and Chico to not less than thirty thousand people." He continued this frenetic schedule through the academic year. In addition to his teaching duties in the agricultural and medical colleges of the university, Carr taught in the preparatory department, the Mechanic Arts College, and the unaffiliated Deaf, Dumb, and Blind Asylum. On top of all that were the public lectures: he traveled in excess of three thousand miles more to deliver sixty-one lectures in San Francisco, Alameda County, Stanislaus, Contra Costa, Sacramento, Solano, and Napa County. In addition to speaking on agriculture and "our industrial interests," he tried to convince his audiences of the value of the state university to the people. In this effort he claimed universal success.[14] Regents, professors, and farmers agreed that the state university should provide practical services to a large number of regular California citizens.

Eventually the outreach programs that emerged after the Civil War evolved into a new element of the university curriculum proper. Universities began to establish extension schools in the 1870s. These served the same purpose as lectures in a church or agricultural fair: they brought higher education to working Americans who otherwise would not have enrolled in college. But instead of merely showing up and listening anonymously, attendees now signed a matriculation form, paid a small tuition fee, and earned a diploma. A project that had begun as a way to stretch university learning beyond its growing student population was now folded back into the university, expanding that population still further. California's Mechanic Arts College, offering free evening and weekend classes, fit this model.[15] The State Normal School in Illinois started an extension program in 1873; Johns Hopkins, its Mechanics' Institute in 1879; Cornell University, its Farmers' Institutes in 1886; and the University of Chicago, its Division of University Extension in 1892. In 1891 a new organization called the American Society for Extension Lecturing Courses organized a national convention that brought together colleges, universities, and societies offering extension courses from twenty states. Meanwhile, states established agricultural experiment stations, most of them affiliated with colleges. These research stations taught farmers scientific methods of agriculture.[16] American colleges increasingly provided services directly to their local and state communities.

College Statistics: The New Role of Government

Colleges also developed new connections with the national government. The federal state expanded in response to the war. Though the initial goal of the expansion was to win the military conflict, officials in Washington exerted their new powers in many directions. As trustees and faculties quickly discovered, the changes included a greater federal role in higher education. Colleges and the government began to work together to expand agricultural education, to provide military training, and, through a new federal agency, to gather and disseminate information about education. The localization of higher education discussed in chapter 4 thus went hand in hand with its nationalization. The difficulty of travel and the establishment of new colleges led colleges to enroll more local student populations, but they taught those men and women in cooperation with a larger and more attentive national government. While some elements of federal expansion lasted only until the late 1860s or 1870s, the government's new roles in education became permanent.

The Civil War forced the national government to expand its powers and its administrative structure. Until then, the federal state had remained small and had governed primarily through the apparatus of parties and courts. Now new tasks required new methods. To start with, the Lincoln administration had to raise a large army. The federal, state, and local governments shared the administrative labor of mustering in the troops. By the end of 1861 the War Department had taken charge of providing the army with food, clothing, and arms. In 1863 the need for troops forced Congress to institute the nation's first draft. Meanwhile, in staffing the army the president introduced a new principle of appointment. At first he appointed party loyalists as officers, in keeping with the partisan foundation of the antebellum state. But over time he increasingly appointed expert leaders with no known party affiliation. Partly as a result, for the first time a large number of West Point graduates became officers. This principle of appointment by expertise would form the foundation of the postbellum civilian bureaucracy.

Congress busied itself with the financial needs of the war. It created an income tax to help fund the war, a Bureau of Internal Revenue to collect the tax, and a national banking system and national currency without backing in gold. Looking forward toward Reconstruction, Congress in 1865 established the Bureau of Refugees, Freedmen, and Abandoned Lands (better known as the Freedmen's Bureau) to oversee African Americans' transition from slavery to freedom. After the war ended, the Radical

Republicans' stringent conditions for ex-Confederate states' readmission invoked a new notion of preeminent federal jurisdiction. The Fourteenth (1868) and Fifteenth (1870) Amendments to the Constitution, which enabled federal protection of civil rights and banned racial restrictions on voting, drew on that jurisdiction. The conditions for readmission also necessitated a military presence in the former Confederacy. The federal government thus employed a new national bureaucracy both to fight the war and to rebuild part of the nation in its aftermath.[17]

Over the course of Reconstruction, Congress, the courts, and the president dismantled much of the new bureaucracy. Congress let both the income tax and the Freedmen's Bureau expire in 1872. Though the military served an important function in Radical Reconstruction, it already had collapsed in size by then, from one million in the spring of 1865 to thirty-eight thousand in the fall of 1866. Former Confederates' return to Congress and Republicans' waning support for civil rights in the 1870s ensured a further weakening of the federal government. The U.S. Supreme Court even debilitated the recently ratified Fourteenth Amendment in such rulings as the *Slaughterhouse* decision of 1873. Finally, in 1877 President Rutherford B. Hayes ordered an end to the military bureaucracy in the South.[18]

But postbellum politicians did not fully eradicate the new federal state. It retained some of its new powers. The federal government continued to manage a national banking system and to provide financial backing for railroads and canals. It thereby helped to build national markets for Northern manufacturers and transporters. Furthermore, because this federal support contributed nothing to the Southern economy, some Southern members of Congress advocated increased federal regulation of industry. Congress thus passed the Interstate Commerce Act in 1887 and the Sherman Antitrust Act in 1890.[19] Much as colleges developed long-term reforms that began as immediate responses to national events, the federal government continued to expand as a result of its initial pragmatic response to the secession crisis.

Also, the Civil War's nationalizing impact on American culture had changed how many Americans viewed the federal government. Northerners and Southern blacks had begun to perceive it as serving individual citizens' interests and protecting their freedoms. This perception gave the government the moral authority to play a larger role in Americans' lives. It made Reconstruction possible. At the same time, because the Civil War had established the supremacy of the federal government over the states, the states could no longer (at least in theory) check the power of a congressional majority hostile to some minority group. So national politicians created new congressional committees and executive agencies in an effort to provide the checks on congressional power that states no longer could.[20] Despite the transience of many Civil War and Reconstruction reforms, then, in some areas the state expansion that had begun in wartime continued in peace.

The new bureaucratic agencies served a wide variety of purposes. The organization of the federal government into many discrete, specialized units, in fact, paralleled the development of some colleges into universities with distinct schools and departments. In each case experts in a particular field handled the university's or the government's activities in that field. Some of the agencies expanded or streamlined the government's ability to enforce the law. The Bureau of Internal Revenue continued collecting taxes despite the abolition of the income tax for which Congress had created it. In 1865 the solicitor of the Treasury Department created the Secret Service to fight counterfeiting. And in 1870 Congress created the Department of Justice. Until then, federal lawyers had been dispersed throughout the executive branch without a single supervisor or clear authority over local governments. Now Congress gathered them together in one department under the leadership of the attorney general and with more explicit lines of authority.[21]

One of the most pervasive tasks of the postbellum executive agencies, however, was the collection of information. The political scientist James C. Scott has observed the importance of "seeing" to the functioning of modern states. Before they can effectively distribute resources or regulate their societies, governments must collect information on those societies. Since the nineteenth century, states have embarked on projects to collect that information and thereby to make their societies "legible" to policymakers.[22] The U.S. government began many such projects after the Civil War.

Congress empowered several agencies to collect information in order to enable specific regulatory or distributive policies. New laws in 1868 and 1874 empowered revenue agents to collect records from individuals under investigation for nonpayment of taxes. The Comstock Law of 1873 authorized the Post Office Department to investigate and prosecute individuals and organizations that sent obscene material through the mail. And the Interior Department's Pension Bureau, in addition to administering the unprecedented number of war pensions that followed the Civil War, made sure that recipients deserved them. For veterans that meant confirming and classifying disabilities and gauging moral character. Physicians examined candidates and reported to the bureau on both counts; such undesirable behaviors as drinking and smoking hurt one's application. For widows it meant an inspection of marital relationships. A widow had to prove her marriage by presenting official documents or else having family members and acquaintances interviewed. Even after winning a pension, a recipient remained subject to government supervision in the form of biennial medical examinations for veterans and continued inquiries into widows' marital status; widows who remarried lost their pensions.[23] The government had begun to keep watch over Americans' most private activities.

The collection of statistics also became a major government function in the 1860s. This function formed an important part of the effort by governments in both North America and Europe to see their societies and make them legible. The word *statistic*, in fact, comes from the word *state*. Statistics are gathered, and required, by the state.[24] Before the Civil War, the U.S. government's only major statistical work had been the decennial census. Even that had not warranted a permanent agency: every ten years Congress had created, then dissolved, a temporary body to carry out the necessary labor.[25] Now politicians decided that the state needed more extensive and frequent data in order to govern.

National governments fulfilled the need for more data by establishing permanent statistical agencies. France, Great Britain, and some German states had them by the mid-1830s. The United States took longer. Here, the Civil War sparked a major new statistical effort, as the War Department tried after Appomattox to calculate the number of Union deaths. The department spent more than twenty years collecting data and revising its total; it created the post of department statistician in the 1880s.[26]

Congress now began building a permanent statistical bureaucracy. At Lincoln's recommendation, it established the Department of Agriculture in 1862 to conduct agricultural research and to collect and publish data on American agriculture. Upon its creation the department issued a report titled "Present Agricultural, Mineral, and Manufacturing Resources of the United States," then each year it published a book full of statistics collected from volunteers around the country. Congress soon created bureaus within the Agriculture Department to order the society it had measured. The Bureau of Animal Husbandry regulated the transport of livestock; the National Board of Health oversaw medical quarantines.[27] The Bureau of Labor, which Congress created within the Interior Department in 1884, performed a similar statistical function for another segment of the nation's economy. Responding to concerns about inconsistencies among states' marriage and divorce laws, Congress in 1887 instructed that agency to compile a volume of statistics on marriage and divorce over the past twenty years. Reflecting their growing faith in the value of statistics to government, legislators promoted the Bureau of Labor to non-cabinet-level departmental status in 1888 and the Department of Agriculture to cabinet-level status in 1889.[28]

Congress also created a bureaucracy to collect data on education. In 1867 it established the Department of Education. As with the Department of Agriculture and the Bureau of Labor, an important part of this agency's job was the distribution to the public of information about America's schools and colleges. Until the Civil War the national government had remained aloof from educational matters. Now the Education Department, along with the Morrill Act and the legislation to supply army officers and arms discussed in chapter 2, gave it a much larger role in education, including higher education. These new activities brought major change both to colleges and to the government. They show clearly that even if some new federal programs ended during Reconstruction, the Civil War produced a major and permanent expansion of federal authority with important consequences for cultural institutions.

Recently, historians have begun to explore in depth the role of education in the development of the American bureaucratic state after the Civil War. Two books show that educational institutions and policies helped to shape the expansion and bureaucratization of the federal government. These works help to incorporate the history of education into the broader history of the late nineteenth century. As a result, they offer new insights into the nature of the developing state. Just as important, they suggest a new way to look at the histories of educational institutions.

Marc R. Nemec, in *Ivory Towers and Nationalist Minds* (2006), uncovers the widespread and deliberate ways in which universities served the nation-state between the Civil War and 1920. They did this primarily through the definition and propagation of disciplinary expertise. The new bureaucratic state that emerged after the Civil War enabled that role. The new agencies relied on authority rooted in the expertise of their employees. When it was established in 1901, for example, the Agriculture Department's Bureau of Forestry could not effectively supervise America's forests unless it employed trained officers and unless Americans accepted those officers' authoritative knowledge. University leaders, anxious to prove their institutions' relevance, saw an opportunity to provide a major service to the state. They established schools of forestry, both to train government experts and to conduct research that produced those experts' knowledge. Through these and many similar projects designed "to gather, assess, and disseminate expertise," universities proved their value to numerous federal departments and agencies in areas from agriculture to commerce and from weather to public health. By the turn of the century, universities had become indispensable to the expansion of the bureaucratic state. The initiative for that new role, Nemec argues, came primarily from university leaders who needed to justify their incipient institutions.[29]

Williamjames Hull Hoffer, by contrast, looks at congressional initiatives to build a relationship between the government and colleges. In *To Enlarge the Machinery of Government* (2007) he examines legislators' decisions to create a bureaucracy that observed, supported, and eventually regulated educational and other institutions. By so doing, he revises the narrative of state expansion. The historiographic debate previously focused on whether the modern state began in the 1860s or the 1890s. Hoffer, through his look at postbellum policies and agencies, including the Morrill Act and the Department of Education, argues for a more complex model of change involving not one new state but two. The modern regulatory state appeared in the Progressive Era, but it was preceded by a different bureaucratic state between the 1850s and the 1890s. Through their debates over these agencies and policies, congressmen built a type of state defined by the "sponsorship, supervision, and standardization" of education and other elements of society.[30]

Each stage of involvement in education, Hoffer argues, further empowered the federal state. The Civil War convinced congressmen that the government needed both to "sponsor" and to "supervise" (by which he means collect information on) key aspects of American life. They therefore created the Agriculture Department and passed the Morrill Act. The Freedmen's Bureau constituted a more activist form of regulation. Finally, congressmen exercised their new power of standardization by consolidating government lawyers into the Justice Department and by creating the Education Department.[31] Hoffer thus uses educational policy to learn about the developing federal state.

These two books point to a third line of inquiry. If the relationship between the growing state and higher education can teach us about that state, it also can teach us about institutions of higher education. Besides providing experts for bureaucratic offices (which happened primarily at a few elite universities), colleges responded to the offer of federal funding and to the Department of Education's efforts to collect and distribute information. In effect, they partnered with the department to create a national database of education and to publicize their own accomplishments and programs. One consequence of university outreach was to increase some colleges' visibility in their local communities. The Department of Education helped colleges to publicize themselves on a national level.

The federal government had collected a few statistics on education, including illiteracy rates and numbers of colleges and students, in its censuses since 1840.[32] After the Civil War, as the government expanded its bureaucracy, some politicians and educators began to argue that it should more consistently and thoroughly study educational systems and institutions. Much as new federal activities in the West through the Homestead and Pacific Railroad Acts emerged alongside the funding of agricultural colleges, the expansion of the federal bureaucracy in areas such as the army, pensions, and agriculture emerged alongside an educational bureaucracy. From both within and without the government, Americans now proposed a federal agency charged specifically with the collection and distribution of data on education.

The legal effort to establish an agency for educational statistics began soon after the war with a more radical proposal. Ignatius Donnelly, a Republican from Minnesota, introduced his resolution into the House in December 1865. It began by asserting that "republican institutions" rest upon "the universal intelligence of the people." In an age of nearly universal white manhood suffrage and widespread common schooling, this was nothing radical. But the resolution next declared that "the great disasters which have afflicted the nation and desolated one half its territory are traceable, in a great degree, to the absence of common schools and general education among the people of the lately rebellious States." Donnelly wanted the House officially to attribute the Civil War, "in a great degree," to the small number of public schools in the South.[33]

Then came Donnelly's radical solution. His resolution instructed "the joint committee on reconstruction . . . to inquire into the expediency of establishing . . . a national Bureau of Education, whose duty it shall be to enforce education, without regard to race or color, upon the population of all such States as shall fall below a standard to be established by Congress." He was proposing a total reconception of the federal role in public education and of public education itself. Between 1820 and 1860 many communities in the Northern states had established free primary and secondary schools. A number of states had appointed superintendents and boards to supervise and regulate those schools. But public schooling remained primarily a local effort through which parents shared the cost of their children's education. Urban school systems took a more hierarchical form, but still on a local level.[34] Donnelly proposed just the opposite: a top-down system in which the national government set standards and "enforce[d] education" on any state that failed to meet those national standards. This system, applying equally to black and white children, would be part of the militarily enforced Reconstruction.

Remarkably, Donnelly's resolution passed. With no debate besides an abortive attempt to table the resolution, the House of Representatives voted to blame secession and the Civil War on a lack of schools and to consider a federal system of public education. Radical Republicans' determination to punish former Confederates for secession probably attracted them to the resolution. But nothing came of it. There is no evidence that the joint committee ever discussed it, and the House records did not mention it again.[35]

Donnelly's resolution, however, opened the door to more moderate proposals for a national bureau of education. In December 1865 or January 1866 a Massachusetts representative delivered a memorial from his constituents proposing such a bureau. School superintendents belonging to the National Educational Association, meeting in Washington in February 1866, prepared a similar memorial.[36]

Representative James A. Garfield, a former president of an educational institute and future president of the United States, brought the question before Congress in February 1866. His bill, after some tinkering in committee, came up for debate that June. It proposed to establish "a Department of Education for the purpose of collecting such statistics and facts as shall show the condition and progress of education in the several States and Territories, and of diffusing such information respecting the organization and management of schools and school systems and methods of teaching as shall aid the people of the United States in the establishment and maintenance of efficient school systems, and otherwise promote the cause of education throughout the country." The president would appoint, with the Senate's confirmation, a commissioner of education to head the department. He, in turn, would appoint five clerks. Each year, the commissioner would present to Congress a report of his findings and "recommendations." The first report would also include a historical description of all federal land grants for education.[37] This department would not "enforce" education. It would "collect" and "diffus[e]" information in order to expand and improve educational opportunities.

A department of education was a logical addition to the federal government in the 1860s. Congress recently had involved the government in education through the Morrill Act. Proponents might well have argued that a department of education logically followed. Also, public education had spread through the Northeast and Midwest by then. After the war, public schools for both white and black Americans began to appear in the South. Colleges had been multiplying since the Revolution. The expansion of American education meant that there was more information to keep track of than ever before. The federal government recently had begun to establish itself as the repository for data on other important elements of American life. Certainly these factors helped to bring educational administration to the attention of Congress. But proponents did not use these arguments. Instead, they promoted the bill by drawing its connections with the Civil War and Reconstruction. They used the war, its causes, its consequences, and its goals to justify the expansion of federal power.

The bill aroused heated debate. The federal government already was rapidly expanding; now Garfield proposed giving it a role in a field strongly rooted in state and local control. The first two congressmen to speak laid out the essential arguments for and against the bill. In doing so, they illustrated two competing images of the federal government. Donnelly, not surprisingly, argued in favor of the bill. He painted the national government as a boon to Americans. Government activism could improve individuals' lives and counteract state governments' errors. Andrew J. Rogers, a Democrat from New Jersey, defended an older objection to centralized power: federal action meant interference with the states and with their citizens' freedom. A central political question of the long Civil War era thus crystallized in this debate over a department of education. At the same time, Donnelly and Rogers agreed on one thing. Both described the proposal as a direct response to the Civil War. In 1866 the war remained on everyone's mind. Much as Justin S. Morrill in 1862 had turned the nation's military needs into an argument for his land-grant bill, Donnelly and Rogers framed a department of education as a response to the war. Donnelly argued that it served the needs of Reconstruction; Rogers, that it furthered the wartime abuses of federal power.[38]

Donnelly opened the debate by focusing his colleagues' attention on the war, its causes, and its yet unfinished resolution. "With the first gun fired upon Fort Sumter," he began, "the nation was born into a new life. All that has followed, all that will follow, must be regarded as the natural outgrowth of that great event." With that premise, he searched for the war's causes to guide Congress in passing proper legislation to follow the military victory. The war had begun with treason on the part of "people

[who] have been rendered unfit to wisely govern themselves." Southerners' incapacity for republicanism, in turn, had arisen from the "degradation" and "ignorance" produced by slavery—afflictions that, he implied, affected black and white Southerners alike.

The Northern victory and the Thirteenth Amendment had begun to repair centuries of degradation, but these alone were not enough. White Confederates had surrendered, but they remained hostile toward the government that had brought "civilizing influences" via the battlefield. The former slave was legally free but after years of enslavement lacked the knowledge of how to use his "new powers . . . to his own advantage and the glory of his country." How were the reconstruction of Confederate whites and the recovery of former slaves to be completed? Education, Donnelly argued, could save both peoples of the South. Proper education would make the one-time rebel "love the great nation which lifts him up" and teach the ex-slave to use his freedom for his own good and for the good of his country. Education, in short, would materially benefit the nation and build nationalism.

To accomplish these lofty goals, education needed centralized direction. Previously, Donnelly acknowledged, the United States had left educational matters to the states, "and we have had the rebellion as a consequence." The absence of a central authority permitted regional and local variations in educational opportunity. The Southern states, he claimed, had altogether neglected their obligation to educate their citizens. To illustrate this, he cited the divergent paths of Massachusetts and Virginia. As early as 1642, Massachusetts Bay had required towns to provide for the education of their children. But in 1671 Virginia's governor had boasted about the *absence* of free schools in his colony. These early patterns persisted into the present. The Bay State, with its extensive system of public schooling, enjoyed "intelligence, enterprise, invention, industry, prosperity, liberty, and justice." The Old Dominion, on the other hand, suffered "ignorance, sloth, poverty, oppression, cruelty, slavery, and . . . anarchy." The time had come to eradicate these disparities through a central, national agency.

To further prove his argument, indicative of the type of agency he wanted to create, Donnelly presented a series of statistics. In 1850, he told his listeners, the free states collectively had spent nearly $6 million on public schooling; the slave states, less than $850,000. Americans had learned the hard way that "ignorance and rebellion" are "as parent and child." Ignorance, he argued, "is even more dangerous than slavery." If Congress allowed ignorance to persist, the consequence would be "degrading our people, impeding commerce, destroying manufactures, making brutes of the masses and demagogues of the leaders," and dooming the nation to dissolution within the next fifty years. Furthermore, since other nations looked to the United States as a model of progress, "we hold the destiny of mankind in our hands." To fight ignorance, ensure national prosperity, unite the country, and prevent another civil war and the end of the American experiment, Congress must establish a national department of education. It would complete the work begun on the battlefield, reintegrating the South into the nation and rebuilding that nation around a central government that reached out to expand individual opportunity and halt oppression by the states.

Rogers followed Donnelly's defense of the bill with an equally spirited speech opposing it. The Democrat disagreed with nearly every point his Republican colleague had made—about the causes of the war, about Southerners' intellect, about state versus federal roles in education, and about the nature of the national government. But he, like Donnelly, saw the proposal's genesis in the Civil War. Over the past several years, he pointed out, Congress had established several new bureaus within the government. Some of these were benign and even necessary. The Department of Agriculture, for example, merely collected and distributed information necessary for informed government and efficient farming. Congress had gone too far, however, in expanding the federal bureaucracy. The Freedmen's Bureau, in particular, constituted a much more sinister intrusion of federal power into state matters. Repeating the older image of centralized government as a threat to liberty, Rogers feared its growing power.

A department of education, Rogers argued, would be "a twin sister of" the Freedmen's Bureau. He repeated the comparison throughout his speech. Federal supervision of black freedom, he implied, somehow had led to federal supervision of education. To start with, this was unnecessary. The states were doing just fine educating their children. America already had the best system of education of any country in the history of the world. Even the South had produced highly intelligent men. They, not unschooled ignoramuses, had led the country into civil war. Garfield and Donnelly proposed to waste precious tax money on another unnecessary bureau.

Beyond its needlessness, Rogers claimed, a department of education would expand beyond its charter into a dangerous coercive agency. It might begin by simply observing educational systems and collecting statistics, but it would not stop there. The very process of gathering information would in effect exert a degree of coercion, and inevitably Congress soon would amend the department's charter to give it the explicit power "to control and regulate the educational system of the whole country." The Constitution gave the national government no such authority. Education belonged in the hands of the states and local communities, "without interference, directly or indirectly," from Washington. The bill before the House proposed an act of "philanthropy," of "charity," not of good government. It also set a dangerous precedent. If it passed, Congress would then create additional harmful bureaus. The proposed department of education, Rogers warned, represented "but one more step toward centralization." Whereas Donnelly had promoted the value of statistics and the potential benefits of active, informed government, Rogers warned against centralization and the abuse of power.

Other congressmen continued the debate along those lines. Supporters of the bill, all Republicans, stressed the value of "centralization" and "uniformity." The rebellion born of Southerners' ignorance had taught them the danger of allowing one region to remain behind another in the provision of education. Only educational uniformity could reunite the country and prevent another civil war. As Garfield put it in his closing speech, "It is cheaper to reduce crime than to build jails. School-houses are less expensive than rebellions." Opponents, from both parties, emphasized the potential expense of such a department, the danger of federal intrusion into state matters, and the slippery slope on which the bill would set the nation. One representative worried that the national government would first educate the freedmen, then take over the nation's schools, then take over the churches; a witty colleague repeated his fear of "a Bureau of Religion—which God forbid!" These men expressed firm convictions of the great potential benefit or evil of an expanded federal bureaucracy in education and in general.[39]

The bill passed, though it took a couple of tries. After amending it to reduce the commissioner's salary and the number of clerks, the congressmen rejected it by a vote of 61 to 59. Eleven days later, with no additional debate, they passed it, 80 to 44. It reached the Senate floor eight months later, where it passed after a similar but much shorter debate. President Andrew Johnson signed the bill into law on March 2, 1867.[40] The department's title and non-cabinet-level status caused some confusion, leading Congress to rename it the Office of Education in 1868 (effective 1869), then the Bureau of Education in 1870. Under these names, the agency fell within the Interior Department.[41] Despite changes in nomenclature and hierarchical position, though, the agency survived. The collection of data on education, like that on agriculture, became a permanent activity of the federal government.

The new law referred to "education" in general, but its congressional proponents and detractors alike had referred to common schools as its objects. Only one speaker had explicitly suggested that the department should concern itself with higher education—he referred specifically to normal schools—while two had said or strongly implied that it should not.[42] The law required that the department's first annual report include a history of federal land grants for education, which obviously included the Morrill grants for colleges, but said nothing more about higher education. Yet the agency that formed over the next few years collected data on all levels of education. Some colleges already maintained strong connections with the federal government through the Morrill Act and, just recently, the army-officers amendment of 1866. Now every college, as well as every primary and high school, began to report to the national Department of Education.

Johnson appointed Henry Barnard commissioner of education; the Senate readily approved. Barnard's experience was beyond question. After serving as state superintendent of schools in both Rhode Island and Connecticut, he had become chancellor of the University of Wisconsin and then president of St. John's College in Maryland. Furthermore, he had argued for nearly thirty years that the federal government should collect statistics on education. This made him a logical choice. His political conservatism outside educational issues may also have facilitated his appointment.[43] At the same time, his extensive involvement with both lower and higher education was at odds with Congress's tacit and sometimes explicit view that the department should deal only with lower schools. He would indeed stretch that mandate considerably.

Barnard began sending out requests for information to governments, schools, and other organizations. Once he had collected data on American education, he distributed it to Congress and to the public through a number of publications, the largest being the annual report. Ranging from fewer than six hundred to more than one thousand pages, the annual reports included statistical tables, abstracts of states' and cities' reports, and articles on a huge variety of educational topics. Much of the content focused on primary and secondary schools. The first report, for instance, included an article on New England high schools and academies, one on public education in Prussia, and one titled "The Right and Duty of the State to Establish, Aid, and Supervise Public Schools." The second report, which presented far more statistics, told readers the number of districts, schools, teachers, and students in each state.[44]

From the very beginning, though, the department also collected data on higher education. In this area, Barnard went well beyond the required history of land grants. In the introduction to his first and only report as commissioner, he elaborated on the congressional act that had created the department, outlining in much more detail what he had decided the department should do. His "Schedule of Information Sought" listed fifteen general topics. These included primary schools, secondary schools, colleges, "professional and special" schools, churches and religious organizations, periodicals, and "Penal and Charitable Institutions." Congress had not intended the inclusion of colleges, let alone prisons, but Barnard and his successor, John Eaton Jr., sought and reported data on these elements of American education every year.[45]

The agency developed an extensive array of surveys for institutions of higher education. It sent out distinct forms to men's or coeducational colleges and universities (including their preparatory departments and scientific, agricultural, mining, and engineering schools), women's colleges and seminaries (including their preparatory departments), divinity schools, medical schools, law schools, normal schools, and business colleges. The information sought varied among the forms but usually included the institution's charter date, religious affiliation, faculty size, student population, tuition and fees, and primary benefactor.[46] For the first time, the national government was attempting to assemble data on every institution of higher education in the country.

The Bureau of Education lacked any coercive power to make institutions respond. Nonetheless, they provided the information it sought. Out of 369 colleges known to the bureau, all but 32 responded to the first general survey in 1870. Five years later the bureau was corresponding with more than 600 colleges and more than 4,000 institutions total.[47] The annual reports reflected this large response. The first, 896 pages in length, included nearly 350 pages about postsecondary institutions. The report on federal land grants made up half that. Barnard printed the relevant legislation from every state that had accepted the terms of the Morrill Act, plus the history and curriculum of every college that had received income from the land grants. Another lengthy section described, one by one, the state normal schools in all twenty-three states that had responded to a request for information. In a section on female education, an article described coeducation at Oberlin College.[48]

Later reports, which included the results of the bureau's statistical surveys, reveal even more clearly the extent of its attention to higher education. In addition to brief textual descriptions of every institution within the abstracts of states', territories', and cities' reports, the report for 1875 included 136 pages of statistical tables describing America's colleges and universities, professional and technical schools, and military academies. Legislators and other readers could learn almost anything about any institution, including its tuition, scholarship funds, and student population by gender, class year, and course of study.[49] College faculties and trustees worked with the growing federal government to assemble and disseminate information about their own institutions and American higher education as a whole.

In addition to the hefty annual reports, each year the bureau issued several "circulars of information" and special reports. These addressed more specific topics in education. Of the eighty-nine circulars and special reports issued between 1867 and 1880, twenty-one focused on colleges or vocational schools. Others discussed both lower and higher education. Many of the circulars, like the annual reports, focused on presenting data. In 1872, for example, Eaton issued a ninety-three-page report on American college students and graduates. Full of tables and charts, it told readers such information as the ages at graduation, occupations, and lifespans of alumni of several New England colleges, as well as the geographic origins of current college students throughout the country. Eaton presented the report as a contribution to knowledge that he hoped would "stimulate and direct inquiry." The following year the bureau published an extensive bibliography of "publications by members of certain college-faculties and learned societies." Reflecting the increasing association between college teaching and scholarly research that accompanied the development of universities, the bureau had solicited publication histories from numerous faculties so that it could show "the industrious activity and labors of the college-professors outside the classroom."[50]

Occasionally the commissioner had more normative or advisory goals in mind. By 1872 Eaton had received numerous inquiries about the definition of the term *university*. He also had observed that many institutions named themselves "'universities,' without regard to their character or purpose." To answer correspondents' questions and to combat what he considered misuse of a term, he had a staff member prepare a circular describing the histories, structures, and curricula of what he considered to be the true universities in Europe. Eaton evidently believed that his office had the power to influence institutions' naming decisions. Also in 1872, he published a recommendation that railroad companies receiving federal land grants voluntarily build free schools (for children of all races) in all the towns and cities located within those grants. Neither of Eaton's recommendations seems to have received much attention or had much effect. In making them, though, he took the first and, as the bureau's opponents in Congress had warned, inevitable step beyond collecting information and toward regulating American education. But it was only a first, small step. Not until the twentieth century would the agency begin regularly to advise or regulate schools or colleges.[51]

In the nineteenth century the Bureau of Education restricted its activities almost exclusively to collecting and distributing information. Its commissioners hoped to distribute to a larger audience than just Congress. They sent the annual reports and circulars to various educators and politicians, but the recipients were limited. The government printed twenty thousand copies of the annual report for the years 1870–72, and then an economically minded Congress reduced the print run to five thousand in 1873.[52] About a decade after the bureau's founding, however, an opportunity came along for it to showcase American educational institutions before a large and attentive public.

Colleges, Governments, and the Centennial Exposition of 1876

International expositions had become a common form of celebration and display by the 1870s. They had their roots in European industrial fairs of the eighteenth century, which the French had expanded into large national expositions by the beginning of the nineteenth. Each included hundreds or thousands of exhibits on domestic manufactures. Organizers built temporary structures, developed classification schemes, published catalogues, and handed out awards. Other nations soon copied the French, and in 1851 Great Britain took the idea one step further. In the famous Crystal Palace at Hyde Park, London, the British held the world's first international exposition. They reserved half the space for British exhibits, dividing the other half among other countries. As with the local and national fairs, the emphasis lay on industrial production. Out of thirty exhibit categories, raw materials, machinery, and manufactures made up twenty-nine (the thirtieth was fine arts). Other nations added new categories. A French international exposition in 1867 included lessons on "the best ways to educate man." Austria formalized that aspect, including education as one of the twenty-six categories of exhibits at the Vienna World

Exposition in 1873.[53] Now expositions displayed to the world not only what nations made but also how they trained their children and youths.

The United States joined in. Individual cities and states sent exhibits on their school systems to Vienna. The Bureau of Education, using the same data it had collected for its annual report, prepared an exhibit on American education as a whole. Eaton and, he observed, American educators were anxious to teach the world about the United States' educational accomplishments. Vienna provided a useful forum. The Austrian authorities even awarded the bureau a grand diploma of honor for its exhibit.[54] But the bureau's best opportunity to teach the world and, more important, Americans about recent developments in American education came several years later on domestic soil.

Even as they attended European expositions, Americans were planning one of their own. In 1864 a professor at Wabash College in Indiana suggested in a speech that the United States celebrate its upcoming centennial with an international exposition. He thought it should take place in Philadelphia, the nation's Revolutionary capital. That city's mayor and council liked the idea, as did the Pennsylvania legislature. The legislature lobbied Congress to take charge of the project, and in 1871 Congress established the U.S. Centennial Commission to select a site and organize the event. The commission chose Fairmount Park, and construction of the exposition buildings began in 1874.[55] Individuals, organizations, cities, states, the federal government, and nations around the world began preparing exhibits to display their finest accomplishments to America and the world.

Like European expositions, America's Centennial Exposition aimed first and foremost to celebrate the nation's natural and industrial resources. The Centennial Commission, itself an example of the information-gathering federal bureaucracy that had sprung up since the Civil War, devised an elaborate system to organize material. It defined seven departments: mining and metallurgy, manufactures, education and science, art, machinery, agriculture, and horticulture. These reflected the emphasis on industry. But the inclusion of a department of education and science meant that the country also would display its educational accomplishments. The commission further divided this department into five groups and thirty-five classes. The first group included institutions of formal education. Within that group, one class covered elementary schools; another, high schools and colleges; another, professional schools; and another, educational reports and statistics.[56] The Centennial Exposition, an educational space itself, would teach about the many types of American educational institutions.

The Department of Education and Science gave the Bureau of Education a great opportunity. The Centennial Commission determined the categories of exhibits it would welcome into the exposition, but it left to others the tasks of designing and installing those exhibits. If Eaton could persuade states, cities, and institutions to prepare exhibits on education, he could use the nation's hundredth birthday to broadcast the state of education in the United States to the American and international public. Far more people would attend the Centennial Exposition than would ever read his annual reports or circulars. So, more than two years before the exposition was to open, he set to work.

The commissioner began his campaign to bring schools and colleges to Philadelphia in early 1874. In cooperation with the National Educational Association, the Bureau of Education published a recommendation that every state, city, and educational institution prepare an exhibit on its educational history and current activities. A year later, Eaton sent out circulars to every type of educational institution he could think of, from primary and high schools to colleges, universities, women's seminaries, and professional schools. Through these circulars he tried to make participation as easy as possible. One explained the layout of the exposition and suggested the kinds of materials participants might include in their exhibits. Others were ready-made information sheets with blanks where the institutions could supply their data. These made it easy for institutional leaders to prepare handouts or displays. One sheet covered preparatory departments; another, literary societies; another, laboratories. Eaton wanted institutions to prepare their own histories, so he sent them a detailed description of what information to include and how to organize it. He also sent a sample history of Mount Holyoke for schools, seminaries, and colleges to use as a model. In addition to all this mail, he enlisted prominent educators to visit institutions and boards of education on behalf of the bureau. In person, these envoys prodded educators to participate.[57]

By the time the Centennial Exposition opened in May 1876, national, state, and local efforts had assembled extensive exhibits on education. These exhibits served both as a culmination of the bureau's work at collecting and disseminating information and as a celebration of the changes the Civil War had brought to America's colleges. The bureau presented far more information to far more people than it ever had before. Its audience finally expanded beyond politicians and educators. The exhibits themselves emphasized several of the changes in education, including higher education, over the past fifteen years: the emergence of universities, the diversification of students, and the collection of statistics. Taken together, these exhibits highlighted the two central themes of higher-education reform during the long Civil War era: increased federal involvement and rapid change in the South. In the final year of that era, the exposition served as a fitting capstone to and reflection on a period of educational transformation.

Owing to the exposition's decentralized system of arrangement, the education exhibits were spread around the entire grounds. The Centennial Commission assigned each state its own exhibit space. Because public schooling remained primarily a state and local project, public schools set up their exhibits with their states. The Bureau of Education instructed private institutions to do the same. Some individuals set up educational exhibits in their own small buildings. Distributed among these many locations and buildings, these exhibits added up to more material on American education than had ever been assembled before.[58]

The Government Building reflected the new federal bureaucracy Congress had created since the Civil War. Many agencies produced exhibits, a dozen of which included content about education. The Department of Agriculture, for example, displayed statistics on technical schools. The Smithsonian Institution displayed minerals, animals, and Native American artifacts from its museum collection. The Geological and Geographical Surveys of the Territories, the Bureau of the Coast Survey, the Bureau of the Signal Service, the Internal Revenue Bureau, the Medical Department of the Army, and the Post Office Department also had exhibits related to education.[59] These varied exhibits revealed the federal government's expanding role in education.

The most important of the government's exhibits on education, of course, belonged to the Bureau of Education. Besides inviting states, communities, and institutions to prepare exhibits, Eaton and his staff also had prepared one themselves. Leaving most of the details to state, local, and private displays, Eaton described the federal exhibit as merely "an outline" of American education. Like the annual reports, this outline showed that the bureau had been closely watching the nation's schools and colleges. Visitors encountered, for example, student work from Native American and white schools; models of school buildings; catalogues, histories, and photographs of higher-education institutions; maps showing the locations of kindergartens and of men's and women's colleges; and campus maps drawn by college students.[60]

The bureau also used Philadelphia to inform the public about its own work over the past nine years. Shelves displayed every annual report and circular since the bureau's founding. Visitors could find virtually any statistic the government knew about education. Eaton even brought along the original manuscript reports that institutions had submitted to the bureau. Clearly proud of the federal government's work collecting data on education, Eaton used this opportunity to inform a vacationing national audience about both the state of American education and the state of government involvement.[61]

Eaton had put most of his energy, however, into encouraging the states to exhibit. Because the bureau's exhibit was only an outline, the states, cities, and institutions had to furnish the main content—and they did. Twenty-four states, plus the District of Columbia and the Indian Territory, contributed exhibits the exposition organizers classified within the first group of the Department of Education and Science. The fourteen states that did not included eight of the eleven states of the former Confederacy. Their omission was both logical and revealing. Colleges in the South had suffered greatly from the tremors of war and the economic challenges that had followed it. Institutions such as the University of South Carolina, working hard to develop new curricula and attract new students, had more pressing tasks than preparing an exposition display. Of the Northern and Southern states that did contribute exhibits on educational institutions, all but two, which displayed only museum artifacts, included presentations on schools or colleges.[62] State governments, local communities, and individual institutions taught exposition-goers about how they educated their children and youths.

Exhibits on primary and secondary schools included a great variety of materials. Some states, like the federal bureau, made statistics a major part of their displays. They too had come to value statistics as a measure of success and a tool by which governments could spread information. Kentucky, for example, distributed a pamphlet giving separate statistics for its white and black public-school systems. Indiana erected the most complete statistical presentation, impressing the exposition judges with its pamphlets, "charts, banners, and tablets, and revolving cases of ingenious construction." These presented historical and contemporary data on public schools, colleges, the press, and state and local revenue for education.[63]

Besides the statistics, visitors encountered a variety of creative and visually impressive exhibits. Indiana's display included models of a log schoolhouse and the State Normal School and no fewer than 166 volumes of examination papers from fifteen thousand students in fifty school districts and thirteen colleges across the state. Pennsylvania designed perhaps the most creative exhibit of primary schools, erecting its own circular building just for exhibits on education. The various displays filled alcoves off a central hall. Moving among the alcoves, one could view the historical progress of public education in Pennsylvania. First came a log schoolhouse of the eighteenth century, complete with an ink-soiled desk, a leather strap for discipline, and a teacher's frayed coat. Next came a modern schoolhouse of stone and cement filled with the newest desks and scientific specimens. Two other alcoves taught visitors about the fifteen schools the Keystone State had set up for the orphans of Civil War soldiers. Most interesting of all, women from Pennsylvania, New York, and Massachusetts pooled their funds to build a kindergarten building. After selecting sixteen children from a Philadelphia orphanage to fill the room, they held class three times a week. They put the orphans on display to show visitors what went on in a kindergarten.[64]

Higher education was also on display. Eaton's numerous mailings had worked: colleges, universities, and normal schools throughout the nation had prepared exhibits as diverse, though not as large, as those about public schools. They used the Centennial Exposition to educate the American public about how they had changed—not since the Revolution, but since the Civil War. Both new institutions and old ones that had enlarged their missions and curricula proudly showed off in Philadelphia what was new in American higher education.

Southern exhibits, though few, displayed some of the newest forms of higher education. Of the mere five institutions from the former Confederacy that appeared in Philadelphia, all were young and innovative. They illustrated two major postbellum developments in Southern higher education: teacher education and higher education for blacks. Four Tennessee institutions prepared small displays: black Fisk University brought publications, campus illustrations, and student work, while the Colored Training School (probably a normal school), the South Normal School, and the University of Nashville's new white normal school displayed photographs. From Virginia came a much more extensive presentation by the Hampton Normal and Agricultural Institute. Besides photographs and paintings, this black institution's exhibit included issues of the student newspaper and student-made industrial and agricultural goods. Visitors to Philadelphia learned nothing of the opportunities for Southern blacks at the reconstructed University of South Carolina, but they did learn something about black and white teacher education in the Upper South.[65] The Civil War's impact on Southern education was very clear.

A few exhibits from the border states helped to fill in the Southern picture. The Lincoln Institute, a normal school for African Americans founded by black veterans in Missouri, prepared a volume that included student coursework and a photograph of the students and faculty. And the University of Missouri's faculty, probably stimulated by Eaton's correspondence, had begun thinking about how to represent the university back in the fall of 1875. A faculty committee had decided to prepare illustrations of the campus grounds and buildings, along with a "Historical Chart." After the curators authorized three hundred dollars for an exhibit, the professors added to that single chart more extensive documents describing the founding and recent history of the university. The exposition judges came away from these publications impressed with the university's successful rebirth and growth after the damage it had suffered during the war—precisely the impression President Read, who had directed that growth and who served on the faculty's Centennial Exhibit Committee, probably wanted to make.[66] Having accomplished his goal of a decade earlier—to build a well-funded university with schools of arts, science, and a variety of occupations—he could now, on his retirement from the presidency,[67] celebrate by broadcasting his accomplishment beyond the campus and state to the American public. The judges, at least, were happy to congratulate him.

The small number of institutions represented gave visitors to the Centennial Exposition a skewed picture of Southern higher education. They indicated more extensive change than actually had occurred since the Civil War. The large majority of institutions in the former Confederacy still enrolled only whites, but most of those represented at Philadelphia educated blacks. Similarly, most institutions in the South still taught only men or only women, but all or nearly all those exhibiting at Philadelphia were coeducational. Single-gender institutions chose not to exhibit. This is especially curious because a Wesleyan professor took a group of students to Philadelphia to see the exposition. They easily could have brought along material about their college to display but apparently did not.[68] Southern institutions that had made it through the war without changing were invisible to exposition visitors, who saw only the new, the innovative, the distinctively postbellum.

A much larger and more representative array of Northern colleges

Fig. 11. Lafayette College exhibit at the Centennial Exposition of 1876. (Special Collections and College Archives, Skillman Library, Lafayette College)

produced exhibits. These also emphasized institutions' innovative elements, such as scientific and vocational courses, university structures, faculty research, and military training. For instance, eleven of Pennsylvania's twenty-nine universities and classical colleges, as well as a number of the state's independent professional schools, were represented. Haverford College focused on professors' research, displaying physics diagrams, architectural models, and the original letters of Pennsylvania's founder, William Penn. Lafayette College emphasized both its educational and its research activities, particularly in science (fig. 11). Photographs of its laboratories and scientific equipment complemented mineralogical, botanical, and zoological specimens from the college's collections. Lincoln University displayed photographs, maps, curricular charts, and examination papers from its African American students. Lincoln also included "two series of ten photographs of native Africans, the first taken upon entrance, the second after two years of study,—a most instructive exhibit," according to the judges.[69] Perhaps, in an era when science tried to define the abilities of racial groups, Lincoln's faculty or trustees hoped to prove the transformative power of education on students of a supposedly inferior race.

Massachusetts provided one of the largest collections of higher-education exhibits. Six normal schools, two technical institutes, four theological seminaries, one college of pharmacy, one college of dentistry, three colleges or seminaries for women, and six men's classical colleges or universities set up displays in the Main Building. The Massachusetts Institute of Technology (MIT), one of the Bay State's two land-grant colleges, represented itself in Philadelphia almost entirely through student work. Besides about fifty theses and hundreds of drawings, its exhibit featured the products of students' practical work in their scientific and occupational studies. Chemistry students had made synthesized fluids; architecture students, models and building plans; and engineering students, machine parts. In addition, MIT's student cadets went to Philadelphia under the command of their military teacher. The Worcester Free Institute similarly displayed its students' work in chemistry, engineering, and physics.[70] Fourteen years after the Morrill Act, with Americans placing increasing value on military preparedness and practical, marketable training, these schools showed exposition-goers the skills, products, and technologies their graduates were contributing to the country.

Women's higher education figured prominently in the Massachusetts section. Mount Holyoke, Wellesley College, and Smith College all prepared exhibits. The principal herself, along with another teacher, tended Mount Holyoke's. Though less elaborate or creative than some colleges'—they consisted of photographs, diagrams, catalogues, and other printed documents—these exhibits successfully conveyed the institutions' merit and accomplishments. They sufficiently impressed the exposition judges that, but for the absence of examples of student work, those judges would have given them a prize.[71]

Harvard University took advantage of the Centennial Exposition to show the American public its recent growth. Making sure that no one thought of Harvard as merely an old college, the new university set up an exhibit for each of its many schools: academic, scientific, divinity, law, medical, dental, and agricultural. The Museum of Comparative Zoology, itself created in part to spread knowledge of science beyond the students and faculty, displayed its publications and a bust of Professor Louis Agassiz.[72]

Not every Northern college was represented at Philadelphia. Cornell

College had no exhibit. Six Northern states joined the eight Southern ones that erected no education exhibits at all. Not surprisingly, given the distance, those included all three states west of the Rocky Mountains. But the University of California did appear at the exposition, just barely. In February 1876 the regents received a letter from the Central Pacific Railroad Company. The railroad was assembling "a collection of the varied products of this State" to display at Philadelphia and asked the state university to contribute "such specimens in mineralogy and paleontology, and other branches, as can safely be lent." The regents, appreciating the value of a good exhibit on California's natural history, agreed to send "ores, minerals[,] etc., from the University museum." Then in April a letter arrived from the California Immigrant Union, whose agent offered to distribute circulars of the university at the exposition and elsewhere.[73] The regents' reply has not survived, but it is unlikely that they would have refused free advertising.

Though the regents acted only passively, and probably few visitors to Philadelphia even noticed the University of California's small presence, that school did in much smaller quantity essentially the same things as Harvard. It both informed the national public about its educational activity and extended its museum to a larger, more distant audience. These contributions to the Centennial Exposition highlighted the university's efforts to educate both enrolled students and the wider public through multiple schools and outreach programs. They also highlighted the university's status as a state institution through the inclusion of its museum specimens in an exhibit on "the varied products of this State." The University of California, like other colleges, showed visitors to the exposition how it had grown and expanded its mission over the past decade and a half.

Higher education and the state had grown together. Between 1861 and 1876 both universities and the federal government had built themselves into extensive arrays of specialized units. Both had committed themselves to research and to the spread of information. Both, through the opening of admissions and the expansion of the electorate, had diversified their constituencies. Cooperation between them was a logical component of their mutual growth. Universities trained the bureaucrats who staffed executive agencies; Congress allocated money and other resources for practical curricula; universities extended learning to a larger portion of the American people; and the Bureau of Education coordinated the collection of information about education and its distribution to politicians and the general public. Colleges thus entered the public space, in both senses of the term, to a greater extent than ever before.

By developing close relationships with their local communities and with the federal government, colleges not only entered the public space but also helped to expand it. The federal government already had begun to play a larger role in Americans' lives. Now colleges, key cultural institutions, simultaneously served a much larger clientele through outreach and cooperated directly with state and federal governments. These two projects were hardly distinct. The University of California used state and federal resources to teach farmers new agricultural techniques. The University of South Carolina offered lectures in a local church while taking state money and reporting on its activities to the Bureau of Education. Publicly oriented colleges—against the wishes of conservatives such as Andrew Rogers—provided an arena for the expansion of federal power and drew more people into the public space and, through the colleges, an indirect relationship with the government.

At Philadelphia, both colleges and the government exhibited their new public roles. Americans learned there about the many educational developments of the Civil War era. The changes in colleges' curricula and students, as well as in their relationships with the government, stood on display. It took little scrutiny on the part of exhibition-goers to see that these recent changes had grown out of federal expansion and the presence of armies in the South. Both the national government and higher education, Americans learned, had in several ways been shaped by the Civil War.

Conclusion

When the Civil War began, higher education in America comprised chiefly small colleges that taught students an abstract curriculum rooted in the classical languages and mathematics. In the North they attracted students from a broad range of social classes who wished to become ministers, doctors, lawyers, or teachers. In the South they enrolled primarily the children of the plantation elite. Men and women in the South attended different colleges; blacks attended none. Students often traveled across state borders to reach college. The federal government did not play a major role in education. State governments had founded some colleges but usually had left them to operate and raise funds on their own.

The war both engaged and challenged these colleges. Male students left to enlist in the Union and Confederate armies. Women replaced brothers who had left farms to enlist or remained on campus knitting socks for the soldiers. Monetary inflation and the presence of armies forced additional students to withdraw. Some Southern colleges suffered physical destruction, while others endured military takeover as bases or hospitals. Meanwhile, Congress made the federal government a patron of higher education by passing the Morrill Land-Grant College Act. When the war ended, Northern colleges quickly regained their students. Southern colleges, many of which had closed, faced a much greater struggle.

As Southern colleges prepared to rebuild and reopen after the war, they thought about what curricula and institutional structures would best help them to survive in the postbellum economy and society. Some decided on multicollegiate universities offering classical, professional, and practical degree programs, along with outreach programs such as public lectures. These universities, they believed, would attract the most students and, through modular tuition policies, extract the most income from those students. Classical colleges such as South Carolina College and the University of Missouri thus reinvented themselves as comprehensive universities. Pointing to wartime damage, the University of Missouri persuaded the state government to fund its transition from college to university. It and other colleges became modern state universities, with funding and direction from their state governments, for the first time.

Both to maximize income and to address the social changes that accompanied the Civil War and Reconstruction, Southern colleges diversified their student populations. In the late 1860s and 1870s they began to admit more students of limited financial means, including both elites who now had less wealth and nontraditional students attracted by the new practical courses. Previously male colleges became coeducational, pushed in that direction by the need to train teachers for the new public school systems. The University of South Carolina, controlled by a Reconstruction legislature, even admitted African Americans for the first time. That change did not last, but access for poor whites did. Blacks' education survived primarily in separate institutions. The difficulty of traveling in wartime began a trend in both Southern and Northern colleges toward enrolling primarily local students. Southern universities, in both their curricula and their student populations, came more closely to resemble Northern ones.

Meanwhile, as the federal government expanded during and after the Civil War, it began to play a larger role in higher education. The Morrill Act of 1862 provided indirect federal funding for colleges teaching agriculture and mechanics. Because of the wartime context, Congress required that funded colleges also teach military tactics. After the war, Congress voted to assign army officers to civilian colleges to drill and teach their students. Colleges readily accepted the offer, partnering with the government to add a new component to the college curriculum. Some colleges and state governments also offered a free education to war veterans, especially injured ones, and to the orphans of men who had died in the war.

Federal involvement in education culminated in the creation of the Department (later Bureau) of Education in 1867. The government began to collect information from colleges, schools, and other educational institutions to prepare and disseminate an ongoing statistical portrait of education in the United States. In 1876 the federal government and individual colleges worked together to display the condition of, and recent developments in, higher education to a national audience at the Centen-

CONCLUSION

nial Exposition in Philadelphia. There Americans outside college communities learned about many of the reforms in curricula, admissions, and government involvement that had transpired over the past fifteen years. They learned how different higher education was from before the Civil War.

The story of higher education in the 1860s and 1870s exemplifies the profound impact the Civil War had on American life. That impact went well beyond military, political, and economic developments to include a variety of changes in cultural institutions that had little obvious connection with battles. In important ways the Civil War created modern America, including modern higher education. Civil War–era impulses toward nationalization, democratization, equality of opportunity, civil rights, and organization all affected colleges. The expansion of the federal government and physical damage and political restructuring in the South dramatically affected their goals, activities, and constituencies. Although limited reforms had begun before 1860, the events of the war and Reconstruction years accelerated some changes, initiated or reversed others, and spread still others to new locations. By forging closer relationships between colleges and governments and local communities and by inducing colleges to serve the needs of more people in more ways, these events gave colleges a more important role in American life. The Civil War was a watershed for higher education.

This story also reveals the longevity of the war's effects. Historians sometimes question whether the war's impact outlasted Reconstruction. They point out, most importantly, that Redemption governments sharply curtailed the rights of Southern blacks and that Congress and the courts contracted some parts of the newly expanded federal government as the nineteenth century progressed. The end of civil rights directly affected colleges, including the de-integrated South Carolina College. As during the war and Reconstruction, colleges continued in the 1880s and thereafter to adapt to serve and survive in a constantly evolving nation. Some of the most radical reforms, such as integration, could not survive once the social and political atmosphere that had enabled them disappeared.

But most of the changes to higher education that grew out of the Civil War era lasted well beyond 1877. Comprehensive universities became an important component of American higher education through the nineteenth and twentieth centuries. Following the example of Robert E. Lee, who had become president of Washington College in 1865, many former Confederate officers accepted positions as college presidents or faculty chairs after Reconstruction. These men, who had witnessed firsthand the Confederacy's industrial inferiority and inability to supply its soldiers, determined to build an industrialized New South by expanding scientific and practical courses in their institutions. Under their leadership, several state universities and land-grant colleges followed the path that the Universities of South Carolina and Missouri had taken during Reconstruction. These veterans' students, who became the next generation of Southern university leaders at the turn of the century, continued to expand vocational programs and to win state funding for public universities. The Second Morrill Act of 1890 provided additional federal funding that helped to put those and other universities on a firm financial footing.[1]

Meanwhile, the agrarian populist movement of the 1880s and 1890s pressed state governments both for agricultural colleges and for outreach through experiment stations and extension courses. Though some populists distrusted so-called expert academics, organizations such as the Grange, the Farmers' Alliance, and the Farmers' Association in South Carolina demanded that states promote the educational and economic interests of farmers. The Farmers' Association, for example, under the leadership of Governor Ben Tillman, successfully lobbied South Carolina's legislature to establish an experiment station in 1886. Fearing that South Carolina College was providing insufficient practical training, Tillman also called for the establishment of another free agricultural college; it opened in 1893 as Clemson Agricultural College. By 1887 at least fourteen states had publicly funded experiment stations. After Congress provided federal money for them through the Hatch Act of that year, those multiplied and expanded.[2] The Southern university leaders who were augmenting vocational curricular offerings also fought for the creation of experiment stations, extension courses, public lectures, and museums.[3] Through the establishment of modern state universities and of outreach programs, educational institutions and the public built new connections with each other.

Colleges also continued to open admissions. The temptation to focus on Reconstruction's short-lived racial consequences, to the exclusion of others, can obscure the important and more durable reforms it brought to class and gendered opportunities. The availability of higher education to lower-class Americans increased in an era of populist political involvement. Women's higher education, especially in coeducational colleges, continued to expand. And though racially mixed education did not fare well, after 1890 many states did fund separate black colleges to comply

CONCLUSION

with the equal-support clause of the Second Morrill Act.[4] War veterans, of course, did not remain a major part of student populations during the thirty-three years of official peace that followed the Civil War. But free college for veterans resumed after twentieth-century wars, eventually at the expense of the federal government. Student populations also continued to become more local. Partly owing to the expansion of urban comprehensive universities, about eight in ten students attended college in their home states after World War I, a further increase over the seven in ten during Reconstruction.[5]

Popular imagery of higher education continued to spread. After studying colleges at the Centennial Exposition, Americans started to form a common romantic image of a college. Not surprisingly, the northeastern schools that had come in such large numbers to the exposition played a disproportionate role in shaping that image. By the turn of the century it had evolved into one of ivy, gothic architecture, and football. Colleges' new visibility and in particular their positive, prestigious image combined with other factors to prompt more Americans to seek a college education.[6]

The federal government continued to play an active role in higher education through the Hatch Act, the Second Morrill Act, and the Bureau of Education. The bureau expanded its activities, adding a monograph series on the history of education to its annual reports and supplementary statistics. After the Second Morrill Act, Congress created a new clerkship in the bureau to handle the reports that law required of land-grant colleges. The holder of this post was the first federal officer charged exclusively with activities related to higher education.[7] Policymakers knew that many Americans still distrusted federal intrusion into state and local matters, so they placed limits on federal educational power: the Second Morrill Act permitted racial segregation, and the Bureau of Education remained powerless to regulate. But the trend in the 1880s and 1890s, as in the 1860s and 1870s, was toward a greater federal role.

The link between civil higher education and military service strengthened after Reconstruction. The former Confederate officers whom many Southern colleges now hired to lead them promoted military training on campus. Amid an increasingly militarized national culture, Congress in the 1880s and 1890s expanded the officer-professor program to provide military instructors to more colleges. In 1916, just before the United States entered World War I, the National Defense Act gave that program a new form and a new name: the Reserve Officers' Training Corps (ROTC). Now students who elected for a military education alongside their civil studies received commissions upon graduation and joined the newly formed Officers' Reserve Corps (ORC). The army could call upon the ORC in times of military need. One hundred ninety-one colleges had organized ROTC units by June 1919; more than one hundred thousand men passed through the program between the world wars.[8] The Civil War had shown policymakers the need to prepare young men for a military emergency, and they had turned to civilian colleges to do so. By the middle of the twentieth century this nationwide partnership was training scholar-soldiers on a grand scale. Comprehensive universities, outreach programs, practical curricula, affordable institutions, diverse students, popular attention, government involvement, and military training all had begun owing to the war but continued long afterward. Higher education in the late nineteenth century and beyond was in all these ways largely a product of the Civil War.

A look at wars of the twentieth century suggests some general conclusions about the effects of modern wars on higher education in America. Both world wars have received more thorough attention by historians of education than the Civil War. That scholarship suggests interesting parallels with the nineteenth-century conflict. All three wars pulled college communities into wartime service to the state, in some aspects willingly and in others without a choice. All three precipitated the diversification and, to a much greater extent in the twentieth century, growth of college student populations. All three ended with the enrollment of veteran students drawing on government financial aid. And all three sparked an integration of civil and military education.

Students and professors reacted to World War I with the same initial mixed opinions and eventual unity as in the Civil War. Before 1917 campus opinion was divided but vocal. Most faculty members who commented on the matter viewed it as a simple one of right and wrong: America should join the Allies. Many students, on the other hand, participated in peace demonstrations. Once Germany began attacking American ships, though, campus opinion united along with the rest of the nation in a loud call for war. Over the next eighteen months, as in the Civil War, colleges served the needs of the state. Later historians have criticized professors for sacrificing objectivity and academic freedom to state service. Historians during the war, for example, prepared publications for the Committee on Public Information and designed new high-school curricula for

CONCLUSION

the Bureau of Education. Like some of their predecessors in the 1860s, these professors sought through their work for the government to intensify popular support for the war. Colleges also fired a number of professors owing to suspicions of a lack of patriotism arising from their German birth or ancestry or from their unpopular opinions about the war.

Finally, in 1918, the War Department announced the government's greatest intrusion ever into civilian colleges. Owing to the need for soldiers, the military took over most colleges and drafted their male students. Officers arrived at every college that enrolled at least one hundred men over eighteen to teach military lessons. All male students were to head off to war within a year. The policy took effect at 516 colleges on October 1. Had the war not ended a month later, the military soon would have drained those colleges. This policy went far beyond the various campus takeovers and the state and national drafts during the Civil War. And though the armistice limited its effect, military education continued at colleges in the form of the ROTC. Three hundred eighty-two colleges taught military science by 1930; 197 of those required it of male students.[9] As in the 1860s and 1870s, wartime government takeovers gave way to government-sponsored military training.

World War I, like the Civil War, also brought new students to college. College leaders and government officials again drew explicit connections between higher education and concrete national needs. After the Civil War, Americans had begun to see higher education as useful to specific vocations, such as engineering, agriculture, and teaching. Now they increasingly came to see a bachelor's degree in the natural or social sciences as a useful qualification for work in business or government. Employers, like wartime bureaucrats, viewed college men and women as experts, regardless of the extent of their work experience. For the first time most Americans attached a practical value to higher education. Wisconsin, meanwhile, helped veterans obtain that education by waiving their tuition at the state university. The economic value of a degree and Wisconsin's program, along with the increasingly positive popular image of a college, attracted young people. Even more than in the 1860s and 1870s, the size and diversity of America's college-going population increased during and after World War I. Institutions expanded and multiplied to keep up.[10]

It all happened again in the 1940s. As Europe entered another great war, American students and professors divided into isolationist and interventionist camps. Students, in particular, developed a vocal antiwar movement. But after Japan bombed Pearl Harbor on December 7, 1941, campuses closed ranks to call for retaliation against Japan and the defeat of fascism. Debate gave way to patriotic support for the war.[11] Under the nation's third draft, college students and alumni served in large numbers.

As in the Civil War and World War I, new policies during World War II brought colleges and the federal government into a closer relationship. The government organized what one historian has labeled "a military-educational network." During the war, the War Department developed educational programs for the soldiers in Europe and Asia. Officials believed that these programs, which included literacy training and college-level correspondence courses, would improve soldiers' psychological adjustment and thereby make them more effective combatants. Officials also believed that the educational programs, which incorporated pro-American propaganda and included professional training, would instill democratic values and shore up enthusiasm for the war. As the war ended, the army set up Post-Hostility Schools in Europe and Asia to help soldiers readjust to civilian life. Soldiers studied agriculture, business, education, and other subjects under teachers who included many professors from American colleges.[12]

Having experienced college-level education while in Europe and Asia, millions of soldiers began to see higher education as an important part of American citizenship. Congress aimed to satisfy their desire for college with the GI Bill of Rights. Like a few states in the 1860s and 1910s, the federal government now funded up to four years of education for any veteran with ninety days of continuous service and an honorable discharge. Half of all veterans—7.8 million men and women—took advantage of the bill's educational provisions, including 2.2 million at the college or university level. During the 1947–48 academic year nearly half of all college students in the United States were veterans. Many institutions continued to exclude African Americans, but black veterans nonetheless took advantage of the GI Bill, often at historically black colleges and universities. Between 1940 and 1950 the proportion of blacks among American college students more than tripled.[13]

The GI Bill combined with the expansion of secondary education and the increased value of a college degree as a job qualification to facilitate a vast expansion in the college-going population after World War II. In 1949 America's colleges enrolled 2.5 million students, one million more than at any time before the war. Schools and the mass media started encouraging parents to send their children to college. Higher education became typical, an expected part of life for most Americans, rather than a privilege for very few.[14] As in the 1860s and the 1910s, a war had forged a stronger relationship between colleges and the government, a relationship that made college accessible to and desirable for new groups of Americans.

These parallels among the Civil War, World War I, and World War II reveal much about the impact of modern wars generally on higher education. But the comparison with twentieth-century wars also highlights what was unique about the Civil War. Unlike any war since, it sparked the formation of a major new type of institution, the Southern comprehensive university. It also stood out by marking the *first* major tightening of college-government relations and, in the South, the *first* major increase in the accessibility of higher education. The location of the conflict on American soil and the reconstruction of the Southern polity and society afterward helped to produce this unique impact. So did the timing of the war during a transformation of higher education in the North. The war brought that transformation to the South. More than any other conflict, the Civil War reshaped not only American politics but also some of the nation's most important social relationships and cultural institutions.

The very challenges the war posed to institutions' survival forced them to make changes that in retrospect we may describe as modernization. This story reminds us of a lesson that historians have recognized for antebellum colleges but less often have applied to the postbellum period: one of the defining features of higher education in the nineteenth century was its fragility. Colleges' survival was not guaranteed in the most prosperous and peaceful of times. It was yet more imperiled amid war or the economic uncertainty that followed the war in the South. The need to survive drove the decisions of professors, trustees, and state legislators. Amid colleges' dearth of students, the financial woes of Southern planters, the physical remnants of battles, and the federal government's new attention to educational matters, those policymakers reconstructed the college campus to serve new constituents and new educational purposes. These, they believed, promised the best chance of survival in postbellum America. As a result, they created practical curricula, military courses, comprehensive universities, diverse student populations, financial-aid programs, government partnerships, and outreach initiatives—features that became emblematic of American higher education in the twentieth century.

Notes

Abbreviations

BL	Bancroft Library, University of California, Berkeley
CCA	Cornell College Archives
DML	Charles Franklin Doe Memorial Library, University of California, Berkeley
GL	Monroe C. Gutman Library, Harvard Graduate School of Education
HUA	Harvard University Archives
MHCA	Mount Holyoke College Archives
PMFA	Phi Mu Fraternity Archives
SCL	South Caroliniana Library, University of South Carolina
UCA	University of California Archives
UMA	University of Missouri Archives
UMSC	University of Missouri Special Collections
USCA	University of South Carolina Archives
WCA	Wesleyan College Archives
WHMC	Western Historical Manuscript Collection, University of Missouri, Columbia
WML	Harry Elkins Widener Memorial Library, Harvard College

Introduction

1. Margaret Mitchell's book tells us that Scarlett attended a female academy but makes no mention of colleges for women. Mitchell, *Gone with the Wind*, 4.

2. Harriman, "Bachelor's Degree," 301–2; Stout, "University Men," 377, 394–400; Gummere, "Colonial Reactions," 55–59, 63–67, 71–72; Herbst, *From Crisis to Crisis*, 1–2; Robson, *Educating Republicans*, 7, 12; Hoeveler, *American Mind*, 32, 54; Herbst, "Professional Education," 139.

3. Burke, *Collegiate Populations*, 54.

4. Trow, "Comparative Perspectives," 280.

5. Rothblatt and Trow, "Government Policies," 174–87; Trow, "In Praise of Weakness," 10–14, 16–20; Roche, *Colonial Colleges*, chaps. 2–7, esp. 165–71; Hoeveler, *American Mind*, chaps. 10–11; Herbst, *From Crisis to Crisis*, 144–48, 204–5, 237–43; Robson, *Educating Republicans*, 143, 227–51. John S. Whitehead argues that state control continued through the antebellum years, though state patronage ceased. Whitehead, *Separation of College and State*, esp. 88 and chap. 3.

6. Trow, "In Praise of Weakness," 13–16; Curti and Nash, *Philanthropy*, 46–47, 50–52; Boorstin, *Americans*, chap. 20; Rudolph, *American College and University*, 53–57; Blodgett, "Finney's Oberlin," 41–44.

7. Heywood, *Cornell College*, 13–23, 29–30.

8. Edu. B. Walsworth and J. A. Benton, extract from records of Presbytery of San Francisco and Congregational Association of California, 10–12 May 1853, Documents of the College of California, folder 7f, UCA; Samuel H. Willey, *Farewell Discourse Delivered in the Howard Street Presbyterian Church, on Sabbath Morning, April 27th, 1862* (San Francisco: Towne & Bacon, 1862), 16–19, in *California Miscellany*, BL.

9. Burke, *Collegiate Populations*, 25.

10. Thelin, *Higher Education*, 42, 79; Malkmus, "Small Towns," 34–35; Ogren, *State Normal School*, 1–2; Herbst, "Professional Education," 139–40.

11. Rothblatt and Trow, "Government Policies," 181–83; U.S. Department of the Interior, *Statistics*, 509.

12. Rudy, *Building America's Schools and Colleges*, 16–17; Hollis, *University of South Carolina*, 1:22; Stephens, *University of Missouri*, 4, 13–14, 23–24; Burke, *Collegiate Populations*, 299–318.

13. Michigan, in 1838, gave its new state university $100,000 in the form of a loan rather than a gift. Geiger, "Introduction," 19–20; Peckham, *University of Michigan*, 20.

14. This figure, from the national census, may exaggerate the number of colleges. Other pages of the same census report give slightly lower figures. The historian Colin B. Burke's finding of 241 colleges founded between 1800 and 1860, while probably incomplete, suggests that the actual total lay somewhere in between. By 1870 the federal Bureau of Education had identified 369 colleges. U.S. Department of the Interior, *Statistics*, 505, xiv, 503; Burke, *Collegiate Populations*, 14; U.S. Bureau of Education, report, 1870, 506–17.

15. *American Almanac*, 232–35.

16. Calculating the proportion of Americans who attended college is extraordinarily difficult. The federal government tabulated little data before 1870 and imperfect data thereafter. The figure 1% is an average of Burke's estimate for men in 1860 (1.33%) and Barbara Miller Solomon's estimate for women in 1870 (0.7%). It probably excludes students who attended only colleges' primary or preparatory departments. Burke, *Collegiate Populations*, 55; Solomon, *Educated Women*, 64.

17. Gummere, "Colonial Reactions," 59.

18. Ogren, *State Normal School*, 16–25; Kaestle, *Pillars of the Republic*, 127–31;

Allmendinger, *Paupers and Scholars*, chap. 1; Geiger, "Introduction," 20–21; Burke, *Collegiate Populations*, 119, 124–26; Glover, *Southern Sons*, 55–57; Wagoner, "Honor and Dishonor," 167–68, 170; Wakelyn, "Antebellum College Life," 109–10, 112; Sugrue, "'We Desired Our Future Rulers,'" 92.

19. Fletcher, *History of Oberlin*, 1:169–78, 120, 375–77, 2:524–36; Malkmus, "Small Towns," 39; McGinnis, *Wilberforce University*, 36, 39; Gems, Borish, and Pfister, *Sports in American History*, 123; Cornelius, "When I Can Read," 18, 32–34, 37–42; Sears, *Kentucky Abolitionists*, chaps. 5–6; Peck, *Berea's First 125 Years*, 12–19; Sugrue, "'We Desired Our Future Rulers,'" 97; E. Smith, *From Whence Cometh My Help*, 11–12; Schwalbe, *Remembering Reet and Shine*, 18; Moss, *Schooling Citizens*, chap. 2.

20. Malkmus, "Small Towns," 33–39; Bishop, *History of Cornell*, 55; Geiger, "'Superior Instruction of Women,'" 183, 187–88; Farnham, *Southern Belle*, 3–4, 11–12, 72; Akers, *Wesleyan College*, 10–11, 45; Rable, *Civil Wars*, 18–22; Heywood, *Cornell College*, 23.

21. Nash, *Women's Education*, 5–7; U.S. Department of the Interior, *Mount Holyoke*, 10, WML; Nash, "'Salutary Rivalry,'" 169–70; *Catalogues of the College of California and of the Seminary for Young Ladies*, 20, 24, 2, 19, Andover-Harvard Theological Library, Harvard Divinity School.

22. Kaestle, *Pillars of the Republic*, 120–21, 193; Trow, "Comparative Perspectives," 288; Tyack and Hansot, *Learning Together*, 121–22.

23. Rudolph, *American College and University*, 281–82; catalogue of Cornell College, 1858–59, 1860–66, CCA; J. W. Lathrop, B. McAlester, and Henry Sheeny, commission report, 16 Feb. 1863, 1–2, Civil War Damage by Federal Troops Folder, UMA.

24. Rudolph, *Curriculum*, 54–85; Farnham, *Southern Belle*, 68–74, 92–93; Kelley, *Learning to Stand and Speak*, 28, 37, 39; Nash, *Women's Education*, 82–87; Nash, "'Salutary Rivalry,'" 177–78; U.S. Department of the Interior, *Mount Holyoke*, 14–15; catalogue of Wesleyan Female College, 1860–61, 27, in [Bass], *Catalogues. Wesleyan Female College, 1848 to 1881*, WCA; Burke, *Collegiate Populations*, 70–71. For the small number of seniors relative to freshmen, see also the antebellum catalogues for all colleges in this study.

25. Herbst, "Professional Education," 139–40; Pace, *Halls of Honor*, 12–13.

26. Pangle and Pangle, *Learning of Liberty*, 166–67, 159–61; Wagoner, *Jefferson and Education*, 130, 137–39; Frost, *Thinking Confederates*, 20–21.

27. *The Substance of Two Reports of the Faculty of Amherst College to the Board of Trustees, with the doings of the Board Thereon* (Amherst, MA: Carter & Adams, 1827), quoted in Guralnick, *Science*, 27 (quotation); Rudolph, *American College and University*, 123–24.

28. Pak, "Yale Report of 1828," 30, 34–35, 45–47; Guralnick, *Science*, 29–33; Rudolph, *American College and University*, 130–35, Yale Report quoted on 132.

29. Herbst, "Professional Education," 139–40; Geiger, "Useful Knowledge," 155, 158–59.

30. Curti, "American Scholar," 257–58, 250–51, 256 (quotation).

31. This figure excludes 134 commercial or business colleges. U.S. Bureau of Education, report, 1877, pt. 1, 487–543, 366–75.

32. Emerson, *Journals*, 194.

33. On the continuities between antebellum and postbellum reform, see Geiger, "Multipurpose Colleges," 128; Guralnick, *Science*, 150–51; and Thelin, *Higher Education*, 82, 87–88. On the Morrill Land-Grant College Act of 1862 as a break with the past, see Eddy, *Colleges*, chap. 2, esp. 44–45; Nevins, *State Universities*, 22, 136; Edmond, *Magnificent Charter*, chap. 2; and Cross, *Justin Smith Morrill*, 77, 87–89. On the Morrill Act as less than a major break, see Ross, *Democracy's College*, 46, 66–67. On the origins of the research university, see chapter 2.

34. Rudy, *Campus*, chap. 2; Pace, *Halls of Honor*, chap. 5; Stetar, "In Search of a Direction"; Thelin, *Higher Education*, 74–75; Trow, "Elite to Mass to Universal Access," 270. Dan R. Frost discusses the war's impact on the educational philosophy of Confederate officers who became university leaders after Reconstruction. Other studies of colleges and the war focus on a single state or institution and do not explore in depth the long-term consequences of the war or the connections between the war and educational reform. See Frost, *Thinking Confederates*; Chessman, *Ohio Colleges*; Dunbar, *Michigan Institutions*; and Jordan, *Charlottesville*. Several books chronicle the war experiences of student enlistees. See Eliot, *West Point*; Waugh, *Class of 1846*; Lubetkin, *Union College's Class of 1868*; Conrad, *Young Lions*; Poirier, "By the Blood of Our Alumni"; Floyd and Gibson, *Boys Who Went to War*; Miller, *Harvard's Civil War*; Schmidt, *Notre Dame*; and Trimpi, *Crimson Confederates*.

35. See Handlin and Handlin, *American College and American Culture*, 65; and Horowitz, *Campus Life*, 49.

36. Veysey, *American University*, 21, 9; Rudolph, *American College and University*, 241–47; C. Lucas, *American Higher Education*, 147–48, quotation from 148.

37. George Ticknor to George T. Curtis, 30 July 1869, in Ticknor, *Life, Letters, and Journals*, 485.

38. For several perspectives on emancipation, the first two emphasizing Reconstruction's revolutionary but impermanent nature and the latter two emphasizing its resilient impact, see McPherson, *Battle Cry of Freedom*; Foner, *Reconstruction*; Hahn, *Nation under Our Feet*; and Ranney, *In the Wake of Slavery*. On nationalism and federal expansion, see chapters 4 and 5. On equal opportunity, free labor, and democracy, see Burton, *Age of Lincoln*, 8, 84, 219–20; Calhoun, *Conceiving a New Republic*, 53; and Schild, "'War Upon the First Principle,'" 54–55, 57–59, 67.

39. Nelson and Sheriff, *People at War*, 105–6.

40. See Rable, *Civil Wars*; Bynam, *Unruly Women*; Whites, *Civil War*; Faust, *Mothers of Invention*; and Silber, *Daughters of the Union*.

41. See Fredrickson, *Inner Civil War*; Gallman, *North Fights the Civil War*; and Mobley, *Weary of War*. Studies of Southern communities and regions and of guerrilla warfare have helped break down the somewhat artificial barrier between the home and war fronts. See B. Wills, *War Hits Home*; Sarris, *Separate Civil War*; and Sutherland, *Savage Conflict*.

42. Gallman, *North Fights the Civil War*, 91, 194; Gallagher, *Confederate War*, 55.

43. Beckert, *Monied Metropolis*, esp. pt. 2; Wells, *Civil War Time*. On reading, see Zboray and Zboray, "Cannonballs and Books." On families, see Taylor, *Divided*

Family; Sheehan-Dean, *Why Confederates Fought*; McClurken, *Take Care of the Living*; and Morsman, *Big House after Slavery*. On children and black schooling, see Marten, *Children's Civil War*; Marten, *Children for the Union*; Bardaglio, "On the Border"; Drago, *Confederate Phoenix*; and Butchart, *Schooling the Freed People*. On religion, see Miller, Stout, and Wilson, *Religion*; Noll, *Civil War*; and Rable, *God's Almost Chosen Peoples*. On machine politics, see Einhorn, "Civil War"; and Bernstein, *Draft Riots*. For broader discussions of the Civil War's impact on civilian life, see Joan E. Cashin, editor's introduction to *War Was You and Me*; and Nelson and Sheriff, *People at War*, esp. introduction and chaps. 11–12.

44. Trow, "In Praise of Weakness"; Malkmus, "Small Towns"; Curti and Nash, *Philanthropy*, chap. 3.

45. I do not include military academies, which obviously had a unique relationship with the war. Because hardly any historically black colleges existed before the Civil War, I cannot trace the war's effect on them. The emancipation of black slaves made their postbellum foundings possible.

46. For consistency when presenting regional statistics, I classify states according to their slave status at the beginning of the war. I include West Virginia and the District of Columbia, for example, in the South.

ONE. Dwellers beside the Sea

1. Banks, *Memories*, 1–2, 26, 29–31, 36, 41–42.

2. Anna C. Edwards, "War Time at Mt. Holyoke," MS, prepared for a meeting of the Mount Holyoke Alumnae of Hampshire County, Amherst, MA, 1908, 2–5, quotation from 2, Civil War Folder, MHCA.

3. Ellen C. Parsons, "Mount Holyoke in War Time. Tense Days of Student Life. Recollections of a Graduate," photocopy of clipping from *Springfield (MA) Sunday Republican*, 6 Oct. 1912, Civil War Folder, MHCA; Wooley and Peters, "Election of 1860"; U.S. Department of the Interior, *Mount Holyoke*, 23–24, WML; [Kathleen M. (Carruth) Phipps], "The Mount Holyoke of the Sixties," TS, [1927], 3, Kathleen M. Carruth Papers, MHCA; Mrs. Douglass, "Looking Backward," *Mount Holyoke Alumnae Quarterly*, Jan. 1927, 197, photocopy, Mary A. Lawrence Papers, MHCA; MS, article copied from "Summary of the Public Intelligence," *North American*, 17 Nov. 1860, Henrietta M. Woodford Papers, folder 2, MHCA.

4. E. Parsons, "Mount Holyoke in War Time"; Edwards, "War Time at Mt. Holyoke," 3, 14–15, quotation from 15.

5. Glover, *Southern Sons*, 51–56, 58. Catalogue of South Carolina College, 1861, 12–16, Catalogue of Trustees, Faculty and Students Collection; Clariosophic Literary Society Records, minutes, vol. 18, 10 Nov. 1860 (quotation); and faculty minutes of South Carolina College, vol. 7, 11 Feb. 1861, all in USCA.

6. O. P. Fitzgerald, *Judge Longstreet*, 73, 107–8, SCL; Sugrue, "'We Desired Our Future Rulers,'" 104–14; Frost, *Thinking Confederates*, 20 (quotation), 127n10.

7. See McLachlan, "Choice of Hercules"; and Thomas S. Harding, *College Literary Societies*.

8. Thomas S. Harding, *College Literary Societies*, chaps. 8, 10, 12; Clariosophic Literary Society Records, minutes, vol. 18, 9 Mar. 1861; Euphradian Literary Society Records, minutes, vol. 9, 20 Oct. 1860, USCA. The Clariosophic Literary Society did debate one question explicitly about the Confederacy in February 1861, but a careless secretary omitted the key word from the minutes: "Will the establishment of be beneficial to the Southern Confederacy?" Clariosophic Literary Society Records, minutes, vol. 18, 23 Feb. 1861.

9. H. H. Rood, "Effect of the Civil war upon the College," MS of speech, [1880s], 2, William Fletcher King Papers, Speeches Folder, CCA. Catalogue of Cornell College, 1860–61, 7–20, CCA. Amphictyon Society minutes, 27 Apr. 1860, 25 Jan., 5 Apr. 1861, CCA (quotations); see also entries for 1 Mar. and 8 May 1861. Cornell's Philomathean Society for women never formally discussed sectional issues before mid-November 1860, and no minutes between then and December 1864 have survived. Philomathean Society minutes, 1857–60, CCA.

10. University of Virginia Library Geospatial and Statistical Data Center, "Historical Census Browser"; McPherson, *Battle Cry of Freedom*, 290–93.

11. Athenaean Literary Society Papers, 6 Apr., 17, 24 Nov. 1860, 11 Jan. 1861, quotations from the latter two dates, WHMC.

12. Ibid., 19 Apr., 13 Dec. 1861 (quotation).

13. Editors' Table, *Harvard Magazine*, Apr. 1861, 279–80, WML.

14. Edwards, "War Time at Mt. Holyoke," 9, 3–5.

15. Hewlett, letter to the editor.

16. Faust, *Sacred Circle*, esp. chaps. 5–6.

17. Longstreet, *Shall South Carolina Begin the War?*, 1–3, quotations from 1, SCL.

18. Ibid., 1–4, emphasis in original.

19. Ibid., 1.

20. *Annual Concert. Wesleyan Female College. Tuesday Evening, July 9th, 1861* ([Macon, GA]: Journal & Messenger, [1861]), in *Catalogues, Wesleyan Female College, 1842 to 1867*, WCA; "The Danger of Delay," *Philomathean Gazette*, [1861], 38, PMFA; Stephens, *University of Missouri*, 190n31, 153.

21. C. Sigourney Knox, "Columbia College," 117–18, 121–22; E. Owen Simpson, "Kenyon College," 130; J. Watson Coxe, "Troy University," 151; and Forrest F. Emerson, "Brown University," 111 (quotation), all in *University Quarterly*, July 1861, WML. F. W. Bailey, "Dartmouth College," ibid., Oct. 1861, 294.

22. [A. Stetson], Editors' Table, *Harvard Magazine*, May 1861, 316–18, quotations from 316, 317.

23. [E. W.] McC[abe], Editors' Table, ibid., June 1861, 358–60. See also A. Stetson, Editors' Table, ibid., July 1861, 363–64.

24. Jas. B. Hedge to A. A. Bauman, 7 Apr. 1924, Wartime Cornell Box, Civil War Folder, CCA; Rood, "Effect of the Civil war," 3.

25. California contributed 15,725 volunteers to the Union forces. Masich, *Civil War in Arizona*, 10.

26. Martin Kellogg, "Report of Progress for the 2nd Term, 1861–2," report no. 6, adopted 26 May 1862, [2–3], Reports of the College of California, 1858–66, UCA;

catalogue of the College of California, 1861–62, 4–5, and 1862–63, 5–7, in *Pamphlets on the College of California*, UCA.

27. See, in *University Quarterly*, July 1861, Emerson, "Brown University," 110–11; Knox, "Columbia College," 116–17; Wm. C. Winslow, "Hamilton College," 123; Simpson, "Kenyon College," 129; J. E. Pierce, "Middlebury College," 141; Henry E. Alvord, "Norwich University," 143; J. H. Laird, "Oberlin College," 148; Coxe, "Troy University," 151; George F. Mills, "Williams College," 159; and "Yale College," 163. In ibid., Oct. 1861, see Bailey, "Dartmouth College," 295; H. L. Curtiss, "Kenyon College," 305; William H. Fleek, "Marietta College," 310; and Henry P. Boyden, "Yale College," 320. And see also Lubetkin, *Union College's Class of 1868*, 70.

28. [Stetson], Editors' Table, 316–18; White, *Oliver Wendell Holmes, Jr.*, 11–12, 15–16.

29. Annual report of the president of Harvard College, 1860–61, 3–4, HUA; Lincoln, diary, esp. 27 Apr. and 1 May 1861, HUA; [Stetson], Editors' Table, 318–19, quotation from 319; faculty records of Harvard University, vol. 16, 22, 29 Apr., 6 May 1861, HUA; Bixby et al., record of students desiring military instruction, HUA; Harvard Corporation formal minutes, vol. 10, 27 Apr. 1861, HUA.

30. Morison, *Three Centuries of Harvard*, 303n. F. Brown, *Harvard Students*. F. Brown, "Harvard University," WML. Trimpi, *Crimson Confederates*, 375, 379. Catalogue of Harvard University, 1st terms, 1860–61, 104; 1861–62, 83–88; 1862–63, 98; 1863–64, 81–87, WML.

31. Rood, "Effect of the Civil war," 4a–4b, quotation from 4a; King, *Reminiscences*, 209–10.

32. "Report of the Trustees of Cornell College to the Upper Iowa Annual Conference," MS, [1862], 3, 1 (quotation), William Fletcher King Papers, Upper Iowa M. E. Conference Folder, CCA.

33. Including the primary department does not change the majority gender. Catalogue of Cornell College, 1860–61, 7–20; 1861–62, 6–16; 1862–63, 5–13; 1863–64, 5–20; 1864–65, 5–20; 1865–66, 5–21. In a later speech or paper, a student from this time gave slightly different enrollment numbers for the war years, but his numbers show the same patterns. Rood, "Effect of the Civil war," 5.

34. Pace, *Halls of Honor*, 113; Rudy, *Campus*, 70.

35. King, *Reminiscences*, 213–14; "Recollections of Olive Burr Fellows [and Alice Fellows Rigby]," ca. 1897, TS prepared by Alice Rigby Moore, 30 Apr. 1950, 33, Samuel Fellows Box, CCA; Foster, "Early Recollections of Cornell College," 88, CCA (quotation).

36. Catalogue of Cornell College, 1862–63, 11–12; 1863–64, 18–20; 1864–65, 18–20. The preparatory department also included many older males who did enlist. Rood, "Effect of the Civil war," 4b–6.

37. Tulloch, *Debate*, 157; Farnham, *Southern Belle*, 18–19.

38. Faculty minutes of South Carolina College, vol. 7, 4 Mar. 1861; Iredell Jones, memoir, quoted in Matalene and Reynolds, *Carolina Voices*, 38.

39. A. B. Longstreet, "President Longstreet's Report," [May 1861], and M. LaBorde, "Dr. LaBorde's Report," in trustees minutes of South Carolina College,

vol. 7, 27 Nov. 1861 and 7 May 1862, USCA; faculty minutes of South Carolina College, vol. 7, 7 Oct. 1861. See also Robert Armstrong Harllee to parents, 9 Apr.–18 May 1861, in Matalene and Reynolds, *Carolina Voices*, 38–40.

40. A. B. Longstreet, "President Longstreet's Report," [Nov. 1861], and Longstreet to Gov. Pickens, 11 Nov. 1861, in trustees minutes of South Carolina College, vol. 7, 27 Nov. 1861; LaBorde, "Dr. LaBorde's Report"; A. B. Longstreet to trustees of the South Carolina College, May 1861, Augustus Baldwin Longstreet Papers, folder 2, SCL; student petition and memorandum from Maximilian LaBorde, in Matalene and Reynolds, *Carolina Voices*, 40–41; catalogue of South Carolina College, 1861, 16, and 1862, 6.

41. Rudy, *Campus*, 171, 86–87, 67–69; Pace, *Halls of Honor*, 103–4; Eliot, *Yale*, 16, 20; Geary, *We Need Men*, 3–5, 49, 52, 66–67; Jordan, *Charlottesville*, 75–76; Battle, *University of North Carolina*, 732–35.

42. LaBorde, "Dr. LaBorde's Report"; M. La Borde, "Report of Dr. M. La Borde," in trustees minutes of South Carolina College, vol. 7, 26 Nov. 1862.

43. "Recollections of Olive Burr Fellows," 26; Rood, "Effect of the Civil war," 5.

44. E. Parsons, "Mount Holyoke in War Time"; Edwards, "War Time at Mt. Holyoke," 13, 17 (quotation). See also Douglass, "Looking Backward," 197–98.

45. Stephens, *University of Missouri*, 150. *Oration, Poem, and Speeches*, 34, WML. "Amherst College," 369; Frank J. Dingley, "Bowdoin College," 376; and H. S. Smith, "Trinity College," 427, all in *University Quarterly*, Apr. 1861. Emerson, "Brown University," 110; Winslow, "Hamilton College," 123; Simpson, "Kenyon College," 129–30; Pierce, "Middlebury College," 141; Laird, "Oberlin College," 148, 150; Coxe, "Troy University," 154; John Butler, "Union College," 157–58; Mills, "Williams College," 159–60; and "Yale College," 163–64, all in ibid., July 1861. Frederic N. Huston, "Bowdoin College," 288; Bailey, "Dartmouth College," 294; Fleek, "Marietta College," 310; and Boyden, "Yale College," all in ibid., Oct. 1861.

46. Rudy, *Campus*, 88–89; Pace, *Halls of Honor*, 104–6; Chessman, *Ohio Colleges*, 16–17.

47. Banks, *Memories*, 32–34, 37.

48. Hall, *Women*, 7–8, 11, 225–73, 54–55, 59; Faust, *Mothers of Invention*, 202–4; Leonard, *All the Daring*, 199–200, 310n2, 238–41, 260–63, 266–72.

49. Banks, *Memories*, 33–34, 36–37, quotations from 34, 37.

50. Andrea G. Radke-Moss makes this argument for noncollegiate women's militarism during the war and students' drilling later in the century in *Bright Epoch*, 224–25.

51. *Soldiers' Concert! In the Chapel of the Wesleyan Female College, On Friday Evening, July 5th, 1861, A Select Choir of Fifty Singers, from the Various College Singing Classes, Will perform the beautiful Operetta, The Flower Queen! For the Benefit of the Soldiers Aid Society of Macon* ([Macon, GA]: Telegraph, [1861]), in *Catalogues, Wesleyan Female College, 1842 to 1867*; Frances Peabody, "These Many Years (The Bellamy Collection of Catalogues)," *Wesleyan Alumnae*, Oct. 1925, 14, WCA.

52. Sarah Parsons, "Mount Holyoke during the Civil War," MS of speech, Jan. 1908, [3–4], Civil War Folder, MHCA; Mary (Haynes) Lane, "Mount Holyoke's Golden Age," read at the meeting of the Hampshire County Mount Holyoke Alum-

nae Association, Hatfield, MA, 26 Oct. 1907, TS, 9, Mary Haynes Lane Papers, box 1, ser. 2, folder 3, MHCA.

53. Edwards, "War Time at Mt. Holyoke," 11–12; E. Parsons, "Mount Holyoke in War Time" (quotation); S. Parsons, "Mount Holyoke during the Civil War," 2–3; [Phipps], "Mount Holyoke of the Sixties," 2–3; Henrietta [Woodford] to Mr. and Mrs. Zerah Woodford, 15 May 1861, TS, Henrietta M. Woodford Papers, folder 2, MHCA; "Selections from the Journal of Annie L. Lane," ed. Charles Lane Hanson, 24 Dec. 1861, TS 1953, Anne L. Lane Papers, folder 2, MHCA; Lane, "Mount Holyoke's Golden Age," 7.

54. Andrew Wright to Nellie Favre, 18 Mar. 1863, quoted in Fitch, "'Look for the Silver Lining,'" 5, MHCA; Chessman, *Ohio Colleges*, 17.

55. "Selections from the Journal of Annie L. Lane," 20 July 1862.

56. See, e.g., [Phipps], "Mount Holyoke of the Sixties," 2; Sarah [Stow] to Mr. and Mrs. Humphrey, 4 Feb. 1864, Sarah D. (Locke) Stow Papers, ser. A, folder 2, MHCA; Mrs. S. D. Stoddard, Principal's Report, 17 July 1867, 6–7, Principals and Presidents, Copies of Reports, folder 1, MHCA.

57. Edwards, "War Time at Mt. Holyoke," 11; "Selections from the Journal of Annie L. Lane," 4 Feb. 1862; Belle [Thomas] to [Walter Thomas], 23 and 27 Sept. 1864, transcripts, Belle Thomas Papers, ser. 1, folder 5, MHCA; Mary Augusta Monroe, diary, 17 May 1864, TS prepared by Eleanor Ibetson Wiedman, 1987, Mary A. Monroe Papers, folder 2, MHCA; E. Parsons, "Mount Holyoke in War Time."

58. Jean Oliphant, "Wesleyan College Presents Sidney Lanier, Flutist," *Wesleyan Alumnae*, Jan. 1925, 4, 6; Fitzpatrick, recollections, 18; Clarke, *Lanier*, 25.

59. Nelson and Sheriff, *People at War*, 153–55; Curti, "American Scholar," 250–51, 256–57; Trimpi, *Crimson Confederates*, 95; McPherson, *Battle Cry of Freedom*, 659, 850; catalogue of the College of California, 1860–61, 2, and 1861–62, 2; Willey, "Roll of the College of California," 14, DML; Chaffin, *Pathfinder*, 456–57; Frost, *Thinking Confederates*, 35; annual report of the president of Harvard College, 1860–61, 10–11, and 1861–62, 4; Stephens, *University of Missouri*, 159.

60. Venable, *Campaign*, 1, SCL; faculty minutes of the University of South Carolina, vol. 7, 28 Nov. 1867, USCA.

61. Marten, *Children's Civil War*, 87–100; Marten, *Children for the Union*, 67–76; Drago, *Confederate Phoenix*, 30–35; Sheehan-Dean, *Why Confederates Fought*, 133, 191.

62. Robt. W. Barnwell Jr. to F. W. Pickens and Board of Trustees, 28 Sept. 1861, folder 3 (quotation); trustees to Barnwell, 28 Sept. 1861, folder 3 (quotation); Barnwell to trustees, 2 Dec. 1861, folder 2 (quotation); and Barnwell to M. Laborde, May 1862, folder 3, all in Robert Woodward Barnwell (1831–1863) Papers, SCL. See also catalogue of South Carolina College, 1861, 5.

63. Hollis, *University of South Carolina*, 2:5; Neuffer, "Professor Who Saved Carolina," 3, SCL; LaBorde, *Dr. LaBorde's Report*, [1], SCL.

64. LeConte, *Instructions*, SCL; Le Conte, *Autobiography*, 183–84; Trimpi, *Crimson Confederates*, 157–58; LeConte, *How to Make Salt*, 10, SCL; Le Conte, "Memoir of John Le Conte," 376.

65. Curti and Nash, *Philanthropy*, esp. chaps. 3–4.

66. Martin Kellogg, "Report to the Executive Committee of the Board of Trustees of the College of California," report no. 4, 1861, [8–12, 15], quotations from [12], [11], [15], Reports of the College of California, 1858–66. See also Rood, "Effect of the Civil war," 1.

67. Thornton and Ekelund, *Tariffs, Blockades, and Inflation,* 71, 75, 73.

68. "Recollections of Olive Burr Fellows," 29; E. Parsons, "Mount Holyoke in War Time"; S. Parsons, "Mount Holyoke during the Civil War," [5].

69. Annual report of the president of Harvard College, 1863–64, 14; trustees minutes of Mount Holyoke Female Seminary, 20, 21 July 1864, MHCA; Belle [Thomas] to [Walter Thomas], 28 July 1864, transcript, Belle Thomas Papers, ser. 1, folder 1.

70. Fitzpatrick, recollections, 18; Banks, *Memories,* 33, 38–39; Napier, recollections, 17; Sallie Love Banks Marston, introduction to Banks, *Memories;* catalogue of Wesleyan Female College, 1859–60, 21, and 1863–64, 14, in [Bass], *Catalogues. Wesleyan Female College, 1848 to 1881,* WCA; trustees minutes of Wesleyan Female College, 27, 29 Aug. 1864, WCA.

71. Pennsylvania College in Gettysburg suffered minor damage from the nearby battle and briefly saw service as a Confederate hospital. Rudy, *Campus,* 75.

72. Godson et al., *College of William & Mary,* 1:289–90, 333–35, 2:443–44; Kale, *Hark Upon the Gale,* 85–89, 93, 97; Hollis, *University of South Carolina,* 2:5; Floyd and Gibson, *Boys Who Went to War,* 15; Rudy, *Campus,* 85; G. Anderson, "Columbian College"; J. M. Bonnell, "Report of the President," in trustees minutes of Wesleyan Female College, 11 July 1864; trustees minutes of Wesleyan Female College, 11 July 1864, 18 Mar. 1865; Jordan, *Charlottesville,* 46; Lyndon, recollections, 15; Trudeau, *Southern Storm,* 70.

73. La Borde, "Report of Dr. M. La Borde." See also faculty minutes of South Carolina College, vol. 7, 6 Oct. 1862; W. J. Rivers, "South Carolina College. This History of its Foundation, Rise and Fall. An Address Before the National Education Association," newspaper clipping, [1876], in scrapbook, Fisk P. Brewer Papers, SCL.

74. Trustees resolution, [25 Nov. 1863], Civil War Folder, USCA; Neuffer, "Professor Who Saved Carolina," 3; Wm —— [illegible] S—— [illegible] and Thomas Jordan to N. S. Crowell and M. La Borde, 19 June 1863, Civil War Folder, USCA; executive committee report, 2 Dec. 1863, Civil War Folder, USCA; M. La Borde to Gov. Bonham, 4 May 1864, Maximilian La Borde Papers, folder 5, SCL; Hollis, *University of South Carolina,* 2:4–6.

75. Neuffer, "Professor Who Saved Carolina," 3; John LeConte to C. O. Martindate Jr., 24 Sept. 1890, John LeConte Papers, folder 3, SCL; [Joseph LeConte], "A Journal of Three Months Personal Experience During the Last Days of the Confederacy," MS, 24 Feb. 1865, Joseph LeConte Papers, SCL; Le Conte, *Autobiography,* 226–27; M. Lucas, *Sherman,* chaps. 4–6, esp. 100–101; Simms, *City Laid Waste,* esp. 101–2, 96.

76. Kennett, *Marching Through Georgia,* 264–87; Carnahan, *Lincoln on Trial,* 35–43, 89–96; Grimsley, *Hard Hand of War,* 3–4, 149–51, 190–93, 196–204.

77. Floyd and Gibson, *Boys Who Went to War,* 15.

78. R. O. Tyler to Lt. Thomas Britton, 14 Sept. 1866; G. Walker Sand to E. W. Everson, 23 Feb. 1874; John [Obr?] Lynch to Captain C. A. [Alligovie?] and A. A. [Quuper?], 25 Nov. 1874; Sand to Everson, 19 Sept. 1874; unsigned letter to Hon. J. K. Jillson, 24 Nov. 1873; and James Davis to University Faculty, 30 May 1874, all in Civil War Folder, USCA; Hollis, *University of South Carolina*, 2:5.

79. *Columbia Statesman*, 5 July 1861, quoted in Switzler, "University of the State of Missouri," 194, UMA (quotations); Viles, *University of Missouri*, 100; McPherson, *Battle Cry of Freedom*, 290–93, 350–54, 783–88.

80. J. W. Lathrop, B. McAlester, and Henry Sheeny, commission report, 16 Feb. 1863, 1–2; "Soldiers Held University During Civil War," *Missouri Alumnus*, 15 Apr. 1918, 225; and Tim Hausman, "Federal Troop Occupation of the University of Missouri During the American Civil War and the University's Quest for Damages, 1861–1915," unpublished student paper, 11 Dec. 2003, 3–4, all in Civil War Damage by Federal Troops Folder, UMA; catalogue of the University of Missouri, 1860–61, 6–10, UMA; Viles, *University of Missouri*, 105; Lowry, *University of the State of Missouri*, 24.

81. U.S. Bureau of Education, *University of Missouri*, 22; Stephens, *University of Missouri*, 157–59.

82. Switzler, "University of the State of Missouri," 216; "Soldiers Held University," 225; Lathrop, McAlester, and Sheeny, commission report, 16 Feb. 1863, 1–4; Hausman, "Federal Troop Occupation," 5–6.

83. Rudy, *Campus*, chap. 5.

84. Longstreet, *Fast-Day Sermon*, 6–12, quotation from 12, SCL.

85. Amphictyon Society minutes, 22 May, 3 Oct. 1862, 16 Jan. 1863.

86. Wubben, *Civil War Iowa*, 114.

87. "Are We Loyal?" *Harvard Magazine*, Apr. 1863, 268–69, emphasis in original.

88. Stella Marshall, "Senior Composition," read at Wesleyan Female College, July 1864, emphasis in original, Commencement Essays/Compositions Collection, Commencement Composition of Stella Marshall Folder, WCA.

89. A. U. Bradbury, "Hamilton College," *University Quarterly*, Oct. 1861, 303.

90. [Phipps], "Mount Holyoke of the Sixties," 3; Ella Burton Scarborough, "Memories," *Wesleyan Alumnae*, July 1925, 28 (quotation); Banks, *Memories*, 31–32, 37.

91. E. Parsons, "Mount Holyoke in War Time." See also Napier, recollections, 17.

92. E. Parsons, "Mount Holyoke in War Time"; LaBorde, "Dr. LaBorde's Report."

93. Foster, "Early Recollections of Cornell College," 89; untitled MS, [ca. 1878], William Fletcher King Papers, Scholarships, General Folder, CCA; Wm. F. King, handwritten note in Rood, "Effects of the Civil war," 9; *Minutes for the Board of Trustees*, 26 June 1864, 16 May 1865, CCA.

TWO. The Curriculum

1. Abraham Lincoln, "Milwaukee Address on Agriculture," in U.S. Bureau of Agricultural Economics, *Washington, Jefferson, Lincoln*, 80–87, quotations from 80 and 87, emphasis in original.

2. Cross, *Justin Smith Morrill*, 1, 6–12, 77–78; Geiger, "Useful Knowledge," 155, 158–59; Ross, *Democracy's College*, chap. 2; Eddy, *Colleges*, 11–20; Nevins, *State Universities*, 13–16; Edmond, *Magnificent Charter*, 5, 7–14; Bishop, *History of Cornell*, 52–56.

3. Nevins, *State Universities*, 13–14.

4. Morrill, *Speech of Hon. Justin S. Morrill*, 15, 4–8; Ross, *Democracy's College*, 45–47, 56–60; Eddy, *Colleges*, 30–32; Edmond, *Magnificent Charter*, 21; Cross, *Justin Smith Morrill*, 79–83; James Buchanan, quoted in Rudy, *Building America's Schools and Colleges*, 20.

5. *Statutes at Large* 12 (1863): 503–5, 14 (1868): 208.

6. Morrill, *Agricultural Colleges*, 2–8, quotation from 2; *Statutes at Large* 12 (1863): 504.

7. Morrill, *Agricultural Colleges*, 1.

8. Ibid., 1–2.

9. Ibid., 7–8, quotation from 7.

10. *Congressional Globe*, 37th Cong., 2nd sess. (1862), esp. 1025, 1951, 1971, 2840.

11. Ibid., 2432, 2769–70, 2187, 2248–50, 2275–77, 2328–29, 2366, 2394–96, 2440–43, 2625–34, 3062.

12. Higginbotham, "Military Education," 30, 40–45; Preston, *Military Education*, 22; Watson, *Military Education*, 1–2; Geiger, "Useful Knowledge," 155; Andrew, *Long Gray Lines*, 10–11, 15; Conrad, *Young Lions*, 3–5, 7–9; J. Green, *Military Education*, 1, 3, 12, 41, 200; Sugrue, "'We Desired Our Future Rulers,'" 95; Morison, *Three Centuries of Harvard*, 214–15; Brereton, *Educating the U.S. Army*, xii–xiii.

13. Roche, *Colonial Colleges*, 10–12, 47, 59–60; Novak, *Rights of Youth*, esp. chap. 3; Sugrue, "'We Desired Our Future Rulers,'" 95–102; Wagoner, "Honor and Dishonor," 173–76.

14. Eddy, *Colleges*, 47–50.

15. *Announcement of the Mining and Agricultural College*, 7; Trustees of the College of California, *Memorial*, 3; and catalogue of the College of California, 1863–64, 18, in *Pamphlets on the College of California*, all in UCA.

16. Trustees of the College of California, *Memorial*, 1–7; Wm. P. Blake to the President and Board of Trustees of the College of Cala., 20 May 1864, in Letter Book of the College of California, folder 32, UCA; W. D. Harwood et al., "A State University," *College Echo*, Jan. 1868, [2], UCA.

17. Blake to President and Trustees. Catalogue of the College of California, 1864–65, 16; 1865–66, 16; 1866–67, 16; 1867–68, 16.

18. Eddy, *Colleges*, 47–50; Ross, *Democracy's College*, 69–72.

19. Catalogue of the College of California, 1866–67, 31, 6–7, 22–27.

20. The regents, who included many Democrats, also revealed their political sympathies by selecting a former Democratic presidential candidate to head the university—in contrast to the College of California's trustees, who once had included the former Republican presidential candidate John C. Frémont. Regents minutes of the University of California, 10 Nov. 1868, UC Regents Collection, box 4, folder 11, UCA; [Samuel H. Willey] to Rev. Dr. Baldwin, 1 Sept. 1869, handwritten

copy, Documents of the College of California, folder 10, UCA; Gustavus Schulte, *A Glance from a German Standpoint at the State University of California, Particularly, and the Educational Systems of America and Germany, Comparatively* (San Francisco: Bacon, 1871), 13–15, in *Pamphlets on the College of California*.

21. "State University. Important Legislation for its Benefit—Fund for its Support," newspaper clipping, [1870], UC Regents Collection, box 3, Legislature, 1872, 1876 Folder; Henry Durant, Quarterly Report, 6 Dec. 1870, 2–3, UC Regents Collection, box 4, folder 8; Martin Kellogg to H. H. Haight, 4 Jan. 1871, in letter book, 52, Office of the Registrar Records, box 5, folder 5, UCA; Martin Kellogg, "Relative to Duties of Professors," 30 Mar. 1871, [3], UC Regents Collection, box 2, folder 12 (quotation); Robert E. C. Stearns, *Annual Report of the Board of Regents of the University of California, For the Year Ending May 31st, 1875. With Supplemental Financial Statements to July 1, 1875* (Berkeley: Univ. Press, 1875), 18, UC Regents Collection, box 1, folder 7; E. S. Carr, report "to the President and Board of Regents," 10 Nov. 1870, 2, UC Regents Collection, box 1, folder 5; Henry Durant, "Schedule of Studies Pursued in University & Text-Books used," 7 Apr. 1871, UC Regents Collection, box 2, folder 12; and "State University. Annual Meeting of the Regents," newspaper clipping, 1 June 1873, UC Regents Collection, box 1, folder 4.

22. Carr, report "to the President and Board of Regents," 2. A disenchanted former professor claimed that many worried about the establishment of compulsory drilling, which he felt made the university resemble a military academy. But the peripatetic agriculture professor was in a better position to gauge public opinion. Schulte, *Glance from a German Standpoint*, 14.

23. Frost, *Thinking Confederates*, 129n29, 26, 29.

24. *Congressional Globe*, 39th Cong., 1st sess. (1866), 1381, emphasis in original.

25. Ibid.

26. Ibid., 1381, 3683–4281 passim, 4296.

27. Adjutant General's Office, *Official Army Register*, 1873, 179, and 1876, 225; E. D. Townsend to Lieut. Isaac T. Webster, 2 Sept. 1874, and Townsend to Geo. G. Wright, 29 June 1876, Wartime Cornell Box, Cornell Cadets Folder, CCA.

28. *Statutes at Large* 16 (1871): 320. The 1870 law placed no geographical or numerical restrictions on the retired officers. The War Department, however, capped the total number of officers, active and retired, at the maximum given in the law of 1866. Adjutant General's Office, *Official Army Register*, 1874–82; J. D. Cameron to the President of Cornell College, 10 Aug. 1876, Wartime Cornell Box, Cornell Cadets Folder.

29. *Statutes at Large* 16 (1871): 373; A. V. Dyer, *In Relation to Arms for Colleges, Under Joint Resolution of May 4, 1870*, Ordnance Office, War Department, Circular No. 10 ([Washington, DC: GPO, 1 July 1870]), [1–2], Wartime Cornell Box, Cornell Cadets Folder; Ordnance Office, War Department, *Announcement of Regulations Governing Issue of Military Officers and Equipment to Colleges and Universities* (Washington, DC: [GPO], 24 June 1876), 2–3, UC Regents Collection, box 3, folder 22. Presumably the War Department counted only male students when calculating the number of muskets.

30. Worthington, "Antecedent Education," 185–87; Clemente, *For King and Kaiser!*, xiii, 1, 82; Van Dyke, *Russian Imperial Military Doctrine*, 57–63.

31. Catalogue of the University of Missouri, 1867–68, 24.

32. The army's register of officers did not list teaching appointments before 1873. Adjutant General's Office, *Official Army Register*, 1873–77, esp. 1873, 179, and 1874, 224.

33. B. F. Whittmore, "Report," in trustees minutes of the University of South Carolina, vol. 8, 21 Dec. 1874, USCA; Adjutant General's Office, *Official Army Register*, 1875, 226, and 1876, 225; catalogue of the University of South Carolina, 1876, 5, Catalogue of Trustees, Faculty and Students Collection, USCA.

34. As before, Congress explicitly limited only the number of *active* officers assigned to colleges. But the War Department, interpreting the law to apply to retired officers as well, appointed exactly thirty total. *U.S. Statutes at Large* 19 (1877): 74; Adjutant General's Office, *Official Army Register*, 1877–82, esp. 1877, 226, and 1878, 223.

35. Ross, *Democracy's College*, 125–26.

36. Robert Lincoln to Wm. Porcher Miles, 7 Jan. 1882, Civil War Folder, USCA.

37. Switzler, "University of the State of Missouri," 231, UMA.

38. Catalogue of the University of Missouri, 1867–68, 24, and 1868–69, 4, 23. University of the State of Missouri, report containing catalogue, 1870, 17; 1871, 36, 59; 1872, 35, UMA. Faculty records of the University of Missouri, 16 Oct. 1868, 8 Jan. 1869, 2 Apr. 1870, UMA; Adjutant General's Office, *Official Army Register*, 1873, 179.

39. James A. Pack to Chas. P. Williams, 31 Jan. 1876, School of Mines and Metallurgy Papers, folder 33, WHMC.

40. Faculty records of the University of Missouri, 9 Oct. 1872, 26 Feb., 26 Mar., 16 Apr. 1870, 30 Nov. 1872, 7 Feb. 1873; University of the State of Missouri, report containing catalogue, 1871, 59, and 1872, 55.

41. Faculty records of the University of Missouri, 8 Jan. 1869, 3 May 1870, 19 Oct. 1872, 10 June 1870, and 1869–73 passim.

42. Unsigned letter to Sec. of War, 5 Dec. 1876; regents minutes of the University of California, 5 Dec. 1876, 6, 21 Mar. 1877; and G. G. Greenough to John Le Conte, 16 Mar. 1877, all in UC Regents Collection, box 3, folder 22. Robt. E. C. Stearns, *Annual Report of the Board of Regents of the University of California, For the Year Ending June 30, 1877, with Detailed Financial Statements To July 1, 1877* (San Francisco: Carmany, 1877), 6, UC Regents Collection, box 1, folder 8. Adjutant General's Office, *Official Army Register*, 1878, 223.

43. O. O. Howard to William F. King, 8 Sept. 1871; C. C. Campbell to the President [Ulysses S. Grant], 20 Feb. 1872; and Baker to President King, 9 May 1872, all in Wartime Cornell Box, Cornell Cadets Folder. King, faculty report, in *Trustee Minutes*, 18 June 1872, CCA. Faculty minutes of Cornell College, 4 Nov. 1872, CCA.

44. Wm. W. Belknap to King, 1 Feb. 1873, Wartime Cornell Box, Cornell Cadets Folder; faculty minutes of Cornell College, 10 Feb., 24 Mar., 7 Apr. 1873; Adjutant General's Office, *Official Army Register*, 1874, 224.

45. Baker to Wm. F. King, 11 Feb., 31 Mar. 1873; Baker to Rev[.] Pres[iden]t King, 4 Apr. 1873; and S. I. Benét to Wm. F. King, 12 May 1873, all in Wartime

NOTES TO PAGES 68-71

Cornell Box, Cornell Cadets Folder. Dyer, "In Relation to Arms for Colleges." —— [illegible], Rock Island Arsenal, IL, to W. F. King, 27 June 1873, William Fletcher King Papers, Construction—misc. campus Folder, CCA. Faculty minutes of Cornell College, 20 Jan., 1 Feb. 1876.

46. Faculty minutes of Cornell College, 12 Jan., 16 Mar. 1874; catalogue of Cornell College, 1876–77, CCA.

47. Faculty minutes of Cornell College, 5 May, 15, 29 Sept. 1873, 14 Sept. 1874, 12 Apr. 1875, quotation from 29 Sept. 1873, emphasis in original.

48. Radke-Moss, *Bright Epoch*, 227–28, 238–40; J. P. Tandberg and H. F. M. Dahl, Editorials, *Manitou Messenger*, Nov. 1890, 125, and O. O. Fugleskjel and Agnes Mellby, eds., College Crumbs, ibid., 126, both in Shaw-Olson Center for College History, St. Olaf College; Stephens, *University of Missouri*, 285; Olson and Olson, *University of Missouri*, 20.

49. Faculty minutes of Cornell College, 2 May, 17 Sept. 1873, 23 Apr., 14 Sept. 1874, 25 Nov., 23 Oct. 1876, and 1873–76 passim, quotations from 25 Nov. and 23 Oct. 1876.

50. F. W. Lister, "Military Drill," *Magenta*, 26 Mar. 1875; catalogue of Harvard University, 1874–75, 18, WML; Drill, "Harvard Rifle Corps," *Magenta*, 9 Apr. 1875; untitled, *Crimson*, 4 June 1875 and 25 Feb. 1876; "H. R. C.," ibid., 9 Nov. 1877; untitled, ibid., 25 Oct. 1878.

51. Hollis, *University of South Carolina*, 2:35, 43.

52. *Statutes at Large* 15 (1869): 25–26; Hollis, *University of South Carolina*, 2:61–63; "A Military Professorship," reprinted from *Orangeburg Citizen*, [1872?], clipping in scrapbook, Fisk P. Brewer Papers, SCL.

53. C. Bruce Walker, *Prospectus of the University of South Carolina. MDCCCLXVI* (Columbia: Office of the Southern Presbyterian Review, 1866), 5–13, Catalogue of Trustees, Faculty and Students Collection. *By-Laws of the University of South Carolina, as Revised and Adopted by The Board of Trustees, at the Annual Meeting in 1866. To Which Are Prefixed the Act to Establish the University of South Carolina, and the Subsequent Act in Amendment Thereto; and to Which Are Annexed Regulations of the Library Committee, and Also, Regulations of the Faculty of the University* (Columbia: Deane, 1867), 3–4, Catalogue of Trustees, Faculty and Students Collection. Catalogue of the University of South Carolina, 1867, 4; 1868, 15; 1869, 25; 1870, 3; 1871, 4; 1872, 15, Catalogue of Trustees, Faculty and Students Collection. *Re-Organization of the University of South Carolina, in 1873, and Catalogue for 1872–'73* (n.p., [1873?]), 4–5, Catalogue of Trustees, Faculty and Students Collection. Hollis, *University of South Carolina*, 2:32–34. E. P. Alexander, "Report of the Professor of Mathematics, Civil & Mil'ry Engineering & Construction," in trustees minutes of the University of South Carolina, vol. 7, 9 May 1866.

54. Zuczek, *State of Rebellion*, 28–31, 53–61, 74–75, 78–82, 88–108; Williamson, *After Slavery*, 254–66, 372–73; Martinez, *Carpetbaggers*, 24–25, 7, 111–14, 123, 66–76, 133–57, 163–87.

55. Nelson and Sheriff, *People at War*, 208.

56. "A Military Professorship." Another Friend of Education, "The Military

Professorship"; Educators of Aiken, South Carolina, "Teaching Versus Fighting," emphasis in original; and Blank Cartridge, "The Military Professorship," all in *Columbia (SC) Daily Union-Herald*, Dec. 1874, clippings in scrapbook, Fisk P. Brewer Papers.

57. Whittmore, "Report"; "Resolution by Prof Brewer In Faculty meeting Jan'y 30 1875 Applied E. V. Everson Sec Fac," Civil War Folder, USCA; Adjutant General's Office, *Official Army Register*, 1875, 226, and 1876, 225; catalogue of the University of South Carolina, 1876, 5.

58. Adjutant General's Office, *Official Army Register*, 1873, 179; 1874, 224; 1878, 223; 1879, 249.

59. Beckert, *Monied Metropolis*, 232–34, 296–97; Hoganson, *Fighting for American Manhood*, esp. 20–21, 109–10; Higham, "Reorientation," 26, 31–32.

60. Geiger, "Multipurpose Colleges," 139–41; Malkmus, "Small Towns," 64–65; Coulter, *College Life*, 186; annual report of the president of Harvard College, 1869–70, 10–11.

61. Hofstadter and Metzger, *Academic Freedom*, 228–31, 261–62; Tobias, *Old Dartmouth on Trial*, 23, 26; Guralnick, *Science*, 142, 144; Schuster and Finkelstein, *American Faculty*, 24–25; Jencks and Riesman, *Academic Revolution*, 1, 6.

62. Axtell, "Death of the Liberal Arts College," 347; Geiger, "Multipurpose Colleges," 130; Thelin, *Higher Education*, 90–97, 105. See also Leslie, *Gentlemen and Scholars*.

63. On the fluidity of terminology in the nineteenth century, see Veysey, *American University*, 11–12; Whitehead, *Separation of College and State*, esp. 1, 7; Mattingly, "Structures Over Time," 44–46; Rothblatt and Trow, "Government Policies," 210; and Malkmus, "Small Towns," 41.

64. Veysey, *American University*, introduction and chaps. 2–4, quotation from 181; Thelin, *Higher Education*, 103.

65. Veysey, *American University*, introduction; Thelin, *Higher Education*, 87–90, 103–6; Reuben, *Modern University*, 4–5 and chaps. 2–4. See also Hofstadter and Metzger, *Academic Freedom*, chaps. 7–8; Jencks and Riesman, *Academic Revolution*, 12–21; Geiger, *To Advance Knowledge*, chap. 1; Turner and Bernard, "German Model"; Kerr, *Uses of the University*, 2–18; Rodgers, *Atlantic Crossings*, 85–86, 88–89, 97–98, 103–5; Singer, *Adventures Abroad*, 56–60; Tobias, *Old Dartmouth on Trial*, 13–14; and Roberts and Turner, *Sacred and the Secular*, esp. chaps. 1–3.

66. Morison, *Three Centuries of Harvard*, 160, 167–68, 242, 238, 264–65, 279.

67. Annual report of the president of Harvard College, 1861–62, 5; 1862–63, 7; 1864–65, 5, HUA. Catalogue of Harvard University, 1868–69, 1st term, 97–100; 1865–66, 1st term, 81; 1870–71, 106. Harvard Corporation formal minutes, vol. 10, 26 Aug. 1865, 23 Feb. 1861, HUA.

68. Annual report of the president of Harvard College, 1870–71, 11–21, quotation from 12.

69. Ibid., 1861–62, 4; 1862–63, 10; 1870–71, 22–23, 26–28. Harvard Corporation formal minutes, vol. 11, 4 Oct. 1870. Harvard overseers formal minutes, vol. 10, 5 Oct. 1870, 6 June 1871, Records of the Board of Overseers, HUA.

70. Catalogue of Harvard University, 1871–72, 2nd ed., 110–17; annual report of the president of Harvard College, 1869–70, 10–11.

71. Announcement of the Mining and Agricultural College, 6–7.

72. Stadtman, University of California, 26–27; Blake to President and Trustees.

73. W. E. Brown, Report of the Secretary, 3, BL; Professor [Ezra S.] Carr, "The University," San Francisco Daily Chronicle, 27 Sept. 1874, 1, clipping, UC Regents Collection, box 1, folder 5; Andrew J. Moulder, Report of the Regents of the University of California, Relative to the Operations and Progress of the Institution ([Sacramento]: Springer, [1872]), 6, in Pamphlets on the College of California; Harwood et al., "State University," [2]; Martin Kellogg, speech, quoted in "The State University. Celebration of Charter Day at Berkeley," San Francisco Daily Evening Post, 24 Mar. 1876, clipping, in Kellogg, Papers and Addresses, item 4, UCA.

74. [Samuel H. Willey], "Statement touching the Simmons purchase and the College Homestead," report no. 54, 4 Dec. 1866, [1–8]; [Samuel H. Willey], "Report, 1864–5," report no. 55, 19; and [Samuel H. Willey], report no. 40, May 1865, [4–5], all in Reports of the College of California, 1858–66, UCA.

75. Quotation from Board of Trustees of the College of California, resolution, Aug. 1867, quoted in Andrew J. Moulder to president and trustees of the College of California, 6 Apr. 1869, Documents of the College of California, folder 8, item 1; and from W. E. Brown, Report of the Secretary, 3–4. See also S. H. Willey, "Vice President's Report. July 1869," 4, 8–9, Documents of the College of California, folder 9; S. H. Willey, memoranda on transfer of College of California to University of California, 1888, 4, Documents of the College of California, folder 2; Moulder, Report of the Regents, 6; Harwood et al., "State University," [2]; and Kellogg, speech, quoted in "The State University."

76. [Willey] to Baldwin, 1 Sept. 1869.

77. Carr, "The University," 1–2, 4; Moulder, Report of the Regents, 6, 8; Moulder to president and trustees; Willey to Baldwin, 1 Sept. 1869; W. E. Brown, Report of the Secretary, 4; Willey, "Vice President's Report," 9; Willey, memoranda on transfer, 26–27, 31–33, 49–50, 57–58; J. Crockett et al., newspaper clipping of California Supreme Court decision, Documents of the College of California, folder 8, item 7.

78. The regents had tried opening the Mechanic Arts College on the Oakland campus in 1869, but not a single student had enrolled. Ezra S. Carr to A. J. Moulder, 6 Jan. 1870, UCA; Moulder, Report of the Regents, 11; John LeConte to Haight, 30 July 1870, UC Regents Collection, box 3, folder 21; Henry Durant, Quarterly Report, 6 Dec. 1870; E. Durant to Mr. Hallidic, 23 Nov. 1870, UC Regents Collection, box 3, folder 21; A. S. Hallidic to Moulder, 29 June 1871, UC Regents Collection, box 3, folder 21; Henry Durant, Quarterly Report, 7 Mar. 1871, [1], UC Regents Collection, box 4, folder 8; Schulte, Glance from a German Standpoint, 28–29; Michael Lynch et al., "Resolutions of Students at Large of Mechanics Arts College University of California," 15 July 1871, [1], UC Regents Collection, box 3, folder 21.

79. "Statement from the Faculty of Toland Medical College," [1870], [2], box 5, folder 11; Board of Regents of the University of California, Extracts from Minutes, 2 Aug. 1870, box 5, folder 11; "State University. Annual Meeting of the Regents,"

newspaper clipping, 1 June 1873; E. F. Bunnell and R. Cutlar to the Board of Regents of the University of California, 15 Aug. 1873, box 5, folder 6; Board of Regents of the University of California, Notes from Records, 17 Dec. 1873, box 5, folder 6; and John LeConte, Memorial to Board of Regents, [2 Dec. 1875], box 3, folder 10, all in UC Regents Collection.

80. Rudy, *Campus*, 98.

81. Thelin, *Higher Education*, 103.

82. Ibid., 103–6, 141, 150–54, quotation from 104.

83. Ibid., 105, 150–52; Angelo, "Social Transformation," 291, 265–67; Crenshaw, *General Lee's College*, 161–62. See also Finnegan and Cullaty, "YMCA Universities," 47–48, 53–58, 60–64. Joseph M. Stetar observes the Civil War's stimulus to utilitarian curricula at additional schools in the South but declines to call these comprehensive institutions universities because of their limited emphasis on research. Stetar, "In Search of a Direction."

84. These figures include first degrees in law, engineering, agriculture, mining, architecture, pedagogy, music, painting, medicine, dentistry, pharmacy, veterinary medicine, and divinity. They exclude bachelor of science degrees, some of which represented work in engineering, agriculture, or other vocational subjects. U.S. Bureau of Education, report, 1889–90, 776–77; Ross, *Democracy's College*, 159–61.

85. Thelin, *Higher Education*, 108–9, 104–5, 51; Angelo, "Social Transformation," 263; Finnegan and Cullaty, "YMCA Universities," 47–48, 58–59. Several older books, cited in n. 2 above, discuss institutions' use of land-grant funds but do not discuss these institutions more generally as a distinct type of university.

86. Angelo, "Social Transformation," 263; Finnegan and Cullaty, "YMCA Universities," 59, 61.

87. See chapter 1.

88. A. B. Longstreet to Trustees of the South Carolina College, May 1861, Augustus Baldwin Longstreet Papers, folder 2, SCL; paper dated ca. 1861, 19th Century Manuscript Collection Presidents' Papers, no. 73, USCA; Venable, *Campaign*, 1, SCL; faculty minutes of the University of South Carolina, vol. 7, 28 Nov. 1867, USCA; paper dated 2 Dec. 1863, [1], Civil War Folder, USCA; C. Bruce Walker, *Treasurer's Report to the Honorable Board of Trustees of the South Carolina College, November 1, 1863* (Columbia: Pelham, 1863), 4, Catalogue of Trustees, Faculty and Students Collection; C. Bruce Walker, *Treasurer's Report to the Honorable Board of Trustees of the University of South Carolina, November, 1866* (Columbia: Selby, 1866), 11, Catalogue of Trustees, Faculty and Students Collection; Hollis, *University of South Carolina*, 2:5–6.

89. Unsigned letter to Brevt Maj. Genl. A. Ames, 16 Jan. 1866, Civil War Folder, USCA; Hollis, *University of South Carolina*, 2:22; G. Walker Sand to E. W. Everson, 23 Feb. 1874, Civil War Folder, USCA; John [Obr?] Lynch to Captain C. A. [Alligovie?] and A. A. [Quuper?], 25 Nov. 1874, Civil War Folder, USCA; Sand to Everson, 19 Sept. 1874, Civil War Folder, USCA; unsigned letter to Hon. J. K. Jillson, 24 Nov. 1873, Civil War Folder, USCA; Neuffer, "Professor Who Saved Carolina," 3, SCL; catalogue of South Carolina College, 1862, 5; *By-Laws of the University of South Carolina . . . 1866*, 5, 12; R. W. Barnwell, "Report of the Chairman of the Faculty," in

trustees minutes of the University of South Carolina, vol. 7, 9 May 1866; trustees minutes of the University of South Carolina, vol. 7, 19 Dec. 1865; catalogue of the University of South Carolina, 1867, 4.

90. See Benjamin F. Perry, quoted in E. Green, *University of South Carolina*, 82, and in Hollis, *University of South Carolina*, 2:9.

91. "An Act to Establish the University of South Carolina," 19 Dec. 1865, in *By-Laws of the University of South Carolina . . . 1866*, 3–5; Walker, *Prospectus*, 3, 14; Hollis, *University of South Carolina*, 2:15–16, 25.

92. Catalogue of South Carolina College, 1861, 5, 9, and 1862, 5.

93. Walker, *Prospectus*, 3, 5–13; "Act to Establish the University of South Carolina," 3–4, quotation from 4; catalogue of the University of South Carolina, 1867, 4; W. J. Rivers, "South Carolina College. This History of its Foundation, Rise and Fall. An Address Before the National Education Association," newspaper clipping, [1876], in scrapbook, Fisk P. Brewer Papers; Alexander, "Report of the Professor of Mathematics"; Joseph LeConte, "Report of the Professor of Chemistry, Pharmacy, Mineralogy & Geology," in trustees minutes of the University of South Carolina, vol. 7, 9 May 1866; Le Conte, *Autobiography*, 235.

94. "An Act to amend the Act establishing the University of South Carolina," 20 Dec. 1866, in *By-Laws of the University of South Carolina . . . 1866*, 6; catalogue of the University of South Carolina, 1867, 4–5; Hollis, *University of South Carolina*, 2:15.

95. Walker, *Prospectus*, 5, 15; *By-Laws of the University of South Carolina . . . 1866*, 4, 17; W. J. Rivers, "Report of Professor of Ancient Languages and Literature," in trustees minutes of the University of South Carolina, vol. 7, 9 May 1866.

96. "Act to Establish the University of South Carolina," 3.

97. Nemec, *Ivory Towers*, 117. Catalogue of South Carolina College, 1860, 19; 1861, 17; 1862, 11.

98. Walker, *Prospectus*, 5; Barnwell, "Report of the Chairman of the Faculty"; Rivers, "Report of Professor of Ancient Languages and Literature"; *By-Laws of the University of South Carolina . . . 1866*, 15; trustees minutes of the University of South Carolina, vol. 7, 11 Nov. 1866.

99. J. J. Wright, "The South Carolina University," public letter to W. B. Nash and members of the state senate Finance Committee, newspaper clipping, 3 Mar. 1875, in scrapbook, Fisk P. Brewer Papers; catalogue of South Carolina College, 1862, 18; Walker, *Prospectus*, 15; catalogue of the University of South Carolina, 1869, 47; Rivers, "South Carolina College"; Perry, quoted in E. Green, *University of South Carolina*, 82, quotations from the latter two sources.

100. Wright, "South Carolina University"; R. W. Barnwell, "Report of the Chairman of the Faculty," in trustees minutes of the University of South Carolina, vol. 7, 11 Nov. 1866; Walker, *Treasurer's Report, 1866*, 11; "Act to Establish the University of South Carolina," 4.

101. Switzler, "University of the State of Missouri," 213, 216; Lynch, diary, 26 Nov. 1865, WHMC. See also chapter 1.

102. Lowry, *University of the State of Missouri*, 30–31; Viles, *University of Missouri*, 108; Switzler, "University of the State of Missouri," 211–12; John H. Lathrop,

"Report of President Lathrop," 1866, quoted in Switzler, "University of the State of Missouri," 217.

103. *Journal of the Missouri State Convention*, 3–4, 15, 196–97, 199–203, 277, 279–80, 272, quotations from 196 and 272.

104. Read, *Address on Education*, 13–14, 6–8, 3, WML (quotations); U.S. Bureau of Education, *University of Missouri*, 24–26; Switzler, "University of the State of Missouri," 229–31; Lowry, *University of the State of Missouri*, 30–32.

105. The university had established a medical department in 1845 but had discontinued it soon thereafter. Catalogue of the University of Missouri, 1858–59, 18, 27; 1859–60, 4–7; 1860–61, 3.

106. Daniel Read, fragment of report, Daniel Read Papers, folder 14, WHMC.

107. Switzler, "University of the State of Missouri," 231, 245. Catalogue of the University of Missouri, 1866–67, 20; 1867–68, 22; 1869–70, 11–15, 26–27; 1871–72, 20. U.S. Bureau of Education, *University of Missouri*, 26–27. "Agricultural College. Historical," *University Missourian*, May 1872, 5, UMSC. "Formal Opening of the School of Mines," *University Missourian*, Nov. 1871, 4, originally published in *Rolla Herald*. University of the State of Missouri, report containing catalogue, 1873, 54–55.

108. Executive committee minutes, 17 Nov. 1870, and Daniel Read to the Executive Committee, 5 Nov. 1870, Board of Curators Executive Board Papers, box 1, folder 1, UMA; Jas. S. Rollins to B. Gratz Brown, 20 June 1871, UMC, University General, Dedications, Event Programs, Correspondence, Speeches and Photographs Collection, box 1, folder 1, UMA; Laura V. Clark to R. L. Hill, 7 June 1926, University of Missouri Papers, Collection C0181, folder 3, WHMC. The mining school, in Rolla, shared a new building with the local public school. "Formal Opening of the School of Mines," 4.

109. Wright, *Transylvania*, 187–88, 194–200; Peter and Peter, *Transylvania University*, 172, 174–77; Conkin, *Gone with the Ivy*, 6, 8–10, 17–18, 24, 43, 54–56; McGaw, *Vanderbilt*, 10–11, 13.

110. Financial troubles forced Washington and Lee to reduce its applied-science curricula in the 1870s. Frost, *Thinking Confederates*, 41, 68, 73; Crenshaw, *General Lee's College*, 147, 134, 137–38, 160–65, 149–50, 176, 182–86, 227–28.

THREE. Admissions: Race, Class, Gender

1. Grandison Harris to D. H. Chamberlain, 4 Oct. 1876, 19th Century Manuscripts Collection, Miscellaneous Student Documents, pt. 1, USCA.

2. Harris, formerly an enslaved procurer of corpses at the Medical College of Georgia, now worked as a salaried porter there in addition to his judicial duties. Allen, "Grandison Harris, Sr.," 194–96.

3. Trow, "Mass to Universal Higher Education," 3; *Circular of the State Normal School*, 7–8, GL; *Catalogue of the State Normal School*, 9, 11, GL.

4. Nemec, *Ivory Towers*, 110–17. On South Carolina College's waiving the entrance test, see chapter 2.

5. Malkmus, "Small Towns," 35–37, 46–47.

6. Allmendinger, *Paupers and Scholars*, 8–18 and chaps. 4–5; Burke, *Collegiate Populations*, 129–31, 135; Horowitz, *Campus Life*, 56–62, 193.

7. [Stephen N. Fellows], MS of address, [1882], 3, Samuel Fellows Box (quotation); Amphictyon Society minutes, 2, 15 Apr., 27 May, 3 June 1864; and Philomathean Society minutes, 18 Jan., 28 Feb. 1867, all in CCA. On restrictions on women and on social mixing, see faculty minutes of Cornell College, 7 Sept., 9 Oct. 1871, 20 Mar. 1868, 20 Mar. 1874, CCA.

8. "Recollections of Olive Burr Fellows [and Alice Fellows Rigby]," ca. 1897, TS prepared by Alice Rigby Moore, 30 Apr. 1950, 31, Samuel Fellows Box; faculty minutes of Cornell College, 2 May, 4 Apr. 1869, 1 Apr. 1872, 30 Oct. 1871; catalogue of Cornell College, 1858–59, 1860–77, esp. 1871–72, 4, CCA; [Fellows], MS of address, 3–4.

9. *Register of the University of California*, 1870–71, 31, WML; Clifford, "Equally in View," xv, 1–2; Tyack and Hansot, *Learning Together*, 49; Kelley, *Learning to Stand and Speak*, 2; Martin Kellogg, speech, quoted in "The State University. Celebration of Charter Day at Berkeley," *San Francisco Daily Evening Post*, 24 Mar. 1876, clipping, in Kellogg, *Papers and Addresses*, item 4, UCA (quotation).

10. Abraham Lincoln, "Gettysburg Address," in G. Wills, *Lincoln at Gettysburg*, 263.

11. Geiger, "'Superior Instruction of Women,'" 186; Solomon, *Educated Women*, 50, 47; Conable, *Women at Cornell*, 55, 43, 52–53, 65, 74.

12. Albert Stetson, "Harvard University," *Undergraduate*, Jan. 1861, 172, WML. Annual report of the president of Harvard College, 1869–70, 19, 29–30, HUA. Harvard overseers formal minutes, vol. 10, 17 Feb., 11 Mar. 1863, Records of the Board of Overseers, HUA. Catalogue of Harvard University, 1869–70, 1st term, 102–3; 1870–71, 108; 1871–72, 2nd ed., 108–9; 1873–74, 169–71, WML. Harvard Corporation formal minutes, vol. 10, 31 Mar. 1866, and vol. 11, 25 Feb. 1870, 28 Apr. 1871, HUA. Horowitz, *Alma Mater*, 95. Kimball, *Modern Professional Education*, 274–75, 277–78.

13. Mounter, "Richard Theodore Greener," 131–33.

14. The trustees did not record the reasoning behind their decision to admit blacks in either 1858 or 1871. *Minutes for the Board of Trustees*, 13 Sept. 1858, 12 July 1859, 14 June 1870, CCA; Heywood, *Cornell College*, 60–64; faculty minutes of Cornell College, 4 Nov. 1872.

15. Photograph of Memorial Hall waiters, 1875, HUA.

16. Julia E. Ward, "Report for 1873," 2 July 1873, 16, photocopy, Principals and Presidents, Copies of Reports, folder 1, MHCA; Mary Haynes Lane, "Mt. Holyoke Seminary and College: Paper read at the Meeting of the National Alumnæ Association at the late Commencement," *Hampshire County (MA) Gazette*, 9 July 1889, [2], photocopy of clipping, Mary Haynes Lane Papers, box 1, ser. 2, folder 3, MHCA; "Our Educational System," newspaper clipping, [1870–77], in Kellogg, *Papers and Addresses*, item 1; annual report of the president of Harvard College, 1863–64, 14–15, quotation from 15.

17. Mary Ellis, Principal's Report, 3 July 1872, 5, photocopy, Principals and Pres-

idents, Copies of Reports, folder 1. Theodore Bradley to Rev. Mr. Durant, 21 Sept. [1870?]; Mrs. G. E. Childs to Robert Stearns, 29 June 1877; Eugene F. Ewell to Board of Regens. [Regents] of the State University, n.d.; and E. T. Barber to Prof. Bolanger, 8 Nov. 1872, all in UC Regents Collection, box 1, folder 2, UCA. C. C. Kinsey to A. J. Moulder, 29 Mar. 1871, UC Regents Collection, box 2, folder 12.

18. The AES severely reduced the number of its beneficiaries in the 1840s. In the 1870s it began to give much of its aid money directly to colleges for distribution to students through their growing financial-aid programs. Allmendinger, *Paupers and Scholars*, 76.

19. Annual report of the president of Harvard College, 1860–61, 5, 14; 1861–62, 10–12, fund quotation from 11; 1862–63, 4, 13; 1863–64, 8, 10, 14–15, housing quotation from 15; 1864–65, 4–6; 1865–66, 4–6; 1867–68, 7; agricultural-tuition quotation from 1870–71, 28 (also in catalogue of Harvard University, 1871–72, 2nd ed., 108). Faculty records of Harvard University, vol. 18, 10 Oct. 1870, HUA. Thernstrom, "'Poor but Hopefull Scholars,'" 123. Catalogue of Harvard University, 1862–63, 1st term, 38.

20. Quotations from trustees minutes of Mount Holyoke Female Seminary, 5 July 1871, MHCA; Ward, "Report for 1873," 5; Julia E. Ward, "Report for 1874," 1 July 1874, 4–5, and "Report for 1875," 30 June 1875, 4, photocopies, Principals and Presidents, Copies of Reports, folders 1 and 2; [Julia E. Ward], "Report for 1876," 21 June 1876, 6–8, photocopy, ibid., folder 2; Andrew J. Moulder, *Report of the Regents of the University of California, Relative to the Operations and Progress of the Institution* ([Sacramento]: Springer, [1872]), 7, in *Pamphlets on the College of California*, UCA; *Prospectus of the University of California*, 26, WML; *Register of the University of California*, 1870–71, 65.

21. "Cornell College," MS, [ca. 1875], William Fletcher King Papers, Advertising Folder, CCA; Mary Ellis and Julia E. Ward, Annual Report, 5 July 1871, 7, photocopy, Principals and Presidents, Copies of Reports, folder 1; Ellis, Principal's Report, 3 July 1872, 5; Julia E. Ward, "Report for 1877," 20 June 1877, 1, photocopy, Principals and Presidents, Copies of Reports, folder 2; faculty minutes of Cornell College, 21 Dec. 1876; "Recollections of Olive Burr Fellows," 28–30, 33; Foster, "Early Recollections of Cornell College," CCA; "Short Lived Graduates," *Collegian*, 1 Sept. 1870, 1, CCA; Ezra S. Carr, report to Board of Regents of the University of California, 18 July 1871, 4, UC Regents Collection, box 1, folder 5; Professor [Ezra S.] Carr, "The University," *San Francisco Daily Chronicle*, 27 Sept. 1874, 5, clipping, UC Regents Collection, box 1, folder 5.

22. Dew, *Apostles of Disunion*, 54, 56–58, 78–81.

23. Cornelius, "When I Can Read," 18, 32–34, 37–42.

24. Folmsbee, "Blount College," 27–28, 30; Montgomery, Folmsbee, and Greene, *To Foster Knowledge*, 11–13; Nobles, *College for Mississippians*; Akers, *Wesleyan College*, 10–11, 45; Farnham, *Southern Belle*, 15–32, 2–3; Jabour, *Scarlett's Sisters*, 52–55. Margaret A. Nash argues that antebellum Americans viewed academics as a "separate . . . realm" in which gender differences mattered little. Nash, *Women's Education*, 1 (quotation), 5–8.

25. See chapter 1.

26. University of Virginia Geospatial and Statistical Data Center, "Historical Census Browser."

27. The figure 219 includes students enrolled in the regular preparatory or collegiate course; it excludes students who studied only music, drawing and painting, or ornamental work. Trustees minutes of Wesleyan Female College, 9 July 1861, WCA; catalogue of Wesleyan Female College, 1860–61, 13–21, in [Bass], *Catalogues. Wesleyan Female College, 1848 to 1881*, WCA.

28. Francis Peabody, "These Many Years (The Bellamy Collection of Catalogues)," *Wesleyan Alumnae*, Oct. 1925, 14, WCA.

29. Banks, *Memories*, 61.

30. Catalogue of Wesleyan Female College, 1860–65; Banks, *Memories*, 31–32, 37; Ella Burton Scarborough, "Memories," *Wesleyan Alumnae*, July 1925, 28 (quotation). See also Marion Elder Jones, review of *The Portal of Wonderland*, by Mary Culler White, ibid., Apr. 1925, 13.

31. Thornton and Ekelund, *Tariffs, Blockades, and Inflation*, 74.

32. Trustees minutes of Wesleyan Female College, 15 Feb., 8 July, 28 Nov. 1862; J. M. Bonnell, "Report of the President," in trustees minutes of Wesleyan Female College, 29 June 1863.

33. The cost of books, the one additional required expense, varied by course. Catalogue of Wesleyan Female College, 1860–61, 30.

34. Ibid., 1862–63, 21, 5–12, 16.

35. Trustees minutes of Wesleyan Female College, 2 May 1863; Thornton and Ekelund, *Tariffs, Blockades, and Inflation*, 73–74.

36. Bonnell, "Report of the President," 29 June 1863.

37. Trustees minutes of Wesleyan Female College, 30 June 1863, 20 Aug. 1863, 12 July 1864.

38. Catalogue of Wesleyan Female College, 1863–64, 14; trustees minutes of Wesleyan Female College, 27, 29 Aug., 5 Nov. 1864, 18 Mar. 1865, quotation from 27 Aug. 1864, emphasis in original.

39. The drop was probably even more dramatic. The catalogue for 1863–64 cited an enrollment of 244 in the literary department, 175 in the ornamental department, and 25 taking drawing and painting classes (these groups overlapped). The next year's catalogue gave 112 as the enrollment in what formerly had been known as the literary department; the other programs appear to have ceased operation temporarily. Catalogue of Wesleyan Female College, 1861–62, 5–10, 13; 1862–63, 5–12, 16; 1863–64, 4–11; 1864–65, 5–10.

40. Scarborough, "Memories," 28.

41. Trustees minutes of Wesleyan Female College, 11 July 1865; catalogue of Wesleyan Female College, 1865–71.

42. Jean Oliphant, "Wesleyan College Presents Sidney Lanier, Flutist," *Wesleyan Alumnae*, Jan. 1925, 10.

43. Leila F. Wood, "Composition," June 1877, [4], in Commencement Essays/Compositions Collection, Leila F. Wood Folder, WCA.

44. Annie R. Barron, "In search of a Subject," 1875, [7–8], in Commencement Essays/Compositions Collection, Annie E. [sic] Barron Folder.

45. Faculty minutes of Wesleyan Female College, Sept. 1866, quoted in untitled article in "College Days in the South," [5], WCA.

46. Catalogue of Wesleyan Female College, 1865–75, esp. 1865–66, 25.

47. For trustees' identities, see ibid., 1865–66, 3.

48. Tyack and Hansot, *Learning Together*, 49.

49. Eugenia Jones, "Hard Times," July 1875, [1–9], quotations from [2], [1], [8], in Commencement Essays/Compositions Collection, Senior Composition, "Hard Times" Envelope.

50. Farnham, *Southern Belle*, 181–82.

51. Catalogue of Wesleyan Female College, 1875–76, 31.

52. Farnham, *Southern Belle*, 18; catalogue of the University of Missouri, 1858–59, 16, UMA.

53. Quinn, *Edgar Allen Poe*, chaps. 1–2 and pp. 99, 109–12, 114, Poe quoted on 110.

54. Catalogue of the University of Missouri, 1859–60, 11; *American Almanac*, 235.

55. "Scholarship Funds with Principal Invested," [1], Student Welfare/Student Aid Collection, folder 1, UMA. See also University of the State of Missouri, report containing catalogue, 1870–71, 61, UMA.

56. Catalogue of the University of Missouri, 1859–60, 11.

57. Wagoner, "Honor and Dishonor," 168n37.

58. See chapter 1.

59. Switzler, "University of the State of Missouri," UMA.

60. Catalogue of the University of Missouri, 1860–61, 6–10; Switzler, "University of the State of Missouri," 195; Viles, *University of Missouri*, 105.

61. Switzler, "University of the State of Missouri," 205, 207; catalogue of the University of Missouri, 1862–65, 21.

62. Ranney, *In the Wake of Slavery*, 91–92; Glymph, "Freedpeople and Ex-Masters," 48–50, 61–64; Fields, "Capitalist Agriculture," 79, 81–83, 86–87; M. Fitzgerald, *Splendid Failure*, 58.

63. M. Fitzgerald, *Splendid Failure*, 56–58, 61; Ranney, *In the Wake of Slavery*, 92–94; Glymph, "Freedpeople and Ex-Masters," 50–52, 61–64; Fields, "Capitalist Agriculture," 80–81, 86–87; Woodman, "Reconstruction of the Cotton Plantation," 109–10, 112.

64. "Agricultural College. Historical," *University Missourian*, May 1872, 5, UMSC (quotation); University of the State of Missouri, report containing catalogue, 1871, 55.

65. Catalogue of the University of Missouri, 1866–67, 17–18; Switzler, "University of the State of Missouri," 238 (quotation).

66. James S. Rollins, quoted in "Honor to Whom Honor Is Due," *University Missourian*, Apr. 1872, 4; "A Free University," ibid., Feb. 1872, 4; University of the State of Missouri, report containing catalogue, 1871, 68; "Appropriation Bill," *University*

Missourian, Apr. 1872, 6; Foner, *Reconstruction*, 28–29, 234–35; Parrish, *History of Missouri*, 114, 140, 246, 265, 182, 238.

67. "Appropriation Bill"; "Honor to Whom Honor Is Due"; and "Free University," quotations from the latter two sources.

68. The catalogue listed 622 students for 1872–73 but omitted the normal students. Forty-two had attended that college the previous year. University of the State of Missouri, report containing catalogue, 1872, 36–43; 1873, 44–55, 75–78.

69. Eddy, *Colleges*, 66–68.

70. Catalogue of the University of Missouri, 1868–69, 33–34; Switzler, "University of the State of Missouri," 268–69; University of the State of Missouri, report containing catalogue, 1871, 68–69; "Local Department," *University Missourian*, Sept. 1871, 7.

71. University of the State of Missouri, report containing catalogue, 1870, 36 (quotation); "Free Students to the School of Mines," *University Missourian*, Jan. 1872, 8, originally published in *Rolla Herald*; T. C. Wilson to Henri [Chomeau], 13 Mar. 1874, Henri Chomeau Papers, folder 4, WHMC.

72. "Free University." See also Switzler, "University of the State of Missouri," 239–40.

73. Solomon, *Educated Women*, 45–47; Ogren, *State Normal School*, 65–66; catalogue of the University of Missouri, 1867–68, 22, and 1868–69, 10; University of the State of Missouri, report containing catalogue, 1870, 35, 43.

74. University of the State of Missouri, report containing catalogue, 1872, 23–26, quotations from 24 and 26; faculty records of the University of Missouri, 4 May 1876, UMA. See also "First Women Graduates, Missouri University," University of Missouri at Columbia Papers, Collection C1708, WHMC; Laura Varner Clark to [R. L. Hill], 25 Aug. 1926, University of Missouri Papers, Collection C0181, folder 3, WHMC.

75. Cornelius, *"When I Can Read,"* 32–34, 37–42; U.S. Department of the Interior, *Statistics*, 507; drawing in newspaper clipping, [1860s?], in scrapbook, ca. 1870–1909, William James Rivers Papers, SCL.

76. Catalogue of South Carolina College, 1860, 26; 1861, 24; 1862, 18, Catalogue of Trustees, Faculty and Students Collection, USCA. *American Almanac*, 235. Hollis, *University of South Carolina*, 1:263.

77. Catalogue of South Carolina College, 1860, 24; 1861, 22; 1862, 16. See also faculty minutes of South Carolina College, vol. 7, 4 Feb., 21 Oct., 4 Nov. 1861, 3 Feb. 1862, USCA.

78. Catalogue of South Carolina College, 1860, 25; 1861, 23; 1862, 17. E. Green, *University of South Carolina*, 66. Clariosophic Literary Society minutes, vol. 18, 9 Mar. 1861, USCA.

79. See chapter 1. Quotations from M. LaBorde, "Dr. LaBorde's Report," in trustees minutes of South Carolina College, vol. 7, 7 May 1862, USCA; and faculty minutes of South Carolina College, vol. 7, 17 Mar. 1862.

80. R. W. Barnwell, "Report of the Chairman of the Faculty," trustees minutes of South Carolina College, vol. 7, 11 Nov. 1866. See also chapter 2.

81. R. W. Barnwell, "Report of the Chairman of the Faculty," and W. J. Rivers, "Report of Professor of Ancient Languages and Literature," trustees minutes of South Carolina College, vol. 7, 9 May 1866; John Calhoun Sellers to Edwin Green, 1912, in Matalene and Reynolds, *Carolina Voices*, 54 (quotation). See also other faculty reports, trustees minutes of South Carolina College, vol. 7, 9 May 1866; and Charles Hutson, memoirs, quoted in Matalene and Reynolds, *Carolina Voices*, 52.

82. The figure $320 presumes enrollment in three schools of the university, the normal course load. C. Bruce Walker, *Prospectus of the University of South Carolina. MDCCCLXVI* (Columbia: Office of the Southern Presbyterian Review, 1866), 5, 15, Catalogue of Trustees, Faculty and Students Collection, USCA.

83. Thornton and Ekelund, *Tariffs, Blockades, and Inflation*, 71.

84. E. Green, *University of South Carolina*, 89; faculty minutes of the University of South Carolina, vol. 7, 8 June 1867, USCA; Walker, *Prospectus*, 14; catalogue of the University of South Carolina, 1870, 5–6, and 1871, 7–8, Catalogue of Trustees, Faculty and Students Collection; W. J. Rivers, "South Carolina College. This History of its Foundation, Rise and Fall. An Address Before the National Education Association," newspaper clipping, [1876], in scrapbook, Fisk P. Brewer Papers, SCL.

85. Joseph LeConte, "Report of the Professor of Chemistry, Pharmacy, Mineralogy & Geology"; John LeConte, "Report of the Professor of Nat. & Mech. Philos. & Astronomy"; E. P. Alexander, "Report of the Professor of Mathematics, Civil & Mil'ry Engineering & Construction"; Rivers, "Report of Professor of Ancient Languages and Literature"; and M. LaBorde, "Report of the Professor of Rhetoric, Criticism, Elocution, & Engl. Lang. & Lit.," in trustees minutes of the University of South Carolina, vol. 7, 9 May 1866, USCA.

86. Jas. Wood Davidson to G. H. McMaster, 14 Jan. 1868, James Wood Davidson Papers, folder 2, SCL; Cyrus D. Melton to Robert W. Barnwell, 26 Nov. 1872, in 19th Century Manuscripts Collection, Faculty Papers (quotation).

87. Williamson, *After Slavery*, 396, 357, 362, 260–61, 266–67, 144–45; Holt, *Black over White*, 96–97, 131, 153, 143–44; Edward Crossland to George Crossland, 24 Nov. 1868 and 27 Feb. 1869, in Matalene and Reynolds, *Carolina Voices*, 56.

88. E. Smith, *From Whence Cometh My Help*, 13–17; Schwalbe, *Remembering Reet and Shine*, 18; U.S. Census Bureau, "1870 United States Federal Census," Schedule 1 for Macon, GA, 231.

89. Other black colleges did not officially exclude whites, but few or none enrolled. Peck, *Berea's First 125 Years*, 12–19, 24–25, 31, 40–42; Sears, *Utopian Experiment*, 39, 41–46, 55, 167; Richardson, *Christian Reconstruction*, 134–35, 132, 193–94, 124.

90. Span, *Cotton Field*, 132–33; Frost, *Thinking Confederates*, 75, 77–78.

91. Morgan and Preston, *Edge of Campus*, 3, 9; Leflar, *First 100 Years*, 273; Frost, *Thinking Confederates*, 78.

92. Hollis, *University of South Carolina*, 2:63; trustees minutes of the University of South Carolina, vol. 8, 10 Oct. 1873 (quotation).

93. Murray, *Race Ideals*, 7; catalogue of the University of South Carolina, 1876, 9.

94. Trustees minutes of the University of South Carolina, vol. 7, 16 Apr. 1873 (quotations), and vol. 8, 10 Oct. 1873.

95. A number of historians have explored the roles of gender and of women in Reconstruction. Most have focused on ways in which black and white Southern women tried to preserve or modify domestic structures and economic conditions, rather than on women's gaining access to traditionally masculine institutions. See Edwards, *Gendered Strife and Confusion;* O'Donovan, *Becoming Free;* and Farmer-Kaiser, *Freedwomen.* Others have linked Reconstruction with heightened efforts to win voting or property rights for women. See DuBois, *Feminism and Suffrage,* esp. p. 19 and chaps. 2–3, 6; and Ranney, *In the Wake of Slavery,* chap. 9.

96. J. Anderson, *Education of Blacks,* 30–31, 36; Ogren, *State Normal School,* 56, 59–61, 67, 46.

97. *Circular of the State Normal School,* 11, 7 (quotation), 5; *Catalogue of the State Normal School,* 15–16, 5, 9, 18–19, quotation from 15; Mortimer A. Warren, report, 31 May 1877, quoted in Matalene and Reynolds, *Carolina Voices,* 65.

98. Catalogue of the University of South Carolina, 1872, 47; Simmons, *Men of Mark,* 878–80.

99. Trustees minutes of the University of South Carolina, vol. 8, 10 Oct. 1873; *Re-Organization of the University of South Carolina, in 1873, and Catalogue for 1872–'73* (n.p., [1873?]), 18, Catalogue of Trustees, Faculty and Students Collection (quotation). See also catalogue of the University of South Carolina, 24 May 1875, [1]; 1876, 26; 1877, 26, Catalogue of Trustees, Faculty and Students Collection.

100. J. Anderson, *Education of Blacks,* 8, 18–19; Williamson, *After Slavery,* 219.

101. Students, letter to the editor, *Columbia Daily Union-Herald,* [Feb. 1875?], in scrapbook, Fisk P. Brewer Papers.

102. Trustees minutes of the University of South Carolina, vol. 8, 10 Oct. 1873; Cornelius Chapman Scott, "When Negroes Attended the University," *Columbia State,* 8 May 1911, quoted in Matalene and Reynolds, *Carolina Voices,* 57–59; Mortimer A. Warren, report, 20 June 1876, quoted in ibid., 64; Mounter, "Richard Theodore Greener," 134–35, 142–43; B. B. Babbitt, *Report of the Chairman of the Faculty of the University of South Carolina, in Response to A Resolution of the House of Representatives and of the Senate, Passed February 18, 1875* (Columbia: Republican, 1875), 19–52, 56–57, Catalogue of Trustees, Faculty and Students Collection; catalogue of the University of South Carolina, 1876, 26; University of Virginia Geospatial and Statistical Data Center, "Historical Census Browser." See also T. McCants Stewart, letter to the editor, *Washington New National Era,* 16 Apr. 1874, in Matalene and Reynolds, *Carolina Voices,* 61.

103. Tindall, *South Carolina Negroes,* 56–57, 204–5.

104. Trustees minutes of the University of South Carolina, vol. 8, 3, 10, 28 Oct. 1873; "The Phœnix and the University," 16 Oct. 1873, and "The Phœnix Answered. A Vigorous and Caustic Reply—Some Hard Stubborn Facts—The Policy of the Party in the Matter of the State University Fully Vindicated," 3 Jan. 1874, newspaper clippings in scrapbook, Fisk P. Brewer Papers; "The School Question in South Carolina," newspaper clipping, 31 May 1877, in scrapbook, Fisk P. Brewer Papers;

Rivers, "South Carolina College" (quotation); Trimpi, *Crimson Confederates*, 364; *Re-Organization*, 4–5; catalogue dated 24 May 1875, 2; Scott, "When Negroes Attended the University," 57–59; Stewart, letter to *Washington New National Era*, 16 Apr. 1874, 61. According to a newspaper from much later, by 1876 blacks made up about 90% of the student body. Clipping, *Greenwood (SC) Index-Journal*, in Reconstruction Subject File, USCA. It is unclear where white students went after they withdrew from the university. They may have moved to nearby colleges. One year after the admission of blacks, the combined student populations of the other white colleges in South Carolina increased by about 9%. Erskine College, eighty miles to the west, nearly doubled in size, from 72 to 134. A year later, though, enrollment fell at nearly every college in the state. U.S. Bureau of Education, report, 1874, 680–81, 190; 1875, 725, 735; 1876, 706, 715–16.

105. Fisk Brewer, report on the admission of black students (1876), quoted in Matalene and Reynolds, *Carolina Voices*, 65; T. McCants Stewart, letter to the editor, *Washington New National Era*, 9 July 1874, in ibid., 61 (quotation); letter to the editor, *Columbia Daily Union-Herald*, 10 Feb. 1875, quoted in ibid., 62 (quotation).

106. South Carolina University, *Act and Summary of Act Relating to State Scholarships* (n.p., [1873?]), Catalogue of Trustees, Faculty and Students Collection; *Re-Organization*, 18–20; Babbitt, *Report*, 16–18; [G.?] J. Reynolds and J. J. Holland to Hon. Gentlemen of the Faculty, 29 Apr. 1876, 19th Century Manuscripts Collection, Miscellaneous Student Documents, Petitions on Behalf of Suspended Students; Heard, *From Slavery to Bishopric*, 37 (quotation).

107. Babbitt, *Report*, 13–15. I calculated this figure based on twenty dollars per month per student for ten months per year, as indicated in trustees minutes of the University of South Carolina, vol. 8, 17 June 1874.

108. E. J. Sawyer et al. to the President and Faculty of the University of S.C., 9 Oct. 1875, and Whitefield McKinlay et al. to the Hon. President and Members of the Faculty of the U.S.C., 27 May 1876, both in 19th Century Manuscripts Collection, Miscellaneous Student Documents, Misc. Petitions.

109. Martinez, *Carpetbaggers*, 206–13; Holt, *Black over White*, 175–211; Zuczek, *State of Rebellion*, chap. 9; Williamson, *After Slavery*, 258, 272, 405–16.

110. Benjn. B. Babbit to Wade Hampton, 11 Aug. 1879, quotation from [1], Benjamin B. Babbitt Papers, USCA; trustees minutes of the University of South Carolina, vol. 9, 30 July 1877; Hollis, *University of South Carolina*, 2:94; catalogue of the South Carolina College of Agriculture and Mechanics, 1881–82, Catalogue of Trustees, Faculty and Students Collection; Miles, *How to Improve Education*.

111. E. Green, *University of South Carolina*, 122, 113; Hollis, *University of South Carolina*, 2:80, 145; Wallenstein, "Higher Education," 13–14.

112. Hollis, *University of South Carolina*, 2:61–63; Potts, *South Carolina State College*, 1–3, 9–11; Tindall, *South Carolina Negroes*, 226–28; Williamson, *After Slavery*, 220–23.

113. Catalogue of South Carolina College, 1882–83, 25–28, 36–39; Eugene Whitefield Dabbs to parents, 11 Oct., 12, 28 Nov. 1880, quoted in Matalene and Reynolds, *Carolina Voices*, 67, 69; Charles Coker Wilson, Forum Club paper, in ibid., 66.

114. Catalogue of South Carolina College, 1882–83, 46; Dabbs to parents, 11 Oct. 1880, 67.

115. These calculations exclude a few colleges that included board in their reported tuition figures and use the mean tuition for colleges that reported multiple figures. I cannot calculate an exact mean tuition for 1870, because most tuition figures that year are given by the term, without specifying how many terms made up a year. Assuming that every one of these colleges used semesters or trimesters, the average annual tuition for all colleges fell between $121 and $158. U.S. Bureau of Education, report, 1870, 506–17; 1880, 640–51 and 664–75.

FOUR. Admissions: Geography, Service, Morality

1. Lynch, diary, esp. front flyleaf, 18, 27 Sept., 13 Oct., 24 Sept., 12 Nov., 16 Sept. 1865, and cash account at end, WHMC.

2. Frederickson, *Inner Civil War*, 184–86; McPherson, *Battle Cry of Freedom*, 859; G. Wills, *Lincoln at Gettysburg*, 145–47; Lawson, *Patriot Fires*, 3, 11–13, 181, 184–85; Onuf and Onuf, *Nations, Markets, and War*, prologue; Stout, *Upon the Altar*, xvii–xxii, 249–51, 458–59.

3. Wiebe, *Search for Order*, xiii, 2–10. For a similar argument for localism during the war, see Gallman, *North Fights the Civil War*, 31, 123, 171–72, 180, 182, 188.

4. See Burke, *Collegiate Populations*.

5. Unless otherwise stated, all changes within a region are statistically significant at the $\alpha = 0.05$ confidence level. As elsewhere in this book, the term *South* refers to the District of Columbia and all states that were slave states in 1861.

6. Catalogue of South Carolina College, 1860, 12–17, Catalogue of Trustees, Faculty and Students Collection, USCA; catalogue of Wesleyan Female College, 1860–61, 13–21, in [Bass], *Catalogues. Wesleyan Female College, 1848 to 1881*, WCA.

7. U.S. Department of the Interior, *Mount Holyoke*, WML; catalogue of Harvard University, 1860–61, 1st term, 10–26, 51–52, 56–62, 72–74, 81, WML; Burke, *Collegiate Populations*, 109; Thernstrom, "'Poor but Hopefull Scholars,'" 117; Trimpi, *Crimson Confederates*, 375–76.

8. Catalogue of Cornell College, 1858–59, 7–15, CCA.

9. U.S. Bureau of Education, *Vital Statistics of College Graduates*, 45–70.

10. Kiddle and Schem, *Cyclopædia of Education*, 443, 617.

11. University of the State of Missouri, report containing catalogue, 1871–72, 36–42, 62–63, UMA; catalogue of Harvard University, 1876–77.

12. Michael Lynch et al., "Resolutions of Students at Large of Mechanics Arts College University of California," 15 July 1871, [1], [3] (quotation), UC Regents Collection, box 3, folder 21, UCA.

13. *American Almanac*, 235.

14. *Placer (County, CA) Herald*, 27 July 1867, quoted in "Oakland College School," *College Echo*, Feb. 1868, tipped in between 4 and 5, UCA. See also *San Francisco Evening Bulletin*, 14 June 1867, quoted in ibid.

15. *Oakland College School*, 17, BL.

16. Martin Kellogg, speech, quoted in "The State University. Celebration of Charter Day at Berkeley," *San Francisco Daily Evening Post*, 24 Mar. 1876, clipping, in Kellogg, *Papers and Addresses*, item 4, UCA.

17. "State University. Important Legislation for its Benefit—Fund for its Support," newspaper clipping, [1870], UC Regents Collection, box 3, Legislature, 1872, 1876 Folder; "Resolutions of Academic Senate Relative to Competitive Scholarships, & Branch of Mechanic Arts College in S.F.," 1870, UC Regents Collection, box 4, folder 17 (quotation); *State University School*, BL.

18. Catalogue of the College of California, 1866–67, 6–7, and 1867–68, 7–8, 23–29, in *Pamphlets on the College of California*, UCA; *Register of the University of California. Department of Letters and Science*, 7–13, WML.

19. Read, *Address of Daniel Read*, 19. "A Free University," *University Missourian*, Feb. 1872, 4, UMSC. "Honor to Whom Honor Is Due," ibid., Apr. 1872, 4. University of the State of Missouri, report containing catalogue, 1871–72, 36–42, 62–63; 1872–73, 44–54, 75–77; 1876–77, 26.

20. The figures in this paragraph exclude those taking only classes in music, drawing, painting, or ornamental work, whose places of origin the catalogues did not identify. Catalogue of Wesleyan Female College, 1863–64, 4–11.

21. Iobst, *Civil War Macon*, chaps. 8–9, pp. 308–20, 346–55; McPherson, *Battle Cry of Freedom*, 743–55, 773–74; Trudeau, *Southern Storm*, 34, 38, 70, chaps. 10–13; catalogue of Wesleyan Female College, 1863–64, 13; Lyndon, recollections, 15.

22. The music and art programs, whose students are excluded from enrollment figures by geography for 1863–64, apparently no longer existed in 1864–65. Catalogue of Wesleyan Female College, 1863–64, 4–11; 1864–65, 5–10.

23. Ibid., 1864–77.

24. Leila A. Ross, "Of all sad words of tongue or pen / The saddest are these, it might have been," 1871, [2], in Commencement Essays/Compositions Collection, Mary C. Fears and Leila A. Ross Folder, WCA. See also Eugenia Jones, "Hard Times," July 1875, [5], in Commencement Essays/Compositions Collection, Senior Composition, "Hard Times" envelope, WCA; and U.S. Census Bureau, "1870 United States Federal Census," Schedule 1 for Macon, GA.

25. Catalogue of South Carolina College, 1860, 12–17; 1861, 12–16. U.S. Census Bureau, "1860 United States Federal Census," Schedule 1 for Columbia, SC, 102–6.

26. M. LaBorde, "Dr. LaBorde's Report," in trustees minutes of South Carolina College, vol. 7, 7 May 1862, USCA.

27. Catalogue of the University of South Carolina, 1867–72, Catalogue of Trustees, Faculty and Students Collection.

28. Trustees minutes of the University of South Carolina, vol. 8, 10 Oct. 1873; catalogue of the University of South Carolina, 24 May 1875, [1], Catalogue of Trustees, Faculty and Students Collection.

29. Hahn, *Nation under Our Feet*, esp. chap. 4.

30. Michigan had established both public schools and an affordable state university by 1841, then eliminated university tuition for Michigan residents a decade later. *Re-Organization of the University of South Carolina, in 1873*, and *Catalogue for*

1872–'73 (n.p., [1873?]), 18, Catalogue of Trustees, Faculty and Students Collection; Roper, "Radical Mission," 9; Peckham, *University of Michigan*, 17, 24, 26.

31. Catalogue of the University of South Carolina, 1876, 7–14. These percentages exclude the normal school, for which enrollment numbers from that year have not survived. In the fall of 1874 it enrolled twenty from Columbia and eleven from elsewhere in the state. *Catalogue of the State Normal School*, 21, GL.

32. Catalogue of the South Carolina College of Agriculture and Mechanics, 1881–82, Catalogue of Trustees, Faculty and Students Collection, 8–10; catalogue of South Carolina College, 1882–83, 18–23, quoted note handwritten on 22.

33. Catalogue of Cornell College, 1858–59, 1860–77.

34. See Lubetkin, *Union College's Class of 1868*, 13, 36, 40, 67; and chapter 1.

35. Bishop, *History of Cornell*, 121; Trimpi, *Crimson Confederates*, 375.

36. Altschuler and Blemin, *GI Bill*, 7–8, 13–18; Oberly, "Gray-Haired Lobbyists," 35–36, 56.

37. Skocpol, *Protecting Soldiers and Mothers*, 106–11, 139–40; McClintock, "Civil War Pensions," 463–64, 458; Logue, *To Appomattox and Beyond*, 89–91, 123–24; Altschuler and Blemin, *GI Bill*, 18–19, 216n12; Davies, "Mexican War Veterans," 225–26; McClurken, *Take Care of the Living*, 143–56.

38. Jordan, *Charlottesville*, 76–77; Rudy, *Campus*, 71, 91; Frost, *Thinking Confederates*, 91–92; Leflar, *First 100 Years*, 5.

39. Rudy, *Campus*, 70–71, 91, announcement quoted on 70; Chessman, *Ohio Colleges*, 27. See also chapter 1.

40. *Minutes for the Board of Trustees*, 26 June 1864, 16 May, 27 June 1865, 1 June 1869, CCA; King, *Reminiscences*, 210–15; Wm. F. King, handwritten note on H. H. Rood, "Effect of the Civil war upon the College," MS of speech, [1880s], 9, William Fletcher King Papers, Speeches Folder, CCA (quotation); untitled MS, [ca. 1878], William Fletcher King Papers, Scholarships, General Folder, CCA; Foster, "Early Recollections of Cornell College," 89, CCA; catalogue of Cornell College, 1864–78; *Trustee Minutes*, 18 Jan. 1895, 8 Jan. 1897, 24–25 Apr. 1902, CCA.

41. King, *Reminiscences*, 214; Rood, "Effect of the Civil war," 7–8 (quotation).

42. Burke, *Collegiate Populations*, 127, 102; H. H. Freer, "Class of Sixty-Nine," *Collegian*, 1 Nov. 1869, [3], CCA; Sam. J. Smyth, "History of the Class of '72, as read by Sam. J. Smyth, at the Adelphian Class Exercises," ibid., 1 July 1872, 4. The imprecise figures result from Burke's rounding technique. See also Allmendinger, *Paupers and Scholars*, 10, 134–35, 138.

43. [Julia E. Ward], "Report for 1876," 21 June 1876, 4–5, photocopy, Principals and Presidents, Copies of Reports, folder 1, MHCA.

44. B. B. Babbitt, *Report of the Chairman of the Faculty of the University of South Carolina, in Response to A Resolution of the House of Representatives and of the Senate, Passed February 18, 1875* (Columbia: Republican, 1875), 7 (quotation), 58–59, Catalogue of Trustees, Faculty and Students Collection.

45. Ellen C. Parsons, "Mount Holyoke in War Time. Tense Days of Student Life. Recollections of a Graduate," photocopy of clipping from *Springfield (MA) Sunday Republican*, 6 Oct. 1912, Civil War Folder, MHCA; Belle [Thomas] to [Walter

Thomas], 7 Aug. 1864, Belle Thomas Papers, ser. 1, folder 5, and archival register, MHCA; catalogue of Harvard University, 1869–70, 103; University of the State of Missouri, report containing catalogue, 1872, 39–42.

46. Faculty minutes of Cornell College, 20–31 Mar. 1868, 7–11 Dec. 1871, 7 Oct. 1872, CCA.

47. Rudolph, *American College and University,* chap. 4; Findlay, "Agency, Denominations, and the Western Colleges," 119–21, 125.

48. Geiger, "Introduction," 20; Sugrue, "'We Desired Our Future Rulers,'" 103–4; catalogue of South Carolina College, 1860, 20 (quotation).

49. Catalogue of the College of California, 1860–61, 5, 1862–63, 8; *By-Laws of the University of South Carolina, as Revised and Adopted by The Board of Trustees, at the Annual Meeting in 1866. To Which Are Prefixed the Act to Establish the University of South Carolina, and the Subsequent Act in Amendment Thereto; and to Which Are Annexed Regulations of the Library Committee, and Also, Regulations of the Faculty of the University* (Columbia: Deane, 1867), 15, Catalogue of Trustees, Faculty and Students Collection; *Regulations of the Faculty* (n.p., [1875]), 10, Catalogue of Trustees, Faculty and Students Collection; catalogue of Harvard University, 1865–66, 1st term, 81, and 1871–72, 2nd ed., 105; *Annual Catalogue of the Mount Holyoke Female Seminary,* 1859–77.

50. Catalogue of the University of South Carolina, 1866–76; *By-Laws of the University of South Carolina . . . 1866,* 26; *By-Laws of the University of South Carolina . . . 1869,* 27, SCL.

51. *Circular of the State Normal School,* 7–8, quotation from 7, GL; *Catalogue of the State Normal School,* 18.

52. Faculty records of the University of Missouri, 25 Sept. 1869, 6 Sept. 1870, 1 Dec. 1876 (quotation), UMA.

53. Harvard Corporation formal minutes, vol. 11, 1, 28 Sept. 1869, HUA; Harvard overseers formal minutes, vol. 10, 2, 9, 16, 30 Sept. 1869, Records of the Board of Overseers, HUA; faculty records of Harvard University, vol. 18, 4 Oct. 1869, 4 Apr. 1870, HUA.

54. Catalogue of Cornell College, 1860–77; [Stephen N. Fellows], MS of address, [1882], 6, Samuel Fellows Box, CCA (quotation); "Cornell College," MS, [ca. 1875], William Fletcher King Papers, Advertising Folder, CCA; faculty minutes of Cornell College, 18 Feb. 1868, 10 Feb. 1869.

55. Freer, "Class of Sixty-Nine," [3]; Philomathean Society minutes, 1865–77 passim, CCA; Amphictyon Society minutes, 1864–74 passim, CCA; editorial, *Collegian,* 1 Mar. 1873, 4.

56. Catalogue of Wesleyan Female College, 1860–77; 1874–75, 33, and 1875–77 (quotation); Banks, *Memories,* 39; "What We Have Observed and Heard," *Philomathean Gazette,* [1869–77], PMFA (quotation).

57. "Selections from the Journal of Annie L. Lane," ed. Charles Lane Hanson, 6 Jan. 1862, TS 1953, Anne L. Lane Papers, folder 2 (quotation); Brown, "Fourscore Plus," 81; trustees minutes of Mount Holyoke Female Seminary, 10 Feb. 1875; and Mary O. Nutting, Principal's Annual Report, 4 July 1870, 2–3, photocopy, Principals and Presidents, Copies of Reports, folder 1, all in MHCA.

58. Mary (Haynes) Lane, "Mount Holyoke's Golden Age," read at the meeting of the Hampshire County Mount Holyoke Alumnae Association, Hatfield, MA, 26 Oct. 1907, TS, 7, Mary Haynes Lane Papers, box 1, ser. 2, folder 3, MHCA; [Edward N.] Kirk, quoted therein, 8.

59. Sarah [Stow] to Mr. & Mrs. Humphrey, 26 Sept. and 4 Feb. 1864, Sarah D. (Locke) Stow Papers, ser. A, folders 3 and 2, MHCA; "Selections from the Journal of Annie L. Lane," 21 Sept. 1861 and 12 Oct. 1862; Lane, "Mount Holyoke's Golden Age," 9; Mary Augusta Monroe, diary, 14 Feb. 1874, TS prepared by Eleanor Ibetson Wiedman, 1987, Mary A. Monroe Papers, folder 2, MHCA; Mary O. Nutting, Principal's Annual Report, 4 July 1870, 1–2 (quotation); Mary Ellis and Julia E. Ward, Annual Report, 5 July 1871, 5, photocopy, Principals and Presidents, Copies of Reports, folder 1, MHCA.

60. Catalogue of the College of California, 1860–61, 5, 1862–63, 8, 16; *The College of California* ([Oakland?], [1863?]), 4–5, in *California Miscellany*, BL; faculty records of the College of California, 26 Feb. 1863, 23 Feb. 1866, UCA; "Town and Country," *Oakland Daily News*, 2 Nov. 1866, [3], DML; Rowell, *Journal of a Voyage*, 16 July 1858, UCA; *Oakland College School*, 18 (quotation).

61. Catalogue of the College of California, 1861–67; Martin Kellogg, "Report of Progress for the 2nd Term, 1861–2," report no. 6, adopted 26 May 1862, [4], Reports of the College of California, 1858–66, UCA; Martin Kellogg, report no. 27, 1864, Reports of the College of California; faculty records of the College of California, 3 Mar. 1865; Samuel H. Willey, *Farewell Discourse Delivered in the Howard Street Presbyterian Church, on Sabbath Morning, April 27th, 1862* (San Francisco: Towne & Bacon, 1862), 20 (quotation), in *California Miscellany*.

62. [Samuel H. Willey] to Rev. Dr. Baldwin, 1 Sept. 1869, handwritten copy, Documents of the College of California, folder 10, UCA; *Register of the University of California*, 1870–71, 31, 39, 48, and 1872–73, 16, 20, WML.

63. Reuben, *Modern University*; Roberts and Turner, *Sacred and the Secular*; Stetar, "In Search of a Direction," 348–54.

64. Four percent is an adjustment of a figure from a historical report by the National Center for Education Statistics. Five percent is Burke's calculation for both colleges and professional schools. Both figures probably exclude students who attended only colleges' primary or preparatory departments. Snyder, *American Education*, 76. Burke, "Expansion," 111; see also 112 and 115.

65. Levine, *American College*, esp. chaps. 1–2. See also Clark, "Piggy Goes to Harvard," esp. 2–6.

FIVE. College, Community, and Nation

1. John W. Hoyt, "Group XXVIII. Educational Systems, Methods, and Libraries," in U.S. Centennial Commission, *Reports and Awards*, 82, 78.

2. Burke, *Collegiate Populations*, 25; Boorstin, *Americans*, chap. 20; Trow, "In Praise of Weakness," 11–12, 14–16; Whitehead, *Separation of College and State*, 9–15.

3. *Oxford English Dictionary*, 3rd ed., s.v. "public," http://dictionary.oed.com.ezp2.harvard.edu/ (accessed 13 Nov. 2007).

4. Creese, *Extension of University Teaching*, 25–38; Woytanowitz, *University Extension*, 17–23, 3–4; Shinagel, "Gates Unbarred," 4–23. In 1883 the Chautauqua Circle became a degree-granting university. Creese, *Extension of University Teaching*, 32.

5. Jas. Wood Davidson, Columbia Contributorial, *Yorkville (SC) Enquirer*, 21, 28 Nov. 1867, 16, 23, 30 Jan., 13, 20, 27 Feb., 5, 12, 26 Mar., 2, 30 Apr., 7, 14 May 1868, George A. Smathers Libraries, University of Florida, Gainesville; Charles Hutson, memoirs, quoted in Matalene and Reynolds, *Carolina Voices*, 53.

6. "Lecture Courses" and review quotations from "Lectures," newspaper clippings, [Mar. 1875] and [1875], in scrapbook, Fisk P. Brewer Papers, SCL.

7. University of Missouri, *Public Lectures*, 3 (quotations), 5, WML; U.S. Bureau of Education, *University of Missouri*, 49.

8. "Agricultural College. Historical," *University Missourian*, May 1872, 5, UMSC.

9. P. Hubbard, W. L. Lenon, and Edwin W. Stephan to the Hon. Executive Committee of the University of Missouri, 17 July 1874, Board of Curators Executive Board Papers, box 1, folder 1, UMA; R. L. Tadd to Hon. [Pane?] Hubbard, 17 July 1874, University of Missouri Papers, Collection C0181, folder 3, WHMC.

10. Creese, *Extension of University Teaching*, 37 (including Daniel Coit Gilman quotation); Woytanowitz, *University Extension*, 21; Harvard Corporation formal minutes, vol. 10, 26 Jan. 1861, HUA (technology quotation); *Reports of the Peabody Museum*, esp. first report (1868), 5–6, HUA.

11. Hoyt, "Group XXVIII," 42–44; Louis Agassiz, quoted in Winsor, *Reading the Shape of Nature*, 11; Albert Stetson, "Harvard University," *Undergraduate*, Jan. 1861, 172, WML; Brevities, *Magenta*, 5 Dec. 1873.

12. Joseph LeConte, "Report of the Results of First Excursion of the Scientific Party of the University," appendix to *Annual Report of the Board of Regents of the University of California, For the Year Ending May 31st, 1875. With Supplemental Financial Statements to July 1, 1875*, by Robert E. C. Stearns (Berkeley: Univ. Press, 1875), 27, UC Regents Collection, box 1, folder 7, UCA; Board of Regents of the University of California, resolution, 14 Mar. 1876, [1], UC Regents Collection, box 2, folder 7; Le Conte, *Religion and Science*, 3–4.

13. Board of Regents of the University of California, resolution, 21 June 1870, quoted in Professor [Ezra S.] Carr, "The University," *San Francisco Daily Chronicle*, 27 Sept. 1874, 2–3, quotation from 2, clipping, UC Regents Collection, box 1, folder 5; faculty records of the College of California, 14 Oct. 1862, UCA.

14. E. S. Carr, report "to the President and Board of Regents," 10 Nov. 1870, 1–2, quotations from 1; Ezra S. Carr, report to Board of Regents of the University of California, 18 July 1871, 1–2; and Faculty of the University of California, *What is the Course of Study in the University of California, in Agriculture and the Mechanic Arts* (n.p., 1874), all in UC Regents Collection, box 1, folder 5.

15. See chapter 2.

16. Creese, *Extension of University Teaching*, 37–38, 40, 43–45; Woytanowitz, *University Extension*, 21, 43–45; R. Smith, *People's Colleges*, viii, 18–20.

17. Bensel, *Yankee Leviathan*, 2–4, 122–24, 169; Skowronek, *New American*

State, 30; McPherson, *Battle Cry of Freedom*, 322–24, 600; DeCanio, "State Autonomy," 121–22; Polsky, "'Mr. Lincoln's Army' Revisited," 178; Williams, "Military Leadership," 27; Cross, *Justin Smith Morrill*, 61–62; Nelson, *Roots of American Bureaucracy*; Spackman, "Beyond the Federal Consensus," 51.

18. Bensel, *Yankee Leviathan*, 333; Hoffer, *To Enlarge the Machinery*, 88; Foner, *Reconstruction*, 148; Lawson, *Patriot Fires*, 181–82. On Hayes's order, see chapter 3.

19. Bensel, *Yankee Leviathan*, 416–19, 423–24, 15–16.

20. Lawson, *Patriot Fires*, 184; Nelson, *Roots of American Bureaucracy*, 158–59. See also DeCanio, "State Autonomy."

21. Hoffer, *To Enlarge the Machinery*, 61, 103–8.

22. Scott, *Seeing Like a State*, introduction and pt. 1.

23. Kersch, "Constitutional Privacy Rights," 66; Carpenter, *Forging of Bureaucratic Autonomy*, 2, 84–85; Logue and Blanck, *Race, Ethnicity, and Disability*, 32–33, 19; Skocpol, *Protecting Soldiers and Mothers*, 106–7; McClintock, "Civil War Pensions," 471–76.

24. The seventeenth-century word *statistic*, or *statisticum*, meant "pertaining to statists or to statecraft" before it acquired its quantitative sense in the late eighteenth century. *Oxford English Dictionary*, 3rd ed., s.v. "statistics," http://dictionary.oed.com.ezp2.harvard.edu/ (accessed 13 Nov. 2007). See also Desrosières, *Politics of Large Numbers*, 173, 179.

25. Not until 1902 did Congress establish a permanent Census Bureau. Desrosières, *Politics of Large Numbers*, 190. Small early statistical projects included collecting statistics on agriculture, a minor job of the commissioner of patents beginning in 1839. Baker et al., *Century of Service*, 5–9.

26. Desrosières, *Politics of Large Numbers*, 147–48, 167–69, 179; Faust, *This Republic of Suffering*, 254–55.

27. Abraham Lincoln, "First Annual Message to Congress, December 3, 1861" and "Second Annual Message to Congress, December 1, 1862," quoted in U.S. Bureau of Agricultural Economics, *Washington, Jefferson, Lincoln*, 88–89; T. Swann Harding, *Two Blades of Grass*, 21, 27–28; Hadwiger, *Politics of Agricultural Research*, 15; Harrison, "'Weakened Spring of Government' Revisited," 64–65; Baker et al., *Century of Service*, 1, 11–15.

28. Hoffer, *To Enlarge the Machinery*, 152–56, 169–71; Goldberg and Moye, *First Hundred Years of Labor Statistics*, 3–4; Cott, *Public Vows*, 110; U.S. Department of Labor, *Report on Marriage and Divorce*, esp. 5, 9; Baker et al., *Century of Service*, 29–30.

29. Nemec, *Ivory Towers*, 1–2, 6–7, 20, 30 (quotation), 77–142 passim, 216–17. See also Rodgers, *Atlantic Crossings*, 108–10.

30. Hoffer, *To Enlarge the Machinery*, x–xii, quotation from xi.

31. Ibid., xi–xii, 38–43, 54, 88, 90, 104–5, 117.

32. University of Virginia Geospatial and Statistical Data Center, "Historical Census Browser"; U.S. Department of the Interior, *Statistics*, xiv, 502–9.

33. *Congressional Globe*, 39th Cong., 1st sess. (1865), 60.

34. Ibid. (quotation); Kaestle, *Pillars of the Republic*, 113–22; Tyack and Hansot, *Learning Together*, 56–59, 79–81.

NOTES TO PAGES 168-177

35. *Congressional Globe*, 39th Cong., 1st sess. (1865), 61; Warren, *To Enforce Education*, 79.

36. *Congressional Globe*, 39th Cong., 1st sess. (1866), 835, 3044; Judd, *Research*, 2–4; U.S. Bureau of Education, *National Bureau of Education*, 1–3.

37. *Congressional Globe*, 39th Cong., 1st sess. (1866), 835, 2966 (quotations); Peskin, *Garfield*, 49–53.

38. My source for this and the following eight paragraphs is *Congressional Globe*, 39th Cong., 1st sess. (1866), 2966–70.

39. Ibid., 3044–51, quotations from 3045, 3044, 3050, 3048.

40. Ibid., 1st sess. (1866), 3049, 3051, 3269–70, and 2nd sess. (1867), 1842–43, 1893; *Statutes at Large* 14 (1868): 434.

41. *Statutes at Large* 15 (1869): 106; 16 (1871): 242.

42. *Congressional Globe*, 39th Cong., 1st sess. (1866), 3048, 3047, and 2nd sess. (1867), 1842–43.

43. Steiner, *Life of Henry Barnard*, esp. 107–9; Judd, *Research*, 2–4; D. Smith, *Bureau of Education*, 1–2; Curti, *Social Ideas*, 140–41.

44. U.S. Bureau of Education, *Index*, 3; U.S. Department of Education, *Report of the Commissioner*, 403–32, 433–522, 311–68; U.S. Bureau of Education, report, 1870, 504.

45. U.S. Department of Education, *Report of the Commissioner*, ix–xxii, quotations from xiii, xviii. See also U.S. Bureau of Education, "Inquiries Respecting Universities and Colleges," form IX, 1877 ([Washington, DC]: [GPO], 1877), UC Regents Collection, box 2, folder 13.

46. U.S. Bureau of Education, *American Education*, 63–67, 73–74.

47. The figures for colleges exclude independent professional schools and those agricultural or scientific schools that the bureau did not classify as colleges. U.S. Bureau of Education, report, 1870, 506–17; see also 518–29. U.S. Bureau of Education, *National Bureau of Education*, 5–8.

48. U.S. Department of Education, *Report of the Commissioner*, 129–310, 657–810, 385–400.

49. U.S. Bureau of Education, report, 1875, 5–518 passim, 587–605, 702–96, 960–81.

50. U.S. Bureau of Education, *List of Publications*, 41–43, 50–51, 220 (quotation); U.S. Department of Education, *Report of the Commissioner*, xxxiii–xl; U.S. Bureau of Education, *Inquiry*, 7–70, quotation from 7.

51. U.S. Bureau of Education, *German and Other Foreign Universities*, quotation from 3; [U.S. Bureau of Education], *Suggestions for a Free School Policy*; Lykes, *Higher Education*, 40, 43–45.

52. U.S. Bureau of Education, *National Bureau of Education*, 16n.

53. Giberti, *Designing the Centennial*, 2–9, 12, 15.

54. Hoyt, "Group XXVIII," 4, 19, 69; John Eaton to the Pres. Cornell College, 11 Dec. 1872, William Fletcher King Papers, Advertising Folder, CCA; U.S. Bureau of Education, *National Bureau of Education*, 13.

55. Post, *1876*, 11; Ingram, *Centennial Exposition*, 41–46, 73.

56. Giberti, *Designing the Centennial*, chap. 1, esp. p. 27; U.S. Centennial Commission, *Official Catalogue*, pt. 1, 27–45, esp. 33; U.S. Centennial Commission, *Reports and Awards*, vii–viii.

57. Hoyt, "Group XXVIII," 4–6; U.S. Department of the Interior, *Mount Holyoke*, esp. 3–4 and insert before 1, WML.

58. Giberti, *Designing the Centennial*, 16–18; Hoyt, "Group XXVIII," 6, 2–3; U.S. Centennial Commission, *Official Catalogue*, pt. 1, 321–37.

59. U.S. Centennial Commission, *Official Catalogue*, pt. 3, 79; Hoyt, "Group XXVIII," 7–19.

60. Hoyt, "Group XXVIII," 6–7, Eaton quoted on 6; U.S. Centennial Commission, *Official Catalogue*, pt. 3, 78.

61. Hoyt, "Group XXVIII," 7–9; U.S. Centennial Commission, *Official Catalogue*, pt. 3, 78.

62. Hoyt, "Group XXVIII," 19–97.

63. Ibid., 33–34, 26–29, quotation from 27; Sir Charles Reed, "Common Schools in the United States," in U.S. Centennial Commission, *Reports and Awards*, 224; U.S. Centennial Commission, *Official Catalogue*, pt. 1, 322–23; Norton, *Frank Leslie's Illustrated Historical Register*, 267.

64. Hoyt, "Group XXVIII," 27–31, 75, 84–85, 78; U.S. Centennial Commission, *Official Catalogue*, pt. 1, 322, 236; Norton, *Frank Leslie's Illustrated Historical Register*, 266–67; Reed, "Common Schools," 221–22; Ingram, *Centennial Exposition*, 714–15, 717.

65. Hoyt, "Group XXVIII," 88, 90; U.S. Centennial Commission, *Official Catalogue*, pt. 1, 322–23.

66. Lincoln Institute Centennial Exhibit, 1876, Manuscript, Archives, and Rare Book Library, Emory University. Faculty records of the University of Missouri, 8 Oct., 5 Nov. 1875, UMA. Switzler, "University of the State of Missouri," 498, UMA. Hoyt, "Group XXVIII," 57–58; on other border states, see 35, 37, 91–93.

67. U.S. Bureau of Education, *University of Missouri*, 17n.

68. Class Notes, *Wesleyan Alumnae*, Apr. 1925, 32, WCA.

69. Hoyt, "Group XXVIII," 80–84.

70. Ibid., 44–48, 50; Reed, "Common Schools," 217, 221; U.S. Centennial Commission, *Official Catalogue*, pt. 1, 322, 324–25; Ross, *Democracy's College*, 127.

71. Hoyt, "Group XXVIII," 47–48; U.S. Centennial Commission, *Official Catalogue*, pt. 1, 324.

72. Hoyt, "Group XXVIII," 50, 42; U.S. Centennial Commission, *Official Catalogue*, pt. 1, 324.

73. B. B. Redding to Regents of the State University, 8 Feb. 1876, UC Regents Collection, box 2, folder 7; Board of Regents, resolution, 14 Mar. 1876; Wm. H. Martin to R. E. L. Sterns [Stearns], 19 Apr. 1876, UC Regents Collection, box 1, folder 2.

Conclusion

1. Frost, *Thinking Confederates*, 37–48, 80, 90, 97–101, 108–11; Dennis, *Lessons in Progress*, 3, 5–8, 19, 74–75, 80–83, 101, 131–36, 220–27, 142.

2. Gelber, *University and the People*, 3–8, 14–15, 103–8, 165, 25–29, 79–81; Sanders, *Roots of Reform*, 316–24; Simkins, *Pitchfork Ben Tillman*, 112; Ross, *Democracy's College*, 138–40; Eddy, *Colleges*, 94–100; Edmond, *Magnificent Charter*, 39–45; Hollis, *University of South Carolina*, 2:133–36, 148–53, 167; Kantrowitz, *Ben Tillman*, 117–18, 127–28.

3. Dennis, *Lessons in Progress*, 74–75, 166–68, 233–35; Frost, *Thinking Confederates*, 85.

4. Solomon, *Educated Women*, 44, 63; Frost, *Thinking Confederates*, 101, 112–13.

5. Levine, *American College*, 75, 230n8.

6. Casey, "Romantic Campus"; Thelin, *Cultivation of Ivy*, chaps. 1–3; Clark, "Piggy Goes to Harvard"; Levine, *American College*, 13–21, 32–41.

7. Lykes, *Higher Education*, 16–18, 21.

8. Frost, *Thinking Confederates*, 92–94; Neiberg, *Making Citizen-Soldiers*, 22–26, 28–29; Lyons and Masland, *Education and Military Leadership*, 36–43; Currie, *Twice the Citizen*, 28–29.

9. Rudy, *Campus*, 101–23, esp. 121–22; Gruber, *Mars and Minerva*, 255, 124–29, 174, 213, 215–16.

10. Levine, *American College*, 19, 23–24, 32–41.

11. Rudy, *Campus*, chap. 4, esp. 148–49.

12. Loss, "'Most Wonderful Thing,'" 864 (quotation), 870, 875–78, 880–86.

13. Ibid., 886–89; Altschuler and Blemin, *GI Bill*, 86, 128–29; Hunter, "Howard University," 67.

14. Trow, "Mass to Universal Higher Education," 3; Loss, "'Most Wonderful Thing,'" 889.

Bibliography

Archival Sources

Andover-Harvard Theological Library, Harvard
Divinity School, Cambridge, MA

Catalogues of the College of California and of the Seminary for Young Ladies, at Oakland, for the Year 1855–'6: With the Anniversary Oration, by the Rev. W. A. Scott, D.D. San Francisco: Monson & Valentine, 1856. Sprague Pamphlet Collection.

Bancroft Library, University of California, Berkeley

Brown, W. E. *Report of the Secretary of the Board of Directors of the Agricultural, Mining and Mechanical Arts College. November 7, 1867.* Sacramento: Gelwicks, 1867.
California Miscellany.
Oakland College School. Preparatory Department of the College of California, Twelfth Street, Oakland, California. 1867–'68. San Francisco: Towne & Bacon, 1868.
State University School, Late Oakland College School, Preparatory to the University of California, Twelfth Street, Oakland, California. 1869–'70. San Francisco: Excelsior & Bacon, 1870.

Charles Franklin Doe Memorial Library, University of California, Berkeley

Oakland Daily News, 1866.
Willey, S. H. "Roll of the College of California." *Berkeleyan*, Feb. 1874, 14.

Cornell College Archives, Mount Vernon, IA

Amphictyon Society minutes, 1860–74.
Catalogue of Cornell College, 1858–59, 1860–78. Various publishers, 1859–78. Titled variously *Annual Catalogue of the Officers and Students of Cornell College, Mt. Vernon, Linn County, Iowa* (academic year 1858–59); *Catalogue of Cornell College, Mt. Vernon, Linn Co., Iowa* (1860–63); *Catalogue of Cornell College* (1863–75); and *Catalogue of Cornell College, Mount Vernon, Iowa* (1875–76).
Collegian, 1869–77.

BIBLIOGRAPHY

Faculty minutes of Cornell College, 1866–77.
Fellows, Samuel. Box. Presidents' Papers Collection.
Foster, John Onesimus. "Early Recollections of Cornell College, Mount Vernon, Iowa." 1916. Bound typescript.
King, William Fletcher. Papers. Presidents' Papers Collection.
Minutes for the Board of Trustees 9/20/1854 to 6/21/1871. Microsoft Word file.
Philomathean Society minutes, 1859–77.
Trustee Minutes, 1872–1915. Microsoft Word file.
Wartime Cornell. Box.

George A. Smathers Libraries, University of Florida, Gainesville

Yorkville (SC) Inquirer, 1867–68.

Harry Elkins Widener Memorial Library, Harvard College, Cambridge, MA

Brown, Francis H. "Harvard University in the War of 1861–1865." *Harvard Graduates Magazine*, Mar. 1902, 402–13.
Catalogue of Harvard University, 1860–77. Cambridge, MA: various publishers, 1860–77. Titled variously *A Catalogue of the Officers and Students of Harvard University* (academic years 1860–72); and *The Harvard University Catalogue* (1872–77).
Harvard Magazine, 1860–64.
Oration, Poem, and Speeches, Delivered at the General Alumni Meeting, Held at the College of California, Oakland, Cal., Tuesday, May 31st, 1864. San Francisco: Bancroft, 1864.
Prospectus of the University of California. 1869–1870. San Francisco: Turnbull & Smith, [1869].
Read, Daniel. *Address on Education, Delivered in the House of Representatives of Missouri, by Dr. Daniel Read, President of the State University, January 18, 1867*. Jefferson City, MO: Foster, 1867.
Register of the University of California, 1870–71, 1874–77. Various publishers, 1870, 1874–76.
Register of the University of California. Department of Letters and Science. 1872–73. Oakland, 1873.
Undergraduate, Jan. 1860. Continued by *University Quarterly*.
U.S. Department of the Interior. *Historical Sketch of Mount Holyoke Seminary. Founded at South Hadley, Mass., in 1837*. By Mary O. Nutting. Washington, DC: GPO, 1876. In Mount Holyoke College.
University of Missouri. *Public Lectures Delivered in the Chapel of the University of the State of Missouri, Columbia, Missouri, by Members of the Faculty. 1878–79. Course II. Volume I.* Columbia: Statesman, 1879.
University Quarterly, 1860–61. Continues *Undergraduate*.

Harvard University Archives, Cambridge, MA

Annual report of the president of Harvard College, 1862–77. By C. C. Felton (academic year 1860–61), Thomas Hill and A. P. Peabody (1861–62), Hill

BIBLIOGRAPHY

(1862–68), Peabody (1868–69), and Charles W. Eliot (1869–77). Cambridge, MA: various publishers, 1862–78. Titled variously *Annual Report of the President of Harvard College to the Overseers, Exhibiting the State of the Institution* (academic years 1862–69); and *Annual Report of the President of Harvard College* (1869–77).

Bixby, Charles Lee, et al. Record of students desiring military instruction. 1861.

Faculty records of Harvard University. Vols. 16–18. 1860–72. Photocopies.

Harvard Corporation formal minutes. Vols. 10–11, 1860–73. Records of the Harvard Corporation. Photocopies.

Harvard overseers formal minutes. Vols. 9–10, 1860–71. Records of the Board of Overseers. Photocopies.

Lincoln, Arthur. Diary. Vol. 1. 1861–62.

Photograph of Memorial Hall waiters. 1875.

Reports of the Peabody Museum of American Archæology and Ethnology in Connection with Harvard University. Vol. 1, 1868–1876. Salem, MA: Salem, 1876.

Manuscript, Archives, and Rare Book Library, Emory University, Atlanta, GA

Lincoln Institute Centennial Exhibit. 1876.

Monroe C. Gutman Library, Harvard Graduate School of Education, Cambridge, MA

Catalogue of the State Normal School, 1875, at Columbia, S.C. Columbia: Columbia Union, [ca. 1875].

Circular of the State Normal School, at Columbia, South Carolina. [Columbia]: Republican, [1873 or 1874].

Mount Holyoke College Archives, South Hadley, MA

Annual Catalogue of the Mount Holyoke Female Seminary, in South Hadley, Mass., 1859–77. Various publishers, 1860–77.

Brown, Mary Ella (Spooner). "Fourscore Plus: The Autobiography of a Country Girl." [Ca. 1935–40]. Typescript. Mary Ella Spooner Papers, box 1, folder 4. Faculty and Staff Collection.

Carruth, Kathleen M., Papers.

Civil War Folder. Mount Holyoke College War Collection.

Fiske, Louise M., Papers.

Fitch, Jane A. "'Look for the Silver Lining'—Mount Holyoke Seminary during the Civil War." Undergraduate essay, Mount Holyoke College, 1977. Jane A. Fitch Papers, folder 1.

Lane, Anne L., Papers.

Lane, Mary Haynes. Papers.

Lawrence, Mary A., Papers.

Monroe, Mary A., Papers.

Principals and Presidents, Copies of Reports.

Stow, Sarah D. (Locke). Papers. Faculty and Staff Collection.

BIBLIOGRAPHY

Thomas, Belle. Papers.
Trustees minutes of Mount Holyoke Female Seminary, 1860–77.
Woodford, Henrietta M., Papers.

Phi Mu Fraternity Archives, Peachtree City, GA.

Philomathean Gazette (Wesleyan Female College), ca. 1857–77. Transcription, [1930s].

Shaw-Olson Center for College History, St. Olaf College, Northfield, MN

Manitou Messenger, Nov. 1890.

South Caroliniana Library, University of South Carolina, Columbia

Barnwell, Robert Woodward (1831–1863). Papers.
Brewer, Fisk P., Papers.
By-Laws of the University of South Carolina, as Revised and Adopted by the Board of Trustees, at a Meeting Held June 21, 1869. To Which Are Prefixed the Act to Establish the University of South Carolina, and the subsequent Acts in amendment thereto; and to Which Are Annexed Regulations of the Library Committee, and, Also, Regulations of the Faculty of the University. Columbia: Denny, 1869.
Davidson, James Wood. Papers.
Fitzgerald, O. P. *Judge Longstreet. A Life Sketch.* Nashville: Printed for the author by Publishing House of the Methodist Episcopal Church, South, 1891.
LaBorde, M. *Dr. LaBorde's Report. Published by Order of the Central Association.* N.p., n.d.
La Borde, Maximilian. Papers.
LeConte, John. *How to Make Salt from Sea-Water.* Columbia, SC: Pelham, 1862.
LeConte, John. Papers.
LeConte, Joseph. *Instructions for the Manufacture of Saltpetre.* Columbia, SC: Pelham, 1862.
LeConte, Joseph. Papers.
Longstreet, A. B. *Fast-Day Sermon: Delivered in the Washington Street Methodist Episcopal Church, Columbia, S.C., June 13, 1861.* Columbia: Townsend & North, 1861.
———. *Shall South Carolina Begin the War?* N.p., [1861].
Longstreet, Augustus Baldwin. Papers.
Miles, Wm. Porcher. *How to Improve Education in our Common Schools. Address Before the Normal Institute Of South Carolina.* Charleston: News and Courier, 1882. Pamphlet SoCar 378.757U So8p.
Neuffer, Claude H. "The Professor Who Saved Carolina: Old Buildings on Campus Remain Because M. LaBorde Halted Sherman's Vandals." N.d. Bound typescript.
Rivers, William James. Papers.
Venable, C. S. *The Campaign from the Wilderness to Petersburg. Address of Col. C. S. Venable, (Formerly of Gen. R. E. Lee's Staff,) of the University of Virginia, Before the Virginia Division of the Army of Northern Virginia, At their Annual Meeting, held in the Virginia State Capitol, at Richmond, Thursday Evening, Oct. 30th, 1873.* Richmond: Gary, 1879.

BIBLIOGRAPHY

University of California Archives, Berkeley

Announcement of the Mining and Agricultural College, San Francisco, 1863–4. San Francisco: Towne & Bacon, 1864.
College Echo, Jan.–June 1868.
Documents of the College of California.
Faculty records of the College of California, 1861–69.
Kellogg, Martin. *Papers and Addresses.* Vol. 1. 1873–93.
Letter Book of the College of California, 1849–67.
Office of the Registrar Records, 1869–1948.
Pamphlets on the College of California.
Reports of the College of California, 1858–66.
Rowell, Wm. K. *Journal of a Voyage to California.* 1858. Typescript.
Trustees of the College of California. *Memorial.* [Oakland?], 1864.
UC Regents Collection.

University of Missouri Archives, Columbia

Board of Curators Executive Board. Papers.
Catalogue of the University of Missouri, 1859–69. Various publishers, 1860–69. Titled variously *Annual Catalogue of the Officers and Students of the University of Missouri* (academic year 1859–60); *Annual Catalogue of the Officers and Students of the University of Missouri, for the Year ending July 4, 1861; Together with a List of Former Officers; Catalogue of the Officers and Students of the University of Missouri, for the Years Ending June 1862, –3–4 and 5. Together with a List of Former Officers and of the Graduates of the Institution; Catalogue of the Officers and Students of the University of Missouri, for the Year ending June, 1866. Together with a List of former Officers and Graduates of the Institution;* and *Annual Announcement of the University of the State of Missouri, Containing Catalogue of Officers and Students* (1866–69).
Civil War Damage by Federal Troops Folder. Buildings, Landmarks & Construction Collection.
Faculty records of the University of Missouri, 1860–77. Director of Admissions & Registrar Collection.
Student Welfare/Student Aid Collection.
Switzler, William F. "History of the University of the State of Missouri (Located at Columbia, Mo.) From March 3, 1811 to January 1, 1904. Also of The College of Agriculture and Mechanic Arts of Missouri (at Columbia, Mo.) And of The School of Mines and Metallurgy. (at Rolla, Mo.) Departments of the University, from their foundation in 1870 to 1904. Continued from the latter date to 19___ by _____." Typescript. Wm. F. Switzler's *A History of the Univ. of the State of Mo. . . .* , box 3, Members Papers, Board of Curators Collection.
UMC, University General, Dedications, Event Programs, Correspondence, Speeches and Photographs Collection.
University of the State of Missouri. Report containing catalogue, 1870–77. Various publishers, 1870–77. Titled variously *Report Containing Catalogue and*

BIBLIOGRAPHY

Announcements (academic year 1869–70); *Report by the Curators to the Governor Containing Catalogue, Announcements, and Other Matter Pertaining to the University* (1870–76); and *Report to his Excellency, the Governor, of the Thirty-Fifth Missouri State University Catalogue, 1876–1877. Founded, 1820—Organized, 1840.*

University of Missouri Special Collections, Columbia

University Missourian, 1871–73.

University of South Carolina Archives, Columbia

Babbitt, Benjamin B., Papers.
Catalogue of Trustees, Faculty and Students Collection.
Civil War Folder.
Clariosophic Literary Society Records (including minutes). Vols. 12–61.
Euphradian Literary Society Records (including minutes). Vols. 5–37.
Faculty minutes of South Carolina College/the University of South Carolina. Vols. 7–8, 1860–73.
19th Century Manuscript Collection Presidents' Papers.
19th Century Manuscripts Collection.
Reconstruction Subject File.
Trustees minutes of South Carolina College/the University of South Carolina. Vols. 6–9, 1861–82.

Wesleyan College Archives, Macon, GA

[Bass, Mrs. William C.]. *Catalogues. Wesleyan Female College, 1848 to 1881.*
Catalogues, Wesleyan Female College, 1842 to 1867.
"College Days in the South During the Sixties at Wesleyan College Macon, Georgia." Special issue, *Bulletin of Wesleyan College*, Sept. 1957.
Commencement Essays/Compositions Collection.
Trustees minutes of Wesleyan Female College, 1860–71.
Wesleyan Alumnae, 1925–40.

Western Historical Manuscript Collection, University of Missouri, Columbia

Athenaean Literary Society Papers. Box 1, vol. 2, 1860–62.
Chomeau, Henri. Papers.
Lynch, William H., Diary. 1865.
Read, Daniel. Papers.
School of Mines and Metallurgy Papers.
University of Missouri at Columbia Papers. Collection C1708.
University of Missouri Papers. Collection C0181.

Federal and Other Widely Published Primary Sources

Adjutant General's Office. *Official Army Register, 1873–82*. [Washington, DC: GPO, 1873–82].

BIBLIOGRAPHY

The American Almanac and Repository of Useful Knowledge, for the Year 1861. Boston: Crosby, Nichols, Lee, 1861.

Banks, Sallie Love. *Memories.* With an introduction by Sallie Love Banks Marston. Pasadena, CA: House of Printing, 1969.

Brown, Francis H. *Harvard Students in the War of 1861–1865: A Record of Services Rendered in the Army and Navy of the United States by the Graduates and Students of Harvard College and the Professional Schools.* Boston: Cupples, Upham, 1886.

Congressional Globe. 46 vols. Washington, DC, 1834–73.

Crimson (Harvard University), 1875–78. http://www.thecrimson.com/archives.aspx (accessed 12 Mar. 2008). Continues *Magenta*.

Emerson, Ralph Waldo. *Journals of Ralph Waldo Emerson with Annotations.* Edited by Emerson and Waldo Emerson Forbes. Vol. 10. Boston: Houghton Mifflin, 1914.

Fitzpatrick, Lizzie Massey. Recollections. In Lamb, *History of Phi Mu*, 18. Originally published in *Aglaia* (Phi Mu Fraternity), Jan. 1928.

Heard, William H. *From Slavery to Bishopric in the A.M.E. Church: An Autobiography.* Philadelphia: A.M.E. Book Concern, 1924.

Hewlett, E. Molyneaux. Letter to the editor. *New York Times*, 23 Feb. 1916.

Ingram, J. S. *The Centennial Exposition.* Philadelphia: Hubbard Bros., 1876. Facsimile reprint, New York: Arno, 1976.

Journal of the Missouri State Convention, Held at the City of St. Louis, January 6–April 10, 1865. St. Louis: Missouri Democrat, 1865.

Kiddle, Henry, and Alexander J. Schem, eds. *The Cyclopædia of Education: A Dictionary of Information for the Use of Teachers, School Officers, Parents, and Others.* New York: Steiger, 1877.

King, William Fletcher. *Reminiscences.* New York: Abington, 1915.

Le Conte, Joseph. *The Autobiography of Joseph Le Conte.* Edited by William Dallam Armes. New York: Appleton, 1903.

———. "Memoir of John Le Conte, 1818–1891." *Biographical Memoirs* (National Academy of Sciences) 4 (1895): 369–93.

———. *Religion and Science: A Series of Sunday Lectures on the Relation of Natural and Revealed Religion, or the Truths Revealed in Nature and Scripture.* New York: Appleton, 1875.

Lyndon, Lucy Lundie. Recollections. In Lamb, *History of Phi Mu*, 15–16. Originally published in *Aglaia* (Phi Mu Fraternity), Mar. 1937.

Magenta (Harvard University), 1874–75. http://www.thecrimson.com/archives.aspx (accessed 12 Mar. 2008). Continued by *Crimson*.

Matalene, Carolyn B., and Katherine C. Reynolds, eds. *Carolina Voices: Two Hundred Years of Student Experiences.* Columbia: Univ. of South Carolina Press, 2001.

Mitchell, Margaret. *Gone with the Wind.* New York: Macmillan, 1936.

Morrill, Justin S. *Agricultural Colleges. Speech of Hon. Justin S. Morrill, of Vermont, in the House of Representatives, June 6, 1862.* N.p., [1862].

———. *Speech of Hon. Justin S. Morrill, of Vermont, on the Bill Granting Lands for Agricultural Colleges; Delivered in the House of Representatives, April 20, 1858.* Washington, DC: Congressional Globe, 1858.

BIBLIOGRAPHY

Murray, George W. *Race Ideals: Effects, Cause, and Remedy for the Afro-American Race Troubles.* N.p., 1910.

Napier, Bessie Reid. Recollections. In Lamb, *History of Phi Mu,* 17. Originally published in *Aglaia* (Phi Mu Fraternity), [1927?].

Norton, Frank H., ed. *Frank Leslie's Illustrated Historical Register of the Centennial Exposition, 1876.* New York: Frank Leslie's, 1877. Facsimile reprint, New York: Paddington, 1974.

Read, Daniel. *Address of Daniel Read, President of the State University of Missouri. Delivered in the Hall of the House of Representatives, in Accordance with an Invitation of Both Houses, Wednesday Evening, Feb. 17th, 1869.* Indianapolis: Conner, 1869.

Simmons, William J. *Men of Mark: Eminent, Progressive and Rising.* Cleveland, OH: Rewell, 1887.

Simms, William Gilmore. *A City Laid Waste: The Capture, Sack, and Destruction of the City of Columbia.* Edited by David Aiken. Columbia: Univ. of South Carolina Press, 2005.

Statutes at Large of the United States of America, 1789–1873. 17 vols. Boston, 1845–73.

Ticknor, George. *Life, Letters, and Journals of George Ticknor.* Edited by [George S. Hillard]. Vol. 2. London: Sampson Low, Marston, Searle, & Rivington, 1876.

U.S. Bureau of Agricultural Economics. *Washington, Jefferson, Lincoln, and Agriculture.* [Washington, DC], 1937.

U.S. Bureau of Education. *American Education at the International Exposition to Be Held at Vienna in 1873.* Prepared by John Eaton Jr. Circulars of Information. Washington, DC: GPO, Nov. 1872.

———. *German and Other Foreign Universities.* Prepared by Herman Jacobson. Circulars of Information. Washington, DC: GPO, Jan. 1872.

———. *Historical Sketch of the University of Missouri, Prepared at the Request of the United States Commissioner of Education by the Late Daniel Read, LL.D., President of the University.* Historical Sketches of the Universities and Colleges of the United States. Washington, DC: GPO, 1883.

———. *Index to the Reports of the Commissioner of Education: 1867–1907.* Bulletin no. 407. Washington, DC: GPO, 1909.

———. *Inquiry Concerning the Vital Statistics of College Graduates. . . .* Prepared by John Eaton Jr. Circulars of Information. Washington, DC: GPO, Mar. 1872.

———. *List of Publications of the United States Bureau of Education, 1867–1907.* Bulletin no. 385. Washington, DC: GPO, 1908.

———. *The National Bureau of Education: Its History, Work, and Limitations.* By Alex. Shiras. Washington, DC: GPO, 1875.

———. Report of the commissioner of education, 1870–77, 1880, 1889–90. Prepared by John Eaton Jr. (1870–77, 1880) and William T. Harris (1889–90). Washington, DC: GPO, 1870–79, 1882, 1893. Titled variously *Report of the Commissioner of Education Made to the Secretary of the Interior for the Year 1870, With Accompanying Papers;* and *Report of the Commissioner of Education* (reports for 1871–77, 1880, 1889–90).

BIBLIOGRAPHY

[U.S. Bureau of Education]. *Suggestions for a Free School Policy for United States Land Grantees.* [Washington, DC?, 1872?].

U.S. Census Bureau. "1860 United States Federal Census." Schedule 1 for Columbia, SC. http://search.ancestry.com/Browse/view.aspx?dbid=7667&path=South+Carolina.Richland.Columbia.

———. "1870 United States Federal Census." Schedule 1 for Macon, GA. http://search.ancestry.com/Browse/view.aspx?dbid=7163&path=Georgia.Bibb.Macon.

U.S. Centennial Commission. *International Exhibition. 1876. Official Catalogue.* Pt. 1, *Main Building and Annexes.* Rev. ed. Philadelphia: Nagle, for the Centennial Catalogue Co., 1876.

———. *International Exhibition. 1876: Official Catalogue.* Pt. 3, *Machinery Hall, Annexes, and Special Buildings. Department V.—Machinery.* 2nd & rev. ed. Philadelphia: Nagle, for the Centennial Catalogue Co., 1876.

———. *International Exhibition, 1876. Reports and Awards: Group XXVIII.* Edited by Francis A. Walker. Philadelphia: Lippincott, 1878.

U.S. Department of Education. *Report of the Commissioner of Education, with Circulars and Documents Accompanying the Same; Submitted to the Senate and House of Representatives June 2, 1868.* By Henry Barnard. Washington, DC: GPO, 1868.

U.S. Department of Labor. *A Report on Marriage and Divorce in the United States, 1867 to 1886; Including an Appendix Relating to Marriage and Divorce in Certain Countries of Europe.* By Carroll D. Wright. Washington, DC: GPO, 1889.

U.S. Department of the Interior. *Statistics of the United States, (Including Mortality, Property, &c.,) in 1860; Compiled from the Original Returns and Being the Final Exhibit of the Eighth Census, Under the Direction of the Secretary of the Interior.* Prepared by J. M. Edmunds. Washington, DC: GPO, 1866.

U.S. Statutes at Large 19 (1877).

University of Virginia Geospatial and Statistical Data Center. "Historical Census Browser." http://mapserver.lib.virginia.edu/index.html (accessed 6 Jan. 2007).

Secondary Sources

Akers, Samuel Luttrell. *The First Hundred Years of Wesleyan College, 1836–1936.* Macon, GA: Beehive/Stinehour, 1976.

Allen, Lane. "Grandison Harris, Sr.: Slave, Resurrectionist and Judge." *Bulletin of the Georgia Academy of Science* 34, no. 4 (1976): 192–99.

Allmendinger, David F., Jr. *Paupers and Scholars: The Transformation of Student Life in Nineteenth-Century New England.* New York: St. Martin's, 1975.

Altschuler, Glenn C., and Stuart M. Blemin. *The GI Bill: A New Deal for Veterans.* New York: Oxford Univ. Press, 2009.

Anderson, G. David. "Columbian College and the Civil War." *GW Magazine,* Spring/Summer 2006. http://www.gwu.edu/~magazine/archive/2006_spring/docs/feature_civilwar.html.

BIBLIOGRAPHY

Anderson, James D. *The Education of Blacks in the South, 1860–1935.* Chapel Hill: Univ. of North Carolina Press, 1988.

Andrew, Rod, Jr. *Long Gray Lines: The Southern Military School Tradition, 1839–1915.* Chapel Hill: Univ. of North Carolina Press, 2001.

Angelo, Richard. "The Social Transformation of American Higher Education." In Jarausch, *Transformation of Higher Learning*, 261–92.

Axtell, James. "The Death of the Liberal Arts College." *History of Education Quarterly* 11, no. 4 (1971): 339–52.

Baker, Gladys L., Wayne D. Rasmussen, Vivian Wiser, and Jane M. Porter. *Century of Service: The First 100 Years of the Department of Agriculture.* [Washington, DC]: U.S. Department of Agriculture Centennial Committee, [1963].

Bardaglio, Peter W. "On the Border: White Children and the Politics of War in Maryland." In Cashin, *War Was You and Me*, 313–31.

Battle, Kemp P. *History of the University of North Carolina.* Vol. 1, *From Its Beginning to the Death of President Swain, 1789–1868.* Raleigh, NC: Edwards & Broughton, 1907.

Beckert, Sven. *The Monied Metropolis: New York City and the Consolidation of the American Bourgeoisie, 1850–1896.* Cambridge: Cambridge Univ. Press, 2001.

Bensel, Richard Franklin. *Yankee Leviathan: The Origins of Central State Authority in America, 1859–1877.* New York: Cambridge Univ. Press, 1990.

Bernstein, Iver. *The New York City Draft Riots: Their Significance for American Society and Politics in the Age of the Civil War.* New York: Oxford Univ. Press, 1990.

Bishop, Morris. *A History of Cornell.* Ithaca, NY: Cornell Univ. Press, 1962.

Blodgett, Geoffrey. "Finney's Oberlin." 1975. Reprinted in *Oberlin History: Essays and Impressions*, 37–51. Oberlin, OH: Oberlin College, 2006.

Boorstin, Daniel J. *The Americans: The National Experience.* New York: Random House, 1965.

Brereton, T. R. *Educating the U.S. Army: Arthur L. Wagner and Reform, 1875–1905.* Lincoln: Univ. of Nebraska Press, 2000.

Burke, Colin B. *American Collegiate Populations: A Test of the Traditional View.* New York: New York Univ. Press, 1982.

———. "The Expansion of American Higher Education." In Jarausch, *Transformation of Higher Learning*, 108–30.

Burton, Oliver Vernon. *The Age of Lincoln.* New York: Hill & Wang, 2007.

Butchart, Ronald E. *Schooling the Freed People: Teaching, Learning, and the Struggle for Black Freedom, 1861–1876.* Chapel Hill: Univ. of North Carolina Press, 2010.

Bynam, Victoria E. *Unruly Women: The Politics of Social and Sexual Control in the Old South.* Chapel Hill: Univ. of North Carolina Press, 1992.

Calhoun, Charles W. *Conceiving a New Republic: The Republican Party and the Southern Question, 1869–1900.* Lawrence: Univ. Press of Kansas, 2006.

Carnahan, Burrus M. *Lincoln on Trial: Southern Civilians and the Law of War.* Lexington: Univ. Press of Kentucky, 2010.

Carpenter, Daniel P. *The Forging of Bureaucratic Autonomy: Reputations, Networks,* and *Policy Innovation in Executive Agencies, 1862–1928.* Princeton, NJ: Princeton Univ. Press, 2001.

Casey, Brian William. "Romantic Campus: Emotion and the American College, 1880–1940." Ph.D. diss., Harvard University, 2000.

Cashin, Joan E., ed. *The War Was You and Me: Civilians and the American Civil War.* Princeton, NJ: Princeton Univ. Press, 2002.

Chaffin, Tom. *Pathfinder: John Charles Frémont and the Course of American Empire.* New York: Hill & Wang, 2002.

Chessman, G. Wallace. *Ohio Colleges and the Civil War.* [Columbus]: Ohio State Univ. Press for the Ohio Historical Society, 1963.

Clark, Daniel A. "Piggy Goes to Harvard: Mass Magazines, the Middle Class, and the Re-Conceptualization of College for a Corporate Age, 1895–1910." *Perspectives on the History of Higher Education* 24 (2005): 1–40.

Clarke, George Herbert. *Some Reminiscences and Early Letters of Sidney Lanier.* Macon, GA: Burke, 1907.

Clemente, Steven E. *For King and Kaiser! The Making of the Prussian Army Officer, 1860–1914.* New York: Greenwood, 1992.

Clifford, Geraldine Jonçich. *"Equally in View": The University of California, Its Women, and the Schools.* Berkeley: University of California Center for Studies in Higher Education/Institute of Governmental Studies, 1995.

Conable, Charlotte Williams. *Women at Cornell: The Myth of Equal Education.* Ithaca, NY: Cornell Univ. Press, 1977.

Conkin, Paul K. *Gone with the Ivy: A Biography of Vanderbilt University.* With the assistance of Henry Lee Swint and Patricia S. Miletich. Knoxville: Univ. of Tennessee Press, 1985.

Conrad, James Lee. *The Young Lions: Confederate Cadets at War.* Mechanicsburg, PA: Stackpole, 1997.

Cornelius, Janet Duitsman. *"When I Can Read My Title Clear": Literacy, Slavery, and Religion in the Antebellum South.* Columbia: Univ. of South Carolina Press, 1991.

Cott, Nancy F. *Public Vows: A History of Marriage and the Nation.* Cambridge, MA: Harvard Univ. Press, 2000.

Coulter, E. Merton. *College Life in the Old South.* New York: Macmillan, 1928.

Creese, James. *The Extension of University Teaching.* New York: American Association for Adult Education, 1941.

Crenshaw, Ollinger. *General Lee's College: The Rise and Growth of Washington and Lee University.* New York: Random House, 1969.

Cross, Coy F., II. *Justin Smith Morrill: Father of the Land-Grant Colleges.* East Lansing: Michigan State Univ. Press, 1999.

Currie, James T. *Twice the Citizen: A History of the United States Army Reserve, 1908–1995.* 2nd rev. & exp. ed. Department of the Army Pamphlet 140–14. Washington, DC: Army Reserve Office of the Chief/GPO, 1997.

Curti, Merle. "The American Scholar in Three Wars." *Journal of the History of Ideas* 3, no. 3 (1942): 241–64.

———. *The Social Ideas of American Educators: With New Chapter on the Last*

BIBLIOGRAPHY

Twenty-Five Years. Paterson, NJ: Littlefield, Adams/American Historical Society Commission on the Social Sciences, 1959.

Curti, Merle, and Roderick Nash. *Philanthropy in the Shaping of American Higher Education.* New Brunswick, NJ: Rutgers Univ. Press, 1965.

Davies, Wallace E. "The Mexican War Veterans as an Organized Group." *Mississippi Valley Historical Review* 35, no. 2 (1948): 221–38.

DeCanio, Samuel. "State Autonomy and American Political Development: How Mass Democracy Promoted State Power." *Studies in American Political Development* 19, no. 2 (2005): 117–36.

Dennis, Michael. *Lessons in Progress: State Universities and Progressivism in the New South, 1880–1920.* Urbana: Univ. of Illinois Press, 2001.

Desrosières, Alain. *The Politics of Large Numbers: A History of Statistical Reasoning.* Translated by Camille Naish. Cambridge, MA: Harvard Univ. Press, 1998.

Dew, Charles B. *Apostles of Disunion: Southern Secession Commissioners and the Causes of the Civil War.* Charlottesville: Univ. of Virginia Press, 2001.

Drago, Edmund L. *Confederate Phoenix: Rebel Children and Their Families in South Carolina.* New York: Fordham Univ. Press, 2008.

DuBois, Ellen Carol. *Feminism and Suffrage: The Emergence of an Independent Women's Movement in America, 1848–1869.* Ithaca, NY: Cornell Univ. Press, 1978.

Dunbar, Willis F., ed. *Michigan Institutions of Higher Education in the Civil War.* Lansing: Michigan Civil War Centennial Observance Commission, 1964.

Eddy, Edward Danforth, Jr. *Colleges for Our Land and Time: The Land-Grant Idea in American Education.* New York: Harper & Bros., 1957.

Edmond, J. B. *The Magnificent Charter: The Origin and Role of the Morrill Land-Grant Colleges and Universities.* Hicksville, NY: Exposition, 1978.

Edwards, Laura F. *Gendered Strife and Confusion: The Political Culture of Reconstruction.* Urbana: Univ. of Illinois Press, 1997.

Einhorn, Robin L. "The Civil War and Municipal Government in Chicago." In *Towards a Social History of the American Civil War: Exploratory Essays,* edited by Maris Vinovskis, 117–38. Cambridge: Cambridge Univ. Press, 1990.

Eliot, Ellsworth, Jr. *West Point in the Confederacy.* New York: Baker, 1941.

———. *Yale in the Civil War.* New Haven, CT: Yale Univ. Press, 1932.

Farmer-Kaiser, Mary. *Freedwomen and the Freedmen's Bureau: Race, Gender, & Public Policy in the Age of Emancipation.* New York: Fordham Univ. Press, 2010.

Farnham, Christie Anne. *The Education of the Southern Belle: Higher Education and Student Socialization in the Antebellum South.* New York: New York Univ. Press, 1994.

Faust, Drew Gilpin. *Mothers of Invention: Women of the Slaveholding South in the American Civil War.* 1996. New York: Vintage, 1997.

———. *A Sacred Circle: The Dilemma of the Intellectual in the Old South, 1840–1860.* Baltimore: Johns Hopkins Univ. Press, 1977.

———. *This Republic of Suffering: Death and the American Civil War.* New York: Knopf, 2008.

Fields, Barbara Jeanne. "The Advent of Capitalist Agriculture: The New South in a Bourgeois World." In Glymph and Kushma, *Essays on the Postbellum Southern Economy*, 73–94.

Findlay, James. "Agency, Denominations, and the Western Colleges, 1830–1860: Some Connections between Evangelicalism and American Higher Education." In Geiger, *American College*, 115–26.

Finnegan, Dorothy E., and Brian Cullaty. "Origins of the YMCA Universities: Organizational Adaptations in Urban Education." *History of Higher Education Annual* 21 (2001): 47–77.

Fitzgerald, Michael W. *Splendid Failure: Postwar Reconstruction in the American South*. Chicago: Dee, 2007.

Fletcher, Robert Samuel. *A History of Oberlin College from Its Foundation through the Civil War*. 2 vols. Oberlin, OH: Oberlin College, 1943.

Floyd, William C., and Paul Gibson. *The Boys Who Went to War from Cumberland University, 1861–1865*. Gettysburg, PA: Thomas, 2001.

Folmsbee, Stanley J. "Blount College and East Tennessee College, 1794–1840: The First Predecessors of the University of Tennessee." *East Tennessee Historical Society's Publication* 17 (1945): 22–50.

Foner, Eric. *Reconstruction: America's Unfinished Revolution, 1863–1877*. New York: Harper & Row, 1988.

Frederickson, George M. *The Inner Civil War: Northern Intellectuals and the Crisis of the Union*. New York: Harper & Row, 1965.

Frost, Dan R. *Thinking Confederates: Academia and the Idea of Progress in the New South*. Knoxville: Univ. of Tennessee Press, 2000.

Gallagher, Gary W. *The Confederate War*. Cambridge, MA: Harvard Univ. Press, 1997.

Gallman, J. Matthew. *The North Fights the Civil War: The Home Front*. Chicago: Dee, 1994.

Geary, James W. *We Need Men: The Union Draft in the Civil War*. Dekalb: Northern Illinois Univ. Press, 1991.

Geiger, Roger, ed. *The American College in the Nineteenth Century*. Nashville: Vanderbilt Univ. Press, 2000.

———. "The Era of Multipurpose Colleges in American Higher Education, 1850–1890." In Geiger, *American College*, 127–52.

———. "Introduction: New Themes in the History of Nineteenth-Century Colleges." In Geiger, *American College*, 1–36.

———. "Research, Graduate Education, and the Ecology of American Universities: An Interpretive History." In Rothblatt and Wittrock, *European and American University*, 234–62.

———. "The Rise and Fall of Useful Knowledge: Higher Education for Science, Agriculture, and the Mechanic Arts, 1850–1875." In Geiger, *American College*, 153–68.

———. "The 'Superior Instruction of Women,' 1836–1890." In Geiger, *American College*, 183–95.

———. *To Advance Knowledge: The Growth of American Research Universities, 1900–1940*. New York: Oxford Univ. Press, 1982.

BIBLIOGRAPHY

Gelber, Scott M. *The University and the People: Envisioning American Higher Education in an Era of Populist Protest.* Madison: Univ. of Wisconsin Press, 2011.

Gems, Gerald R., Linda J. Borish, and Gertrud Pfister. *Sports in American History: From Colonization to Globalization.* Champaign, IL: Human Kinetics, 2008.

Giberti, Bruno. *Designing the Centennial: A History of the 1876 International Exhibition in Philadelphia.* Lexington: Univ. Press of Kentucky, 2002.

Glover, Lorri. *Southern Sons: Becoming Men in the New Nation.* Baltimore: Johns Hopkins Univ. Press, 2007.

Glymph, Thavolia. "Freedpeople and Ex-Masters: Shaping a New Order in the Postbellum South, 1865–1868." In Glymph and Kushma, *Essays on the Postbellum Southern Economy,* 48–72.

Glymph, Thavolia, and John J. Kushma, eds. *Essays on the Postbellum Southern Economy.* Walter Prescott Webb Memorial Lectures 18. College Station: Texas A&M Univ. Press for Univ. of Texas at Arlington, 1985.

Godson, Susan H., Ludwell H. Johnson, Richard B. Sherman, Thad W. Tate, and Helen C. Walker. *The College of William & Mary: A History.* 2 vols. Williamsburg, VA: King & Queen, 1993.

Goldberg, Joseph P., and William T. Moye. *The First Hundred Years of the Bureau of Labor Statistics.* [Washington, DC]: U.S. Bureau of Labor Statistics, 1985.

Goode, James Moore. "The Confederate University: The Forgotten Institution of the American Civil War." Master's thesis, University of Virginia, 1966.

Green, Edwin L. *A History of the University of South Carolina.* Columbia, SC: State, 1916.

Green, Jennifer R. *Military Education and the Emerging Middle Class in the Old South.* New York: Cambridge Univ. Press, 2008.

Grimsley, Mark. *The Hard Hand of War: Union Military Policy toward Southern Civilians, 1861–1865.* Cambridge: Cambridge Univ. Press, 1995.

Gruber, Carol S. *Mars and Minerva: World War I and the Uses of Higher Learning in America.* Baton Rouge: Louisiana State Univ. Press, 1975.

Gummere, Richard M. "Colonial Reactions to a Classical Education." In *The American Colonial Mind and the Classical Tradition: Essays in Comparative Culture,* 55–75. Cambridge, MA: Harvard Univ. Press, 1963.

Guralnick, Stanley M. *Science and the Ante-bellum American College.* Philadelphia: American Philosophical Society, 1975.

Hadwiger, Don F. *The Politics of Agricultural Research.* Lincoln: Univ. of Nebraska Press, 1982.

Hahn, Steven. *A Nation under Our Feet: Black Political Struggles in the Rural South from Slavery to the Great Migration.* Cambridge, MA: Belknap Press of Harvard Univ. Press, 2003.

Hall, Richard D. *Women on the Civil War Battlefront.* Lawrence: Univ. Press of Kansas, 2006.

Handlin, Oscar, and Mary Handlin. *The American College and American Culture: Socialization as a Function of Higher Education.* New York: McGraw Hill, 1970.

Harding, T. Swann. *Two Blades of Grass: A History of Scientific Development in the U.S.*

BIBLIOGRAPHY

Department of Agriculture. Norman: Univ. of Oklahoma Press, 1947. Facsimile reprint, New York: Arno, 1980.
Harding, Thomas S. *College Literary Societies: Their Contribution to Higher Education in the United States, 1815–1876*. New York: Pageant, 1971.
Harriman, Philip L. "The Bachelor's Degree." *Journal of Higher Education* 7, no. 3 (1936): 301–7.
Harrison, Robert. "The 'Weakened Spring of Government' Revisited: The Growth of Federal Power in the Late Nineteenth Century." In Jeffreys-Jones and Collins, *Growth of Federal Power*, 62–75.
Herbst, Jurgen. *From Crisis to Crisis: American College Government, 1636–1819*. Cambridge, MA: Harvard Univ. Press, 1982.
———. "Rethinking American Professional Education." *History of Higher Education Annual* 21 (2001): 137–48.
Heywood, C. William. *Cornell College: A Sesquicentennial History, 1853–2003*. Vol. 1. Cedar Rapids, IA: WDG, 2004.
Higginbotham, Don. "Military Education before West Point." In *Thomas Jefferson's Military Academy: Founding West Point*, edited by Robert M. S. McDonald, 23–53. Charlottesville: Univ. of Virginia Press, 2004.
Higgs, Robert. *Crisis and Leviathan: Critical Episodes in the Growth of American Government*. New York: Pacific Research Institute for Public Policy/Oxford Univ. Press, 1987.
Higham, John. "The Reorientation of American Culture in the 1890's." In *The Origins of Modern Consciousness*, edited by John Weiss, 25–48. Detroit: Wayne State Univ. Press, 1965.
Hoeveler, J. David. *Creating the American Mind: Intellect and Politics in the Colonial Colleges*. Lanham, MD: Rowman & Littlefield, 2002.
Hoffer, Williamjames Hull. *To Enlarge the Machinery of Government: Congressional Debates and the Growth of the American State, 1858–1891*. Baltimore: Johns Hopkins Univ. Press, 2007.
Hofstadter, Richard, and Walter P. Metzger. *The Development of Academic Freedom in the United States*. New York: Columbia Univ. Press, 1955.
Hoganson, Kristin L. *Fighting for American Manhood: How Gender Politics Provoked the Spanish-American and Philippine-American Wars*. New Haven, CT: Yale Univ. Press, 1998.
Hollis, Daniel Walker. *University of South Carolina*. 2 vols. Columbia: Univ. of South Carolina Press, 1951.
Holt, Thomas. *Black over White: Negro Political Leadership in South Carolina during Reconstruction*. Urbana: Univ. of Illinois Press, 1977.
Horowitz, Helen Lefkowitz. *Alma Mater: Design and Experience in the Women's Colleges from Their Nineteenth-Century Beginnings to the 1930s*. New York: Knopf, 1985.
———. *Campus Life: Undergraduate Cultures from the End of the Eighteenth Century to the Present*. Chicago: Univ. of Chicago Press, 1987.
Hunt, Robert. *The Good Men Who Won the War: Army of the Cumberland Veterans and Emancipation Memory*. Tuscaloosa: Univ. of Alabama Press, 2010.

BIBLIOGRAPHY

Hunter, Gregory. "Howard University: 'Capstone of Negro Education' during World War II." *Journal of Negro History* 79, no. 1 (1994): 54–70.

Iobst, Richard W. *Civil War Macon: The History of a Confederate City.* Macon, GA: Mercer Univ. Press, 1999.

Jabour, Anya. *Scarlett's Sisters: Young Women in the Old South.* Chapel Hill: Univ. of North Carolina Press, 2007.

Jarausch, Konrad H., ed. *The Transformation of Higher Learning, 1860–1930: Expansion, Diversification, Social Opening, and Professionalization in England, Germany, Russia, and the United States.* Chicago: Univ. of Chicago Press, 1983.

Jeffreys-Jones, Rhondri, and Bruce Collins, eds. *The Growth of Federal Power in American History.* Dekalb: Northern Illinois Univ. Press, 1983.

Jencks, Christopher, and David Riesman. *The Academic Revolution.* Garden City, NY: Doubleday, 1968.

Jordan, Ervin L., Jr. *Charlottesville and the University of Virginia in the Civil War.* Lynchburg, VA: Howard, 1988.

Judd, Charles H. *Research in the United States Office of Education.* U.S. Advisory Committee on Education Staff Study no. 19. Washington, DC: GPO, 1939.

Kaestle, Carl F. *Pillars of the Republic: Common Schools and American Society, 1780–1860.* New York: Hill & Wang, 1983.

Kale, Wilford. *Hark Upon the Gale: An Illustrated History of the College of William and Mary.* Norfolk, VA: Donning, 1985.

Kantrowitz, Stephen. *Ben Tillman and the Reconstruction of White Supremacy.* Chapel Hill: Univ. of North Carolina Press, 2000.

Kelley, Mary. *Learning to Stand and Speak: Women, Education, and Public Life in America's Republic.* Chapel Hill: Univ. of North Carolina Press, 2006.

Kennett, Lee. *Marching Through Georgia: The Story of Soldiers and Civilians during Sherman's Campaign.* New York: HarperCollins, 1995.

Kerr, Clark. *The Uses of the University.* The Godkin Lectures at Harvard University. Cambridge, MA: Harvard Univ. Press, 1964.

Kersch, Ken I. "The Reconstruction of Constitutional Privacy Rights and the New American State." *Studies in American Political Development* 16, no. 1 (2002): 61–87.

Kimball, Bruce A. *The Inception of Modern Professional Education: C. C. Langdell, 1826–1906.* Chapel Hill: Univ. of North Carolina Press, 2009.

Lamb, Annadell Craig. *The History of Phi Mu: The First 150 Years.* Tucker, GA: Phi Mu Fraternity, 2002.

Lancaster, James Dean, Jr. "Howard College During the Civil War and Reconstruction 1860–1873." Master's thesis, Samfund University, 1974.

Lawson, Melinda. *Patriot Fires: Forging a New American Nationalism in the Civil War North.* Lawrence: Univ. Press of Kansas, 2002.

Leflar, Robert A. *The First 100 Years: Centennial History of the University of Arkansas.* Fayetteville: University of Arkansas Foundation, 1972.

Leonard, Elizabeth D. *All the Daring of the Soldier: Women of the Civil War Armies.* New York: Norton, 1999.

BIBLIOGRAPHY

Leslie, W. Bruce. *Gentlemen and Scholars: College and Community in the "Age of the University," 1865–1917.* University Park: Pennsylvania State Univ. Press, 1992.

Levine, David O. *The American College and the Culture of Aspiration, 1915–1940.* Ithaca, NY: Cornell Univ. Press, 1986.

Logue, Larry M. *To Appomattox and Beyond: The Civil War Soldier in War and Peace.* Chicago: Dee, 1996.

Logue, Larry M., and Peter Blanck. *Race, Ethnicity, and Disability: Veterans and Benefits in Post–Civil War America.* New York: Cambridge Univ. Press, 2010.

Loss, Christopher P. "'The Most Wonderful Thing Has Happened to Me in the Army': Psychology, Citizenship, and American Higher Education in World War II." *Journal of American History* 92, no. 3 (2005): 864–91.

Lowry, Thos. Jefferson. *A Sketch of the University of the State of Missouri.* Columbia, MO: Herald, [1890].

Lubetkin, M. John. *Union College's Class of 1868: The Unique Experiences of Some Average Americans.* McLean, VA: privately printed, 1995.

Lucas, Christopher J. *American Higher Education: A History.* 2nd ed. New York: Palgrave Macmillan, 2006.

Lucas, Marion Brunson. *Sherman and the Burning of Columbia.* College Station: Texas A&M Univ. Press, 1976.

Lykes, Richard Wayne. *Higher Education and the United States Office of Education (1867–1953).* Washington, DC: Bureau of Postsecondary Education, 1975.

Lyons, Gene M., and John W. Masland. *Education and Military Leadership: A Study of the R.O.T.C.* Princeton, NJ: Princeton Univ. Press, 1959.

Malkmus, Doris. "Small Towns, Small Sects, and Coeducation in Midwestern Colleges, 1853–1861." *History of Higher Education Annual* 22 (2002): 33–65.

Marten, James. *Children for the Union: The War Spirit and the Northern Home Front.* Chicago: Dee, 2004.

———. *The Children's Civil War.* Chapel Hill: Univ. of North Carolina Press, 1998.

Martinez, J. Michael. *Carpetbaggers, Cavalry, and the Ku Klux Klan: Exposing the Invisible Empire during Reconstruction.* London: Rowman & Littlefield, 2007.

Masich, Andrew E. *The Civil War in Arizona: The Story of the California Volunteers, 1861–1865.* Norman: Univ. of Oklahoma Press, 2006.

Mattingly, Paul H. "Structures Over Time: Institutional History." In *Historical Inquiry in Education: A Research Agenda,* edited by John Hardin Best, 34–55. Washington, DC: American Educational Research Association, 1983.

McClintock, Megan J. "Civil War Pensions and the Reconstruction of Union Families." *Journal of American History* 83, no. 2 (1996): 456–80.

McClurken, Jeffrey W. *Take Care of the Living: Reconstructing Confederate Veteran Families in Virginia.* Charlottesville: Univ. of Virginia Press, 2009.

McGaw, Robert A. *A Brief History of Vanderbilt University.* Centennial ed. Nashville: Vanderbilt University, 1973.

McGinnis, Frederick A. *A History and an Interpretation of Wilberforce University.* Wilberforce, OH: Brown, 1941.

McLachlan, James. "The *Choice of Hercules*: American Student Societies in the Early

19th Century." In *The University in Society,* edited by Lawrence Stone, 2:449–94. Princeton, NJ: Princeton Univ. Press, 1974.

McPherson, James M. *Battle Cry of Freedom: The Civil War Era.* New York: Ballantine, 1988.

Miller, Randall M., Harry S. Stout, and Charles Reagan Wilson, eds. *Religion and the American Civil War.* New York: Oxford Univ. Press, 1998.

Miller, Richard F. *Harvard's Civil War: A History of the Twentieth Massachusetts Volunteer Infantry.* Hanover, NH: Univ. Press of New England, 2005.

Mobley, Joe A. *Weary of War: Life on the Confederate Home Front.* Westport, CT: Praeger, 2008.

Montgomery, James Riley, Stanley J. Folmsbee, and Lee Seifert Greene. *To Foster Knowledge: A History of the University of Tennessee, 1794–1970.* Knoxville: Univ. of Tennessee Press, 1970.

Morgan, Gordon D., and Izola Preston. *The Edge of Campus: A Journal of the Black Experience at the University of Arkansas.* Fayetteville: Univ. of Arkansas Press, 1990.

Morison, Samuel Eliot. *Three Centuries of Harvard, 1636–1936.* Cambridge, MA: Harvard Univ. Press, 1936.

Morsman, Amy Feely. *The Big House after Slavery: Virginia Plantation Families and Their Postbellum Domestic Experiment.* Charlottesville: Univ. of Virginia Press, 2010.

Moss, Hilary J. *Schooling Citizens: The Struggle for African American Education in Antebellum America.* Chicago: Univ. of Chicago Press, 2009.

Mounter, Michael Robert. "Richard Theodore Greener and the African American Individual in a Black and White World." In *At Freedom's Door: African American Founding Fathers and Lawyers in Reconstruction South Carolina,* edited by James Lowell Underwood and W. Lewis Burke, 130–65. Columbia: Univ. of South Carolina Press, 2000.

Nash, Margaret A. "'A Salutary Rivalry': The Growth of Higher Education for Women in Oxford, Ohio, 1855–1867." In Geiger, *American College,* 169–82.

———. *Women's Education in the United States, 1780–1840.* New York: Palgrave Macmillan, 2005.

Neiberg, Michael S. *Making Citizen-Soldiers: ROTC and the Ideology of American Military Service.* Cambridge, MA: Harvard Univ. Press, 2000.

Nelson, Scott Reynolds, and Carol Sheriff. *A People at War: Civilians and Soldiers in America's Civil War, 1854–1877.* New York: Oxford Univ. Press, 2007.

Nelson, William E. *The Roots of American Bureaucracy, 1830–1900.* Cambridge, MA: Harvard Univ. Press, 1982.

Nemec, Mark R. *Ivory Towers and Nationalist Minds: Universities, Leadership, and the Development of the American State.* Ann Arbor: Univ. of Michigan Press, 2006.

Nevins, Allan. *The State Universities and Democracy.* Urbana: Univ. of Illinois Press, 1962.

Nobles, Lewis. *A College for Mississippians: The Story of Mississippi College.* New York: Newcomer Society in North America, 1976.

Noll, Mark A. *The Civil War as a Theological Crisis*. Chapel Hill: Univ. of North Carolina Press, 2006.

Novak, Steven J. *The Rights of Youth: American Colleges and Student Revolt, 1798–1815*. Cambridge, MA: Harvard Univ. Press, 1977.

Oberly, James W. "Gray-Haired Lobbyists: War of 1812 Veterans and the Politics of Bounty Land Grants." *Journal of the Early Republic* 5, no. 1 (1985): 35–58.

O'Donovan, Susan Eva. *Becoming Free in the Cotton South*. Cambridge, MA: Harvard Univ. Press, 2007.

Ogren, Christine A. *The American State Normal School: "An Instrument of Great Good."* New York: Palgrave Macmillan, 2005.

Olson, James, and Vera Olson. *The University of Missouri: An Illustrated History*. Columbia: Univ. of Missouri Press, 1988.

Onuf, Nicholas, and Peter Onuf. *Nations, Markets, and War: Modern History and the American Civil War*. Charlottesville: Univ. of Virginia Press, 2006.

Pace, Robert F. *Halls of Honor: College Men in the Old South*. Baton Rouge: Louisiana State Univ. Press, 2004.

Pak, Michael S. "The Yale Report of 1828: A New Reading and New Implications." *History of Education Quarterly* 48, no. 1 (2008): 30–57.

Pangle, Lorraine Smith, and Thomas L. Pangle. *The Learning of Liberty: The Educational Ideas of the American Founders*. Lawrence: Univ. Press of Kansas, 1993.

Parrish, William E. *A History of Missouri*. Vol. 3, *1860 to 1875*. Columbia: Univ. of Missouri Press, 1973.

Peck, Elizabeth S. *Berea's First 125 Years, 1855–1980*. New ed. Lexington: Univ. Press of Kentucky, 1982.

Peckham, Howard H. *The Making of the University of Michigan, 1817–1992*. 175th anniv. ed. Edited and updated by Margaret L. Steneck and Nicholas H. Steneck. Ann Arbor: University of Michigan Bentley Historical Library, 1994.

Peskin, Allan. *Garfield: A Biography*. Kent, OH: Kent State Univ. Press, 1978.

Peter, Robert, and Johanna Peter. *Transylvania University: Its Origin, Rise, Decline, and Fall*. Louisville, KY: Morton, 1896.

Poirier, Robert G. *"By the Blood of Our Alumni": Norwich University Citizen Soldiers in the Army of the Potomac*. Iowa City: Savas, 1999.

Polsky, Andrew J. "'Mr. Lincoln's Army' Revisited: Partisanship, Institutional Position, and Union Army Command, 1861–1865." *Studies in American Political Development* 16, no. 2 (2002): 176–207.

Post, Robert C., ed. *1876: A Centennial Exhibition*. Washington, DC: National Museum of History and Technology, 1976.

Potts, John F., Sr. *A History of South Carolina State College, 1896–1978*. Orangeburg: South Carolina State College, 1978.

Preston, Richard A. *Perspectives in the History of Military Education and Professionalism*. Harmon Memorial Lectures in Military History 22. [Colorado Springs?], CO: U.S. Air Force Academy, 1980.

Quinn, Arthur Hobson. *Edgar Allen Poe: A Critical Biography*. New York: Appleton-Century-Crofts, 1941.

BIBLIOGRAPHY

Rable, George C. *Civil Wars: Women and the Crisis of Southern Nationalism.* Urbana: Univ. of Illinois Press, 1989.

———. *God's Almost Chosen Peoples: A Religious History of the American Civil War.* Chapel Hill: Univ. of North Carolina Press, 2010.

Radke-Moss, Andrea G. *Bright Epoch: Women and Coeducation in the American West.* Lincoln: Univ. of Nebraska Press, 2008.

Ranney, Joseph A. *In the Wake of Slavery: Civil War, Civil Rights, and the Reconstruction of Southern Law.* Westport, CT: Praeger, 2006.

Reuben, Julie. *The Making of the Modern University: Intellectual Transformation and the Marginalization of Morality.* Chicago: Univ. of Chicago Press, 1996.

Richardson, Joe M. *Christian Reconstruction: The American Missionary Association and Southern Blacks, 1861–1890.* Athens: Univ. of Georgia Press, 1986.

Roberts, Jon H., and James Turner. *The Sacred and the Secular University.* Princeton, NJ: Princeton Univ. Press, 2000.

Robson, David W. *Educating Republicans: The College in the Era of the American Revolution, 1750–1800.* Westport, CT: Greenwood, 1985.

Roche, John F. *The Colonial Colleges in the War for American Independence.* Millwood, NY: Associated Faculty Press, 1986.

Rodgers, Daniel T. *Atlantic Crossings: Social Politics in a Progressive Age.* Cambridge, MA: Belknap Press of Harvard Univ. Press, 1998.

Roper, John H. "The Radical Mission: The University of South Carolina in Reconstruction." Master's thesis, University of North Carolina, 1973.

Ross, Earle D. *Democracy's College: The Land-Grant Movement in the Formative Stage.* Ames: Iowa State Univ. Press, 1942.

Rothblatt, Sheldon, and Martin Trow. "Government Policies and Higher Education: A Comparison of Britain and the United States, 1630–1860." In *Social Research and Social Reform: Essays in Honour of A. H. Halsey,* edited by Colin Crouch and Anthony Heath, 173–216. New York: Oxford Univ. Press, 1992.

Rothblatt, Sheldon, and Björn Wittrock, eds. *The European and American University since 1800: Historical and Sociological Essays.* New York: Cambridge Univ. Press, 1993.

Rudolph, Frederick. *The American College and University: A History.* New York: Knopf, 1962.

———. *Curriculum: A History of the American Undergraduate Course of Study since 1636.* San Francisco: Jossey-Bass, 1978.

Rudy, Willis. *Building America's Schools and Colleges: The Federal Contribution.* Cranbury, NJ: Cornwall, 2003.

———. *The Campus and a Nation in Crisis: From the American Revolution to Vietnam.* Madison, WI: Farleigh Dickinson Univ. Press, 1996.

Sanders, Elizabeth. *Roots of Reform: Farmers, Workers, and the American State, 1877–1917.* Chicago: Univ. of Chicago Press, 1999.

Sarris, Jonathan Dean. *A Separate Civil War: Communities in Conflict in the Mountain South.* Charlottesville: Univ. of Virginia Press, 2006.

Schild, Georg. "'A War Upon the First Principle of Popular Government': Abraham

Lincoln and the Development of American Democracy during the Civil War." In *The American Experience of War*, edited by Schild, 53–68. Paderborn, Germany: Ferdinand Schöningh, 2010.

Schmidt, James M. *Notre Dame and the Civil War: Marching Onward to Victory.* Charleston, SC: History Press, 2010.

Schuster, Jack H., and Martin J. Finkelstein. *The American Faculty: The Restructuring of Academic Work and Careers.* Baltimore: Johns Hopkins Univ. Press, 2006.

Schwalbe, Michael. *Remembering Reet and Shine: Two Black Men, One Struggle.* Jackson: Univ. Press of Mississippi, 2004.

Scott, James C. *Seeing Like a State: How Certain Schemes to Improve the Human Condition Have Failed.* New Haven, CT: Yale Univ. Press, 1998.

Sears, Richard. *The Kentucky Abolitionists in the Midst of Slavery, 1854–1864: Exiles for Freedom.* Lewiston, NY: Mellen, 1993.

———. *A Utopian Experiment in Kentucky: Integration and Social Equality at Berea, 1866–1904.* Westport, CT: Greenwood, 1996.

Sheehan-Dean, Aaron. *Why Confederates Fought: Family and Nation in Civil War Virginia.* Chapel Hill: Univ. of North Carolina Press, 2007.

Shinagel, Michael. *"The Gates Unbarred": A History of University Extension at Harvard, 1910–2009.* Hollis, NH: Puritan, 2009.

Silber, Nina. *Daughters of the Union: Northern Women Fight the Civil War.* Cambridge, MA: Harvard Univ. Press, 2005.

Simkins, Francis Butler. *Pitchfork Ben Tillman, South Carolinian.* 1944. Reprint, Columbia: Univ. of South Carolina Press, 2002.

Singer, Sandra L. *Adventures Abroad: North American Women at German-Speaking Universities, 1868–1915.* Westport, CT: Praeger, 2003.

Skocpol, Theda. *Protecting Soldiers and Mothers: The Political Origins of Social Policy in the United States.* Cambridge, MA: Belknap Press of Harvard Univ. Press, 1992.

Skowronek, Stephen. *Building a New American State: The Expansion of National Administrative Capacities, 1877–1920.* New York: Cambridge Univ. Press, 1982.

Smith, Darrell Hevenor. *The Bureau of Education: Its History, Activities and Organization.* Baltimore: Johns Hopkins Press, 1923.

Smith, Ethel Morgan. *From Whence Cometh My Help: The African American Community at Hollins College.* Columbia: Univ. of Missouri Press, 2000.

Smith, Ruby Green. *The People's Colleges: A History of the New York State Extension Service in Cornell University and the State, 1876–1948.* Ithaca, NY: Cornell Univ. Press, 1949.

Snyder, Thomas D., ed. *120 Years of American Education: A Statistical Portrait.* Washington, DC: National Center for Education Statistics, 1993.

Solomon, Barbara Miller. *In the Company of Educated Women: A History of Women and Higher Education in America.* New Haven, CT: Yale Univ. Press, 1985.

Spackman, S. G. F. "Beyond the Federal Consensus: A Doctrine of National Power." In Jeffreys-Jones and Collins, *Growth of Federal Power*, 49–61.

Span, Christopher M. *From Cotton Field to Schoolhouse: African American Education in Mississippi, 1862–1875.* Chapel Hill: Univ. of North Carolina Press, 2009.

BIBLIOGRAPHY

Stadtman, Verne A. *The University of California, 1868–1968*. New York: McGraw-Hill, 1970.

Steiner, Bernard C. *Life of Henry Barnard: The First United States Commissioner of Education, 1867–1870*. U.S. Bureau of Education Bulletin no. 8 for 1919. Washington, DC: GPO, 1919.

Stephens, Frank F. *A History of the University of Missouri*. Columbia: Univ. of Missouri Press, 1962.

Stetar, Joseph M. "In Search of a Direction: Southern Higher Education after the Civil War." *History of Education Quarterly* 25, no. 3 (1985): 341–67.

Stout, Harry S. "University Men in New England, 1620–1669: A Demographic Analysis." *Journal of Interdisciplinary History* 4, no. 3 (1974): 375–400.

———. *Upon the Altar of the Nation: A Moral History of the American Civil War*. New York: Viking, 2006.

Stratton, Julius, and Loretta H. Mannix. *Mind and Hand: The Birth of MIT*. Cambridge, MA: MIT Press, 2005.

Sugrue, Michael. "'We Desired Our Future Rulers to Be Educated Men': South Carolina College, the Defense of Slavery, and the Development of Secessionist Politics." In Geiger, *American College*, 91–114.

Sutherland, Daniel E. *A Savage Conflict: The Decisive Role of Guerrillas in the American Civil War*. Chapel Hill: Univ. of North Carolina Press, 2009.

Taylor, Amy Murrell. *The Divided Family in Civil War America*. Chapel Hill: Univ. of North Carolina Press, 2005.

Thelin, John R. *The Cultivation of Ivy: A Saga of the College in America*. Cambridge, MA: Schenkman, 1976.

———. *A History of American Higher Education*. Baltimore: Johns Hopkins Univ. Press, 2004.

Thernstrom, Stephan. "'Poor but Hopefull Scholars.'" In *Glimpses of the Harvard Past*, by Bernard Bailyn, Donald Fleming, Oscar Handlin, and Thernstrom, 115–28. Cambridge, MA: Harvard Univ. Press, 1986.

Thornton, Mark, and Robert B. Ekelund Jr. *Tariffs, Blockades, and Inflation: The Economics of the Civil War*. Wilmington, DE: SR Books, 2004.

Tindall, George Brown. *South Carolina Negroes, 1877–1900*. 1952. Columbia: Univ. of South Carolina Press, 2003.

Tobias, Marilyn. *Old Dartmouth on Trial: The Transformation of the Academic Community in Nineteenth-Century America*. New York: New York Univ. Press, 1982.

Trimpi, Helen P. *Crimson Confederates: Harvard Men Who Fought for the South*. Knoxville: Univ. of Tennessee Press, 2010.

Trow, Martin. "Comparative Perspectives on British and American Higher Education." In Rothblatt and Wittrock, *European and American University*, 280–302.

———. "In Praise of Weakness: Chartering, the University of the United States, and Dartmouth College." *Higher Education Policy* 16, no. 1 (2003): 9–26.

———. "Reflections on the Transition from Elite to Mass to Universal Access: Forms and Phases of Higher Education in Modern Societies since WWII." In *International Handbook of Higher Education*, edited by James J. F. Forest and Philip G.

BIBLIOGRAPHY

Altbach, pt. 1, *Global Themes and Contemporary Challenges*, 243–80. Dordrecht, Netherlands: Springer, 2006.

———. "Reflections on the Transition from Mass to Universal Higher Education." *Dædalus* 99, no. 1 (1970): 1–42.

Trudeau, Noah Andre. *Southern Storm: Sherman's March to the Sea*. New York: Harper, 2008.

Tulloch, Hugh. *The Debate on the American Civil War Era*. New York: Manchester Univ. Press, 1999.

Turner, James, and Paul Bernard. "The German Model and the Graduate School: The University of Michigan and the Origin Myth of the American University." In Geiger, *American College*, 221–41.

Tyack, David, and Elisabeth Hansot. *Learning Together: A History of Coeducation in American Schools*. New Haven, CT: Yale Univ. Press; New York: Russell Sage Foundation, 1990.

Van Dyke, Carl. *Russian Imperial Military Doctrine and Education, 1832–1914*. New York: Greenwood, 1990.

Veysey, Laurence R. *The Emergence of the American University*. Chicago: Univ. of Chicago Press, 1965.

Viles, Jonas. *The University of Missouri: A Centennial History*. Columbia: University of Missouri, 1939.

Wagoner, Jennings L., Jr. "Honor and Dishonor at Mr. Jefferson's University: The Antebellum Years." *History of Education Quarterly* 26, no. 2 (1986): 155–79.

———. *Jefferson and Education*. [Charlottesville, VA]: Thomas Jefferson Foundation; Chapel Hill: Univ. of North Carolina Press, 2004.

Wakelyn, Jon L. "Antebellum College Life and the Relations between Fathers and Sons." In *The Web of Southern Social Relations: Women, Family, and Education*, edited by Walter J. Fraser Jr., R. Frank Saunders Jr., and Wakelyn, 107–26. Athens: Univ. of Georgia Press, 1985.

Wallenstein, Peter. "Higher Education and Civil Rights: South Carolina, 1860s–1960s." *History of Higher Education Annual* 23 (2003–4): 1–22.

Warren, Donald R. *To Enforce Education: A History of the Founding Years of the United States Office of Education*. Detroit: Wayne State Univ. Press, 1974.

Watson, Cynthia A. *Military Education: A Reference Handbook*. Westport, CT: Praeger Security International, 2007.

Waugh, John C. *The Class of 1846: From West Point to Appomattox; Stonewall Jackson, George McClellan and Their Brothers*. New York: Warner Books, 1994.

Wells, Cheryl A. *Civil War Time: Temporality and Identity in America, 1861–1865*. Athens: Univ. of Georgia Press, 2005.

White, G. Edward. *Oliver Wendell Holmes, Jr.* New York: Oxford Univ. Press, 2006.

Whitehead, John S. *The Separation of College and State: Columbia, Dartmouth, Harvard, and Yale, 1776–1876*. New Haven, CT: Yale Univ. Press, 1973.

Whites, LeeAnn. *The Civil War as a Crisis in Gender: Augusta, Georgia, 1860–1890*. Athens: Univ. of Georgia Press, 1995.

Wiebe, Robert H. *The Search for Order, 1877–1920*. New York: Hill & Wang, 1967.

BIBLIOGRAPHY

Williams, T. Harry. "The Military Leadership of North and South." In *Why the North Won the Civil War*, edited by David Donald, 23–48. [Baton Rouge]: Louisiana State Univ. Press, 1960.

Williamson, Joel. *After Slavery: The Negro in South Carolina during Reconstruction, 1861–1877*. Chapel Hill: Univ. of North Carolina Press, 1965.

Wills, Brian Steel. *The War Hits Home: The Civil War in Southeastern Virginia*. Charlottesville: Univ. of Virginia Press, 2001.

Wills, Garry. *Lincoln at Gettysburg: The Words That Remade America*. New York: Simon & Schuster, 1992.

Winsor, Mary P. *Reading the Shape of Nature: Comparative Zoology at the Agassiz Museum*. Chicago: Univ. of Chicago Press, 1991.

Woodman, Harold D. "The Reconstruction of the Cotton Plantation in the New South." In Glymph and Kushma, *Essays on the Postbellum Southern Economy*, 95–119.

Wooley, John, and Gerhard Peters. "Election of 1860." American Presidency Project. http://www.presidency.ucsb.edu/showelection.php?year=1860 (accessed 16 May 2010).

Worthington, Ian. "Antecedent Education and Officer Recruitment: The Origins and Early Development of the Public School–Army Relationship." *Military Affairs* 41, no. 4 (1977): 183–89.

Woytanowitz, George M. *University Extension: The Early Years in the United States, 1885–1915*. Iowa City: National University Extension Association/American College Testing Program, 1974.

Wright, John D., Jr. *Transylvania: Tutor to the West*. Lexington: Univ. Press of Kentucky, 1975.

Wubben, Hubert H. *Civil War Iowa and the Copperhead Movement*. Ames: Iowa State Univ. Press, 1980.

Zboray, Ronald J., and Mary Saracino Zboray. "Cannonballs and Books: Reading and the Disruption of Social Ties on the New England Home Front." In Cashin, *War Was You and Me*, 237–61.

Zuczek, Richard. *State of Rebellion: Reconstruction in South Carolina*. Columbia: Univ. of South Carolina Press, 1996.

Index

Aberdeen Female College, 19–20, 36
academic criteria for admission, 75, 83–84, 92–93, 117
Adelphian Society (Cornell College), 31
admissions criteria, 17, 83, 92–93, 146–47. *See also* academic criteria for admission; moral education and criteria for admission; social criteria for admission
African Americans: as college staff, 6–7, 49, 98, 101, 104, 118, 216n2; as freedpeople, 1, 12, 13, 92, 98, 110, 120, 121, 123, 124, 140, 145, 156, 161–62, 170, 171; as militiamen, 70, 71, 118; as politicians, 70, 71, 115, 118, 119, 120, 123, 156; as professors, 6, 26, 119, 123; as slaves, 1, 6–7, 19, 24, 37, 49, 101, 104, 109, 115, 120, 123, 216n2; as students, 6, 11, 16, 69, 70, 71–72, 85, 92, 93, 94, 97–98, 100–102, 115, 118–25, 126, 127, 140, 145, 153, 156, 167–68, 169, 170, 176, 181–82, 183–84, 188, 190–91, 194, 224n104; as teachers, 121, 123; as trustees, 119; as veterans and normal school founders, 182. *See also* slavery
African Methodist Episcopal Church, 156–57, 186
Agassiz, Louis, 97, 158–59, 184

age in college admissions, 112, 129, 145–46, 147, 175
Agricultural and Mechanical College (Kentucky), 89
Agricultural and Mechanical College (University of Missouri), 87, 111, 112, 113, 114, 133, 157
Agricultural College (University of California), 78, 159–60
agricultural education, 11, 16, 52–53, 54–57, 59–60, 65, 70, 74, 76, 77, 78, 79, 83, 86, 87, 89, 90–91, 97, 99, 100–101, 111, 112, 113, 114, 126–27, 133, 154, 159–60, 161, 167, 174, 179, 184, 186, 188, 190, 194, 214n84
agricultural experiment stations, 160, 186, 190
agricultural fairs, 52, 159–60
Aiken, S.C., teachers, 71
Alabama Female Institute, 108
Allegheny College, 4
American Education Society (AES), 95, 98, 218n18
American Journal of Science and Arts, 10
American Literary, Scientific, and Military Academy, 58
American Revolution, 3–4, 26, 57, 58, 142
American Society for Extension Learning Courses, 160

259

INDEX

Amherst College, 4, 9, 49, 123
Amphictyon Society (Cornell College), 24, 31, 48, 96, 149
antebellum colleges, 1–2, 4–11, 22–23, 25–26, 54, 58, 73, 90, 94–95, 101, 103–4, 108–10, 115–16, 119–20, 130–32, 136–37, 138, 141, 145, 147, 153, 198n14, 198n16, 218n24
Appomattox Court House, Va., surrender at, 50
architectural education, 77, 183, 184, 214n84
Arkansas Industrial University, 64, 119, 143
Arkansas veterans' children–education law (1868), 143
arms-supply joint resolution (1870), 63, 65, 67, 90–91, 154, 165, 209n29
army, Union. See U.S. Army
army-officers amendment (1866), 62–65, 67–68, 71–72, 90–91, 154, 165, 173, 188, 209n28, 210n32
army-officers amendment, act amending (1876), 64–65, 210n34
army-officers amendment, acts amending (1880s–1890s), 191
army-officers (retired) law (1870), 63–65, 90–91, 154, 165, 188, 209n28, 210n32
art education, 184, 214n84, 219n27, 219n39, 226n20, 226n22
Association of American Universities, 76, 79
Astronomical Observatory (Harvard), 76
Athenaean Literary Society (University of Missouri), 24–25, 28, 128
Atlanta, capture of, 105, 137
Austria, 176–77
automotive education, 80

bachelor of arts degree, 2–3, 5, 7, 8, 9–10, 73, 74, 77, 78, 81, 82, 83, 89–90, 103, 111, 117
banking system, national, 161, 162
Baptist Church, 6, 123
Barnard, Henry, 173–74

Barnwell, Robert W., Jr., 40–41
Barnwell, Robert W., Sr., 81, 123–24
Bates College, 97
Beckert, Sven, 13
Bell, John, 22
Berea College, 6, 118–19
Berryman College, 19
"Blank Cartridge" (pseud.), 71
blockade of Confederate ports, 41, 43
Blount College, 103. See also East Tennessee University
Bonnell, John M., 37, 104, 105
Bonnell Blues (Wesleyan), 37, 59
Boone County, Mo.: poorhouse and hospital of, 157–58; University of Missouri's relationships with, 87, 109, 157–58
Bowdoin College, 40, 71
Boylston Prize for Oratory (Harvard), 97
Breckinridge, John C., 22
Broun, William L., 40
Brown University, 28
Buchanan, James, 26, 27, 55
buildings as part of educational reform, 55, 87, 99, 112–13, 157, 181
Burke, Colin B., 130–32, 198n14, 198n16, 229n64
Burton, Clara, 49, 104, 106
Burton, Ella, 49, 104, 106
business and commercial education, 89–90, 174, 194, 199n31
Bussey Institution (Harvard), 76, 77, 97, 184

California College of Dentistry (University of California), 78
California College of Pharmacy (University of California), 78
California Immigrant Union, 185
Cambridge Arsenal, 30
Carr, Ezra S., 61, 159–60, 209n22
Carruth, Kathleen M., 49
Centennial Exhibit Committee (University of Missouri), 182
Centennial Exposition, 152, 154, 177–85, 186, 188–89, 191

260

INDEX

Central Association for the Relief of South Carolina Soldiers, 41
Central Pacific Railroad Company, 185
Chamberlain, Joshua L., 40
Charleston Harbor: anticipated invasion of, 34, 41. *See also* Fort Sumter
Chautauqua Literary and Scientific Circle, 156
Church of England, 2
Citadel, 58
Civil War, causes of, 26–28, 167, 168, 169–71, 172
Claflin University, 70, 71, 118, 126, 127
Clariosophic Literary Society (South Carolina College), 202n8
classical curriculum. *See* bachelor of arts degree
class in college admissions, 6, 7, 10, 11, 16, 43, 54, 55–56, 74, 78, 80, 81–83, 84, 90–91, 95, 98–102, 103–4, 108–13, 114–16, 117–18, 121, 123, 124–25, 126–27, 133, 138, 140, 141, 152, 187, 188, 190
Clemson Agricultural College, 190
closures of colleges. *See* Southern colleges, closures of during Civil War; State Normal School (South Carolina), closure of after Reconstruction; survival as reason for educational reform; University of South Carolina, closure and expulsion of blacks and women from
code of war, Union, 40, 45
coeducation and coeducational colleges, 6, 7, 29, 30, 32, 49, 94–97, 102–3, 113–14, 119, 121, 137, 146, 152, 174, 182, 188, 190. *See also specific institutions*
College Cadets (South Carolina College), 34, 37, 58–59
College Drill Club (Harvard), 31, 37
College of California, 15, 42, 50–51, 59–60, 77–78, 208n20; founding of, 5; geographic origins of students at, 134, 135; military education at, 37, 58–60, 69, 77; military service of trustee and possibly students from, 30, 40, 42; morality and religion at, 148, 151; and Seminary for Young Ladies, 7. *See also* University of California
College of Letters (University of California), 78
College of Letters and Sciences (University of Missouri), 111, 114
College of Normal Instruction (University of Missouri), 87, 111–12, 113–14, 133, 221n68
College of William and Mary, 2, 43
colleges: attendees of as percentage of population, 3, 5–6, 94, 152, 198n16, 229n64; definition of, 2–3, 5, 8, 74; proliferation of, 2, 3, 4–5, 10, 11, 15, 128, 132–33, 161, 169, 198n14, 199n31; roles of in life and culture, 1, 2–3, 6–7, 8, 10, 14, 22–23, 49, 50, 58, 90–91, 101, 103–4, 107, 111, 117, 119–20, 122, 130, 141, 144–45, 152, 154–55, 185–86, 189, 193, 194
College School (College of California; later State University School, University of California), 60, 134, 135, 160
colonial colleges, 2–3, 6, 10
Colored Training School, 181
Columbia, S.C., invasion and burning of, 44–45, 51, 118
Columbia College (Missouri), 108
Columbia College (New York), 28, 40
Columbia (SC) Daily Union-Herald, 71–72
Columbian College, 43
commencements, expression of opinions at, 28, 39, 48–49, 106–7
Committee on Public Information, 192
Comstock Law (1873), 163
Confederate government: colleges' relationships with, 42, 50, 51 (*see also* conscription; Southern colleges, military occupation of); founding of, 23, 24, 27
Confederate Niter and Mining Bureau, 41
Confederate Ordnance Department, 40
Congregational Church, 2, 4–5, 134

INDEX

conscription, 21, 35, 39–40, 49, 53, 116, 139, 161, 193, 194

Copperheads, 48

Cornell, Ezra, 87

Cornell College, 8, 15, 36, 43, 146, 184–85, 202n9; ages of students at, 145, 146; blacks admitted to, 97–98, 217n14; discussion of slavery, secession, and war at, 24, 29, 39, 48; founding of as Iowa Conference Seminary, 5; geographic origins of students at, 132, 141; military education at, 67–68; military service of students from, 29, 31–32, 39; morality and religion at, 146, 148, 149; poor students at, 100; veterans and their orphans as students at, 32, 50, 51, 141, 144–45; women at, 7, 31–32, 51, 68, 95–96, 146, 203n33

Cornell University, 87, 97, 100, 142, 160

correspondence courses, 156, 194

Crimean War, 63

Crystal Palace, 176

cultural diversity, celebration of, 134–35

Cumberland University, 43

currency, national, 161

curricula. *See* bachelor of arts degree; religion, in college curricula and missions; slavery, in college curricula; universities; vocational education; *and specific subjects and types of schools*

Curti, Merle, 11–12, 14, 154

Cutter, Caroline, 36

Darwin, Charles, 75

Davis, Jefferson, 35, 47

Deaf, Dumb, and Blind Asylum, 160

Declaration of Independence, 129

Democratic Party, 22, 69, 112, 123, 125, 126, 169, 171–72, 208n20. *See also* Redemption

denominational colleges, 4–5, 6, 7, 11, 15, 59, 101, 129, 147, 148–52, 153. *See also specific institutions*

Dental School (Harvard), 76, 184

dental schools, 76, 78, 184, 214n84

Department of Analytical and Applied Chemistry (University of Missouri), 87

Department of Education and Science (Centennial Exposition), 177–84

Department of Science and the Arts. *See* Mining and Agricultural College (College of California)

Divinity School (Harvard), 76–77, 97, 184

divinity schools, 76–77, 79, 89, 97, 174, 184, 214n84

Division of University Extension (University of Chicago), 160

doctoral degrees, 52, 77

Donnelly, Ignatius, 167–68, 169–71, 172

Douglass, Frederick, 26

drafts. *See* conscription

duels, 58

Durham, James J., 121, 123

East Tennessee University, 64. *See also* Blount College

Eaton, John, Jr., 174–76, 177, 178–80, 181

economic boom in North after Civil War, 78–79, 99, 100

economic depression in South after Civil War, 2, 80, 82, 110–11, 126, 180, 195

education fund (Mount Holyoke), 99

election of 1860 (national), 14, 22, 23, 25, 26

election of 1868 (South Carolina), 118

election of 1876 (South Carolina and national), 125

elective principle, 9, 74, 77, 83, 84, 106, 116, 117, 148

Eliot, Charles W., 76–77

Emancipation Proclamation, Preliminary (1862), 48

Emerson, Ralph Waldo, 11, 14

Enforcement Acts of 1870 and 1871, 70

engineering education, 11, 52, 55, 59, 65, 70, 74, 77, 78, 79, 80, 82, 84, 87, 89–91, 101, 111, 112, 116, 117, 120, 126–27, 133, 154, 174, 184, 188, 213n78, 214n84

INDEX

England, 3, 63, 156, 164, 176
entrance examinations, 83–84, 93, 117
Erskine College, 224n104
Everett Scholarships (Wesleyan), 104
evolution, 75, 157
expositions, European, 176–77. *See also* Centennial Exposition
extension schools, 156, 160, 190

Farmers' Alliance, 190
Farmers' Association, 190
Farmers' Institute (Cornell University), 160
far western colleges, 5, 7, 20, 29–30, 128, 132–33. *See also specific institutions*
federal government: colleges' relationships with, 2, 4, 11, 15, 16–17, 21, 42, 50, 51, 53, 59, 65, 68, 72–73, 152–55, 161, 165–80, 181–86, 187, 188–89, 191–93, 194–95 (*see also* conscription; land grants, federal, for colleges; Morrill Land-Grant College Act [1862]; Southern colleges, military occupation of; *and arms-supply and army-officers laws*); funding of national development by, 57, 162, 167; growth of during and after Civil War, 12, 13, 15–16, 51, 129–30, 154, 161–73, 185, 188, 189; and public schools, 167–69, 170–74, 175–78, 179–81
Fifteenth Amendment (1870), 162, 185
financial aid, 17, 50, 91, 95, 98–100, 104, 107, 108, 109, 111–13, 115–16, 117, 128–29, 134–35, 137–38, 139, 142, 143–44, 145–46, 152, 175, 188, 191, 192, 193, 194–95, 218n18, 224n107. *See also* tuition and fees; work-study programs
First Iowa Volunteer Infantry, 29, 31
Fisk University, 181
Flower Queen, The (operetta), 38
football, 72, 191
Fort Donelson, capture of, 19
Fort Independence, 30

Fort Sumter, resupply of and firing on, 24, 27–28, 29, 30, 34, 58, 116, 169
Fourteenth Amendment (1868), 130, 162
France, 164, 176
Frances (Burton family slave), 49, 104, 106
Freedmen's Bureau, 161, 162, 166, 171
Freeman Guards (Wesleyan), 37, 59
Frémont, John C., 40, 42, 208n20
French and Indian War, 57
Fristoe, Edward F., 37, 40, 47
Frost, Dan R., 200n34
Fugitive Slave Law (1850), 22, 24
fundraising and philanthropy: for colleges, 42, 75, 78–79, 80, 89, 99, 100, 102, 115; for war effort, 38, 102

Gardiner Lyceum, 54
Garfield, James A., 168, 169, 171, 172
gender in college admissions, 1–2, 6, 7, 11, 15, 21, 29, 31–32, 51, 68, 80, 94–97, 100–103, 108, 113–15, 120–21, 127, 147, 152, 182, 187, 188, 190, 203n33
general beneficiary fund (Harvard), 98–99
geography in college admissions. *See* localization, of higher education
George Washington University. *See* Columbian College
Georgia Female College. *See* Wesleyan Female College
Georgia veterans-education law (1866), 143
Germany, 63, 164; universities in, 12, 17, 74–75, 76, 78, 79, 90, 175
Gettysburg, Battle of, 40, 105
Gettysburg Address, 96–97
GI Bill of Rights (1944), 142, 191, 194–95
Gone with the Wind (book, Mitchell), 197n1
Gone with the Wind (film), 1–2
Grange, 190
Greener, Richard T., 97, 123, 124
Greenough, George G., 67
Grinnell College, 32, 67, 95

INDEX

Halleck, Henry W., 46
Hamilton College, 49
Hampton Normal and Agricultural Institute, 72, 181
"Hard Times" (commencement speech, Jones), 107
Harris, Grandison, 92, 101–2, 140, 216n2
Harvard Magazine, 25, 28–29
Harvard Medical School, 76–77, 97, 184
Harvard University, 4, 8, 12, 15, 25, 43, 73, 146; blacks hired at and admitted to, 6, 26, 97, 98, 123; at Centennial Exposition, 184, 185; development of into university, 76–77, 79, 97, 158–59, 184; discussion of slavery, Confederacy, and war at, 25, 26, 28–29, 48; founding of as Harvard College, 2; geographic origins of students at, 131, 133; military education at, 30–31, 37, 58–59, 62, 69; military service of students and professors from, 28–29, 30, 31, 40, 51; morality and religion at, 148, 149; outreach programs at, 158–59; poor students and financial aid at, 98–99, 100; veterans as students at, 142; women admitted to, 97
Harvard Washington Corps, 58
Hatch Act (1887), 190, 191
Haverford College, 183
Hawaiian students, 134
Hayes, Rutherford B., 125, 162
Hayne, Henry, 123–24
Hewlett, Aaron Molyneaux, 6, 26, 98
high-school diploma, 93
Hill, Thomas, 43, 76, 77, 98, 99
Hispanics, 134, 135
historically black colleges and universities, 6, 7, 70, 71, 94, 98, 118, 119, 123, 126, 127, 153, 181–82, 188, 190–91, 194, 201n45
Hoffer, Williamjames Hull, 166
Holmes, Oliver Wendell, Jr., 30
Homestead Act (1862), 57, 167
Hopkins, Johns, 75
Howard University, 72, 118, 123, 127

Illinois Industrial University, 100
income tax, 161, 162, 163
Indiana-Asbury College, 143
inflation, 16, 21, 41, 42–43, 51, 104–6, 108, 110, 136, 137, 138, 139, 187
Interstate Commerce Act (1887), 162
Iowa Conference Seminary. *See* Cornell College
Iowa militia, 67
Iowa State Agricultural College, 67, 68, 100
Ivory Towers and Nationalist Minds (Nemec), 165

Jefferson, Thomas, 9, 58, 82
Johns Hopkins University, 75–76, 79, 89, 158, 160
Johnson, Andrew, 62–63, 69, 70, 81, 172, 173
Johnson, Richard W., 65
Jones, Eugenia, 107
Judson Institute, 19

Kansas-Nebraska Act (1854), 22
Kellogg, Martin, 42, 96–97, 98, 134
Kentucky University (post-1865), 79–80, 89
Kentucky University (pre-1865), 87, 89
kindergarten, 153, 180, 181
King, William F., 67, 144
knitting and sewing for soldiers, 38–39, 41, 51, 155, 187
Ku Klux Klan, 70–71

LaBorde, Maximilian, 40–41, 44, 45, 81
Ladies' Military Company (Iowa State Agricultural College), 68
Lafayette College, 183
land grants, federal: for colleges, 5, 46, 173, 174 (*see also* Morrill Land-Grant College Act [1862]); for railroads, 57, 167, 175–76
Latin American students, 134, 135
Law College (University of Missouri), 87, 111
Lawrence, Amos A., 95

INDEX

Lawrence Scientific School (Harvard), 76, 97, 158, 184
Lawrence University, 95
Law School (Harvard), 31, 76, 184
law schools, 9, 52, 74, 76, 79, 83, 87, 89, 91, 92, 111, 119, 120, 174, 214n84
LeConte, John, 41, 45
LeConte, Joseph, 41, 159
Lee, Robert E., 40, 50, 89–90, 189
letter writing to soldiers, 39
Lieber, Francis, 40, 45
Lincoln, Abraham, 12–13, 22, 24–25, 27, 28, 29, 39, 48, 52–53, 54, 55, 56, 57, 96–97, 129, 144. *See also* election of 1860 (national)
Lincoln, Robert Todd, 31, 65
Lincoln Institute, 182
Lincoln University, 153, 183
Lister, Frederick W., 69
literacy laws, 6, 102, 115, 120, 145
literary societies, 23–25, 28, 31, 48, 96, 116, 128, 149, 178, 202nn8–9
localization: of American life, 128, 130; of higher education, 128, 130–41, 152, 154, 161, 175, 188, 191, 225n5
Longstreet, Augustus B., 23, 24, 26–27, 34, 47–48, 116
Longstreet, James, 23
Lost Cause, 107
Louisiana State University, 119
Love, Sallie, 19–20, 36, 38, 44, 104, 136, 150
Lowell Institute, 156
Loyalist Publication Society, 40
Lucas, Christopher J., 12
lyceum circuit, 156
Lynch, William H., 128, 142
Lyon, Mary, 98

Macon, Ga.: armory and arsenal at, 137; military actions against, 44, 137
Maine College of Agriculture and the Mechanic Arts, 100
marriage, 7, 103, 106, 107, 108, 114, 146, 148, 164–65
"Marseillaise" (song), 28

Marshall, Stella, 48–49
Massachusetts Bay education law (1642), 170
Massachusetts State Agricultural College, 100
master's degrees, 73, 77, 83, 96
McClellan, George B., 61, 208n20
mechanical education. *See* engineering education
Mechanic Arts College (University of California), 78, 133, 151, 160, 213n78
Mechanics' Institute (Johns Hopkins), 160
Mechanics' Institute of San Francisco, 78, 133
mechanics' institutes, 78, 133, 156, 160
Medical College of Georgia, 216n2
Medical Department (University of Missouri), 87, 157–58
Medical Department of the Army, 179
medical schools, 9, 11, 16, 52, 74, 76–77, 78, 79, 83, 87, 89, 91, 97, 120, 157–58, 174, 184, 214n84, 216n105, 216n2
Mercer University, 23, 143
Methodist Church, 5, 7, 31, 47, 89, 102, 104, 107, 150, 156–57, 186
Methodist Female College, 115
Mexican students, 134, 135
Mexican War, 134, 142
mid-Atlantic colleges, 132. *See also specific institutions*
midwestern colleges, 4–5, 6, 7, 10, 94–95, 100, 128, 132–33, 145. *See also specific institutions*
militarization of American culture, 59, 72–73, 90, 142
Military Department (University of California), 61
military education: at colleges, 16, 17, 30–31, 34, 37, 38, 52–53, 54, 56–57, 58–73, 90–91, 102, 142, 154, 161, 183, 184, 188, 191–92, 193, 195, 204n50, 209n22, 209nn28–29, 210n32, 210n34; in Europe, 63; outside colleges, 55, 56, 57–58, 64, 161, 175, 201n45

INDEX

military occupation of colleges in World War I, 193

military occupation of colleges in Civil War. *See* Pennsylvania College; Southern colleges, military occupation of

military service. *See under* professors; students; trustee; veterans

Milton, John, 156

Mining and Agricultural College (College of California), 59–60, 77

mining and metallurgy education, 59–60, 65, 76, 77, 78, 79, 87, 91, 101, 111, 112, 113, 133, 174, 214n84

ministers' children as students, 104, 107, 137–38, 149

Mississippi College, 103

Missouri as border state, 24, 46, 65

Missouri Constitution of 1865, 85–86

Missouri public-school fund, 86

MIT (Massachusetts Institute of Technology), 184

Mitchell, Margaret, 197n1

modernization, 17, 189–92, 195

moral education and criteria for admission, 75, 93–94, 129, 146–52

Morrill, Justin S., 54–57, 60, 169

Morrill Land-Grant College Act (1862), 11–12, 50, 53, 54, 55–57, 59, 62, 69, 77–78, 80, 82, 85, 86, 87, 89, 90, 100, 112, 126, 134, 140, 154, 165, 166, 168–69, 173, 174, 184, 187, 188, 200n33, 214n85; act amending (1868), 55; joint resolution amending (1867), 70

Morrill land-grant college bill (1857–58), 54–55

Mount Holyoke Female Seminary, 15, 36, 43, 51, 97, 100, 146; ages of students at, 145; and Centennial Exposition, 178, 184; Civil War work by students at, 36, 38–39, 40, 51, 146, 155; discussion of slavery, politics, and war at, 22, 25–26, 49–50; founding of, 7; geographic origins of students at, 131; morality and religion at, 148, 150, 151; poor students and financial aid at, 98, 99, 100

Murray, George W., 120, 123

Museum of Comparative Zoology (Harvard), 158–59, 184

museums, 158–59, 179, 180, 184–85, 190

music education, 38, 43, 214n84, 219n27, 226n20, 226n22

Nash, Margaret A., 218n24

National Academy of Sciences, 40

National Center for Education Statistics, 229n64

National Defense Act (1916), 191–92

National Educational Association, 168, 178

nationalization: of American life, 12–13, 129–30, 162–63, 168–72, 186, 189; of higher education, 90–91, 130, 144–45, 154–55, 189, 193 (*see also* federal government, colleges' relationships with; public attention to and knowledge of colleges)

Native Americans, 179

navigation education, 77

Nemec, Marc R., 165–66

New York Central College, 6, 97

New York State Agricultural College, 54

normal schools. *See* teacher education

Northeastern College, 80

northeastern colleges, 6, 7, 94, 95, 96, 97, 131, 145, 191. *See also* specific institutions

Northern colleges, 2, 23–24, 53, 137, 152; admissions changes at, 6, 31–32, 43, 54, 78, 80, 94–100, 131–35, 187; at Centennial Exposition, 182–85; outreach programs at, 155, 158–60; as universities, 76–79, 80, 90, 183, 184, 185. *See also* specific institutions

nurses. *See under* students

oath of allegiance, Union, 46

Oberlin College, 4–5, 6, 7, 32, 39, 94, 95, 174

266

INDEX

Officers' Reserve Corps, 192
Ohio Home Guard, 37
Ohio University, 143
Ohio veterans-education law (1864), 143
Ohio veterans-education law, law amending (1866), 143
On the Origin of Species (Darwin), 75
outreach programs, 17, 152, 153–60, 186, 187, 190, 192, 195

Pace, Robert F., 12
Pacific Railroad Act (1862), 57, 167
Panamanian student, 135
parallel courses, 9, 10, 73, 90
Parsons, Ellen C., 49–50
Peabody Institute, 156
Penn, William, 183
Pennsylvania College, 206n71
Perry, Benjamin F., 51, 81–82, 84, 116
pharmaceutical education, 78, 82–83, 91, 116, 117, 184, 214n84
philanthropy. *See* fundraising and philanthropy
Philomathean Society (Cornell College), 96, 149, 202n9
physical damage to colleges. *See* Pennsylvania College; Southern colleges, physical damage to
Pickens, Francis W., 34, 35, 42, 44
Placer (County, CA) Herald, 134
planter class, 1, 2, 7, 22–23, 101, 103, 104, 110–11, 114, 115, 117, 119–20, 126, 187
Poe, Edgar Allan, 109
polytechnic education, 80
poor, housing and medical care for, 157–58
poor and middle-class students, 6, 43, 54, 55–56, 66, 74, 78, 80, 81–83, 84, 90–91, 95, 98–101, 104, 107, 108–9, 111–13, 114–16, 117–18, 121–23, 124–25, 126–27, 133, 140, 160, 188, 190
populist movement, 190
Port Royal, invasion of, 34
Post-Hostility Schools, 194

prayer, 39, 149, 150, 151; and mourning for the nation, 22, 26, 150; for soldiers, 39, 40, 41, 150
prayer day for colleges, national, 149, 151
preparatory and primary departments, 8, 32, 37, 58–59, 60, 120, 123, 134, 135, 145, 174, 178, 203n36
Presbyterian Church, 4, 5, 134
"Present Agricultural, Mineral, and Manufacturing Resources of the United States" (report, U.S. Department of Agriculture), 164
presidents (college), conference of, 65
printing and journalism education, 89–90
private nature of colleges. *See* public versus private nature of colleges
private property as military targets, 45
professors: as doctors, 40–41, 44, 155, 157–58; enthusiasm of about Civil War, 28, 29, 31, 39, 41; intellectual contributions of to war effort, 11, 21, 40, 41, 50, 155; military service of, 20, 40–42, 47; as public leaders, 3, 26–27, 29, 39, 47; as teachers and researchers, 73, 74–75, 175, 183
Prussia, 63, 173. *See also* Germany
public attention to and knowledge of colleges, 2, 17, 42, 61, 152–53, 154, 166–67, 168, 173–86, 191, 192, 194–95
public schools, 5, 6, 7–8, 86, 96, 103, 107, 112, 113, 120–21, 122, 135, 140, 143, 159, 167–68, 169, 170–74, 175–78, 179–81, 226n30
public versus private nature of colleges, 4, 21, 43–44, 45, 153–55, 186
pumpkin pie as hardship, 43
Puritans, 2

race in college admissions, 6, 11, 16, 71, 97–98, 100–102, 114–15, 118–27, 138, 140, 147, 152, 181–82, 187, 188, 190–91, 194, 224n104
Radcliffe College (Harvard), 97
Radke-Moss, Andrea G., 204n50

267

INDEX

Read, Daniel, 65, 86, 87, 110, 113, 114, 135, 157, 182
Reconstruction, 12, 16, 129, 134, 136, 189, 200n38; end of, 13, 14, 72, 125, 162; presidential, 69; Radical, 61, 69–71, 92, 118–25, 126, 127, 140, 143, 161–63, 167–68, 169–71, 188; violence in, 69, 70–72
Reconstruction Act of 1867, 70
Redemption, 16, 92, 125–27, 134, 141, 189
refugees in college dormitories, 40, 45–46, 51, 103, 155
refuges from war, colleges as for students, 20, 46, 49, 102
religion: in college curricula and missions, 39, 93–94, 107, 128, 129, 147, 148–52, 159; disestablishment of, 4; government control of feared, 172. *See also* moral education and criteria for admission
Republican Party, 22, 28, 69, 70–71, 112, 118, 122–23, 124, 125, 161–62, 167–68, 169–71, 172, 208n20; ideals and rhetoric of, 12–13, 91, 96–97, 100, 101, 111, 123, 126, 127. *See also* Reconstruction
research. *See* agricultural experiment stations; doctoral degrees; museums; professors, as teachers and researchers; universities, research
revivals, 149, 150
Rifle Corps (Harvard), 69
"Right and Duty of the State to Establish, Aid, and Supervise Public Schools, The" (article, U.S. Department of Education), 173
Roanoke College, 32, 35
Rogers, Andrew J., 169, 171–72, 186
Rollins, James S., 112
ROTC (Reserve Officers' Training Corps), 191–92, 193
Royal Commission on Military Education (United Kingdom), 63
Rudolph, Frederick, 12
Rudy, Willis, 12
Russia, 63

San Francisco Mining and Scientific Press, 134
School of Mathematics, and Civil and Military Engineering and Construction (University of South Carolina), 70, 71, 82, 116, 117, 120
School of Mining and Metallurgy (University of Missouri), 65, 87, 111, 112, 113, 133
School of Mining and Practical Geology (Harvard), 76, 77
science education, 9, 74–75, 76, 77, 82–83, 86, 87, 89–90, 97, 108, 133, 156, 157, 158–59, 174, 178, 181, 182, 183, 184, 185, 190, 214n84
Scott, James C., 163
secession, 26, 42, 167, 168, 169–70; debate over, 23–25
Second Morrill Act (1890), 190–91
Seminary for Young Ladies, 7
sewing. *See* knitting and sewing for soldiers
Shall South Carolina Begin the War? (A. Longstreet), 26–27
Sheffield School of Science (Yale), 60
Sherman, John, 62, 64
Sherman, William T., 62, 118, 144; Atlanta campaign of, 105, 106, 137; marches of through Georgia and South Carolina, 19, 44–45, 51, 106, 137
Sherman Antitrust Act (1890), 162
shipbuilding education, 77
Slaughterhouse decision (1873), 162
slavery: abolition of, 13, 16, 48, 69, 70, 97, 102, 110, 170, 200n38, 201n45; in college curricula, 22, 25–26; debate over, 22–25, 26, 48, 52; as impediment to learning, 86, 170. *See also under* African Americans
small size of colleges, 73, 74, 187
Smith College, 97, 184
Smithsonian Institution, 179
social criteria for admission, 2, 10, 11, 17, 93, 94, 155, 179, 185, 192, 195. *See also* age in college admissions; class in

INDEX

college admissions; gender in college admissions; localization, of higher education; race in college admissions; veterans, as students
social life, regulation of, 96, 146
Sociedad Literaria Castellana de California (College of California), 134, 135
Soldiers' Aid Society of Macon, 38
soldiers-education programs in World War II, 194
Soldiers Fund (Cornell College), 50, 144
Solomon, Barbara Miller, 198n16
South, definition of, 16, 21, 201n46, 225n5
South Carolina, readmission of to Union, 69–70
South Carolina College, 15, 58, 82, 84, 93, 109, 202n8; closure of during Civil War, 34, 35–36, 44, 51, 73, 81, 116; discussion of slavery, war, and Confederacy at, 23, 24, 26–27, 47–48; elite students of, 115–16, 119–20; founding of, 5; geographic origins of students at, 23, 131, 138–39; military contributions of students and professors from, 32, 34–36, 39, 40–41, 58, 116, 155, 158; military education at, 34, 37, 58–59; military occupation of, 44–46, 51, 70, 73, 81, 92, 116; morality and religion at, 147; physical damage to, 45, 73, 92; poor students and financial aid at, 115; —, law enabling (1857), 115–16, 117, 139; veterans as students at, 50, 116. *See also* South Carolina College of Agriculture and Mechanics; University of South Carolina
South Carolina College of Agriculture and Mechanics: geographic origins of students at, 138, 141; opening of as white, male college, 125–26, 189; poor students and practical education at, 126–27, 190. *See also* South Carolina College; University of South Carolina
South Carolina Constitution of 1868, 122
South Carolina Land Commission, 118
South Carolina militia, 70, 71, 118
South Carolina public-accommodations discrimination bill, 118
Southern colleges, 12, 43; admissions changes at, 2, 16, 17, 32, 68, 71, 81–83, 84, 94, 100–127, 130–31, 132–33, 135–41, 147–50, 151–52, 181–82, 187–88, 195; antebellum cultural roles of, 1, 2, 6–7, 22–23, 49, 58, 101, 103–4, 107, 111, 119–20, 122, 141; at Centennial Exposition, 180, 181–82, 185; closures of during Civil War, 2, 19–20, 29, 34, 35–36, 44, 46, 51, 53, 73, 81, 89, 110, 116, 136; military occupation of, 16–17, 21, 43–47, 49, 50, 51, 53–54, 55–57, 66, 70, 73, 81, 85, 92, 110, 114, 116, 139, 187; outreach programs at, 154, 155, 156–58, 187; physical damage to, 2, 12, 16, 21, 43, 45, 51, 53–54, 73, 80, 85, 86, 87, 89, 92, 110, 113, 114, 135, 187–88, 189, 195; as universities, 2, 16–17, 53–54, 73, 75–76, 79–81, 87, 89–90, 100–101, 187–88, 195. *See also specific institutions*
South Normal School, 181
Spanish-American War, 72
Spanish language, 134, 135
State Agricultural College (Michigan), 54
state colleges and universities, 5, 6, 10–11, 15, 17, 54, 59, 61, 65, 73, 77–78, 81–87, 89–90, 99, 100–101, 108–10, 111–12, 113, 114, 115–16, 119–27, 128, 130, 133–35, 140–41, 143, 147, 148, 150–52, 153, 154, 156–58, 185, 186, 187, 188, 190, 192, 195, 198n13. *See also specific institutions*
State Female College (Tennessee), 19
state governments, colleges' relationships with, 4, 5, 11, 21, 42, 50, 51, 67, 68, 121, 128–29, 143, 152, 153, 178, 180, 198n5. *See also* conscription; Morrill Land-Grant College Act (1862); state colleges and universities
State Normal School (Illinois), 160
State Normal School (Indiana), 181

INDEX

State Normal School (South Carolina): academic criteria for admission to, 93, 123; blacks and women admitted to, 101, 115, 120–21; closure of after Reconstruction, 125; founding of by law (1873), 121; geographic origins of students at, 227n31; morality and religion at, 148

statistics, 154, 164–65, 168, 170–72, 173–75, 179, 180, 188, 231n24

Stetar, Joseph M., 12, 214n83

St. John's College, 173

St. Olaf College, 68

Stoneman, George M., Jr., 137

Straight University, 119, 127

Strawberry Festival (Wesleyan), 37, 38

student newspapers, 25, 28–29, 69, 100, 112, 150

students: ambivalence of about Civil War, 47, 48–49; enthusiasm of about Civil War, 25, 28–29, 30–31, 34, 37–38; marriages of, 146, 148; matured by war, 50, 116–17, 148; military service of, 1, 2, 3–4, 16, 20, 21, 28–36, 39, 41–42, 43, 44, 46, 50, 51, 53–54, 58, 67, 81, 95, 110, 116, 138, 187, 191–92, 193; needed at home during Civil War, 36–37, 139, 187; on-campus Civil War work of, 30–31, 34, 37–39, 40, 41, 51, 58–59, 102, 155, 187; as nurses in Civil War, 20, 36, 41, 51

surveying education, 77

survival as reason for educational reform, 14, 53, 80, 94–95, 110, 127, 195

teacher education, 5, 6, 7, 11, 52, 80, 86, 87, 91, 94, 95, 96, 101, 107, 111–12, 113–14, 119, 120–21, 123, 133, 148, 173, 174, 181–82, 184, 187, 188, 194, 214n84, 221n68

teachers' institutes, 160

Temple University, 79, 81

Thelin, John R., 12, 79

Thirteenth Amendment (1865), 69, 70, 170

Thirty-second Missouri Volunteer Infantry (USA), 128

Ticknor, Anna, 156

Ticknor, George, 12, 14

Tillman, Ben, 190

To Enlarge the Machinery of Government (Hoffer), 166

Toland Medical College (later Medical Department, University of California), 78, 160

"To Our Gallant Southern Soldiers" (hymn), 28

Transylvania University, 87, 89

travel, difficulty of during Civil War, 16, 19–20, 21, 91, 104, 128, 130, 136, 137, 138, 139, 161, 188

Trow, Martin, 12

trustee, military service of, 40, 42

Trustees of Dartmouth College v. Woodward (1819), 4

tuition and fees, 99, 109, 115, 225n115; changes in after Civil War, 17, 51, 84, 99, 106, 112–13, 114, 117, 121–22, 126–27, 128, 133–34, 137, 139, 140, 145, 188, 192, 222n82; changes in during Civil War, 43, 100, 105–6, 110, 117, 137; in-state versus out-of-state, 112, 135, 226n30; women's versus men's, 114. *See also* class in college admissions; financial aid

Tulane University, 80

Union College, 9, 10, 141

Union Leagues, 70–71

Unitarianism, 4, 15

United Kingdom, 3, 63, 156, 164, 176

United States (term), 29–30

universities: comprehensive, 2, 16–17, 79–85, 86–91, 92, 100–101, 110, 111, 114, 119, 133, 156, 187–88, 189–90, 191, 192, 195; definition of, 73, 74, 87, 175; emergence of, 9, 11–12, 16–17, 52–53, 73, 147–48, 152, 163, 179, 185–86; research, 74–79, 90, 134, 165–66, 183, 184, 185. *See also specific institutions*

University Cadet Battalion (University of Missouri), 65

INDEX

University Cadets (University of California), 61

University of Alabama, 37, 108

University of California, 208n20; at Centennial Exposition, 185; formation of as state university, 60, 69, 76, 77–78, 134, 140, 151, 159, 185, 213n78; —, Organic Act enabling (1868), 78; geographic origins of students at, 133, 134–35, 140; military education at, 60–61, 67, 68, 209n22; —, law requiring (1870), 61; morality and religion at, 148, 150–51, 159; move from Oakland to Berkeley, 78; outreach programs at, 158, 159–60, 186; poor students and financial aid at, 98, 133; —, laws enabling (1870), 99, 134–35; women admitted to, 96–97. See also College of California

University of Chicago, 160

University of Georgia, 40, 73, 143

University of Louisville, 80

University of Michigan, 5, 109, 198n13, 226n30

University of Mississippi, 119

University of Missouri, 8, 15, 51, 146, 221n68; at Centennial Exposition, 182; closure of during Civil War, 46, 73, 110; development of into university, 73, 80, 81, 87, 110, 111, 114, 140, 157, 182, 188, 216n105; —, constitution (1865) and law (1867) enabling, 85–87; discussion of secession and war at, 24–25, 28; founding of, 5, 46; geographic origins of students at, 133, 135, 140; military education at, 37, 58–59, 65–67; military occupation of, 46–47, 66, 73, 85, 110, 114; military service of students and professors from, 40, 46, 47; morality and religion at, 148; outreach programs at, 157–58; physical damage to, 47, 73, 85, 86, 110, 113, 114, 135, 188; poor students and financial aid at, 101, 109–10, 112–13, 114, 127; —, laws enabling (1867, 1872), 111–12; veterans as students at, 128, 142; women admitted to, 68, 101, 108, 113, 120

University of Nashville, 181

University of Nebraska, 68

University of North Carolina, 35

University of Pennsylvania, 79

University of South Carolina: ages of students at, 145–46; blacks admitted to and hired at, 69, 71–72, 85, 92, 101, 114–15, 119–25, 126, 140, 145–46, 182, 188, 224n104; closure and expulsion of blacks and women from, 69, 85, 125–26, 141, 188, 189; formation of as university, 69–70, 73, 80, 81–85, 87, 92, 116, 156, 180, 188, 222n82; —, law enabling (1865), 82–83; geographic origins of students at, 138, 139–41; law- and medical-school law for (1866), 83; military education at, 64, 69–71; —, law enabling (1874), 71–72; military occupation of, 45, 139; morality and religion at, 148, 159; outreach programs at, 156–57, 186; poor students and financial aid at, 101, 117–18, 121–23, 124–25, 127, 140, 141, 224n107; —, law enabling (1874), 124, 224n107; veterans as students at, 116–17, 141–42. See also South Carolina College; South Carolina College of Agriculture and Mechanics; State Normal School (South Carolina)

University of Virginia, 9, 25, 37, 40, 58, 82, 109, 116, 143, 147

University of Wisconsin, 86, 100, 173

U.S. Army: appointment of officers in, 58, 161; contraction of after Civil War, 61–62, 72, 162; deaths in, 164; raising of for Civil War, 29, 31, 39, 61, 161, 167; use of against labor strikes, 72; use of in Radical Reconstruction, 61, 70, 118, 162. See also conscription; Medical Department of the Army; professors, military service of; Southern colleges, military occupation of; students, military service of

271

INDEX

U.S. Bureau of Animal Husbandry, 164
U.S. Bureau of Education, 15, 127, 132, 161, 166–74, 185–86, 188, 191, 192–93; act assigning name of (1870), 172; and Centennial Exposition, 154, 176, 177, 178–85, 188–89; publications by, 168, 173–76, 191
U.S. bureau of education joint resolution (1865), 167–68
U.S. Bureau of Forestry, 165–66
U.S. Bureau of Internal Revenue, 161, 163, 179
U.S. Bureau of Labor, 164–65
U.S. Bureau of Refugees, Freedmen, and Abandoned Lands. See Freedmen's Bureau
U.S. bureau of religion feared, 172
U.S. Bureau of the Coast Survey, 179
U.S. Bureau of the Signal Service, 179
U.S. census bureaus, 164, 231n25
U.S. Centennial Commission, 177–78, 179, 180
U.S. Christian Commission, 38
U.S. Department of Agriculture, 164, 165, 166, 167, 171, 173, 179
U.S. Department of Education: act creating (1867), 168–73, 174. See also U.S. Bureau of Education
U.S. Department of Justice, 163, 166
U.S. Department of Labor. See U.S. Bureau of Labor
U.S. Department of War, 63–65, 67, 72, 144, 161, 164, 193, 194, 209nn28–29, 210n34
U.S. Geological and Geographical Surveys of the Territories, 179
U.S. Military Academy, 56, 57–58, 161
U.S. National Board of Health, 164
U.S. Office of Education: act assigning name of (1868), 172. See also U.S. Bureau of Education
U.S. Pension Bureau, 142, 163–64, 167
U.S. Post Office Department, 163, 179
U.S. Secret Service, 163
Utah Agricultural College, 68

Valparaiso University, 143
Vanderbilt, Cornelius, 89
Vanderbilt University, 80, 89
Vassar College, 97
Venable, Charles S., 40
veterans: children of as students, 50, 107, 108, 137–38, 143–44, 152, 188; as college leaders and founders, 61, 89–90, 189–90, 182, 191, 200n34, 208n20; government benefits to, 142–43, 163–64, 191, 193, 194–95; as students, 16, 32, 50, 51, 116–17, 128–29, 141–42, 143–45, 146, 147, 152, 188, 191, 193, 194
veterinary education, 214n84
Veysey, Laurence R., 12, 74–75
Vicksburg, Battle of, 105
Vienna World Exposition, 176–77
Vietnam War, 35, 47
Virginia Military Institute, 43, 58
Virginia University Magazine, 25
Virginia veterans-education law (1864), 143
vocational education: at colleges, 10, 11, 17, 52–53, 76, 79, 82–83, 86–87, 89–91, 101, 111, 113, 114, 116, 117, 127, 133, 148, 154, 157, 175, 177, 182, 183, 184, 187–88, 190, 192, 195, 214nn83–84; outside colleges, 3, 5, 8, 10, 79, 175, 177, 178, 183, 184, 232n47. *See also specific subjects and types of schools*

Wabash College, 177
War of 1812, 142
Washington, George, 57
Washington and Lee University. See Washington College
Washington College, 80, 89–90, 189
Webster, Isaac T., 67–68
Wellesley College, 97, 184
Wells, Cheryl A., 13–14
Wesleyan Female College, 8, 15, 19, 43–44, 109, 110, 113, 118, 219n39; admissions as constant at, 101, 102, 103–8, 114, 219n27; at Centennial

INDEX

Exposition, 182; Civil War contributions of, 37, 38, 40, 102, 155; closure of during Civil War, 44, 51; discussion of war and Confederacy at, 28, 48–49; founding of as Georgia Female College, 7, 103; geographic origins of students at, 131, 136–38, 139, 226n20, 226n22; military education at, 37, 38, 59, 68, 102; morality and religion at, 149–50, 151; veterans' orphans admitted for free to, 107, 108, 137–38, 143–44
"When Tyranny Condescending" (song), 28
Whitehead, John S., 198n5
Wiebe, Robert H., 130
Wilberforce University, 6, 94, 98
Williams College, 4
Wisconsin State Agricultural Society, 52
Wisconsin veterans-education law of World War I, 193

women: in Civil War and Reconstruction, 13, 48–49, 120, 223n95; literacy of, 103; military activities of, 37–38, 59, 68, 102, 204n50; as missionaries, 150; as professors, 68, 96; as students, 2, 6, 7, 10, 21, 29, 31–32, 36, 37–39, 43, 51, 53, 68, 78, 80, 94–97, 100–102, 113–15, 120–21, 125–26, 127, 190, 218n24; as teachers, 94, 96, 97, 103, 107, 113–14, 120–21
women's colleges and seminaries, 7, 8, 11, 15, 20, 29, 49–50, 95, 97, 101, 102–4, 115, 137, 149–50, 152, 174, 178, 180, 182, 184. *See also specific institutions*
Worcester Free Institute, 184
work-study programs, 100, 113, 126–27
World War I, 191–93, 194–95
World War II, 11, 93, 142, 193–95

Yale College, 2, 6, 9–10, 35, 60, 62
Yale Report of 1828, 9–10

www.ingramcontent.com/pod-product-compliance
Lightning Source LLC
Chambersburg PA
CBHW021341230426
43666CB00006B/361